INTERNATIONAL MERGERS AND ACQUISITIONS

INTERNATIONAL MERGERS AND ACQUISITIONS

A Country-by-Country Tax Guide

Edited by
Robert Feinschreiber
and
Margaret Kent

John Wiley & Sons, Inc.

This book is printed on acid-free paper.

Copyright © 2002 by John Wiley and Sons, Inc., New York. All rights reserved.

Published simultaneously in Canada.

No part of this publication may be reproduced, stored in a retrieval system or transmitted in any form or by any means, electronic, mechanical, photocopying, recording, scanning or otherwise, except as permitted under Section 107 or 108 of the 1976 United States Copyright Act, without wither the prior written permission of the Publisher, or authorization through payment of the appropriate per-copy fee to the Copyright Clearance Center, 222 Rosewood Drive, Danvers, MA 01923, (978) 750-8400, fax (978) 750-4744. Requests to the Publisher for permission should be addressed to the Permissions Department, John Wiley & Sons, Inc., 605 Third Avenue, New York, NY 10158-0012, (212) 850-6011, fax (212) 850-6008, E-Mail: PERMREQ@WILEY.COM.

This publication is designed to provide accurate and authoritative information in regard to the subject matter covered. It is sold with the understanding that the publisher is not engaged in rendering legal, accounting, or other professional services. If legal advice or other expert assistance is required, the services of a competent professional person should be sought.

Library of Congress Cataloging-in-Publication Data:

International mergers & acquisitions : a country by country tax guide / edited by Robert Feinschreiber and Margaret Kent.
    p. cm.
    Includes index.
    ISBN 0-471-40898-0 (cloth : acid-free paper)
    1. Consolidation and merger of corporations—Taxation. 2. Corporations—Taxation—Law and legislation. I. Title: International mergers and acquisitions. II. Feinschreiber, Robert. III. Kent, Margaret, 1942–
    K4558.M47 I58 2002
    343.06′7—dc21   2001046542

Printed in the United States of America.

10 9 8 7 6 5 4 3 2 1

BECOME A SUBSCRIBER!
Did you purchase this product from a bookstore?

If you did, it's important for you to become a subscriber. John Wiley & Sons, Inc. may publish, on a periodic basis, supplements and new editions to reflect the latest changes in the subject matter that you *need to know* in order to stay competitive in this ever-changing industry. By contacting the Wiley office nearest you, you'll receive any current update at no additional charge. In addition, you'll receive future updates and revised or related volumes on a 30-day examination review.

If you purchased this product directly from John Wiley & Sons, Inc., we have already recorded your subscription for this update service.

To become a subscriber, please call **1-800-225-5945** or send your name, company name (if applicable), address, and the title of the product to:

mailing address: **Supplement Department**
                             John Wiley & Sons, Inc.
                             One Wiley Drive
                             Somerset, NJ 08875

e-mail: **subscriber@wiley.com**
fax: **1-732-302-2300**
online: **www.wiley.com**

For customers outside the United States, please contact the Wiley office nearest you:

Professional & Reference Division
John Wiley & Sons Canada, Ltd.
22 Worcester Road
Rexdale, Ontario M9W 1L1
CANADA
(416) 675-3580
Phone: 1-800-567-4797
Fax: 1-800-565-6802
canada@jwiley.com

John Wiley & Sons, Ltd
Baffins Lane
Chichester
West Sussex, PO19 1UD
ENGLAND
Phone: (44) 1243 779777
Fax: (44) 1243 770638
cs-books@wiley.co.uk

Jacaranda Wiley Ltd.
PRT Division
P.O. Box 174
North Ryde, NSW 2113
AUSTRALIA
Phone: (02) 805-1100
Fax: (02) 805-1597
headoffice@jacwiley.com.au

John Wiley & Sons (SEA) Pte. Ltd.
2 Clementi Loop #02-01
SINGAPORE 129809
Phone: (65) 463-2400
Fax: (65) 463-4604; (65) 463-4605
wiley@singnet.com.sg

*We dedicate this book to our children,
Steven Feinschreiber and Kathryn Hagedorn.*

Robert Feinschreiber
Margaret Kent

Contents

1	Taxation of Mergers and Acquisitions in Argentina *Daniel E. Rybnik, Gustavo Scravaglieri, and Maria Florencia Gaido*	1-1
2	Taxation of Mergers and Acquisitions in Australia *Tim Carberry and Greg Leyden*	2-1
3	Taxation of Mergers and Acquisitions in Azerbaijan *Alum Bati*	3-1
4	Taxation of Mergers and Acquisitions in Canada *Gregory C. Boehmer and Mike Vantil*	4-1
5	Taxation of Mergers and Acquisitions in Finland *Kirsi Hiltunen and Jaakko Sivonen*	5-1
6	Taxation of Mergers and Acquisitions in France *Jean-Marc Girard, Raphael Coin, and Gael Beiniex*	6-1
7	Taxation of Mergers and Acquisitions in Germany *Dieter Endres and Stefan Ditsch*	7-1
8	Taxation of Mergers and Acquisitions in Ireland *Dermot P. Clarke and David J. Rorke*	8-1
9	Taxation of Mergers and Acquisitions in Italy *Robert Lazzarone and Franco Carlo Papa*	9-1
10	Taxation of Mergers and Acquisitions in Japan *Kan Hayashi and Al Zencak*	10-1
11	Taxation of Mergers and Acquisitions in Kazakhstan *Aigoul Kenjebayeva, Joseph Luke, and Abai Shaikenov*	11-1
12	Taxation of Mergers and Acquisitions in Korea *Kyun (Ken) Cook*	12-1
13	Taxation of Mergers and Acquisitions in Mexico *Jaime Gonzales-Bendiksen*	13-1
14	Taxation of Mergers and Acquisitions in the Netherlands *Olaf Ernst van der Donk, George L. Meij, and Carl W. A. Van Suchtelen*	14-1
15	Taxation of Mergers and Acquisitions in Norway *Espen Ommedal*	15-1
16	Taxation of Mergers and Acquisitions in Russia *Joel M. McDonald, Oleg Y. Konnov, and Andrei Shishkov*	16-1

17	Taxation of Mergers and Acquisitions in Spain *Rocío Reyero, Laura Ezquerra, and Adriana Ojeda*	**17-1**
18	Taxation of Mergers and Acquisitions in Ukraine *Oleg V. Batyuk and Vladimir N. Zakhvataev*	**18-1**
19	Taxation of Mergers and Acquisitions in the United Kingdom *Noel N. Davison and Jim Hillian*	**19-1**
20	Taxation of Mergers and Acquisitions in the United States *Marc A. Claybon, Stephen A. Cohen, and Robert B. Feinberg*	**20-1**

About the Editors

Robert Feinscheiber is an attorney and counselor in Miami. His firm concentrates on international transfer pricing. As a partner in the firm of Feinschrieber and Associates, his clients include foreign-owned U.S. businesses, U.S. exporters, and companies facing transfer pricing issues. He received a B.A. from Trinity College in Connecticut, an L.L.B. from Yale, an M.B.A. from Columbia Graduate School of Business, and an L.L.M. in Taxation from New York University. Mr. Feinschreiber was a CPA in Florida.

He has written and edited many books on taxation, including *Foreign Sales Corporations, Fundamentals of International Taxation, Domestic International Sales Corporations, Tax Incentives for U.S. Exports, Tax Depreciation Under the Class Life ADR System, International Tax Planning Today, Subpart F, Earnings & Profits, Allocation and Apportionment of Deductions,* and *International Reorganizations.* Mr. Feinschreiber is also the author of *Tax Reporting for Foreign-Owned U.S. Corporations,* published by John Wiley & Sons, Inc. Mr. Feinschreiber has written many articles on tax and tax-related subjects, especially international taxation. He has been quoted as an authority by *Tax Court, Business Week,* and *Forbes.* He has also been a consultant to several foreign governments.

Mr. Feinschreiber is the editor of the *Interstate Tax Report*. He was the founding editor of the *International Tax Journal,* and has been the editor of *Export Tax Report* and the United States editor of *Tax Haven* and *Shelter Report.* He was formerly the U.S. correspondent for *Tax News Service,* published by the International Bureau of Fiscal Documentation. Robert Feinschreiber and Margaret Kent are editors of *Mergers and Acquisitions: The Monthly Tax Journal* published by Panel Publishers.

He has taught accounting at Yale and law at Wayne State University Law School. He was director of the International Tax Institute. Mr. Feinschreiber has lectured at various tax conferences on such topics as foreign sales corporations, DISC, intercompany pricing, Subpart F, foreign tax credit, the research credit, and depreciation. He has lectured for the American Management Association, International Business Seminars, the International Tax Institute, the World Trade Institute, where he was the Senior International Tax Advisor, and other organizations. He is the editor of *Export Handbook, Transfer Pricing Handbook,* and co-editor of *Import Handbook,* both published by John Wiley & Sons.

Margaret Kent has been an attorney for more than 17 years, focusing on international taxation, but having a wealth of diverse responsibilities.

- Structured the termination of the $2 billion per year aid from Russia to Cuba
- Participated in an earnings & profits study of a large U.S. multinational corporation having two-tier operations in Venezuela

- Structured U.S. business operations of a Brazilian manufacturer to avoid effectively-connected status.
- Examined transfer pricing in Latin American countries
- Defended clients in response to IRS information documents requests and prepared protests
- Brought EEOC claims
- Lectured on FSCs and on escheat
- Challenged assets protection structures for spouses in divorce actions
- Handled probate and probate litigation
- Structured and negotiated prenuptial and postnuptial agreements.

Margaret Kent, Esq. is a graduate of Barry University, B.A., Intstituto Tecnologico de Estudios Superiores de Monterrey, M.A., and University of Miami, J.D.

Robert Feinschreiber and Margaret Kent can be reached at 1121 Crandon Boulevard, Key Biscayne, Florida, Tel: 305-361-5800, Fax: 305-361-7722, e-mail: *multijur@aol.com*.

Preface

As international tax practitioners, we have seen a strong need for a country-by-country mergers and acquisitions tax guide with a U.S. emphasis. *International Mergers and Acquisitions: A Country-by-Country Tax Guide* fills that need by providing the country-specific information required when planning an acquisition.

It is our hope that *Mergers and Acquisitions: A Country-by-Country Tax Guide* will be a central part of your international tax library, joining other volumes in Wiley's international tax handbook series: *The Transfer Pricing Handbook, Transfer Pricing International: A Country-by-Country Guide, The Export Handbook,* and *The Import Handbook,* all edited by Robert Feinschreiber. International tax practitioners should find Wiley's country-by-country guides to be valuable resources, providing insight into the tax minds of America's most important trading partners.

As editors, we sought to provide penetrating analyses of the mergers and acquisitions tax practice in countries important to us. In so doing, we selected experts already known in their own countries. We sought to give each author free opportunity to address the relevant mergers and acquisitions tax issues of significance in that specific country. At the same time, we encouraged the authors to address mergers and acquisitions tax topics such as the following in the author's own country:

- What are the needs of the buyer and seller in the merger or acquisition?
- What parameters apply in deciding whether to transfer assets or stock?
- What ownership and control requirements apply to the merger or acquisition?
- How are taxable and tax free transactions delineated?
- When do basis adjustments apply to the merger or acquisition?
- What carryover attributes apply, including credits and net operating losses?
- When does tax attribution apply to affiliated businesses?
- How are debt and equity determined, and what is its relevance in the mergers and acquisitions context?
- How are capital gains and losses treated in the mergers and acquisitions context?
- How are subsidiaries taken into account during a merger or acquisition?
- To what extent is consolidated returns treatment relevant to mergers and acquisitions treatment?
- How are outbound and inbound mergers and acquisitions treated?

These questions are the same and are most often asked in almost every developed country. The reader is cautioned, however, that while the questions may be the same in each country, the approaches taken by these countries, the taxpayers, and the tax practitioners will substantially differ and could possibly change over time.

                                                                           Robert Feinschreiber
                                                                           Margaret Kent
                                                                           October, 2001

About the Contributors

Alum Bati is a British Barrister with over 20 years experience in law and tax consulting. He is the author of a number of books and articles on taxation and law. Alum is the Amsterdam-based International Bureau of Fiscal Documentation's correspondent in Azerbaijan and his other publications include articles for the *British Tax Review,* the *CCH Journal of Asia Pacific Taxation* and for the *Nikkei Weekly.* Alum co-authored the first edition of two standard works on UK taxation. He is a former Representative Director of Ernst & Young in Azerbaijan (having established its Baku office in 1993) and was, prior to that, British Petroleum's Regional Tax Manager for Japan and Korea (based in Tokyo).

Oleg V. Batyuk is a Partner with Salans Hertzfeld & Heibronn, Kiev. He has worked extensively in structuring international trade and inward investment in Ukraine and as an advisor in Ukrainian lending and bank regulatory issues and capital markets transactions. He contributes articles on a regular basis to international journals on the subjects of legal and tax issues affecting foreign investment in Ukraine.

Gaël Beineix is an Associate within the International Tax Service of HSD Ernst & Young in Paris, France. He specializes in international mergers and acquisitions transactions as well as cross-border reorganizations involving multinational companies, either French or foreign.

Gregory C. Beohmer is the National Director of Ernst & Young's Canadian Mergers & Acquisitions Tax Services Group. He has extensive experience in corporate reorganizations, merger and acquisition structuring, tax due diligence, and financial restructuring transactions.

Tim L. Carberry is a Partner at Ernst & Young, Australia.

Dermot P. Clarke is a Tax Partner to Ernst & Young who specializes in serving multinational high-tech companies and has extensive experience in international tax planning. He sits on several committees advising the Irish Government on tax policy.

Marc A. Claybon is a Manager at Ernst & Young, US and is a member of their National Tax and Mergers and Acquisitions Tax Services groups.

Stephen A. Cohen is a Partner at Ernst & Young, New York. Steve's technical expertise involves corporate reorganizations and spin-offs, as well as other acquisition and disposition techniques. Prior to relocating to the New York area in 1996, Steve was a member of the firm's National Tax Mergers & Acquisitions Group from 1987 through

1996. Before joining the firm, he was an attorney with the IRS Office of Chief Counsel in the Reorganization Branch of the Corporation Tax Division.

Raphaël Coin is an Attorney at law specializing in international taxation and M & A. He is a partner in HSD Ernst and Young in Paris and is involved in cross-border acquisition/reorganization and financing. Before joining the International Tax Service group of Ernst & Young in Paris he was seconded in E&Y in New York and London where he did work more specifically on major French/US and French/UK transactions. He has written articles for international tax publications and lectures at universities and business schools.

Kyun (Ken) Cook is a Senior Tax Partner at Ernst & Young, Seoul, Korea. He is responsible for the firm's international tax and investment services. Mr. Cook has spent the last 22 years in public accounting practice in Korea and North America serving numerous multinational clients making cross-border investments.

Noel N. Davison has worked in International Tax for Ernst & Young for over ten years. He had advised in a wide range of cross-border transactions including acquisitions, mergers, buy-outs, and joint ventures.

Stefan Ditsch is an international Tax Partner in the M & A Tax Group of PricewaterhouseCoopers, Frankfurt. He was on a $2\frac{1}{2}$ years tour at the German Tax Desk of PwC in New York and Washington from 1997 to 1999. His main practice area is tax consulting on international business transactions, reorganizations, and M & A consulting. He is a frequent author and speaker on various matters related to German and international taxation. He is a member of the German Institute of Tax Advisers and of the European-American Tax Institute.

Dieter Endres is an international tax partner at PricewaterhouseCoopers in Frankfurt and head of the firm's tax and legal services in Germany. He has published numerous tax publications and is a frequent speaker at tax conferences in Germany and abroad. Dr. Endres is a member of the German Institute of Tax Advisers, of the international tax committee and the tax reform committee of the German Institute of Chartered Accountants, of the European-American Tax Institute, and of the International Fiscal Association. He is an honorary professor and lecturer on international taxation at Mannheim University.

Laura Ezquerra is a Tax Lawyer with Ernst & Young Spain and specialize in mergers and acquisitions and international tax.

Robert B. Feinberg is the National Director, Mergers & Acquisitions Tax Services at Ernst & Young LLP, United States.

María Florencia Gaido is currently working in the International Tax Services Department at Ernst & Young, Buenos Aires, having previously worked as lawyer in the Tax Law Area for Abeledo Gottheil Abogados and as intern in the Customs and Tax Law Area at Marval, O'Farrell & Mairal.

Jean-Marc Girard is a Partner in the International Tax Services Group of HSD Ernst & Young in Paris. He concentrates on international tax planning for French multina-

About the Contributors

tional companies, on cross-border mergers and acquisitions. Between 1994 and 1997, he was responsible for the French Tax Desk in the International Tax Services of Ernst & Young LLP in Chicago that he created, where he assisted French and U.S. clients involved in cross-border transactions. HSD Ernst & Young is one of the leading firms in France with 300 attorneys, providing services in Business and Tax law.

Jaime Gonzales-Bendiksen is a Partner with Baker & McKenzie in Mexico who specializes in international taxation issues. He is also a member of the International Fiscal Association, where he was president of the Colombia chapter, wrote a national report on Tax Treatment of Computer Software, and was a member of the discussion panels at the annual congresses of Amsterdam (1988) and Delhi (1997). As an advisor to multinational corporations, he has extensive experience in the areas of international tax planning, mergers and acquisitions, permanent establishments, transborder transactions, intercompany pricing, taxation of nonresident entities and individuals, corporate taxation, assets taxes, and VAT.

Kan Hayashi has been serving primarily Japanese multinational clients for their international tax affairs, notably global reorganization and M & A transactions. His experience includes nearly eight years in Singapore and London. Currently, he is actively involved in seminars as well as clients service in connection with the new Japanese taxation for reorganization.

Jim Hillian has a background in accounting and law. He joined Ernst & Young's International Tax Services practice in 1999 and is currently working on secondment at Tite and Lewis, the UK law firm associated with Ernst & Young.

Kirsi Hiltunen is a Partner at Ernst & Young's Helsinki office. Kirsi Hiltunen has more than 11 years of experience advising clients on various transfer pricing and cross-border investment matters. She is heading a transfer pricing team focused on transfer pricing planning and documentation including economic analyses. Furthermore, she has been engaged in international post acquisition reorganizations and tax optimization projects.

Aigoul Kenjebayeva is a Partner with Salans Hertzfeld & Heilbronn, Kazakhstan. Her field of concentration is on corporate, commercial, and natural resources law, with particular emphasis on foreign investment in Kazakhstan and the Caspian Region.

Oleg Y. Konnov is a Senior Associate in the Moscow office of Salans Hertzfeld & Heilbronn. He advises western and Russian clients on Russian tax issues.

Robert Lazzarone is a Partner with Ernst & Young, Italy.

Joseph Luke is a Partner with Salans, Hertzfeld & Heilbronn, Kazakhstan.

Greg Leyden is a Senior Manager with Ernst & Young and is currently at the Australian Tax Desk for the firm in Chicago. Greg has been with Ernst & Young for seven years and previously worked for the Australian Taxation Office.

Joel M. McDonald is a Partner in the London office of Salans Hertzfeld & Heilbronn. He is a former advisor to the Russian Government on tax reform.

George Meij was a tax inspector with the Dutch Revenue for nine years before he joined Ernst & Young in 1986. He has been a Partner with Ernst & Young since 1990. At first he worked in the national practice where he got vast experience in domestic deals. Since early 2000, he has been a member of the International Tax Services M & A practice, with a focus on taxation due diligence. He leads the taxation due diligence team of Ernst & Young in the Netherlands.

Adrianna Ojeda is a Tax Adviser in Ernst & Young who specializes in Mergers and Acquisitions.

Espen Ommedal is a Business Economist, Lawyer, and Partner with Ernst & Young, Norway. At Ernst & Young, he is Director of Law, Vice-Director of Tax, and a member of the National Management team. He is an advisor to several international companies involved in major cross-border transactions.

Franco Carlo Papa joined Ernst & Young Corporate Finance as Partner in charge of M & A, Valuation and IPO operations. He is currently Managing Director of Ernst & Young SpA and Managing Partner of the Corporate Finance Division. Prior to Ernst & Young, Franco Carlo was a Board Member at AFV Sim, responsible for Finance & Venture assignments such as M & As, IPO's, Business Planning, valuations, and consulting on the international funds of the AFV shareholders.

Rocío Reyero is a Partner at Ernst & Young, Madrid who specializes in cross-border transactions.

David J. Rorke is a tax director in Ernst & Young who deals extensively with inward investment to Ireland by multinational companies and with tax due diligence relating to major acquisitions. He also specializes in oil and gas taxation matters.

Daniel Rybnik is a Principal at Ernst & Young Buenos Aires. Before joining E&Y, he was an International Tax Manager at PricewaterhouseCoopers, L.L.P. (formerly Coopers & Lybrand) New York and a Tax Manager at Coopers & Lybrand in Buenos Aires. He is mainly focused on Business Change tax services, including Transfer Pricing, Tax Effective Supply Chain Management, e-business Tax Structuring, Post Merger Integration, and International Tax Planning. He currently manages the E&Y Argentine International Tax Services team.

Gustavo Scravaglieri is a Tax Manager with Ernst & Young, Buenos Aires where he provides tax services to multinational clients doing business in Argentina. His areas of experience include international tax consulting, treatment of inbound and outbound investments, oil and gas and mining industry taxation, transfer pricing, and corporate mergers and acquisitions.

Abai Shaikenov is a Partner with Salans Hertzfeld & Heilbronn, Kazakhstan. His concentration is on corporate, commercial, and natural resources law with an emphasis on tax issues.

Andrei Shishkov is an Associate in the Moscow office of Salans Hertzfeld & Heilbronn. He advises western and Russian clients on Russian tax issues.

About the Contributors

Jaakko Sivonen is a Tax Manager at Ernst & Young, Finland. He was a Presenting Official for the Helsinki Administrative Court from April 1997 to May 2000.

Olaf Ernst van der Donk is a partner in the Amsterdam office of Ernst & Young where he leads the Merger & Acquisition team of the International Tax Services group. His team has been engaged in many high profile transactions from early negotiations to post completion reorganization.

Carl van Suchtelen works in the Amsterdam office of Ernst & Young as part of the Mergers & Acquisitions team. He has worked on a number of high profile transactions from early negotiations to post completion reorganization. Carl's expertise lies on cross-border M & A work for large Multinational Corporations (MNC). He advises both foreign and domestic MNC's on Dutch inbound as well as Dutch outbound transactions.

Mike Vantil is a Senior Manager with Ernst & Young's Mergers & Acquisitions Tax Services Group in Toronto. Prior to joining the M & A Group, Mr. Vantil was with the International Tax Services Group. He has provided many corporate tax clients planning advice including structuring international transactions, mergers and acquisitions, and corporate restructurings.

Vladimir N. Zakhvataev is an Associate in the Kiev office of Salans Hertzfeld & Heilbronn. His areas of concentration include international and domestic arbitration and litigation, legal aspects of foreign investment, acquisitions, commercial transactions, tax law, maritime law, and ship building finance.

Al Zencak is a Senior Tax Manager in the PricewaterhouseCoopers Tokyo International Tax office. He specializes in providing Japanese corporate tax advice for cross-border transactions, with special emphasis on the Japanese corporate tax implications of mergers and acquisition and other corporate reorganization structures.

INTERNATIONAL MERGERS AND ACQUISITIONS

CHAPTER 1

Taxation of Mergers and Acquisitions in Argentina

By Daniel E. Rybnik
Gustavo Scravaglieri
María Florencia Gaido*
International Tax Services, Ernst & Young Argentina

1.1 **Introduction**
1.2 **Tax Law**
    (a) Income Tax
    (b) Tax on Minimum Presumed Income
    (c) Value-Added Tax (VAT)
    (d) Turnover Tax
    (e) Stamp Tax
1.3 **Taxable Acquisitions**
    (a) Asset Acquisitions
    (b) Income Tax
    (c) Value-Added Tax
    (d) Turnover Tax
    (e) Buyers Income Tax
    (f) Buyers VAT
1.4 **Stock Acquisitions**
    (a) Acquisition of Shares of an Argentine Company
    (b) Tax Treatment of the Purchase of Shares for a Foreign Company
    (c) Tax Treatment of the Purchase of Shares by an Argentine Company
1.5 **Tax-Free Reorganizations**
    (a) Definition of Reorganization
    (b) Mergers
    (c) Tax-Free Reorganization Requirements
    (d) Transfer of Rights and Obligations to the Surviving Companies
    (e) Noncompliance
    (f) Other Consequences
    (g) Divisions or Spin-Offs

---

*The Authors wish to thank Eduardo Cariglino, Steve Hodge, and Carlos Casanovas for their invaluable review and comments.

1.6 Sales and Transfers within the Same Business Group
    (a) Tax-Free Reorganization Requirements
    (b) Transfer of Rights and Obligations to the Surviving Companies
    (c) Other Sales and Transfers
1.7 Conclusion
ANNEX 1

1.1 INTRODUCTION

Mergers and acquisitions activity in Argentina developed rapidly under both corporate law and tax law. Economic globalization, the allowance of free foreign investments, and the numerous privatizations since the late 1980s precipitated these mergers and acquisitions changes. We refer to mergers and acquisitions activity as encompassing mergers, spin-offs, and acquisitions of assets within the same economic group.

This chapter analyzes the tax effects of mergers and acquisitions in Argentina. In examining these materials, consider that the manner in which the parties have structured transactions involving the sale of a business historically has been influenced by four major tax factors:

1. The seller's desire to carry out a nontaxable stock sale rather than an asset sale subject to tax at standard corporate rates
2. The buyer's desire to obtain as high a basis as possible for the entity's assets, particularly inventory and depreciable property
3. The ability to avoid recognition of gain at the entity level
4. The possibility to cut off the assumption of past liabilities by the acquiring entity

Tax results are not the only factors that influence the form of a sale and purchase of a business. In many cases, tax results are of lesser importance than nontax factors. A single purchaser for all of the entity's business activities often cannot be located, and one line of business is sold to one purchaser while another line of business is sold to a second purchaser.

In other cases, a purchaser might be unwilling to acquire the stock of a corporation because of its concerns regarding contingent or unascertained liabilities. On the other hand, an asset purchase might be ruled out if the acquired business owns rights that are not assignable. In such a case, the acquisition must be structured as a sale and purchase of stock. Other important factors to consider include rights of dissenting shareholders, securities laws, and the authority of regulatory agencies to approve or disapprove a transaction.

Finally, it must be taken into consideration that, according to Article 31 of the Argentine Companies Act (ACA), no company can take over or maintain participation interest in one or more other companies for an amount exceeding its free reserves and half of its issued capital and legal reserves. A legal reserve is a portion of accumulated earnings that cannot be distributed. To form this reserve, the company must reserve 5 percent of its annual statutory earnings up to 20 percent of its issued capital.

This limitation established by the ACA precludes companies from having participation interest or ownership exceeding its free reserves, generally accumulated earnings. This provision does not apply to financial or investment entities or when such excess in the participation interest or ownership derives from the payment of dividends with shares or through a capitalization of reserves.

If such participation limit has been exceeded, the excess amount will have to be transferred within six months from the date of approval of the balance sheet that demonstrates that the participation limit has been exceeded. Otherwise, the shareholder will lose its ownership rights coming from the exceeding participation interest, such as a right to vote or right to receive dividends.

1.2 TAX LAW

The Argentine Constitution provides three governmental levels—Federal, Provincial and Local, all of whom have tax powers. Constitutional provisions determine the scope in the following way:

- Federal government:
  - On an exclusive and permanent basis: Customs duties.
  - On a permanent basis and together with provincial governments: Value-added tax (VAT) and excise taxes.
  - On a temporary basis: Among others, income tax, tax on minimum presumed income, and tax on personal assets.

- Provincial governments:
  - On a permanent basis: Direct taxes (e.g., stamp taxes).
  - On a permanent basis and together with the federal government: Turnover tax.

- Local governments:
  - In general, their tax power applies only to service fees.

The following is a brief summary of the relevant Argentine federal and provincial taxes.

(a) Income Tax

The Income Tax Act (Law 20628, as amended) is a federal tax. The statute establishes that Argentine residents are subject to tax on their worldwide source income. Non-Argentine residents are subject to tax only on their Argentine-source income through income tax withholdings.

Progressive income tax rates on individuals range from 9 percent to 35 percent. The corporate tax rate is 35 percent, applicable to the net income determined according to the Income Tax Act (ITA).

Resident taxable entities deriving capital gains from the sale of shares are not subject to any special tax nor are they subject to preferential rates. Instead, capital gains are included within the income tax and, consequently, these capital gains are subject to a 35 percent rate, as in the case of ordinary income; however, the gains obtained by individual residents of Argentina from the sale of these shares are not subject to income tax.

(b) Tax on Minimum Presumed Income

The Argentine Tax Reform of 1998 included within its provisions a new tax—the tax on minimum presumed income (TMPI). This tax, which functions similarly to an assets tax, is assessed at a rate of 1 percent over the value of a taxpayer's worldwide assets at the end of the taxpayer's fiscal year, although certain assets are excluded from the tax basis.

The TMPI operates in conjunction with the regular Argentine corporate income tax. Taxpayers are allowed to credit their regular corporate income tax liability against their TMPI liability. In other words, the TMPI is payable only to the extent that a taxpayer's liability under the TMPI exceeds its liability under the regular corporate income tax. The TMPI law also allows for a taxpayer who is required to pay the TMPI in any given year (because its TMPI liability exceeded its income tax liability) to credit the amount paid against its income tax liability in any of the 10 immediately succeeding taxable years.

(c) Value-Added Tax (VAT)

The value-added tax (VAT) is a general tax on consumption that applies within the Argentine territory. VAT is levied on the delivery of goods and/or the providing of services by any individual or legal entity conducting an economic activity in Argentina. VAT applies to the importation of goods and on the importation of services to be used or exploited in Argentina. The tax general rate is 21 percent.

Under the VAT system, the tax is levied at each stage of the manufacturing and distribution process on a noncumulative basis. The accumulation of tax is avoided through the deduction of VAT invoiced to the entity. The entity collects VAT on the total amount invoiced in each monthly tax period, but the entity is entitled to recover the imputed VAT that was invoiced to the entity during the same period.

The credit for imputed VAT may be higher than the amount of VAT due on output. In that event, the entity is not entitled to a refund unless the refund is related to exports. Instead, the excess is credited against future VAT liabilities.

(d) Turnover Tax

Provincial governments impose turnover tax on the gross revenues of businesses. The tax rate varies depending on the type of activity:

- Farming and cattle raising, mining, and other primary activities are taxed at a rate of 1 percent.
- Industrial activities are taxed at a rate of 1.5 percent.
- Commerce and general services are taxed at a rate of 3 percent.
- Financial and intermediary activities are taxed at a rate of 4.9 percent.

The rate is applied to the total amount of gross receipts accrued during the calendar year.

(e) Stamp Tax

Each Argentine province levies its own stamp tax. In the City of Buenos Aires, the federal government levies the stamp tax only on sales of real estate. Consequently, documents entered into within the City of Buenos Aires are not taxable. Transactions that apply elsewhere may be taxed in other jurisdictions. Tax rates vary for each province; the most common rate is 1 percent calculated on the economic value of the instrument.

1.3 TAXABLE ACQUISITIONS

This portion of the analysis deals with the tax aspects of a taxable purchase and sale of the corporate business. The various techniques for tax-free reorganizations are considered in section 1.4.

(a) Asset Acquisitions

The materials in this section deal with the sale of a business that takes the form of a sale of corporate assets. This analysis explores the problems that this form of transaction historically has generated, as well as the currently applicable rules. If a taxable entity sells its business by selling its assets to the purchaser, the transaction is deemed to be a "transfer of a going concern."

Transfers of going concerns are governed by Law 11,867 Transfer of Going Concerns Act (TOGC Act), which sets forth special rules to protect the seller's nontax creditors. The TOGC Act provides a list of elements that constitute a "commercial establishment or going concern for the purpose of any type of transfer thereof." Such items would include the following:

- premises
- inventory stock
- trade name
- logo
- customer portfolio
- right to use the sales premises
- invention patents
- trademarks
- industrial blueprints and models

- honors awarded
- any other rights deriving from the commercial and industrial or artistic property

Under certain circumstances, the transfer of certain assets may be construed as a transfer of a going concern if, upon the sale, the seller is deprived of the means necessary to carry on its business or cannot continue to do business in the same way as it did before such sale.

Notice of the transfer must be published in the *Official Gazette* and in one or more newspapers for a five-day term in order to cut off the assumption of the seller's nontax liabilities to the buyer. The seller's nontax creditors have 10 days as from the last publication to make objections to the transaction. The acquiror is jointly liable for the undetermined federal tax liabilities of the seller. Such joint liability expires at the applicable time frame:

- As from 3 months after the transfer, if the taxpayer notifies the Argentine Revenue Service (ARS) no fewer than 15 days before the transfer
- At any moment in which the ARS considers the seller is solvent enough to settle any unpaid tax, or when the ARS accepts the guarantees offered by the seller

Taxpayers and the Argentine tax authorities must follow the TOGC Act procedure. A tax audit is likely to take place shortly after the taxpayer notified the transfer to the ARS. The purchaser will be jointly liable together with the seller if the transfer is not notified to the ARS; however, in case the seller and purchaser are jointly responsible, the ARS must claim against the seller first, and only afterward make claim against the buyer. Provincial tax laws provide for specific procedures to cut off the buyer's liability for past provincial tax contingencies.

(b) Income Tax

The taxable entity that transfers a going concern must recognize gain or loss from the bulk sale.

(c) Value-Added Tax

The seller must allocate the purchase price to the various assets transferred for VAT purposes. This allocation is generally relevant from the buyers income tax and VAT standpoint. These allocations generally present no problem if the parties have bargained on an asset-by-asset basis, but that is rarely the case. More commonly, the parties bargain for the sale and purchase based on a lump sum price. After the total purchase price has been determined, the parties often then bargain about the allocation among all of the assets. The parties' objectives in this ex-post allocation are largely determined by tax considerations.

If the seller is in a large VAT credit position, it is more desirable for the seller to allocate purchase price to VAT taxable assets and then maximize the utilization of VAT credits. Regarding tangible assets, VAT is applicable at a 21 percent rate

1.3 Taxable Acquisitions

on the sale price of the assets that form part of the going concern, including inventories and so on.

When an improvement is sold within a period of 10 years from the completion of the work, any VAT credits generated by the acquisition of such construction (or by the construction by the taxpayer itself) would have to be refunded. Land does not form part of the base for calculating VAT. As regards the intangible assets that form part of the going concern, such as goodwill, the transfer is not generally subject to VAT. The conditions of the bulk transfer should be analyzed in detail because the transfer of such intangibles might be subject to VAT under certain circumstances.

Two credit situations must be considered:

1. *Credits that produce interest:* VAT must be paid on the amount resulting from the difference between the final value of the receivable and the value at which it was transferred. Therefore, VAT would have to be paid in advance on the credit's total interest not yet accrued.

2. *Credits that do not produce interest:* If the transfer is made at face value, such transfer shall not trigger VAT; however, if the transfer is made at a discount, such difference is taxable.

(d) Turnover Tax

The sale of assets is subject to the turnover tax. In this case, the taxability of these assets depends on the nature of each asset being transferred. Thus, the transfer of the inventory that forms part of the going concern would generally be subject to this tax at approximately 3 percent of the value of such inventory.

The transfer of fixed assets is generally not subject to turnover tax. The exclusion is specifically provided by the law in some jurisdictions, such as the City of Buenos Aires and the provinces of Buenos Aires and Santa Fe. Fixed assets are excluded from the turnover tax base because the fixed assets are those goods the company affects to its own productive development. As such, the sale of these fixed assets does not form part of the company's normal course of business (i.e., of its habitual taxable activity).[1]

Whether the transfer of intangible assets is taxable is debatable. The approach for fixed assets is applicable to this case because the sale of intangibles (like goodwill) does not form part of the company's normal course of business activity. The tax treatment of intangibles may create price allocation inconsistencies between seller and buyer. The seller may benefit from larger amounts being allocated to intangibles. In contrast, the buyer may lose income tax deductions.

(e) Buyer's Income Tax

The seller's allocation of the sale price for VAT purposes is relevant to the buyer because the allocation establishes the tax basis for each of the newly acquired

---

[1] Enrique Bulit Goñi, *Turnover Tax.* Copyright Depalma Buenos Aires, 1986 (page 109).

assets. Goodwill is amortizable under Argentine generally accepted accounting principles (GAAP), but it is not possible to amortize goodwill for income tax purposes. Therefore, purchasers attempt to allocate all or part of a "premium" payment in excess of the value of the assets among all of the assets, rather than allocating the premium solely to goodwill or going concern value.

The purchase and sale of a business is often accompanied by the shareholders' agreement not to compete with the buyer in the specific business field. A covenant not to compete, even though created in the sale transaction, is amortizable over the asset's life. The ARS, however, is not restricted from challenging the taxpayers' allocations.

When the transfer price assigned is higher than the current market price of the related assets, the value considered for tax purposes is the market price. The treatment given by this law to goodwill is applicable to the surplus. Such goodwill is nondeductible. The taxpayer must consider the criteria followed for accounting purposes in order to value the transferred assets. The taxpayer must follow Argentine GAAP in order to determine the taxable results unless an alternative treatment is specially provided for by the tax law. In such a case, the taxpayer must follow this tax treatment.[2]

In other words, the Argentine procedure to value the transferred assets works as a "residual method." Once the market price is determined, the difference between the amount paid and the market price of the transferred assets is treated as goodwill. It is advisable that the tax base of each asset be carefully disclosed in order to avoid potential challenges from the ARS.

(f) Buyer's VAT

VAT paid in an asset transaction does not represent a cost for VAT taxpayers. Instead, the VAT amount is an input VAT to be offset against future output VAT. VAT may result in a real cost if the buyer conducts VAT-exempted transactions or if it is a "time-money value expense." The taxpayer expects to offset the input VAT of the going concern, but it may not be able to do so in the immediate future. Thus, purchasers may prefer to minimize the amount of the price allocated to VAT-taxable assets. Depending on the jurisdiction where the company is located, bulk transfer agreements may be subject to stamp tax.

1.4 STOCK ACQUISITIONS

This section focuses on the alternative form for the sale of a corporate business—the sale of the shares of stock of the corporation. We focus on the tax rules designed for this form of transaction.

One of the prime motivations for a stock sale is that nonresident sellers are accorded an income tax exemption on the entire realized gain. Capital gains on stock sales are accorded other various tax advantages. For a variety of reasons,

---

[2] "Industrias Plásticas DíAccord S.R.L. c/ DGI," TFN Sala A, 12/17/97 confirmed by CNCAF, Sala 1 7/6/00.

1.4 Stock Acquisitions

however, the purchaser often does not want to purchase the stock, but prefers to purchase the assets directly.

- The corporation may have liabilities that the purchaser does not wish to assume indirectly.
- If the assets have a basis lower than their market value, and hence lower than the price to be paid for the business, the assets retain that low basis when ownership of the corporation changes hands. This basis result may be unsatisfactory to the purchaser, especially with respect to inventory or depreciable property.
- A stock purchase involves taking over other tax attributes, such as the tax basis, tax credits, net operating losses carryforwards, and so forth.

(a) Acquisition of Shares of an Argentine Company

From an income tax perspective, the capital gains obtained from the sale of the shares of an Argentine Sociedad Anónima (SA) by non-Argentinean residents are exempt from income tax according to the rules of Decree 2284/91, ratified by Law 24,307. This exemption applies even when the beneficiary transfers such gains abroad. Therefore, the capital gains deriving from this transaction are exempt from income tax for the foreign beneficiary.

In general, real estate transactions are outside the scope of VAT if the entity is not involved in the construction activity. In addition, certain transactions are exempt, such as the sale of shares and other securities and certain sales of intangibles. Consequently, the sale of shares is exempt from VAT. The sale of shares is exempt from turnover tax in the City of Buenos Aires. The transfer of shares of an Argentine SA domiciled in the City of Buenos Aires is not subject to stamp tax.

(b) Tax Treatment of the Purchase of Shares for a Foreign Company

The purchase of an Argentine company's shares by a foreign corporation does not generate any tax effects in Argentina for the foreign corporation. Assuming that the Argentine corporation is an SA by virtue of Executive Order 2284/91[3], the results deriving from the sale of the Argentine corporation's shares by the foreign corporation are expressly exempt from income tax.

Dividends paid by the Argentine corporation to the foreign corporation are not subject to withholding tax in Argentina, regardless of whether paid to residents or nonresidents, as long as the dividends do not exceed accumulated taxable income with certain adjustments. To the extent that a dividend exceeds the payor's accumulated taxable income, the excess amount is generally subject to a 35 percent withholding tax.

The change of ownership of an Argentine corporation's shares does not release the company from any tax and social security liabilities not barred by the statute

---

[3] Ratified by Law 24,307.

of limitation that may exist. In other words, upon purchasing shares from a company, the new investors "acquire" all the tax and social security contingencies of such company. In this regard, and according to local legislation, the actions and powers of the tax authorities to determine and demand the payment of federal taxes are barred by the statute of limitations after five years. The statute of limitations for social security purposes is ten years.

(c) Tax Treatment of the Purchase of Shares by an Argentine Company

The purchase of an Argentine company's shares by an Argentine company does not generate any tax ramifications in Argentina for the purchaser, other than the issues addressed as follows. Special attention should be given to the limitations provided for in the ACA regarding investments made by local companies in other entities.

As explained previously, article 31 of the ACA provides that no company can take over or maintain participation interest in one or more other companies for an amount exceeding its free reserves and half of its issued capital and legal reserves. This limitation established by the ACA precludes companies from having participation interest or ownership exceeding its free reserves, which generally are accumulated earnings. This provision does not apply to financial or investment entities or when such excess in the participation interest or ownership derives from the payment of dividends with shares or through a capitalization of reserves.

The highest value paid on the book value of a company is generally considered as goodwill for the purchaser for accounting purposes. Although this goodwill is not deductible for income tax purposes because this higher value is part of the tax basis of the shares, this amount is generally considered, from an accounting perspective, as an asset subject to amortization.

The effect of the recording of goodwill in the book of an Argentine company must be carefully analyzed because although it is not deductible for tax purposes, the accounting amortization of the goodwill reduces the company's net profits and thus the accounting amortization affects the capacity to distribute dividends to its shareholders.

1.5 TAX-FREE REORGANIZATIONS

In general, the Argentine tax laws permit business transactions involving certain corporate acquisitions and readjustments to be carried out without a tax being incurred by the participating corporations or by their shareholders at the time of the transactions.

(a) Definition of Reorganization

The application of the term *reorganization* is limited to three basic situations set forth in the ITA Section 77. These three situations are the only situations included within the term *reorganization*.

1.5 Tax-Free Reorganizations

- Type (A) **mergers** of preexisting companies through either (1) forming a new company or (2) by absorption of one of them
- Type (B) **spin-off or division** of a company into another or others that jointly continue the operations of the first one
- Type (C) **sales or transfers** from an entity to another which, despite being legally independent, are part of the same business group

When a business reorganization qualifies for tax-free treatment, the tax rights and obligations of the predecessor entities are transferred to the surviving entities—subject to the fulfillment of certain requirements. According to Section 74 of the ACA, another legal type similar to reorganization is called *conversion*. Conversion takes place when a certain company adopts any of the other legal types provided for by the ACA through LLP, corporation, general partnership, and so on. Upon conversion, the company neither is dissolved, nor are its rights and duties altered. Although not considered a tax-free reorganization, conversions are nevertheless not subject to tax.

(b) Mergers

For purposes of the tax-free reorganization regime, a merger of entities is defined by the Income Tax Regulatory Decree as follows:

> *Merger of companies: when 2 (two) or more companies are dissolved without being liquidated in order to form a new company, or when an existing company absorbs another company/ies that is/are dissolved without liquidation, as long as, in the first case, at least 80% (eighty percent) of the new company's capital belongs—upon the merger—to the owners of the preceding companies; and, in the second case, the value of the ownership interest corresponding to the owners of the absorbed company/ies in the absorbing company must be that representing at least 80% (eighty percent) of the capital of the absorbed company/ies.*[4]

According to this definition, the Income Tax Regulatory Decree introduces a capital requirement (i.e., "at least 80%") to the definition provided by the ITA by which the owner of the entity or entities being reorganized must have in the surviving entity or entities in order to qualify for the tax relief.

(c) Tax-Free Reorganization Requirements

The ITA and its regulations establish certain requirements for mergers to be qualified as tax free. These requirements are generally designed to facilitate reorganizations so that tax considerations do not prevent companies from structuring themselves in an efficient manner; however, as with tax-free reorganization provisions in other countries, the rules also prevent taxpayers from using a tax-free reorganization to achieve what is in reality a true sale of business interests. The following section describes these requirements.

---

[4] Article 105 of the Income Tax Regulatory Decree.

Article 77 of the ITA, along with Articles 105 and 108 of the Income Tax Regulatory Decree, establishes the requirements for a merger to be treated as tax free. These requirements are as follows:

1. **Active entity:** As of the reorganization date, the companies being reorganized must be going concerns. This condition is considered to be met when such companies are carrying out the activities stated in the company's charter or, if no longer performing such activities, when they have ceased the activities within 18 months before the reorganization date.

2. **Participation requirement:** The owner(s) of the predecessor entities must maintain an amount of participation in the capital of the surviving company of not less than the participation held at the time of the reorganization (i.e., the afore-mentioned capital requirement) for at least two years from the reorganization date.[5] This requirement does not apply when the surviving entity or entities list their shares on self-regulated stock exchanges. Those entities must maintain such condition for at least two years from the reorganization date.

3. **Holding requirement:** The carryover of net operating losses and the transfer of unused tax exemptions originated in the adoption of the special promotion regimes referred to in clauses 1 and 5 of Article 78 of the ITA tie in the preceding entities and the surviving entities. This relationship occurs because the reorganization is limited to the extent that the owners, partners, or shareholders of the preceding entities, during the two years before the reorganization date, have maintained at least 80 percent of their interest in the preceding entities. This requirement does not apply when the precedent entities list their shares on self-regulated stock exchanges.

4. **Continuity of business activities:** The surviving entities must continue—for a period not less than two years from the reorganization date—any of the activities of the reorganized company or companies or any other activity related thereto (i.e., maintenance of the exploitation within the same industry). Therefore, the goods and/or services produced and/or commercialized by the surviving company or companies must bear characteristics that are essentially similar to those produced and/or commercialized by the preceding company or companies.

5. **Prior activity requirement:** The companies must have carried out the same or related activities during 12 months immediately before the reorganization date or the cessation of such activities, if such cessation occurred within the term of 18 months or, in both cases, during its existence if such term is shorter.

---

[5]This requirement was introduced by Law 25,063 (published in the *Official Bulletin* on December 30, 1998), applicable to the years ending subsequent to December 31, 1998 (following day after the publication of Law 25,063) and from tax year 1998 for individuals and undivided shares. Regarding this requirement, see the following ARS opinion: DICT. 19/85, DATJ (DGI) - 5/09/85.

1.5 Tax-Free Reorganizations

Related activities are those activities that help or supplement an industrial, commercial, or administrative process, or that aim at a purpose or goal related to the other activity, including horizontal and/or vertical integration.

6. **Reporting requirement:** The reorganization must be reported to the ARS within 180 days of the reorganization[6] when, due to the nature of the reorganization, the full transfer of the reorganized company or companies is not made, except in the case of spin-off, the transfer of tax rights and liabilities remain subject to the tax authorities' prior approval.

7. **Publication and Registration requirement:** The following publication and registration requirements set forth in Article 83 of the ACA 19550, as amended, must be satisfied:

- *Publication formalities:* A notice shall be published for three days in the official gazette or legal publications of the province or federal district of each company and in a major newspaper of nationwide circulation in Argentina. The notice must state the following:
    — Name and address of each merging company and data concerning the company's registration with the Public Registry of Commerce
    — Capital of the new company or companies or amount of increase in the capital of the absorbing company
    — Appraisal of assets and liabilities of the merging companies and the appraisal date
    — Name, type of company, and address of the new company, if a new company results from the merger
    — Dates of the prior merger commitment and company decisions approving it.

If any of the merging companies has a branch in another province, publication must also be made in that province to protect the interests of the creditors.

- *Registration:* the merger must be registered with the Public Registry of Commerce in the province of each merging company. As stated under Article 82 of the ACA, the merger takes effect from the date in which the final merger agreement and the new company's bylaws are in place or the absorbing company's capital increase are registered with the Public Registry of Commerce.

    If the reorganization provokes the dissolution of one of the predecessor companies, the company's dissolution must be registered with the appropriate Public Registry of Commerce.

---

[6] General Resolution of the ARS 2245 establishes the information to be supplied in a particular tax report to provide evidence that the requirements of the ITA and the Regulatory Decree have been complied with. Regarding this requirement, see the following ARS opinions: DICT. 48/84, DATJ (DGI)-10/03/84, DICT. 28/86, DATJ (DGI)-10/21/86, DICT. 46/93, DAL (DGI)-09/28/93, and DICT. 127/92, DAT (DGI)-12/10/92.

To comply with the afore-mentioned requirements, the reorganization date is that on which the surviving company or companies start(s) the activity or activities previously carried out by the preceding company or companies.

(d) Transfer of Rights and Obligations to the Surviving Companies

Among others, the more significant tax rights and obligations transferable to the surviving company or companies under the tax-free regime established in Article 78 of the ITA are as follows:

- Carryforward of net operating losses that were not barred by the statute of limitations
- The balances of tax exemptions or special deductions not used by virtue of the limitations on the computable amount for each tax period and that are transferable to future years
- Deferred charges that have not been deducted
- Unused tax exemptions to which the predecessor company or companies would have been entitled by virtue of using of special promotional regimes, provided that the basic conditions considered to grant the benefit are the same for the new company or companies. For these purposes, the applicable regulatory body appointed in the related provision shall issue a decision.
- The tax valuation of fixed assets, inventories, and intangible assets, whichever the value assigned may be for transfer purposes
- Applicable methods to charge income and expenses to the tax period
- Depreciation methods of fixed assets
- Amortization methods of intangible assets

In order to use criteria or methods different from those of the predecessor company or companies, the new company must request prior authorization from the tax authorities, provided that the legal provisions or regulations require so.

(e) Noncompliance

A purported reorganization might not comply with the technical requirements. In such a situation, the reorganization would be considered a taxable disposal of assets by the transferor company or a taxable acquisition of assets by the transferee company. The bulk sale tax treatment would apply. Consequently, the appropriate tax returns should be filed or amended, applying the legal provisions that would have been appropriate if the transaction had been made disregarding the tax-free regime. The taxpayer would need to pay the pertinent tax plus interest and fines.

(f) Other Consequences

For purposes of the TMPI, Article 3 of its Regulatory Decree establishes that when, as a consequence of a tax-free reorganization according to the ITA, the closing of both the reorganized and surviving entity's or entities' financial year

1.5 Tax-Free Reorganizations

occurs in the same fiscal year, the predecessor and surviving entities have to file their tax returns separately. Thus, these parties are taxed on their existing assets at the closing of their financial periods; however, the surviving companies would be able to credit the amount paid for the TMPI by the reorganized companies in proportion to the taxable assets transferred to each surviving entity. This would not generate, in any case, a credit balance in favor of the surviving entity or entities.

According to Article 2 of the VAT law, the transfer of goods made as a result of a business reorganization that qualifies as tax free for income tax purposes is not considered a taxable sale. Thus, tax-free mergers are not levied with VAT. Furthermore, the VAT law establishes that the accumulated VAT credits of the entities being reorganized could be used by the surviving entities. If the merger does not fall within the tax-free reorganization regime, the transfer of assets is subject to the general treatment of the law.

Generally, the stamp tax rules of most Argentine provinces provide that reorganizations that qualify as tax free for income tax purposes are not subject to stamp taxes. In some cases, stamp tax rules do not apply when the entities qualify as certain types of reorganizations for corporate law purposes.

Provincial turnover taxes do not apply to qualifying tax-free reorganizations. Whether a particular reorganization is tax free for turnover tax purposes depends on variables such as the law of the province involved and the details of the reorganization itself. For example, in the City of Buenos Aires, the transfer of assets as a part of a reorganization through mergers, spin-offs, and transfers of going concerns must meet the requirements for tax-free reorganization under the federal income tax law before they can be considered tax free for City of Buenos Aires turnover tax purposes.

(g) Divisions or Spin-Offs

For purposes of the tax-free reorganization regime, a spin-off is defined as follows:[7]

- *When a company destines a portion of its equity to an existing company or participates in the creation of a new company, as long as upon such spin-off or division, the value of the ownership interest corresponding to the spun-off or divided company in the existing company's capital or in the new company is not lower than that representing at least 80% (eighty percent) of the equity used for that purpose.*

- *When a company destines a portion of its equity to create a new company or it is split into new companies which are both legally and economically independent, as long as at least 80% (eighty percent) of the capital of the new company(ies), taken together, belongs to the owners of the preceding company. The spin-off or division implies in all cases the proportional reduction of capital.*

---

[7] Article 105 of the Income Tax Decree.

According to Article 106 of the Income Tax Decree, *in a tax-free division, the transfer of the tax rights (e.g., net operating losses) must be allocated based on the assets transferred on a pro-rata basis.*

The tax attributes that are transferable in a tax-free division are the same as those for mergers. As occurs with mergers, when the tax-free requirements are not complied with, this reorganization would be subject to the same income tax treatment as a taxable merger. This treatment would apply to the extent that the division implies a disposal of assets by one company and their acquisition by another company.

1.6 SALES AND TRANSFERS WITHIN THE SAME BUSINESS GROUP

The sale and transfer between entities that belong to the same economic group is the last kind of reorganization described under Article 77 of the ITA. According to Article 105 of the Regulatory Decree, a business group exists when:

> *80% (eighty percent) or more of the capital of the surviving company belongs to the owner, partners or shareholders of the company being reorganized. In addition, they must individually maintain in the new company, upon conversion, at least 80% (eighty percent) of the capital they owned as of the reorganization date in the preceding company."* [8]

(a) Tax-Free Reorganization Requirements

In the case of business reorganizations that qualify for the afore-mentioned definition, *only points **2, 3** (i.e., holding requirements), **4** (i.e., continuity of business activities), and **7** (i.e., publication and registration requirements set forth by the ACA 19,550)* of the requirements established for tax-free mergers and divisions must be met for intra-group transfers to be qualified as tax free (*see* 5.1.1.2). In other words, the tax-free intra-group transfers have fewer requirements than tax-free mergers and divisions.

A particular issue regarding an intra-group transfer is whether this is the sale/transfer of a "universe" of assets or, instead, the partial sale/transfer of assets from one entity to the other.

It is important to bear in mind in this regard that, as mentioned in Section 5, point 6:

> *When, due to the nature of the reorganization, the full transfer of the reorganized company or companies is not made, except in the case of spin-off, the transfer of tax rights and liabilities shall remain subject to **the tax authorities' prior approval.***

---

[8] Regarding the controversial requirement of the 80 percent of the capital, see the following leading cases: Ponieman Hnos. SAICA, CNACAF (9/06/65) and Lagazzio, Emilio Francisco, CSJN (8/25/72).

1.6 Sales and Transfers within the Same Business Group

Finally, secondary authority, jurisprudence, and ARS opinions maintain that a partial transfer of assets is also a "tax-free reorganization" because in the Argentine tax system, such concept has always comprehended both the transfer of a "universe" of assets and of certain isolated assets.[9]

(b) Transfer of Rights and Obligations to the Surviving Companies

The tax attributes that are transferable in a tax-free transfer of going concerns are the same as those described previously with respect to mergers. Also, *the transfer of the tax rights (e.g., net operating losses) must be allocated based on the net assets transferred (as opposed to assets) on a pro-rata basis.*

(c) Other Sales and Transfers

In the case of other sales and transfers (i.e., those that qualify as tax-free intra-group transfers), the tax rights and obligations are not transferred. When the transfer price assigned is higher than the current market price of the related assets, the value to be considered for tax purposes shall be such market price, and the treatment given by this law to goodwill shall be applicable to the surplus.[10] The consequences with respect to other taxes in this context are the same as those described previously for mergers.

1.7 CONCLUSION

Argentina has been going through a transformation since July 1989, including intense political changes triggered by the reinstatement of democracy in December 1983. The current government policy seeks to reverse six decades of economic decline, which was characterized by the nationalization of all public utilities and excessive regulation of private sector activities. A combination of legal framework, fiscal discipline, consistent monetary and financial policies, rescheduling of the foreign debt, and structural changes in areas including trade liberalization, privatization, and deregulation have strengthened the Argentine economy in recent years.

---

[9] Giuliani Fonrouge, *Business Reorganizations from a Tax Point of View.* Copyright La Ley, Volume 92 (page 423) quoted in Rubén O. Asorey, *Business Reorganization in Argentina.* Copyright 1996 by La Ley, page 94. ARS opinion "Sofitur S.A.", D.A.T., August 1978.

[10] Special tax settlement terms: According to Article 109 of the Income Tax Regulatory Decree, the ARS may grant—at the taxpayer's request—special terms to pay the respective tax, which shall not exceed five years—with or without bond—plus the related interest and the adjustment provided for in Law 11,683 (as amended in 1998), considering the terms and formalities agreed upon for the collection of the credit.

The provisions set forth in this article shall be applicable to the extent that the publication and registration requirements provided for in Law 11,867 are met.

ANNEX I

Reorganization Type	Tax Free (1)	Assumption of Tax Contingencies	Transfer of Rights and Liabilities	Active Entity	Maintainance of Ownership	Two-Year Look-Back (3)	Continuity of Business	Prior Activity	Report to the ARS	Registration (Law No 19550) (6)	Prior Approval of the ARS
Merger Art 77	YES	YES	YES	YES	YES	YES	YES	YES	YES	YES	NO
Taxable Merger	NO	YES	NO	NO	NO	NO	NO	NO	NO	YES	NO
Spin Off Art 77	YES	YES	YES	YES	YES	YES	YES	YES	YES	YES	NO
Taxable Spin Off	NO	YES	NO	NO	NO	NO	NO	NO	NO	YES	NO
Intra-group Assets Transaction	YES	YES	YES	NO	YES	YES	YES	NO	YES	NO	YES (4)
Assets Acquisition (7)	NO	NO (5)	NO	NO	NO	NO	NO	NO	NO	NO	NO
Stock Acquisition	NO (2)	YES	YES	NO	NO	NO	NO	NO	NO	NO	NO
Conversion	YES	YES	YES	NO	NO	NO	NO	NO	NO	YES	NO

(1) Tax-free for purposes of Income Tax and VAT. In general terms, provincial turnover and stamp taxes do not apply to qualifying tax-free reorganizations.
(2) However, if the seller is not an Argentine resident, the transaction would be exempt from Argentine income tax (Decree 2284).
(3) Only required with respect to the transfer of net operative losses and tax incentives.
(4) In case of partial transfers (when, due to the nature of the reorganization, the full transfer of the reorganized company or companies is not made) the transfer of tax rights and liabilities is subjct to the ARS' prior approval.
(5) Only applicable to the transfer of a going concern if within three months after the transfer such transaction is notified to the ARS.
(6) The Argentine Companies Act establishes the fulfillment of this requirement regardless of whether the reorganization qualifies as tax-free or not.
(7) We refer to an assets acquisition that qualifies as a transfer of going concern.

CHAPTER 2

Taxation of Mergers and Acquisitions in Australia

Tim L. Carberry*
Greg Leyden
Ernst & Young, Australia

2.1 **Introduction**
2.2 **Income Tax**
    (a)   General
    (b)   Residence
    (c)   Choice of Entity
    (d)   Calculation of Taxable Income
2.3 **Merger and Acquisition Options in Australia**
2.4 **Asset vs. Scrip Acquisition**
    (a)   Benefits of an Asset Acquisition
    (b)   Benefits of a Scrip Acquisition
2.5 **Asset Acquisition**
    (a)   Trade Debts
    (b)   Inventory
    (c)   Plant and Equipment
    (d)   Employee Entitlements and Other Assumed Liabilities
2.6 **Scrip Acquisition**
    (a)   Purchase of Scrip for Cash
    (b)   Scrip-for-Scrip Acquisition: Issues for the Vendor
    (c)   Scrip-for-Scrip Acquisition: Issues for the Purchaser
    (d)   Purchase of Scrip for both Cash and Issue of Scrip
    (e)   Recoupment of Prior Year Tax Losses
    (f)   Unrealized Losses on Change of Majority Beneficial Ownership
    (g)   Loss Integrity Measures

---

*The authors gratefully acknowledge the assistance of the following:
Richard Czerwik, Senior Manager, National Tax, Melbourne
Richard Goodwin, Manager, International Tax, Melbourne
Ken Goodin, Senior Manager, GST & Transaction Taxes, Melbourne
Cullen Smythe, Manager, GST & Transaction Taxes, Sydney
Leon Loganathan, Senior Manager, GST & Transaction Taxes, Sydney
David Lawson, Principal, Ernst & Young Law, Melbourne
Rod Brown, Associate Lawyer, Ernst & Young Law, Melbourne

(h) Dividends
(i) Capital Gains Tax: Unrealized Liabilities
2.7 Inbound Investment
(a) Capital Gains Tax
(b) Withholding Tax
(c) Thin Capitalization
(d) Transfer Pricing
2.8 Outbound Investment
(a) Financing the Acquisition
(b) Dividends Received
(c) Attribution of Income
2.9 Business Taxation Reform
(a) Consolidation Regime
(b) Thin Capitalization
(c) Debt and Equity Classification
(d) Uniform Entity Regime
2.10 Goods and Services Tax (GST)
(a) Background
(b) Overview of the GST System
(c) Application of GST to Business Reorganizations
2.11 Stamp Duty
(a) Business Acquisitions
(b) Acquisition of Shares
(c) Other Duties
(d) Corporate Reconstruction Examples
2.12 Legal and Regulatory Requirements
(a) Competition Policy: Acquisitions of Australian Businesses
(b) Foreign Exchange Controls

2.1 INTRODUCTION

This chapter addresses Australian mergers and acquisitions taxation issues, with a particular focus on the considerations relevant to nonscrip assets or a scrip acquisition. *Scrip* includes equity in an entity, such as shares in a company or rights or options pertaining to shares in a company or units in a unit trust. Corporations are generally referred to as "companies" in Australia. This chapter addresses the different needs of Australian inbound and outbound investors.

The chapter is divided into the following subjects:

- income tax that incorporates capital gains tax
- goods and services tax
- stamp duty
- legal and regulatory requirements

2.2 Income Tax

Australia is currently undergoing a period of significant business taxation reform. Some of the reform measures that have been recommended will significantly impact business taxation in general, as well as future mergers and acquisitions. These tax reform measures are addressed as part of the discussion of the income tax implications.

2.2 INCOME TAX

(a) General

The federal government in Australia levies income taxes. Although Australia also has state and local governments, these governments do not levy income taxes.

The income tax year in Australia is the year ending June 30, and taxpayers are required to file their income tax returns for periods ending each June 30; however, a taxpayer may seek approval from the Federal Commissioner of Taxation to adopt a different income year-end date (e.g., the year ending December 31 in lieu of the succeeding June 30). This accounting timeframe is known as a *substituted accounting period*. The Commissioner of Taxation generally grants this approval when a foreign parent reports on a date other than June 30.

(b) Residence

Australia generally seeks to impose income tax on Australian residents for their income from all sources. Australia seeks to impose income tax on nonresidents based on their income from Australian sources.

(c) Choice of Entity

This chapter focuses on the tax implications of mergers and acquisitions involving corporate entities in Australia. By way of background, the following is a brief summary of the income tax treatment of alternative types of investment vehicles in Australia.

Companies

Companies are subject to income tax as an entity. The current rate of corporate tax is 34 percent; however, Australia is planning to reduce this corporate tax rate to 30 percent for income years commencing July 1, 2001, or for a substituted accounting period.

Australia has adopted a dividend imputation regime to minimize the incidence of double taxation of company profits. Income tax paid by an Australian resident company on its taxable income will generally give rise to credits known as *imputation credits*. A company will maintain an account known as a *franking account* to record such credits. These credits do not provide any tax relief to the company itself, but they may be passed onto shareholders attached to dividends or distributions paid by the company to its shareholders.

A company distribution from fully taxed profit is known as a fully franked dividend, whereas a distribution from a partially taxed pool of profits is known as a partially franked dividend. If the shareholder is a resident taxpayer, the imputation credits can be used to reduce the income tax payable by the shareholder on such dividends. The treatment of nonresident shareholders is considered separately in a following section. In essence, the payment of tax by a company on its profits is imputed to the shareholder when those after-tax profits are paid to the shareholder.

A company is treated as a resident of Australia if the company is incorporated in Australia or if the company carries on business in Australia and either has its central management and control in Australia or Australian residents have voting power that controls the company.

A registered pooled development fund is a venture capital investment company. A company that is registered as a pooled development fund is subject to lower tax rates of 15 percent on capital gains and unfranked dividends, distributed to shareholders from untaxed profits, or 25 percent for interest or other income. Special tax rules apply to certain types of companies, including life insurance companies, friendly societies, credit unions, and cooperatives.

Trusts

Trusts are generally taxed as flow-through vehicles under Australian income tax law. Nevertheless, trusts are required to prepare a separate trust income tax return disclosing the net income and to whom that income is taxable. In contrast, public trading trusts and corporate unit trusts are taxed as if they were companies. A public unit trust is essentially a unit trust with at least 50 unitholders, which carry on a trading business. A corporate unit trust is a unit trust with at least 50 unitholders, where the trust has received property from a company that is associated with the unitholders under an arrangement.

A superannuation fund is a trust established to principally provide retirement benefits to its members (i.e., a pension fund). A resident superannuation fund is generally subject to income tax at the rate of 15 percent on taxable incomes. Special rules apply to such funds in determining what is included in taxable income. Distributions of taxable income by a trust to a nonresident investor are subject to withholding tax.

Partnerships

A partnership includes an arrangement under which parties jointly receive income. Partnerships are generally treated as flow-through vehicles but are required to file a separate partnership income tax return disclosing partnership income. The individual partners are assessed on their share of the partnership's net income for a tax year or are allowed a deduction for their share of the net loss. Partnerships that are treated as limited partnerships under the general laws of one of the Australian states or territories are taxed as companies.

2.2 Income Tax

A partner in a partnership is treated as having an equitable interest in each of the partnership assets for the purposes of capital gains tax. A change of partners in a partnership may trigger a deemed disposal of an interest in each partnership asset by each preexisting partner, which in turn may trigger a tax liability on any deemed gains arising from such a transaction; however, rollover relief may be claimed in certain circumstances. Rollover relief involves the taxpayer choosing to defer the recognition of a taxation liability in respect of a transaction. Relief is available only when the taxpayer meets several specific conditions.

Joint venture arrangements

Unincorporated joint venture arrangements are arrangements by which the joint venturers share the produce (raw materials or the like) of an operation. Such arrangements are treated as flow-through vehicles. Essentially, each joint venturer is deemed to have incurred its proportionate share of the expenditure of the joint venture and is assessed on any income it makes from the sale or utilization of the product of the venture.

Joint ventures are not required to file separate tax returns. Members of a joint venture have a legal interest in the venture's assets for the purpose of capital gains tax. A change in the members of a joint venture may trigger a deemed disposal of the plant of the joint venture, subject to eligibility to choose rollover relief.

(d) Calculation of Taxable Income

Income tax is imposed on taxable income, which is the sum of assessable income less allowable deductions. Assessable income includes income according to ordinary accounting concepts and statutory income, which includes capital gains. Allowable deductions generally include the expenses of a business necessarily incurred in deriving assessable income; however, allowable deductions exclude expenses incurred in earning exempt income. Allowable deductions also exclude expenses of a private and domestic nature or those that are capital in nature.

As a general rule, a capital expenditure is not deductible; however, various provisions within Australian income tax law allow a deduction for the following:

- A factory plant that produces income can be depreciated over the effective life of the plant unless the plant is acquired under a contract entered on or before September 21, 1999. Accelerated rates may apply to a plant acquired before September 21, 1999.
- The original construction cost of income-producing buildings, such as an office building or factory, and other structural improvements, such as income-producing roads and associated earth works can be amortized at an historical construction cost at 2.5 percent or 4 percent per year.
- Certain capital expenditures on industrial property, limited to copyright, patents, and registered designs, are allowed.

Other intangibles such as goodwill are not amortizable/depreciable for taxation purposes.

The Australian government is considering introducing legislation to amalgamate the various capital allowable regimes outlined previously into a uniform capital allowance regime, based on the effective life of assets. This measure is intended to come into effect on July 1, 2001. Currently, the costs of acquiring a new business are not deductible; however, the uniform capital allowance regime may allow a deduction for limited types of project costs and business acquisition costs.

Capital gains on the disposal of assets are taxed under income tax law, however, a special regime within this law (referred to as capital gains tax provisions) calculates gains to be included within assessable income. The capital gains of companies are taxed at the standard corporate rate.

Australia operates a mixed system of exemption and credits to eliminate the double taxation of foreign-source income received by Australian residents. Double taxation can occur when the same income is subject to tax in the hands of two or more different entities or the same income is taxed in the hands of the same entity by two or more different tax jurisdictions. Australia uses an imputation system to eliminate double taxation of company profits and either the allowance of a foreign tax credit or exemption to eliminate double taxation of foreign-source income.

2.3   MERGER AND ACQUISITION OPTIONS IN AUSTRALIA

In broad terms, a merger or acquisition involves the acquisition of an equity interest in a target company and/or the underlying assets in a target company. Equity interest may include scrip in a company, and underlying assets may include items such as land, plant, or materials held by a target company. In addition, Australian Corporations Law, supplemented by the rules of the Australian Stock Exchange for listed entities, may allow the following types of transactions as part of a scrip or asset acquisition:

- Issue of new scrip by the target company to the purchaser
- Transfer of existing scrip by existing shareholders to the purchaser
- Transfer of assets from a target company to the purchaser
- Scrip-for-scrip transfers
- Merger/demerger of existing corporate entities
- Reorganization of assets within a corporate group

Both the seller and the purchaser often undertake preparatory reorganizations to maximize the potential commercial and tax benefits that can arise from a merger or acquisition. These reorganizations may include the implementation of appropriate steps to allow for the method of financing the proposed acquisition.

The capital gains tax provisions include a wide range of rollover relief. Under these provisions, a taxpayer can choose to defer the recognition of a taxation lia-

2.4 Asset vs. Scrip Acquisition

bility as to a transaction. This relief is available only to taxpayers that meet specific conditions for relief. Rollover relief is generally available when the following conditions occur:

- An individual transfers assets to a company wholly owned by the individual.
- Partners in a partnership transfer assets to a company wholly owned by the partners in proportion to their preexisting partnership interests.
- An asset is transferred among members of a group of wholly owned companies (e.g., from a parent company to its wholly owned subsidiary).
- A newly created company is interposed between a previously existing company and its shareholders, where those shareholders own the interposed entity in the same proportions as their previous shareholding in the previous company.

Australian income tax law does not provide specific capital gains tax relief for business mergers or demergers, although capital gains tax scrip-for-scrip rollover rules may potentially apply. The Australian government is currently considering the introduction of demerger rollover relief rules, with a potential start date of July 1, 2002, as part of its program to reform business taxation.

2.4 ASSET VS. SCRIP ACQUISITION

The key considerations in deciding between a scrip acquisition (i.e., the acquisition of shares or rights or options over shares in a company) and an asset acquisition (i.e., the acquisition of underlying assets held by an entity such as land, plant, or materials) are outlined as follows.

(a) Benefits of an Asset Acquisition:

- The acquiror is free from any exposure to undisclosed liabilities of the target company, such as legal actions and tax liabilities that may arise after the acquisition.
- A significant portion of the purchase price may be structured in a tax-effective manner. The acquisition of underlying assets generally provides greater deductions in either the year of acquisition or subsequent years of income. These greater deductions accrue because deductions are based on the market value of the asset, rather than the written-down value in the hands of the vendor. The cost of acquiring shares is generally not deductible for Australian income tax purposes, and the value of underlying assets is generally not refreshed as a result of an acquisition of shares.

(b) Benefits of a Scrip Acquisition

- Accumulated prior year tax losses of the target company may be utilized if the target company continues to carry on the same business after acquisition.
- Franking credits of the target company may be utilized by the acquiring company.
- Stamp duty is generally lower than on an asset acquisition.

The Australian government is proposing to introduce an income tax consolidation regime that will radically alter the way wholly owned groups are taxed in Australia. If this regime is introduced, the resident parent (head entity) of a consolidated group of companies will be treated as having acquired each of the underlying assets held by each member of the group. The cost of the shares in each member will form the basis of determining the tax value of the underlying assets. Each member can restate the tax basis of the assets of a target company to reflect the share acquisition price. The proposed consolidation regime is discussed in Section 2.9, Business Taxation Reform, of this chapter.

2.5 ASSET ACQUISITION

Each asset and liability acquired needs to be considered for its specific taxation implications. The ability to structure the purchase price of the assets in a tax-effective manner is currently a key advantage of asset acquisitions. Purchasers may want to allocate the purchase price to those assets for which tax deductions are available, either immediately or in future years; however, vendors may not want to allocate the purchase price to particular assets if the allocation results in a taxable gain on the disposal of those assets. As a result, the competing considerations of vendors and purchasers need to be addressed and an agreement reached regarding the allocation of the proceeds among the assets of the business. Specific taxation considerations of an asset acquisition include the taxation treatment of trade debtors, trading stock, plant and equipment, and employee entitlements.

(a) Trade Debts

Debt acquired on the acquisition of a business is generally not deductible if the debt is subsequently written off as bad debt. A bad debt may otherwise give rise to a capital loss, but capital losses can be offset only against capital gains rather than any assessable income. Company trade debt on a share acquisition may give rise to a tax deduction if written off after the acquisition.

(b) Inventory

The purchaser is entitled to an immediate tax deduction for the purchase of inventory. However, if the inventory is still on hand at the end of the year of income, then the value of the inventory on hand (either its cost or market value) is included as an item of assessable income. This add-back adjustment offsets the immediate deduction claimed.

(c) Plant and Equipment

The purchaser of plant and equipment is not entitled to an immediate deduction for the cost of plant and equipment. However, a depreciation deduction is allowed for the cost of the plant, when the plant is owned by an Australian taxpayer and is used for the purpose of producing assessable income. This depreciation deduction is calculated over the remaining effective life of the plant and equipment.

Special provisions allow a depreciation deduction for a plant that is not owned by an Australian taxpayer but the plant is affixed to land to which the taxpayer has a quasi-ownership right. A quasi-ownership right is a government-granted lease over land or some other kind of power over land that was granted by law. For example, such a right is a right granted under a state's mining laws to explore for minerals on land owned by a third party.

The cost allocated to a plant by parties dealing at arm's length is generally the cost that the purchaser is able to depreciate. This can include actual cash outlaid, liabilities assumed, and incidental costs of acquisition, including stamp duty but excluding goods and services tax paid. Assets acquired from exempt entities (governments or charities) may have their depreciable cost imposed by statute based on the notionally written-down original acquisition cost or on the notionally written-down audited book value of the asset in the hands of the vendor. The purchaser needs to estimate the effective life of the plant in order to calculate depreciation deductions. Alternatively, the purchaser can rely on the rates of effective life published by the Australian Commissioner of Taxation.

A key advantage of an asset acquisition over a scrip acquisition is the ability to step up the depreciable base of the plant. However, a plant acquired after September 21, 1999, cannot be depreciated using "accelerated" depreciation rates. *Accelerated depreciation* refers to the use of broad-banded rates of write-off where the rate is generally faster than the pure effective life. For example, an asset with an effective life of five years would have an effective life rate of historical cost depreciation of 20 percent, whereas the broad-banded accelerated rate would have been 40 percent.

(d) Employee Entitlements and Other Assumed Liabilities

When acquiring the assets of a business, the purchaser may undertake to continue the employment of employees and therefore agree to pay their accrued leave entitlements of the employees. These liabilities are generally deductible when paid to employees. The purchaser should carefully examine other assumed liabilities to ensure that they are deductible when paid.

2.6 SCRIP ACQUISITION

The acquisition of scrip in a target company may be structured as follows:

- The purchaser pays cash for the scrip in the target company
- The purchaser issues scrip to the vendor in return for the sale of the vendor's scrip in the target company
- A combination of both

(a) Purchase of Scrip for Cash

In order to reduce any capital gains tax upon a subsequent disposal of scrip, it is desirable for the purchaser to maximize the cost base of the scrip it is acquiring. For Australian capital gains tax purposes, the cost base of scrip includes the following expenditures, which are not otherwise deductible for tax purposes:

- The amount paid by the purchaser for scrip in the target company
- Fees paid to professional advisers, including accountants, lawyers, and brokers, in connection with the acquisition of the scrip
- Stamp duty
- Costs incurred by the purchaser in relation to making a valuation of the target company

The purchaser should identify any nondeductible costs to determine whether these may be included in the cost base of the scrip acquired.

(b) Scrip-for-Scrip Acquisition: Issues for the Vendor

The transfer or assignment of scrip or other property may give rise to a taxable capital gain under Australia's capital gains tax provisions. Under scrip-for-scrip capital gains tax rollover relief rules, where there is an eligible scrip-for-scrip arrangement a vendor can defer a capital gain until it disposes of the replacement scrip received in the purchasing entity, or a related entity.

To be eligible for scrip-for-scrip rollover relief, the following requirements must be satisfied:

- The vendor must have acquired the scrip in the target company after September 19, 1985, the start date for Australia's capital gains tax regime
- The purchaser must become the owner of at least 80 percent of the scrip in the target company under a single arrangement
- All scripholders of the target company must be able to participate in the arrangement
- The vendor must have exchanged its scrip in the target company for scrip in the purchaser or a related entity, which is called *rollover scrip*
- The vendor would otherwise make a capital gain on disposal of its scrip.
- The vendor elects for the rollover relief to apply.

Rollover relief will not apply if the vendor meets the following conditions:

- Is a nonresident or a resident trust for capital gains tax purposes
- Is a resident, but the target entity is a nonresident entity (with less than 300 members) and the acquiror was a nonresident (with less than 300 members)

The capital gain made by the vendor is disregarded when rollover relief requirements are satisfied.

2.6 Scrip Acquisition

The vendor's cost base—the cost of the asset taken into account for tax purposes when determining whether a taxable gain or loss arises on disposal of the asset—in the rollover scrip is equal to the cost base of the vendor's original scrip in the target company. For the purchaser, the cost base of the scrip it has acquired from the vendor is one of the following:

- Equal to the vendor's cost base in the scrip that it has disposed (this is known as *cost base transfer* and occurs only if the vendor has at least a 30 percent interest in both the target company and the acquiring entity)
- The market value of the scrip acquired at the date of acquisition by the purchaser.

(c) Scrip-for-Scrip Acquisition: Issues for the Purchaser

The issue of shares by a purchaser should not give rise to any immediate tax liability. A fresh issue of scrip, in contrast to a transfer of existing scrip on issue, will not constitute a disposal of an asset for capital gains tax purposes. Under the capital gains tax provisions the value of the scrip issued by the purchaser is generally included in determining the capital gains tax cost base of the scrip acquired in the target company. However, this rule does not apply where scrip-for-scrip capital gains tax rollover relief is claimed and the vendor had at least a 30 percent interest in the target company and the acquiring entity.

(d) Purchase of Scrip for both Cash and Issue of Scrip

When the consideration provided by the purchaser for acquisition of scrip in the target company is both cash and the issue of scrip, both of the issues discussed previously apply. However, to the extent that cash is received, scrip-for-scrip capital gains tax rollover relief is not available to the vendor.

(e) Recoupment of Prior Year Tax Losses

A current benefit of a scrip acquisition is that it allows for the recoupment of prior year tax losses (both revenue and capital losses) incurred by the target company. However, when there has been a change in majority underlying beneficial ownership in the loss company, then the company must meet the requirement of the "same business test" in order to recoup its losses. This means a company taken over must carry on the "same business" it conducted immediately before the takeover in the year of income that it seeks to recoup losses.

The Australian Commissioner of Taxation applies a strict interpretation of the "same business" test. The test assesses the identity of the business carried on before and after the change in ownership. Similarity is not sufficient; however, this does not mean the business must be identical in all respects. The test is not satisfied if the target company carries on a new business after the change in ownership or enters into transactions of a kind that it had not entered into before the change of ownership. Prior year trust losses are subject to broadly similar rules, which have been modified to deal with a wider range of ownership structures that may arise for a trust.

(f) Unrealized Losses on Change of Majority Beneficial Ownership

Net unrealized losses of a target company at the time of a change in majority beneficial ownership may also be subject to the same business test when the loss is subsequently realized and the company seeks to use the loss.

(g) Loss Integrity Measures

Consideration also needs to be given to the impact of several loss integrity measures that were introduced by the Australian government as part of a program to reform business taxation. These measures are broadly designed to minimize the opportunities for generating multiple losses within a wholly owned group. The loss integrity measures that need to be considered, in addition to the loss rules noted previously include the following:

- Cost base adjustments to scrip held in companies with accumulated tax losses where there is a change in majority underlying beneficial ownership of the loss company
- Cost base adjustments to shares held in a company, where that company has transferred a tax loss to another group company
- Guaranteeing of losses incurred on the disposal of an asset between group or linked entities

In certain circumstances, a corporate reorganization may trigger the application of these measures. In addition, any due diligence process needs to consider whether a target company may have been previously impacted by these rules.

(h) Dividends

The taxation treatment of the dividends paid by the target company to the purchaser depends on whether the purchaser is a resident or nonresident company.

Resident company purchaser

If the target company is 100 percent owned by another Australian company, or if the target company pays a franked dividend, the resident company shareholder is entitled to a full rebate of tax on the dividend received. Therefore, the dividend is effectively tax free. The Australian government proposes to amend the law to remove this rebate as to group company dividends upon the introduction of a consolidation regime (see section 2.9(a), Consolidation Regime), which has a proposed start date of July 1, 2002. When a target company has a 10 percent or greater interest (but less than 100 percent) in another Australian company, the target company may be entitled to a deduction for unfranked dividends received and taxed in its own hands, where it subsequently pays a dividend to a nonresident shareholder.

2.6 Scrip Acquisition

Nonresident company purchaser

For a nonresident company purchaser, dividend withholding tax is payable if the dividend is paid out of untaxed profits of the target company, known as an *unfranked dividend*. The rate of withholding tax is 30 percent, but if the nonresident shareholder is a resident of a country with which Australia has entered a comprehensive double tax agreement, the rate is generally 15 percent. If the dividend is fully franked (i.e., it is paid out of taxed profits), no withholding tax is payable. When withholding tax is paid, or the dividend is fully franked, the dividend is excluded from the assessable income of the nonresident shareholder and therefore no further Australian tax is payable.

An unfranked dividend may be exempt from dividend withholding tax to the extent that it is subject to a foreign dividend account credit. This regime essentially allows the flow of comparably taxed foreign dividends through Australia without adding an additional layer of Australian withholding tax when the dividend is paid to a nonresident. The regime does this by allowing the Australian shareholding company to accumulate foreign dividend account credits for certain foreign dividends received. Dividends paid to a nonresident by the Australian company are not subject to Australian withholding tax to the extent where foreign dividend account credits are attached to those dividends.

(i) Capital Gains Tax: Unrealized Liabilities

An important consideration when acquiring shares in a company is a comprehensive understanding of any potential unrealized capital gains tax liabilities that may exist within a target company. Current considerations include the following:

Pre-CGT assets

Assets acquired by a target company before September 20, 1985, fall outside the capital gains tax (CGT) regime in Australia and are not subject to this tax on disposal; however, when a takeover or acquisition results in a change of ownership of 50 percent or more of the issued shares of the target company, all assets of the target company that were acquired before September 20, 1985, are deemed to have been acquired on the date the change of ownership occurred for market value. These assets fall within the capital gains tax regime and a capital gain may arise upon subsequent disposal.

Group company rollover assets

The purchaser should also be aware of any assets that the target company acquired from another group company for which capital gains tax group company rollover relief was chosen. Rollover relief may have been chosen when an asset is transferred among members of a group of wholly owned companies (e.g., from a parent company to its wholly owned subsidiary). When the takeover or acquisition occurs, there may be a deemed disposal (i.e., a deemed sale) and reacquisition of these assets by the target company at their market value on the date of the takeover or acquisition. The target company is subject to tax on the capital gain that arises on the deemed disposal of the asset.

The Australian government is currently proposing to amend Australian law to introduce a consolidation regime (see subsection 2.9(a) Consolidation Regime). This regime will affect the capital gains tax implications of share disposals for consolidated groups.

2.7 INBOUND INVESTMENT

This section considers additional issues for non-Australian investors investing into Australia.

(a) Capital Gains Tax

Non-residents of Australia will be subject to tax on the disposal of an asset only if the asset has a "necessary connection" with Australia. Only assets that fall within a limited class will have a necessary connection with Australia. Under a scrip acquisition, the scrip in an Australian resident company or trust will generally have the necessary connection with Australia, and therefore will be subject to capital gains tax upon disposal.

Certain portfolio interests in Australian public companies and unit trusts (less than 10 percent ownership interest in the entity at all times during the last five years before any disposal) may not have a necessary connection with Australia. Under an asset acquisition, all assets used in an Australian permanent establishment will generally have a necessary connection with Australia. When the purchaser is a resident of a country with which Australia has entered into a double tax agreement, it may be possible to structure the acquisition such that Australian income tax is not payable upon a subsequent disposal of the shares. This purchase requires careful tax planning before the acquisition.

The Australian government is seeking to prevent such tax-planning opportunities under its business taxation reform program. Proposed reform measures include the extension of capital gains tax rules to gains on disposal of interposed entities and antitreaty shopping measures. Whether such unilateral measures by Australia will be effective in binding its treaty partners is unclear and may need to be tested in court.

(b) Withholding Tax

Australia generally seeks to tax Australian-source income of a nonresident company at the corporate rate of tax; however, interest, royalty, and dividend income may be subject to withholding tax on the gross total payment. The rate of withholding on interest income is 10 percent. The rate of withholding on royalty income is 30 percent, reduced to 15 percent under most double tax agreements with Australia. Dividend income may be subject to withholding of 30 percent when it is unfranked, is reduced to 15 percent under most double tax agreements

2.8 Outbound Investment

with Australia, or is zero when the dividend is franked or subject to a foreign dividend account credit.

(c) Thin Capitalization

The Australian tax law contains rules that deny deductions for interest paid by an Australian company to the extent that foreign debt, which is borrowed from, or guaranteed by, the nonresident controller, exceeds the foreign equity of the Australian company by a ratio of 2 to 1. These rules are referred to as the "thin capitalization" rules. These rules apply when the nonresident controller owns at least 15 percent of the Australian company and applies only to the interest-bearing related foreign party debt of the Australian company.

It is currently proposed to amend Australia's thin capitalization rules as part of broader business taxation reform (see section 2.9, Business Taxation Reform). Australia also has antidebt creation rules that may apply to deny an interest deduction in certain circumstances involving the transfer of assets. It is proposed that these rules will be repealed with effect from July 1, 2001 upon the introduction of the new thin capitalization rules.

(d) Transfer Pricing

Australia has a complex transfer pricing regime that applies to inbound and outbound investments. These rules allow the Australian Commissioner of Taxation to substitute an arm's length amount when a related party transaction (including transactions with a branch) is not otherwise at arm's length. These rules place onerous compliance obligations on Australian taxpayers.

2.8 OUTBOUND INVESTMENT

For Australian investors seeking to acquire foreign businesses, the following Australian tax implications need to be considered.

(a) Financing the Acquisition

The choice between debt and equity finance may depend on the mode of acquisition of the foreign business and on the jurisdiction of the foreign business.

Share acquisition

When an Australian investor receives dividends from a nonresident company and owns more than 10 percent of the foreign company, the dividend is generally exempt from Australian tax, although some dividends from companies in low-taxed jurisdictions are generally taxable unless the dividend satisfies specific conditions. Because the dividend is exempt from tax, any interest paid on funds borrowed to acquire the shares is not deductible for Australian tax purposes.

Therefore, in these circumstances it may be more tax-effective to finance the acquisition by equity rather than debt. Under recommendations made as part of the business taxation reform process, it is proposed that all interest expenses of an Australian business taxpayer be allowed as a deduction subject to the new thin capitalization rules (see subsection 2.9(b) Thin Capitalization).

Asset acquisition

When an Australian investor acquires the assets of a foreign business, the choice between debt and equity finance may depend on the jurisdiction of the foreign business. Under Australian tax law, business profits of the foreign branch of an Australian company are exempt from tax in Australia if those profits have been subject to tax in a country that has a tax system comparable to Australia. Because the foreign income is exempt from Australian tax, interest paid on debt funding is not deductible for Australian tax purposes.

If the foreign branch income is not exempt from Australian tax, interest paid on borrowed funds is allowed as a tax deduction. However, the interest may be claimed only as a deduction against the foreign-source income. Under business taxation reform, it is proposed that interest expenses incurred in deriving foreign-source income not be quarantined and be allowed as deductions against all income, irrespective of source, subject to the new thin capitalization rules.

(b) Dividends Received

Dividends received by an Australian company from a nonresident company are generally exempt from tax in Australia when the Australian company holds at least 10 percent of the voting power of a nonresident company in certain jurisdictions (including the United States, United Kingdom, France, and Japan). If the Australian company holds less than 10 percent of the voting power of the foreign company, the dividends received are subject to tax in Australia and a credit is allowed for the foreign taxes paid in respect of the dividend. Foreign dividends received by an Australian resident company can give rise to a credit to a foreign dividend account when the Australian company holds at least 10 percent of the voting power in the foreign company. The foreign dividend account can be used to credit unfranked dividends paid to nonresidents to effectively render them free from Australian withholding tax.

(c) Attribution of Income

Australian investors acquiring a foreign company need to be aware of Australia's accrual taxation rules, which are designed to prevent Australian investors from accumulating income and profits in low-tax foreign jurisdictions. The accrual tax rules tax Australian residents on their share of the income or profits derived by a foreign entity that has not been comparably taxed in the foreign jurisdiction and that has not been repatriated to Australia.

2.9 Business Taxation Reform

The accruals taxation system consists of four sets of rules:

- *Controlled foreign company rules,* which apply when an Australian resident owns or controls (together with their associates) at least 40 percent of a foreign company or otherwise controls the foreign company
- *Foreign investment fund rules,* which apply when an Australian resident has an interest in a foreign company or foreign trust
- *Transfer trust rules,* which apply when an Australian resident has transferred property to a foreign trust
- *Trust deeming rules,* which apply when an Australian resident has an interest (including a contingent interest) in a trust

Where an Australian investor acquires a controlling interest in a foreign company, both the controlled foreign company and foreign investment fund rules could potentially apply. Therefore, to avoid double taxation, the foreign investment fund rules do not apply if the controlled foreign company rules also apply to that investment. Income attributed to an Australian resident under the accruals regime and subsequently received is generally exempt from tax on receipt.

2.9 BUSINESS TAXATION REFORM

Australia is currently undergoing a significant period of business taxation reform. Many of the recommendations that have emerged from this reform process will have an impact on merger and acquisition activity in Australia. Those recommendations that have been legislated, and are now law, have been discussed previously where appropriate. Outlined as follows are key recommendations for which legislation has yet to be introduced into the Australian federal parliament, but for which the Australian government has provided in principle support. This discussion does not detail all the proposed changes nor does it provide a comprehensive analysis of the changes.

(a) Consolidation Regime

A major recommendation of Australian business taxation reform is the introduction of a consolidation regime. Exposure draft legislation has recently been released, detailing the rules for consolidation, and it is now proposed that these rules will apply from July 1, 2002. These measures are yet to be introduced into the Australian federal parliament.

Under the consolidation regime, all Australian resident entities (companies and trusts) within the same wholly owned group may elect to be treated as a single entity for income tax purposes. Once the election is made, it is irrevocable. Upon consolidation, the parent (head entity) of the consolidated group becomes the taxpayer for the group, and each wholly owned subsidiary within the group will be treated as if it were a division of the parent for Australian tax purposes.

Thereafter, all intra-group transactions are ignored for tax purposes and the parent assumes the income tax liability for the consolidated group. Partnerships will not be able to be amalgamated into a consolidated group for the purposes of the new regime.

Although consolidation is optional, Australian resident groups will have little choice but to elect to be taxed as a consolidated entity. The benefits that currently exist for wholly owned groups, particularly transfer of tax losses, inter-corporate dividend rebate, and CGT rollover on intra-group transfers of assets, will not be available to groups that do not consolidate.

For inbound investors, the impact of the consolidation regime needs to be carefully considered. When a nonresident ultimately owns an Australian resident group, the exposure draft legislation does not allow the nonresident entity to be the parent of the consolidated group because only Australian resident entities are allowed in the consolidated group. However, it is proposed that when a nonresident had two or more entry points (Australian resident entities) into Australia at September 21, 1999, one of these entities will be allowed to be nominated as a virtual head entity of the entire Australian group. Australian entities acquired after September 21, 1999, on the other hand, must be inserted under a single Australian entry point in order to be consolidated into the Australian Group. For outbound investors, any foreign companies acquired will not be able to be included within the Australian consolidated group under the proposed rules.

The proposed consolidation regime will effectively lift the corporate veil for taxation purposes. Under the proposed rules, consideration paid for a share acquisition will effectively be pushed down to set the taxation cost bases of the underlying assets. This reform may overcome one of the key advantages of an asset acquisition over a scrip acquisition. Under the proposed regime, losses and other credits will be vested in the parent of the consolidated group. Therefore, these tax benefits will be available to a purchaser only when it acquires the parent.

When a consolidated group sells a consolidated entity, the capital gains tax cost bases of the vendor in the shares will be fundamentally equal to the capital gains tax cost bases of the underlying assets. Thus, any capital gain or loss on the sale of a subsidiary in the consolidated group will reflect the capital gains tax cost of the underlying assets of that subsidiary at the time of the sale rather than the nominal cost of the shares in the company. The rules for transition to the consolidation regime are likely to be complex. Groups should carefully examine the final rules in order to decide whether they wish to consolidate, and if they do consolidate, to ensure that they maximize the advantages offered to transitional groups.

(b) Thin Capitalization

Australia currently has thin capitalization rules that apply to Australian taxpayers when a foreign investor directly or indirectly owns at least 15 percent of the investment. These rules prevent foreign-controlled Australian companies and other foreign-controlled Australian businesses from being funded by excessive foreign-related party debt. As a general rule, an affected taxpayer will be funded by excess foreign-related party debt where such debt exceeds the equity in the taxpayer by a ratio of 2 to 1.

2.9 Business Taxation Reform

The business taxation reform process has recommended significant changes to these rules, which will apply from July 1, 2001. For inbound investors, it is proposed that the foreign control test be increased from 15 percent to 50 percent. Under the new regime, most affected taxpayers will have the choice of relying on a safe harbor debt ratio or an arm's length debt ratio in determining whether they have too much debt for the purposes of the thin capitalization regime.

To pass the safe harbor debt ratio, a taxpayer needs a debt ratio in which total interest-bearing debt is less than 75 percent of adjusted net assets. If the taxpayer fails the safe harbor ratio, the taxpayer may apply an arm's length test to determine whether its level of debt is acceptable for thin capitalization purposes. However, this arm's length test is restrictive in how it applies and ignores related-party support to the affected taxpayer.

The proposed thin capitalization rules apply to Australian resident entities with outbound investments to deny a deduction for debt funding where the Australian operations have too much debt. Such taxpayers may also seek to rely on a safe harbor debt amount or an arm's length debt amount in proving that their debt structure in the Australian entities is acceptable. These taxpayers may seek to rely on a worldwide debt structure that they will pass if the debt structure of the Australian business is not more than 120 percent of the level of worldwide debt structure.

(c) Debt and Equity Classification

The new thin capitalization rules also include rules for classifying debt and equity for the purposes of those rules. The debt/equity classification rules will also be used as the basis of deciding whether a payment by a company is interest (and thus potentially deductible) or equity (and thus nondeductible but frankable). These classification rules generally adopt an "economic substance" approach to classifying debt and equity. This approach ignores the legal form of underlying instruments and focuses on the substance of the arrangement.

An interest in a company will be classified as debt when there is a noncontingent obligation to repay at least the original advanced amount, whereas an interest will be equity when there is a contingent obligation to repay the original advanced amount. An obligation will be effectively noncontingent when the repayment is not contingent on the underlying economic performance of the paying entity. Nominal values will generally be used to determine the status of an instrument; however, when the performance period of an instrument exceeds 10 years, a present value analysis is required to decide whether there is a noncontingent obligation to repay at least the original advanced amount.

(d) Uniform Entity Regime

The Australian government has announced that it will no longer proceed with a uniform entity taxation regime. The government will, however, commence a new round of consultations to address perceived tax abuse by trusts.

2.10 GOODS AND SERVICES TAX (GST)

(a) Background

The goods and services tax (GST) is a broad-based consumption tax generally imposed at the rate of 10 percent on the supply of most goods and services in Australia. Australia implemented the GST on July 1, 2000, to replace a range of existing indirect taxes. Due to its nature, GST has implications for all parties involved in business mergers, acquisitions, and reorganizations, when such transactions involve the transfer of assets or shares. In addition, special treatments apply when a business, or parts of a business, may be transferred as a going concern.

(b) Overview of the GST System

The GST regime requires the supplier of any goods or services, other than those specifically excluded from GST, to remit 1/11th of the consideration received for the supply to the Australian Commissioner of Taxation; however, the cost of the tax is usually passed onto the consumer. *Consideration* is a broad term and can include almost any provision of value (e.g., cash, services, forbearance) as an inducement for the supply.

GST is generally paid at each step of the supply chain. All entities registered for GST can usually claim input tax credits from the Australian Commissioner of Taxation for most GST incurred on goods or services needed for their business or enterprise. An input tax credit is essentially a credit for the tax paid on the inward supplies to a business. This credit may be refunded to the registered entity for the tax period (which can be monthly, quarterly, or in some cases, yearly) or offset against GST due on supplies made by the entity during the same period. A supply is a "taxable supply" if it is made by a person who is registered or required to be registered for GST and the supply meets the following criteria:

- Made for some form of consideration
- Made in the course or furtherance of an enterprise
- Connected with Australia

A creditable acquisition is anything acquired solely or partly for a creditable purpose. An acquisition is deemed to be for a creditable purpose if the thing acquired is related to the carrying on of an enterprise. Input tax credits are not available for acquisitions that relate to supplies that would be "input taxed" or that are of a private or domestic nature.

Input-taxed supplies are not subject to GST. However, there is no entitlement to claim input tax credits for GST paid on anything acquired or imported that relates to the making of such supplies. As a consequence of this rule, businesses that make input-taxed supplies may face increased costs under the GST and have to make a commercial decision whether to absorb or pass on these cost increases. Supplies that are input taxed include the following:

2.10 Goods and Services Tax (GST)

- Financial supplies
- Residential rents
- Sales of existing residential property

Some supplies are GST-free. GST does not have to be charged on these supplies, but an input tax credit is available for GST included in the price of acquisitions relating to such supplies. The types of supplies that are GST-free include exports, the first supply of a precious metal, basic food and some health, education, and child care services. In addition, the supply of a business as a going concern is also GST-free, as discussed in a following section.

(c) Application of GST to Business Reorganizations

This section analyzes the GST implications for the following commercial transactions, commonly undertaken by businesses:

- The supply of a going concern
- Buying and selling shares

The supply of a going concern

Generally, the sale of assets or real property constitutes a taxable supply (or is input taxed in the case of existing residential property). Accordingly, the sale is usually subject to GST. However, the GST legislation may permit the sale of assets and real property to be GST-free if it satisfies the meaning of a supply of a "going concern." A supply of a going concern is classed as a supply under an agreement in which the supplier performs the following functions:

- Supplies to the recipient all of the things necessary for the continued operation of an enterprise
- Carries on, or will carry on, the enterprise until the day of the supply (whether or not as part of a larger enterprise carried on by the supplier)

The supply of a going concern is GST-free if it fulfills the following criteria:

- The supply is for consideration.
- The recipient is registered or required to be registered.
- The supplier and the recipient have agreed in writing that the supply is a going concern.

This exemption to GST alleviates the short-term cashflow of paying GST on the supply of a going concern, prior to being able to claim an input tax credit.

Buying and selling shares

GST is not generally levied on buying or selling shares. Such transactions are classified as financial supplies and are generally input taxed; however, a registered party may be able to claim some input tax credits for services associated with a share acquisition.

2.11 STAMP DUTY

Stamp duty is tax imposed by an Australian state government on certain transactions under several "heads of duty," the main one being the transfer of property. A head of duty is essentially the particular set of rules that apply to particular types of transactions. Although broadly similar, each Australian state and territory has its own stamp duty legislation with differing rates and exemptions.

Depending on the type of transaction, duty is imposed either at a fixed amount or at an *ad valorem* rate of duty. An *ad valorem* rate of duty is essentially a variable rate of duty usually imposed as a percentage of the value of the transaction When *ad valorem* duty is levied on property transfers, duty is calculated on the greater of the consideration paid for the property or the unencumbered value of the property.

If a transaction or instrument falls within a head of duty, a liability to duty arises. Examples of the heads of duty include the following:

- Conveyance duty
- Marketable securities duty
- Mortgages and other dealings in loan securities
- Lease duty
- Rent of goods/rental business duty

(a) Business Acquisitions

Conveyance duty, at rates of up to 6 percent, is imposed on property (other than shares) transferred as part of a sale or acquisition of a business. Whether property is liable to duty depends on the nature and location of the property transferred. The term *property* includes real and personal property and encompasses items such as land and buildings, goodwill, intellectual property, plant and equipment, debts, and partnership interests.

For business acquisitions in the Australian states of Queensland and South Australia, all of the business assets acquired are generally liable to conveyance duty; however, in the state of Victoria, only transfers of land and chattels transferred together with land are generally liable to duty. The transfer of goods in the state of New South Wales and the Australian territories, Australian Capital Territory, and the Northern Territory are only liable to conveyance duty if the goods are transferred with other property that is liable to duty, such as land or goodwill.

In practice, the various state and territory revenue authorities generally apportion the value of any goodwill of a business between themselves on a sales/location of customer basis. Accordingly, if a business makes sales to customers in more than one Australian jurisdiction, a stamp duty liability arises on the transfer

2.11 Stamp Duty

of goodwill in each jurisdiction in which sales are made. The treatment of intellectual property can be complex. Whether the transfer of intellectual property is brought to duty depends on the nature of the transaction.

(b) Acquisition of Shares

Stamp duty is imposed on the transfer of marketable securities (securities that can be traded), which includes shares and units in a unit trust (generally a fixed trust where the interest of the beneficiaries are represented by units). A distinction is made between transfers of listed and nonlisted marketable securities. A listed security is generally a security that is listed on a stock exchange.

Stamp duty at the rate of 0.3 percent is payable on the transfer of a listed marketable security. A transfer of an unlisted marketable security generally incurs stamp duty at the rate of 0.6 percent. As with conveyance duty, stamp duty is imposed on the greater of the consideration paid or the unencumbered value of the property transferred. As a result of the intergovernmental agreement between the Commonwealth of Australia and each state and territory, from July 1, 2001, stamp duty is no longer payable on a transfer of listed marketable securities.

In certain circumstances, higher rates of duty (at conveyance rates) may apply to an acquisition of shares or units if the company or unit trust scheme in which the shares or units are being acquired is considered land-rich for stamp duty purposes. Further, in the states of Queensland, Western Australia, and South Australia, conveyance rates of duty may apply to the transfer of units in a unit trust based on the underlying value of the property being transferred.

A company or unit trust scheme is generally considered land-rich if the company or unit trust scheme has the following characteristics:

- It is entitled, either legally or beneficially, to land worth at least A$1 million in a particular Australian jurisdiction.
- Its total landholdings, wherever situated, represent at least 80 percent of the total property owned by the company or unit trust scheme, subject to certain exclusions.

This rule applies to all Australian jurisdictions with the exception of the Northern Territory and the Australian Capital Territory. In the Northern Territory, the threshold is at least A$500,000 worth of land, which represents at least 60 percent of the company's or unit trust scheme's total property. In the Australian Capital Territory, a company or unit trust scheme is considered land-rich if it is entitled, either legally or beneficially, to any land in that territory.

The land-rich provisions apply when there has been an acquisition in a land-rich company or unit trust scheme and that acquisition represents either:

- A majority interest in the company/unit trust scheme; or
- A further interest in the company/unit trust scheme where the acquiring party or persons related to the acquiring party already hold a majority interest.

(c) Other Duties

Several other stamp duty liabilities may arise upon a merger or acquisition. Examples of these duties include duty on the lease/license of property, franchise duty, hire of goods/rental business duty, and mortgage/security duty. The imposition of any or all of these duties depends on the nature and location of the property and the form and substance of the instrument being executed. This forum is too narrow to provide a detailed description of these duties.

(d) Corporate Reconstruction Exemptions

When a merger or acquisition occurs within a corporate group, a stamp duty exemption may be available on application to the relevant state or territory revenue authority. New South Wales, the Australian Capital Territory, Victoria, Queensland, and Western Australia offer stamp duty relief for intra-group acquisitions if certain conditions are met.

A corporate group in New South Wales, the Australian Capital Territory and Victoria may generally obtain stamp duty relief for internal mergers or acquisitions if the following conditions are met:

- The corporate group consists of a parent and corporate subsidiaries that are at least 90 percent beneficially owned, either directly or indirectly, by the parent and over which the parent or other subsidiaries have voting control.
- The members of the corporate group have been members for at least 12 months in New South Wales and the Australian Capital Territory and three years in Victoria before to the transaction or since incorporation.
- In New South Wales and the Australian Capital Territory, the transferee and transferor must remain members of the corporate group for at least 12 months after the transaction, unless disassociation occurs by virtue of certain listed criteria.

No postassociation requirement as to the transferor and transferee exists in Victoria. The only requirement is that the ultimate beneficial ownership of any land held by the transferor or transferee at the time of the transaction remains unchanged for three years after the transaction has occurred. Queensland and Western Australia have more stringent requirements for stamp duty relief. As a consequence relief can be more difficult to obtain in these states.

2.12 LEGAL AND REGULATORY REQUIREMENTS

Foreign investment in Australia is governed by a combination of the Foreign Acquisitions and Takeover Act 1975 (the Act) and the Australian government's foreign investment policy. The Australian government has the power under the Act to block foreign investment proposals that are determined to be contrary to the national interest. This power is used only rarely, and it is widely accepted that Australia welcomes foreign investment.

2.12 Legal and Regulatory Requirements

The Foreign Investment Review Board (FIRB) administers the Australian government's foreign investment policy, including the application of the Act. If a proposed transaction is subject to FIRB scrutiny, a notice (in the prescribed form) must generally be given to the FIRB. The FIRB then reviews the details contained in the notice and recommends appropriate action to the federal government treasurer, who is responsible for making the final determination on foreign investment proposals. Not all proposed investments are subject to review by the FIRB. The types of proposed investments that should be notified to the FIRB include the following:

- Acquisitions of 15 percent or more (or 40 percent or more in aggregate in the case of several foreigners) of the ownership of existing Australian businesses with total assets of more than A$50 million or where the proposal values the business at more than A$50 million
- Proposals to establish new businesses involving a total investment of A$10 million or more
- Portfolio investments in the media of 5 percent or more and all nonportfolio investments irrespective of size
- Takeovers of offshore companies whose Australian subsidiaries or assets are valued at A$50 million or more or account for more than 50 percent of the target company's global assets
- Direct investments by foreign governments or their agencies irrespective of the size of the investment

The Australian government also has specific policies in relation to various industry sectors, such as urban land, airports, and media.

(a) Competition Policy: Acquisitions of Australian Businesses

The Australian Competition and Consumer Commission (ACCC) administers the Australian government's competition policy, which is contained in the Trade Practices Act 1974. Under Section 50 of the Trade Practices Act, acquisitions of shares and acquisitions of assets of a business are prohibited if the acquisition would substantially lessen the competition in a substantial market for goods and services in Australia.

The ACCC's approach to examining mergers and acquisitions is as follows:

1. If the relevant market, as identified by the ACCC, is substantial, market concentration is considered. The ACCC will not investigate the matter further unless the following conditions exist:

   - The resultant combined market share of the four (or fewer) largest firms is 75 percent or more and the merged firm will supply at least 15 percent of the relevant market, and
   - The merged firm will supply 40 percent or more of the market.

2. If the concentration ratios are exceeded, the ACCC considers the level and nature of import competition.

3. If import competition is unlikely to impose an appropriate discipline on the merged firm, the ACCC considers the likelihood of new entrants establishing themselves in the market to inhibit the exercise of market power by the merged firm.

4. If new entrants are unlikely to inhibit market power, the ACCC considers other factors (such as the availability of substitutes and the extent of innovation or product differentiation), which could have an effect on the likely competitive impact of the merger.

The ACCC may authorize acquisitions that would otherwise substantially lessen competition by accepting court-enforceable undertakings. For example, there may be undertakings that certain assets be disposed or that businesses under common ownership be independently operated. To avoid action from the ACCC, proposed acquisitions that might substantially lessen competition should be discussed in advance.

(b) Foreign Exchange Controls

Under Section 39 of the Banking Act 1959, the Australian government has the power to regulate foreign exchange (where it considers it expedient to do so) for purposes including foreign investment in Australia. Until December 1983, a rigorous set of foreign currency restrictions was set out in the Banking (Foreign Exchange) Regulations. On December 12, 1983, the Australian dollar was floated, and the operation of the Banking (Foreign Exchange) Regulations was substantially curtailed by Australia's central bank, the Reserve Bank of Australia, which has the power to grant exemptions from the regulations. This process of granting exemptions from the foreign exchange regulations continued actively through 1984 (and less aggressively in the early 1990s), resulting in Australia's foreign exchange regulations being made essentially inoperative. Foreign exchange controls presently operate in relation to countries such as Iraq, Yugoslavia, the Taliban (Afghanistan), and UNITA (Angola).

CHAPTER 3

Taxation of Mergers and Acquisitions in Azerbaijan

Alum Bati
Salans Hertzfeld & Heilbronn, Azerbaijan

3.1 **Introduction**
3.2 **Overview of the Tax and Legal System in Azerbaijan**
    (a)   Major Types of Taxes
    (b)   The Autonomous Republic of Nakhichevan and Municipalities
    (c)   Transfer Pricing
    (d)   Commercial and Corporate Law
    (e)   Currency Control
    (f)   Anti-Monopoly Regulation
    (g)   Restrictions on Foreign Ownership of Domestic Businesses
3.3 **Analysis of Types of Mergers and Acquisitions**
    (a)   Overview
    (b)   Share Purchases
    (c)   Asset Purchases
    (d)   Reorganizations
3.4 **Financing**
    (a)   Equity
    (b)   Debt
3.5 **Repatriation of Capital and Profits**
    (a)   Management Fees
    (b)   Royalties
    (c)   Interest
    (d)   Leasing
    (e)   Dividends
    (f)   Redemption and Sale of Shares
3.6 **Conclusion**

I. INTRODUCTION

The Azerbaijan Tax Code came to force on January 1, 2001. This Tax Code replaced most existing tax provisions. The Code heralded a major step forward in bringing the tax regime more into line with common practice in developed countries. The Tax Code followed soon after of the new Civil, Civil Procedure,

Administrative Offences, Family, and Criminal Codes, all in force from September 1, 2000, not to mention the new Labor Code, in force from July 1, 1999.

Whenever considering tax issues in Azerbaijan, one cannot lose sight of the country's dependence on the hydrocarbons industry. As a result, Azerbaijan has entered into a whole series of exploration, development, and production sharing agreements (PSAs) with many companies in the oil and gas sector. These PSAs are not limited, in most cases, in their application to the operators of oil and gas fields. Instead, these PSAs apply, for some tax and other purposes, to suppliers of goods and services (subcontractors). This chapter does not attempt to consider these PSAs in any detail.

As with the Russian Federation, the legal and financial infrastructure necessary for sophisticated merger and acquisition strategies is still weak. The 2000 Tax Code introduced various tax provisions relating to mergers and acquisitions, but it is too early to say how these provisions will operate in practice. As a result, investments in Azerbaijan still take the form of relatively simple investment structures. The law is generally stated as of March 31, 2001. All references are to the 2000 Tax Code unless otherwise stated.

This chapter is divided into four main sections.

1. The first section provides an overview of the tax and legal system in Azerbaijan, including areas such as corporate taxes, corporate and commercial law, currency control, and anti-monopoly regulations.

2. The second section analyzes the tax treatment of mergers and acquisitions in Azerbaijan.

3. The third section discusses financing structures that are used in connection with mergers and acquisitions.

4. The fourth section looks at capital and profit repatriation.

3.2 OVERVIEW OF THE TAX AND LEGAL SYSTEM IN AZERBAIJAN

The introduction of the 2000 Tax Code, which came into force on January 1, 2001, was a significant event in the economic and fiscal development of Azerbaijan. The Tax Code introduced a whole series of concepts in taxation, which were either new to Azerbaijan or were barely developed, but it remains to be seen how the Tax Code will work in practice.

The Tax Code does the following:

- Sets out principles to be followed in applying tax legislation.
- Determines the rights and obligations of taxpayers and tax authorities.
- Determines the principles to be applied in the conduct of tax audits by the tax authorities.
- Provides basic rules for the computation of various taxes.

3.2 Overview of the Tax and Legal System in Azerbaijan

The Tax Code has more than replaced the law *On the State Tax Service* and several laws regulating the rules and procedures for the computation and payment of various taxes. The Tax Code has also systematized and elaborated on several important areas, including the following:

- The rights of taxpayers
- General rules for the payment of taxes and financial penalties
- Rules for carrying out tax audits

(a) Major Types of Taxes

Most larger businesses will generally be faced with profits tax, value-added tax (VAT), customs duties, and assets tax. In addition, these larger businesses may have land tax obligations. These larger businesses will have to pay social security and similar contributions and will have to pay the agent obligations to their employees. Certain types of corporate businesses, such as those involved in the production and sale of alcohol and tobacco, are subject to additional excise taxes.

The production sharing agreement (PSA) regime complicates the basic tax system. For instance, subcontractors charge VAT to the operating companies and PSA consortium members at a zero rate. In general, if the subcontractors possess appropriate certificates, they pay VAT at 0 percent.

The subcontractors are known as Foreign Subcontractors if they are foreign companies. These subcontractors pay profits tax on a deemed profit basis through a withholding mechanism. In this case, the effective withholding rates depend on the rate of profits tax and level of deemed profit applicable to the relevant PSA. To date, there are four effective rates of withholding tax: 5 percent, 6.25 percent, 7.5 percent, and 8 percent.

Exhibit 3.1 sets out the major Azerbaijan taxes in a summarized format.

Exhibit 3.1

MAJOR AZERBAIJAN TAXES

Type of tax	Tax base	Tax rate
Profits tax	Net income of Azerbaijan entities and permanent establishments of foreign entities. The profits tax applies to Azerbaijan-source income	27% rate applies to companies not operating under PSAs. Simplified tax procedures applies to small companies with 2% of turnover. Withholding taxes apply to Azerbaijan-source income not earned by an Azerbaijan entity or permanent establishment of a foreign entity

Exhibit 3.1 Major Azerbaijan Taxes (*cont'd*)

Type of tax	Tax base	Tax rate
Value added tax	Turnover from domestic sales of goods and services and value of imported goods	18% for most goods and services; 0% for exports; 0% on goods and services provided under PSAs
Customs duties	Value and/or unit of imported goods	*Ad valorem* rate categories are 0%, 0.5%, 5%, 10%, 15% (proposed) Various per unit rates apply. Some combined *ad valorem* and per unit rates. No customs duties apply to imports for PSA purposes though a customs clearance fee is applicable
Personal income tax	Worldwide income of Azerbaijan residents and Azerbaijan source income of Azerbaijan non-residents	Progressive scale up to 35% (applicable to monthly income over 60,000,000 AZM); 10% applies to Azerbaijan bank interest up to the end of 2001 and dividends from local companies
Social security contributions	Same as for personal income tax but non-Azerbaijan citizens (and employers making payment to them) may be exempt in some cases	30% employer's contribution and 1% employee's contribution to the Social Protection Fund; 2% employer's contribution to the Employment Fund
Invalid duty	Payable on net profit	1% payable to the Fund for the Social Protection of Invalids
Property tax	Average net book value assets	1%
Transit road tax	Tax on the transit of vehicles	Rate depends on type of vehicle, load, cargo etc.
Minerals Resources Tax	On the wholesale price of the mineral extracted	Various rates depending on the nature of the mineral
Excise taxes	Turnover from or units of domestic sales of excisable goods by producers and value of imported excisable goods	*Ad valorem* rates on spirits, brewing yeast, beer, alcohol of any kind, tobacco products, and petroleum products[1]

---

[1] Unit rates are also specified, but it is arguable that these are illegal under the Tax Code.

(b) The Autonomous Republic of Nakhichevan and Municipalities

The autonomous republic of Nakhichevan is a region of the Azerbaijan Republic separated from the main body of the country by a strip of Armenian territory. The Tax Code of Azerbaijan generally applies to the autonomous republic but, other than road transit tax, taxes are paid to the Nakhichevan budget rather than into state coffers.[2] The municipalities have the power to raise profits taxes on enterprises owned by them. They also are entitled to collect certain lesser taxes (e.g., land and property taxes on individuals).[3]

(c) Transfer Pricing

Market price may be substituted for transfer pricing analysis in the following cases:

- Transactions between related persons. including limiting tax deductions for interest on loans[4]
- Barter transactions
- Where the price of goods, works, or services with the same or similar properties is changed by more than 30 percent within a 30-day period

Related persons are defined[5] as physical and legal persons whose relationship may have a direct influence on the economic results of their activities or on the activity of persons whom they represent. The following are regarded as related:

- If one person A directly or indirectly participates in the equity of another B in which the person has at least a 20 percent share or voting rights, A and B are regarded as related.
- If one person A is subordinated to another person B in terms of business position or A is directly or indirectly under the control of B, then A and B are regarded as related.
- A person A who is under the direct or indirect control of another person B is related to any other person C who is also under the control of B.
- A person A who directly or indirectly controls another person B together with a third person C, is regarded as being related to C.
- Family members (as defined in Article 13.2.7 of the Tax Code) are related persons.

Market price is defined as the price resulting from the interaction of supply and demand.[6] The market price is basically determined by prices established in relevant transactions regarding transactions in identical or similar goods (works or

---

[2] Art. 7.
[3] Art. 8.
[4] Cf. Art. 110.
[5] Art. 18.
[6] Art. 14.1.

services) on the day closest to the time of the relevant transaction but not more than 30 days before or after that transaction date.[7] Related party transactions may be taken into account if they have taken place at arm's length.[8]

Market price might not be established by the aforementioned methods. In that event, market price is determined in accordance with regulations established by the Cabinet of Ministers. In that case, accounts are taken as to costs of production or supply as are customary. These costs taken into account for transfer pricing purposes include the costs of transportation, storage, insurance, similar costs, and in establishing market price for transactions between unrelated persons. Additional charges and discounts, regarding deterioration in quality, expiration dates, and so on, will be taken into account based on supply and demand.[9] Notwithstanding these provisions, a taxpayer may submit other evidence in support of its pricing.[10]

The tax authorities, in establishing market price, may have recourse to stock exchange quotations, official information sources, databases of the state and local authorities, information provided by taxpayers, and advertising materials.[11]

(d) Commercial and Corporate Law

Azerbaijan is gradually developing a body of commercial and corporate law. For example, a new Civil Code came into force on September 1, 2000, which provides the legal framework for the major types of business transactions. Nevertheless, many of the laws are still awaiting implementation of regulations, and provisions are often contradictory or ambiguous.

Azerbaijan permits 100 percent foreign-owned subsidiaries in most cases. Two types of legal entities are in common use in Azerbaijan: joint stock companies and limited liability companies. Most mergers and acquisitions involve either of these types of legal entities.

A joint stock company is a legal entity. A shareholder of a joint stock company is generally liable for the debts of the company only up to the amount of the shareholder's investment. A joint stock company may be of a *closed* type, which means that it cannot have more than 50 shareholders.[12] In this case, its shareholders have a preemptive right to acquire shares sold by other shareholders. Alternatively, the joint stock company can use an *open* type. Here the joint stock company can have an unlimited number of shareholders and its shares may be freely traded. Azerbaijan imposes a 0.2 percent duty on the issue of shares in an open-type joint stock company. The Azerbaijan State Securities Commission registers the shares of the joint stock companies.

---

[7] Art. 14.4.
[8] Art. 14.5.
[9] Art. 14.6.
[10] Art. 14.8.
[11] Art. 14.9.
[12] Cf. Cabinet of Ministers' Resolution No. 224, 23 December, 2000.

3.2 Overview of the Tax and Legal System in Azerbaijan

A limited liability company (LLC) is a legal entity established by one or more *participants*. The liability of an LLC for the debts of the company in general is limited to the extent of each participant's investment in the company. Unlike joint stock companies, LLCs do not issue shares but, instead, investors own *participatory interests*. A participant in an LLC has the unilateral right to withdraw from the company at any time and demand redemption of the participatory interest in exchange for the net asset value of the interest. The Azerbaijan State Securities Commission does not register interests in LLCs.

Investors commonly use LLCs. A joint stock company may be more appropriate when more than one shareholder is involved because a participant has a unilateral right to withdraw from an LLC at any time.

A capricious and corrupt judicial enforcement system in Azerbaijan seriously inhibits the protection of creditors and shareholders, as with other parts of the former Soviet Union. For creditors of an entity undergoing a reorganization, Article 58 of the Civil Code provides that the creditors have the right to be notified in writing of the reorganization and to have their debts paid. In the case of a division or split, it is impossible to determine the legal successor. The newly created legal entities will bear joint responsibility to the creditors.

(e) Currency Control

The Azerbaijan currency, the *manat*, is not a fully convertible currency. Unless a party possesses a license to transact in and to accept foreign currency, a transaction taking place within Azerbaijan must be carried out in *manats*. However, subject to the formality of obtaining the consent of the tax authorities, there are no restrictions on the opening of foreign currency bank accounts (normally, in US dollars) or on receiving foreign currency from overseas. (The export of currency is permitted when it is shown that it has previously been imported to Azerbaijan or when the currency represents income on which the company has paid tax.)

No compulsory currency conversion requirements apply in Azerbaijan. However, foreign currency held in an Azerbaijan bank account may be used only for specific purposes (e.g., the purchase of imported goods).

(f) Anti-Monopoly Regulation

Azerbaijan has rather broad anti-monopoly legislation that has a direct impact on a wide range of commercial transactions. A business needs to consider this legislation in any merger or acquisition. A business with a "dominant" market position is subject to several restrictions and controls, including on mergers and acquisitions. A dominant market position is defined as controlling 35 percent of any particular market.

Essentially, the following types of acquisition or reorganization must be referred to the State Anti-Monopoly Committee:

- Those resulting in a new company controlling more than 35 percent of the market in a particular commodity

- Those where the assets of the merged or deconsolidated entity are more than approximately US $448,000
- Those where the liquidation or deconsolidation of an enterprise results in a company with assets exceeding approximately US $298,000, if the established entity controls more than 35 percent of the market in a particular commodity
- Where more than 20 percent of the voting shares in a company are purchased by another. This provision applies if the aggregate balance sheet value of the buying and selling companies exceeds US $448,000 or if the share of the seller or buyer in any particular market exceeds 35 percent or if the purchaser controls the seller. This provision does not apply on the initial establishment of a company.
- Where more than 10 percent of the balance sheet value of fixed production assets and intangible assets is transferred if the aggregate balance sheet value of the transferor and transferee companies exceeds US $448,000 or if the share of the seller or buyer in any particular market exceeds 35 percent or if the purchaser controls the seller.
- If, basically, the acquiror has management or executive authority in the target company if the aggregate balance sheet value of the acquiror and target companies exceeds US $448,000 or if the share of either company in any particular market exceeds 35 percent.

Failure to obtain Anti-Monopoly Committee consent in appropriate circumstances could result in the transaction being declared void and the imposition of fines.[13] All U.S. dollar numbers are approximate values based on exchange rates current at the time of writing (4600 AZM = US $1).

(g) Restrictions on Foreign Ownership of Domestic Businesses

Generally, Azerbaijan does not impose any restrictions on foreign ownership of domestic businesses except in certain limited areas. For instance, foreign ownership in insurance companies may not exceed 49 percent, and the National Bank of Azerbaijan imposes internal limits on the amount of foreign capital permitted in the banking sector.

3.3 ANALYSIS OF TYPES OF MERGERS AND ACQUISITIONS

(a) Overview

Mergers and acquisitions may take place in the following forms:

---

[13] Law (as amended) *On Antimonopoly Activity,* 1993, Art. 13,13-1,18.

3.3 Analysis of Types of Mergers and Acquisitions

- Share purchases
- Asset purchases
- Reorganizations (company reconstructions and amalgamations)

Each of these forms is discussed in more detail as follows; however, the tax rules dealing with the more complex type of merger or acquisition are new, and the civil law provisions are largely untried. As a result, straightforward share or asset purchases are likely to be the norm for some time to come.

(b) Share Purchases

Equity interests in LLC are technically referred to as "participatory interests." Nevertheless, references to "shares" in the following sections, for the sake of convenience, encompasses both equity interests in joint stock companies and LLCs.

Acquisition vehicle

Azerbaijan has no tax consolidation provisions to permit the offset or use by one group company of losses incurred by another. As such, a foreign acquiror will probably use a non-Azerbaijan entity to purchase and hold the shares of the Azerbaijan target company.

Selecting the territory to locate the offshore holding company depends on several factors. The existence of a tax treaty may be one such factor. Dividends paid by an Azerbaijan company are subject to a withholding tax of 10 percent, which is a final tax. Dividends paid to a non-Azerbaijan resident person are subject to a 10 percent withholding tax unless a lower rate is applicable under a double tax treaty.

A summarized list of withholding tax rates for treaties in force or in the process of negotiation is given in Exhibit 3.2. The latter list should, of course, be treated with caution because these treaties are not yet in force and the proposed treaties may never come into existence.

Azerbaijan has no favorable treaties with low-tax territories such as Cyprus. Azerbaijan has antitax avoidance provisions relating to parent companies located in tax havens where the shares are owned by Azerbaijan residents.[14] A person residing in Azerbaijan may be taxed on the income of a nonresident company when the resident owns, directly or indirectly, more than 20 percent of the authorized share capital (or voting shares) of the nonresident and the nonresident is located in a country with a "concessionary" tax regime.

A country with a "concessionary" tax regime is one where the tax rate is 50 percent or less of the rate of profits tax in Azerbaijan or where there is a secrecy of information law relating to financial data, the ownership of property, or of the identity of persons earning income.

---

[14] Art. 128.

Exhibit 3.2

WITHHOLDING TAX RATES UNDER DOUBLE TAX TREATIES

Country	Dividends Note	%	Interest %	Royalties Note	%
CIS					
Russia		10	10		10
Ukraine		10	10		10
Kazakhstan		10	10		10
Uzbekistan		10	10		10
Moldova	US$250,000 investment	8	10		10
	in other cases	15			
Georgia		10	10		10
Belarus		15	10		10
NON-CIS					
United Kingdom	30% or US$300,000 investment	10	10	copyright or artistic works	5
	in other cases	15		in other cases	10
Norway	30% or US$100,000	10	10		10
	in other cases	15			
Turkey		12	10		10
Germany		15	5		0
Treaties under negotiation or signed but not yet in force					
Pakistan		10	10		10
Poland		10	10		10
France		10	10		10
Netherlands	25% or US$300,000	5	10	technology	5
	10% or US$75,000	10		in other cases	10
	in other cases	15			
Belgium	30% and US$500,000	5	10		10
	10% and US$75,000	10			
	in other cases	15			
Austria	25% or US$250,000	5	10	not older than 3 years	5
	25% or US$100,000	10		in other cases	10
	in other cases	15			
Sweden	30% or US$100,000	10	10	copyright or artistic works	5
	in other cases	15		in other cases	10

3.3 Analysis of Types of Mergers and Acquisitions

Legal documentation and filings

The principal legal documentation for a share purchase is normally a basic sales contract. No special contractual provisions are required under Azerbaijan civil law. An acquiror needs to obtain advance permission from the Azerbaijan antimonopoly authorities for any acquisition of more than 20 percent of the voting shares of an Azerbaijan company if the aggregate book value of the assets of the acquiror and the target company exceeds approximately $448,000.

Tax consequences

Taxation of a seller of shares. An Azerbaijan seller of shares in an Azerbaijan company (joint stock company/LLC) is subject to Azerbaijan corporate profits tax (or personal income tax, if the seller is an individual). The tax is imposed on the excess of the selling price over the acquisition price of the shares, including expenses connected with both purchase and sale. It appears that losses on the sale of securities (e.g., shares in a joint stock company) realized by Azerbaijan companies may be offset against profits from other activities. There is no clear statement to this effect in the Tax Code. Indeed, Article 108 states that all expenses connected with the generation of income shall be tax deductible unless otherwise specified, which suggests that losses are not tax deductible at all; however, it is generally believed that losses on the sale of securities will be allowed for tax purposes. A seller of Azerbaijan shares is not liable for VAT or notary/stamp duties.

Taxation of a buyer of shares The buyer of shares in a closed-type joint stock company is liable to pay a modest notary duty. In the case of open-type joint stock companies, a state duty is payable by the issuer on the initial issue, whereas in the case of closed-type companies a notary duty is paid on the subsequent transfer of the shares. No notary duty is payable in the case of the transfer of a share in an LLC.

Advantages and disadvantages of share purchases

The principal advantages of a share purchase are simplicity and the fact that it is well understood by buyers, sellers, and other interested persons. As with any share purchase, the main disadvantages are that a buyer may be acquiring hidden liabilities. A buyer should be cautious in acquiring shares of any Azerbaijan company, but especially one that has undergone privatization, to ensure that the seller has complied with all legal formalities.

(c) Asset Purchases

An asset purchase may either be in the form of the acquisition of individual assets or as the acquisition of "a whole business." There are no special rules under Azerbaijan civil legislation as to the acquisition of a whole business. Strangely enough, the Tax Code, when dealing with VAT, makes the assumption that such an acquisition is possible. In practice, it is unlikely that asset purchases will be structured as acquisitions of a whole business, partly because of legal and tax uncertainties.

Acquisition vehicle

An asset purchase will generally be made through an Azerbaijan company, especially if the purchaser is to acquire land. Foreign persons are not permitted to own land in Azerbaijan. Even an Azerbaijan subsidiary that is directly owned by a foreign person may face difficulty in acquiring land.

Legal documentation and filings

A buyer of assets may be required to obtain preliminary approval from the anti-monopoly authorities (see previous section). Rights over and pertaining to certain assets are subject to registration (e.g., immovable property and ships, cars and aircraft) and perfection of title. The sale of registrable assets is subject to the payment of notary and registration duties.

Tax consequences

Following is a discussion of the tax consequences of an asset purchase to the seller and the buyer.

Taxation of a seller of assets. Two principal taxes may apply to a seller of assets: corporate profits tax and VAT.

As a general rule, a seller of assets is subject to profits tax on the excess, if any, of the selling price of the assets over the seller's net book value for the assets or pool of assets. The following points should be noted:

- *Depreciable fixed assets:* Depreciable fixed assets (i.e., assets with a useful life of more than one year) are divided into five classes. Intangible assets are included as a class of fixed assets, although the definition of fixed assets given in Article 13.2.17 would seem to preclude this. The five classes are as follows:

  1. Buildings and structures—10 percent per year on a reducing balance basis
  2. Machinery, equipment, and computing technology—25 percent per year on a reducing balance basis
  3. Other fixed assets—20 percent per year on a reducing balance basis
  4. Geological survey costs and works preparatory to the extraction of natural resources (including the costs of intangible assets incurred in order to acquire the right to carry out geological surveys and the treatment or exploitation of natural resources[15])—25 percent per year on a reducing balance basis

---

[15] Art. 117.

3.3 Analysis of Types of Mergers and Acquisitions

5. Intangible assets with a life of more than one year[16]—depreciated on a straightline basis over the useful life of the asset or, where the useful life cannot be determined, at 10 percent per year on a reducing balance basis

- Depreciation is calculated for each class of asset, with each building/structure being regarded as a separate class. The residual book value of any class at the end of the previous tax year is increased by purchases during the year or decreased by sales. If the sale of an asset would otherwise cause the relevant class to fall below zero, the excess of proceeds over the amount in the class is treated as taxable income.
- Land, fine art, and other assets that do not deteriorate are not depreciable for tax purposes. Therefore, any gains or losses will be taxable/tax deductible.
- *Capital investment relief:* Capital expenditures by legal entities for production purposes (or for the repayment of bank loans used for capital investment) are deductible from taxable profit.[17] The deductible amount is calculated after reducing the capital expenditures by the amount of depreciation taken to produce expenses for the year. It is unclear whether this is a reference to total depreciation for the year or depreciation for the relevant category of assets, but the tax authorities' interpretation is to total depreciation. In other words, an Azerbaijan company may take a current deduction (less depreciation) for the cost of acquisition of fixed assets. The relief is not available for investment in land or intangible assets.
- A clawback might apply if a business receives relief as to fixed assets or incomplete buildings and the business sells these assets within two years after the year in which the relief was given. In that event, the relief is clawed back, but the clawback cannot exceed the net book value of the assets sold or transferred.
- *Sale of a business as a going concern:* The disposal of all the assets of an enterprise (or independent branch of an enterprise) will not be taxed for VAT purposes in the course of a transaction if the parties apply to the tax authorities in advance. Both the buyer (being registered for VAT) and seller of a business (also being registered for VAT) must make a written application to the tax authorities within 10 days of the sale requiring the application of Article 160 of the Tax Code.[18] The purchaser of the business is deemed to have taken over all the rights and obligations of the enterprise. The seller remains liable for the payment of taxes, interest, and financial penalties in relation to previous periods.
- *Other sales of assets:* Assuming the seller of assets is VAT registered, VAT will generally apply to the sale of assets unless the assets are specifically exempted. The purchase of assets from state enterprises in the process of privatization are considered exempt supplies.

---

[16] See Art. 118.1.
[17] Art. 106.3.
[18] Art. 160(3).

Taxation of a buyer of assets. Four principal taxes are relevant to a buyer of assets:

1. Corporate profits tax
2. VAT
3. Property tax
4. Land tax

Generally speaking, a buyer of assets will account for each acquired asset at its acquisition cost, which may include various expenses connected with the acquisition. The following additional points should be noted:

- For depreciation rates applicable to fixed assets see discussion under "Taxation of a seller of assets" above.
- For capital investment relief, see discussion under "Taxation of a seller of assets" above. If the purchase is financed by a bank loan, then the deduction for interest is taken for each repayment of the loan.

A seller of assets will charge VAT (generally at a rate of 18 percent) to the buyer. The buyer will be able to credit such VAT to the extent the assets purchased are for the purpose of activities that are not exempt or otherwise not chargeable to VAT. If the assets are used in an exempt activity (such as banking), then the VAT is capitalized in the cost of the assets.

For property tax purposes, a buyer of assets will account for each acquired asset at its acquisition cost, which may include various expenses connected with the acquisition. The buyer will be liable for property tax on the average net book value of tangible fixed assets. The generally applicable property tax rate is 1 percent.

Land tax is based on the size, use, and location of land.[19] The following tax rates apply to landowners and land-users:

Agricultural Use: The land tax is 0.3 percent of the nontaxable amount of monthly income (i.e. currently, AZM 300) per one "point"[20] (the "points" being determined by the relevant executive bodies based on the cadastral value of land, regarding its use, geographic location, and quality).[21]

Industrial Use (including use for construction, transport, communication, commercial, and consumer services): Tax is based on the geographic region and use of the land.[22]

---

[19] Art. 206
[20] Art. 206.1
[21] Art. 206.2
[22] Art. 206.3

3.3 Analysis of Types of Mergers and Acquisitions

Advantages and disadvantages of asset purchases

The principal advantage of an asset purchase is that, if asset purchase is properly structured, the buyer does not assume any of the liabilities of the business from which the assets are purchased.

The main disadvantages of an asset purchase are as follows:

- The buyer will normally pay a large amount of VAT on the purchase of the assets. Asset purchases may result in a significant cashflow impact because the buyer may need several months to recover this VAT fully.
- The buyer will be liable for all the liabilities of the business from which the assets are purchased if the asset purchase constitutes the acquisition of "a whole business."[23]

(d) Reorganizations

Reorganizations are dealt with principally by Articles 55 to 58 of the 2000 Civil Code. The legal framework for mergers and divisions as understood in industrialized countries has been in place only since the introduction of the 2000 Civil Code, which has been in force from September 1, 2000. The provisions of the Civil Code have been applied infrequently, if at all, to date. There is considerable uncertainty as to how the Civil Code would apply.

Reorganizations are regarded as being any of the following:

- *Consolidation:* The Civil Code does not define "consolidation." "Consolidation" appears to be, essentially, when two or more entities transfer their businesses to a new entity in exchange for shares in that entity.
- *Deconsolidation:* Deconsolidation appears to be when an existing entity splits into several new entities.
- *Merger:* A merger appears to be the absorption of one business by another.
- *Demerger:* Demerger or division appears to be the splitting off of one business from another.
- *Transformation:* Transformation includes the conversion of a limited liability enterprise into a joint stock company—or of a joint stock company of a closed-type into an open-type company—or vice versa.

Legal documentation and filings

A reorganization is carried out by a resolution of the founders (participants) or by such other body as authorized by the charter of the company. The act of transfer will specify the rights and obligations being transferred. In the case of a consolidation, the rights and obligations of each party are transferred to the newly established entity in accordance with the "Transfer Act." In the case of a merger, the Transfer Act will specify the rights and obligations to be transferred to the absorbing entity.

---

[23] Art. 160.

Unlike in the Russian Federation, there are no established procedures concerning the conclusion of a *merger contract* (providing for the terms of the merger), though these would be expected.

Mergers of Azerbaijan companies require preliminary approval of the antimonopoly authorities if the aggregate book value of the assets of the merged companies exceeds approximately $448,000. Shareholders and participants in closed-type joint stock companies and limited liability enterprises have preemptive rights.

In reorganizations, there are transfers of assets and liabilities between companies and exchanges of shares. As a result of these transactions, the two principal tax issues that arise from reorganizations are the following:

1. The taxation of the reorganized companies and their shareholders
2. The carryover of tax liabilities and tax attributes

Taxation of reorganized companies and their shareholders

Asset-for-share exchanges. A transfer of assets by any person(s) does not create taxable income if the following occurs:[24]

- That person(s) transfers assets to a legal entity in exchange for a participating share in that company. The wording used in the code implies that this relief applies only to limited liability enterprises, although excluding joint stock companies is unlikely to have been the intent.
- That person(s) possesses 100 percent of the participating share(s) in the legal entity directly after the exchange.

The transfers will be on a "no-gain, no-loss" basis. The deemed acquisition value of the asset for the transferee will be equal to the transferor's net book value at the time of the transfer. The value of the shares received by the transferor will be the net book value of the assets transferred less any liabilities also transferred.

This relief is not available (or is only partly available) when the following conditions occur:

- The net book value of assets is less than the amount of liabilities transferred. Relief will be given in this case, but the acquisition cost of the participating share will be treated as being zero.
- The assets transferred have been depreciated in accordance with one of the classes of depreciable assets unless all the assets of that class are transferred together.

---

[24] Art. 146.1.

3.3 Analysis of Types of Mergers and Acquisitions

The relevant article of the Tax Code (Article 146) that deals with asset-for-share exchanges is titled "Establishment of a legal person." As a result, it is possible that the relief will be limited to such situations even though the text of the article itself gives no indication of such limitation.

Exchange of shares. Azerbaijan permits taxpayers to exchange shares if they obtain consent of the authorized tax body that the reorganization is not for the purpose of tax evasion:[25]

1. The exchange of a participating share in one resident legal entity (Company A) for a participating share in another resident legal entity (Company B) is not treated as a taxable event where both Company A and Company B are participants in a reorganization. The shares acquired in Company A will have the same value as the shares exchanged in Company B.[26]

2. The distribution of a participating share in a legal entity will not be treated as a dividend for the parties participating in the reorganization. This situation applies as to a participant of a reorganization in connection with an exchange of participating shares with another legal entity with a participant of the reorganization. The initial value of the shares will be the market value immediately after the distribution.[27]

3. As a general rule, share issues by Azerbaijan open-type joint stock companies are subject to a duty of 0.2 percent assessed on the par value of shares issued.

For tax purposes, a "reorganization" means[28] the following:

- A consolidation between two or more resident legal persons
- An exchange of at least 50 percent of the participating voting shares held by a resident legal person and at least 50 percent of all other participating shares with the participating shares of a participator of the reorganization
- The acquisition by a resident legal person of 50 percent or more of another resident legal person's assets in exchange for nonpreferred participating voting shares in a company that is a participator in a reorganization
- The demerger of a resident legal person into two or more resident legal persons. Read literally, the provision appears to be aimed at deconsolidation.
- The establishment of a new legal person through a demerger
- The distribution to the participants of a legal person of all participating shares held by a legal person in an enterprise and owning at least 50 percent of the participating shares in that enterprise

---

[25] Art. 147. For tax authority consent, see Art. 147.7.6.
[26] Art. 147.4.
[27] Art. 147.5, 147.6.
[28] Art. 147.7.

A "participator of a reorganization" is a resident legal person who is a direct participator of a reorganization and any legal person that owns or is owned by such a participator.[29] An "owner" for this purpose is a person who possesses 50 percent or more of participating voting shares or 50 percent or more of the value of all participating shares.[30]

Carryover of tax liabilities and tax attributes

The successor company or companies in a reorganization with or without a change of legal form succeed(s) to the tax liabilities of the predecessor(s), irrespective of whether the successor company was aware of the liabilities.[31]

The net book value of assets of a successor company in a reorganization will be the same as that of the transferor. This treatment does not apply to fixed assets depreciated in accordance with the rules in the Azerbaijan Tax Code unless all fixed assets of the relevant category are transferred together.[32]

Substantial change of ownership—tax losses. In general, an Azerbaijan company with a net operating loss in a particular year can carry forward the loss for five years. Tax losses may not be carried forward when the ownership of a company changes by more than 50 percent in any year compared to the previous year. There is an exception to this general rule when the entity whose ownership has changed meets the following criteria:

- Continues the same business for the three years after the change.
- Does not begin any new business within one year of the change.

Tax credits. There are no clear rules about tax credits when a transferring company has overpaid taxes, but the Transfer Act may transfer all rights and obligations.[33]

Cost basis of assets and shares. The general cost basis for assets and shares may be summarized as follows:

- Assets received by a transferee company from the transferor company are accounted for at the same net book value as reflected in the transferor company's balance sheet for those assets at the time of the reorganization. No VAT will be chargeable on a transfer of assets that constitutes a contribution to charter capital.[34]

---

[29] Art. 147,8.
[30] Art. 147.9.
[31] Art. 80.
[32] Art. 147.10.
[33] *Civil Code,* 2000, Art. 56.
[34] Art. 164.1.5.

- New shares received in a merger or division in exchange for shares in a reorganized company have a cost base equal to the cost base of the shares exchanged.

Advantages and disadvantages of reorganizations

The principal advantages of tax-free reorganizations are the following:

- Subject to some uncertainty, these reorganizations can be accomplished tax-free.
- No cash is required because the consideration paid is the acquiring company's shares.

The principal disadvantages of tax-free reorganizations are the following:
- Significant uncertainty exists among professionals, judges, and government officials regarding the legal requirements of reorganizations.
- A company that is liquidated is subject to a final audit conducted by the tax authorities. Several hidden liabilities are invariably discovered in this way. This audit process can definitively establish the extent of those hidden liabilities, but it can be a time-consuming affair.
- Capital markets in Azerbaijan are barely developed. As such, shareholders of companies acquired pursuant to a reorganization will generally prefer to receive cash rather than receive shares in another company.

3.4 FINANCING

An acquisition of assets or equity can generally be financed through cash, debt, or shares. Cash is the most likely option in Azerbaijan, though the cash itself may be obtained through taking on more debt. A brief overview of equity and debt financing is given as follows.

(a) Equity

If an Azerbaijan company is the acquiring company, then the shareholders of the Azerbaijan company may, depending on the company's charter, need to adopt a resolution to enable the company to contribute cash to the charter capital of a Azerbaijan company in exchange for shares. The share-issuing company will need to pass a resolution increasing its charter capital. The complexity of the corporate procedures required to make a cash equity contribution depends on the type of Azerbaijan company involved. The procedure is generally more time-consuming for joint stock companies than for LLCs. The foreign company may be the acquiring company. In that event, the taxpayer should consider the impact of the relevant corporate legislation of the jurisdiction in which the foreign company is established.

(b) Debt

Interest and withholding

Interest paid by an Azerbaijan resident legal person or the permanent establishment of a nonresident is subject to a withholding tax at source of 10 percent. This withholding applies on behalf of such establishment where the establishment is associated with income earned from an Azerbaijan source. Withholding tax is not applied to interest paid to Azerbaijan banks or the Azerbaijan permanent establishments of nonresident banks. The withholding tax is a final tax for individuals who are beneficial owners of the interest. Azerbaijan legal entities and permanent establishments of foreign companies are taxable on interest income, but receive a tax credit for the tax withheld upon submission of evidence of withholding.[35]

Interest paid may be deductible when using the cash basis of accounting (or payable when using the accruals basis of accounting) on credits. The interest is deductible if the interest rate as to credit is not higher than 150 percent of the interest rate of the inter-bank credit auction at the time the credit is given.[36] The Tax Code does not make clear whether, if interest exceeds 150 percent, the whole of the interest will be disallowed or only the portion above 150 percent. The Tax Code sets the limit of 150 percent at the date the credit is extended. It is possible, therefore, that interest on loans provided in tranches at floating rates might be deductible one day but not the next. No special treatment is provided in the code for banks or credit institutions.

Shareholder/Related party loans

Defined in Article 18, "related persons" are physical and legal persons whose relationship may have a direct influence on the economic results of their activities or on the activity of persons whom they represent. The following situations are regarded as related:

- A and B are regarded as related if one person A directly or indirectly participates in the equity of another B in which the person has 20 percent share or voting rights.
- A and B are regarded as related if one person A is subordinated to another person B in terms of his business position or A is directly or indirectly under the control of B.
- A person A who is under the direct or indirect control of another person B is related to any other person C who is also under the control of B.
- A person A who directly or indirectly controls another person B together with a third person C, is regarded as being related to C.
- Family members (as defined in Article 13.2.7) are related persons.

---

[35] Interest paid by an Azerbaijan bank to an individual is exempted from withholding tax until the end of 2001 (subject to extension of the exemption). Art. 123.
[36] Art. 110.1.

3.4 Financing

Thin capitalization: Deductible interest on loans between related parties is further limited by applying the following formula:

II + (GI-II-E) 50% = DI

Where:

II is interest income
GI is gross income
E is expenses deductible from gross income (before interest)
DI is the deductible amount

Interest paid by a Azerbaijan company to a foreign lender that is not attributable to a permanent establishment of the foreign lender in Azerbaijan is subject to a 10 percent Azerbaijan withholding tax. This tax is reduced or eliminated under most Azerbaijan tax treaties. It is usually possible to obtain an advance treaty exemption from the withholding tax. The currency control rules permit the repayment of foreign loans and interest in foreign currency. Debt-financing of a subsidiary may have an advantage of spreading tax deductions for capital investments through the capital investment relief discussed previously; however, Azerbaijan may generally provide loans only in Azerbaijan currency.

3.5 REPATRIATION OF CAPITAL AND PROFITS

A foreign investor should be concerned about the repatriation of capital invested as well as profit obtained. Investment made in foreign currency may be repatriated without restriction provided the foreign currency had previously been brought into Azerbaijan through the banking system. Profit may also be repatriated freely in the form of dividends, subject to payment of withholding taxes.

(a) Management Fees

In some cases, foreign investors or their foreign affiliates provide management services to their Azerbaijan subsidiaries. Management fees are generally deductible by the Azerbaijan subsidiary. The management fees are subject to a 15 percent Azerbaijan withholding tax if the services constitute Azerbaijan-source income and do not give rise to a permanent establishment. This tax may be reduced or eliminated under tax treaties. Azerbaijan VAT will generally be withheld from the fees in a form of "reverse charge" if the services are performed in Azerbaijan. The VAT should be creditable by the Azerbaijan subsidiary.

(b) Royalties

A common means by which a foreign investor can extract earnings is through licensing of technology and know-how to their Azerbaijan subsidiaries. The royalty payments under a license will normally be deductible by the Azerbaijan licensee. "Royalty" is defined as payment received for the right to use (or assignment thereof) literary, artistic, or scientific works, software, cinematograph films, patents, trademarks, designs or models, plans, know-how and processes, and information concerning industrial, commercial, or scientific experience. Royalties also include the right to use industrial, commercial, or scientific equipment (or assignment thereof).[37]

Royalty payments are subject to a 10 percent Azerbaijan withholding tax. The rate of withholding tax may be reduced or eliminated under some of Azerbaijan's tax treaties. It is unlikely that the Azerbaijan government would give clearance in advance for applying a reduced treaty rate.

A VAT-registered taxpayer will deduct VAT (and treat as a self-supply) from the amount payable to a nonresident person who is not registered for VAT in Azerbaijan. This treatment applies if the payment relates to the nonresident's performance of works or services in Azerbaijan on behalf of the taxpayer.[38] Services directly connected with immovable property are performed where the property is located. Services connected with movable property are performed where they are actually rendered.

(c) Interest

See Section 3.4(b)

(d) Leasing

The new tax rules relating to finance leases are contained in the Tax Code. As such it is too early to predict the extent of non-PSA-related cross-border leasing in Azerbaijan, which currently is almost nonexistent.

A lessee leasing tangible property under a finance lease agreement will be regarded for tax purposes as the owner of the leased property. Consequently, lease payments will be treated as payments as to a loan made to the lessee.[39] The code does not explicitly say so but, presumably, the lessee will be entitled to depreciation allowances and interest deductions for the asset and the deemed loan interest. This structure could make finance leasing an attractive option for nonresident lessors because payments under finance leases would appear to be subject to a withholding tax of 4 percent of the total payment. This raises several issues. First, if the whole payment is treated as a lease payment, there is an argument that it should be subject to a 10 percent withholding obligation on the full amount by virtue of Article 125.1.7, but one could (and, probably, would) also apply Article 125.1.5, which would give a withholding rate of 15 percent; however, Article 140.4 appears to split the payment into interest and principal components, and so the interest would be taxable at 10 percent under Article 125.1.2. A further difficulty then lies with Article 125.1.3, which provides a

---

[37] Cf. Art. 13.2.23.
[38] Art. 169.
[39] Art. 140.

3.5 Repatriation of Capital and Profits

withholding rate of 4 percent on payments under finance lease transactions. The import of the asset will be VAT exempt, and the lessee should receive depreciation allowances.

A finance lease is defined as a lease in which the following criteria are met:

- The asset is transferred into the ownership of the lessee upon expiration of the lease term or the lessee is entitled to purchase the asset at the end of the lease term at a predetermined price.
- The lease term exceeds 75 percent of the useful life of the leased asset.
- The residual value of the asset after the lease term has expired is less than 20 percent of the market value at the start of the lease.
- The total amount of lease payments equals 90 percent of the asset's market value at the commencement of the lease, except when the lease commences after 75 percent of the useful life of the asset has expired.
- The leased asset has been built for the purpose of the lessee and is not usable by any other person after the expiration of the lease term.

The lease term is the original term of the lease together with any renewal term where the lessee has an option to renew.[40]

A transfer to the lessee of the asset under a finance lease is to be treated as a disposal by the lessor and a purchase by the lessee.[41]

Although the code does not explicitly say so, it is implicit that part of the lease payment under a finance lease will be treated as interest and part as a repayment of the loan. The interest will be determined by the following formula:[42]

$$P \times (C \times 125/100) = I$$

Where:
P = the lease payments paid in each quarter
C = the arithmetic average credit rate established at the inter-bank credit auctions of the National Bank in the previous quarter[43]
I = the interest amount

(e) Dividends

Dividends paid by an Azerbaijan resident enterprise, an Azerbaijan-incorporated entity, are subject to a 10 percent withholding tax at source. This withholding tax is a final tax. Individuals and Azerbaijan legal entities are not subject to further tax on dividend income.[44] Dividends paid to a nonresident shareholders are subject to a 10 percent withholding tax. Dividends are not deductible by the Azerbaijan company. In rare cases, Azerbaijan tax treaties provide for a lesser rate of withholding tax. It is unlikely that the Azerbaijan tax authorities would provide

---

[40] Art. 140.5.
[41] Art. 140.6.
[42] Art. 140.4.
[43] No such rate is set for the U.S. dollar.

clearance in advance for applying a reduced treaty rate. Repayment of a debt by an Azerbaijan company is not subject to Azerbaijan tax.

(f) Redemption and Sale of Shares

The redemption of shares in an Azerbaijan company will be treated as giving rise to Azerbaijan-source income. The tax treatment for that income will be the same as for other types of disposals of equity interests. A redemption of shares requires approval of a shareholders' meeting and notification to creditors;[45] however, there appears to be no withholding mechanism that could be applied to a non-Azeribaijan shareholder whose shares are redeemed. The Azerbaijan tax authorities will no doubt attempt to argue that the 15 percent withholding tax applies.

The proceeds from the disposal of an equity interest in an Azerbaijan company or from the disposal of an equity interest in an entity where at least 50 percent of the value of the shares is derived directly or indirectly from real property in Azerbaijan is regarded as Azerbaijan-source income.[46] The Tax Code is unclear as to whether such income is subject to tax, but it is likely that the tax authorities will argue that the total proceeds are subject to 15 percent withholding tax, unless reduced or eliminated under a double tax treaty.

3.6 CONCLUSION

Azerbaijan's economy, although developing at a reasonable pace, still lacks many of the mechanisms that permit the more complex merger and acquisition strategies. In addition, both the Civil Code and Tax Code have been in force for less than a year, and there is little experience regarding their application in this area.

---

[44] Art. 122.
[45] Civil Code, 2000, Article 105.
[46] Article 13.2.16.6, 13.2.16.13.

CHAPTER 4

Taxation of Mergers and Acquisitions in Canada

Gregory C. Boehmer
Mike Vantil
Mergers & Acquisitions Tax Services, Ernst & Young LLP, Toronto, Canada

4.1 **Introduction**
4.2 **Taxation in Canada**
   (a) General Structure
   (b) Federal and Provincial Structure
   (c) Business Profits and Capital Cost Allowances
   (d) Interest and Taxes
   (e) Federal Part I and Provincial Corporate Income Taxes
   (f) Federal Branch Tax (Part XIV Tax)
   (g) Corporate Capital Tax on Large Corporations (Part I.3 Tax)
   (h) Withholding Tax on Payments to Nonresidents (Part XIII Tax)
   (i) Losses and Other Corporate Tax Attributes
   (j) CCA Rules Upon Acquisition
   (k) Acquisition of Control Rules
4.3 **Alternative Business Structures**
   (a) Direct Sales by Foreign Vendors to Canadian Customers
   (b) Branch/Permanent Establishment in Canada
   (c) Subsidiary Incorporated in Canada
4.4 **Tax Treatment of Capital Gains and Capital Losses**
4.5 **Tax Treatment on Sale of Goodwill and Other Intangibles**
4.6 **Taxation of Dispositions of Taxable Canadian Property by NonResidents**
   (a) Tax Clearance Certificate
   (b) Deposit Procedure
4.7 **Asset Purchase Transactions**
   (a) Double Taxation
   (b) Taxable Canadian Corporation
   (c) International Issues
4.8 **Share Purchase Transactions**
   (a) Nonresident Parties
   (b) Seller's Perspective

(c) Purchaser's Perspective
(d) Excessive Assets
4.9 Profit Repatriation, Cross-Border Paid-Up Capital, and Financing Issues
4.10 Share-for-Share Transactions
(a) Compliance Issues
(b) Selling Corporation's Perspective
(c) Acquiring Coporation's Perspective
4.11 Amalgamation Transactions
4.12 Foreign Purchasers
4.13 Exchangeable Share Transactions
4.14 Proposed FIE Rules
4.15 Financing Costs
4.16 Thin Capitalization Rules

4.1 INTRODUCTION

Generally, foreign and domestic investors have equal status for Canadian income tax purposes. The North American Free Trade Agreement (NAFTA), to which Canada is a member, further commits Canada to this open investment climate. Certain industries restrict levels of foreign ownership:

- Certain financial services (banking, insurance, trust and loan companies)
- Media (publishing, film, videos and music)
- Airlines

Investment Canada applies a notification and review process, and these rules apply depending on the size and the percentage of control over the investee.

Businesses in Canada are most typically carried on through corporations, although a business may be carried on as a proprietorship or through a joint venture or partnership arrangement. A corporation that is incorporated in Canada or resident in Canada is subject to Canadian income tax on its worldwide income. Similarly, a resident proprietor or a partner of a partnership that is a resident in Canada is also taxable by Canada on worldwide income.

Nonresidents are generally subject to Canadian income tax only from the following sources:

- Canadian-source income from businesses carried on in Canada (either carried on directly or through a partnership or joint venture)
- Certain Canadian nonresident withholding taxes on Canadian-source income from property (e.g., rents, royalties, interest and dividends)
- Canadian income tax on the disposition of taxable Canadian property (e.g., shares of Canadian private corporations and Canadian real property)

Canada has an extensive network of bilateral income tax treaties that restrict Canada's ability to tax a nonresident's Canadian-source income and gains. Such treaties generally exempt nonresidents from tax on gains where that income is not principally derived directly or indirectly from Canadian real property. The rate of nonresident withholding taxes is significantly reduced from the 25 percent statutory rate on interest, dividends, and royalties.

From an income tax perspective, acquisitions and divestitures are typically structured as either asset sales or share sales. A Canadian seller may be able to utilize several specific rollover rules to defer tax on gains realized on the disposition of a Canadian business or shares of a corporation. These provisions can apply where the consideration paid to acquire the business or shares includes equity of the acquiror.

4.2 TAXATION IN CANADA

The following is a brief summary of some of the taxation rules in Canada that may be useful in understanding the taxation of Canadian M & A transactions.

(a) General Structure

The federal government of Canada is entitled to levy any type of tax. Each Canadian province has the right to levy direct taxes for provincial purposes. Accordingly, both levels of government can levy income and capital taxes on businesses. Only the federal government (and Quebec in some circumstances), however, may levy withholding taxes on income paid to nonresidents.

The provincial government of Ontario, for example, to circumvent this limitation on withholding tax, requires corporations to add back a portion of the amount paid in computing their taxable income in Ontario. This addback applies to a business carrying on a business in Ontario that makes management fee, rent, or royalty payments to nonresident persons with whom the corporation does not deal at arm's length. The Ontario tax on the amount of the addback effectively represents a withholding tax equivalent to 5 percent on these payments (i.e., where the Ontario corporation is in a taxable position).

(b) Federal and Provincial Structure

Most of the provinces have entered into tax collection agreements with the Canadian federal government. These collection agreements apply to income taxes determined in a manner that is generally consistent with the federal base, enabling the federal government to administer the collection of these taxes. Canada avoids double taxation through abatement from the federal corporate income tax rate. Taxable income earned in a province is abated to allow the province to assess its own corporate income tax.

Currently, three provinces collect their own corporate income tax: Quebec, Ontario, and Alberta. The province of Quebec collects its own personal income tax. Those provinces with separately collected corporate income taxes typically use definitions of income that are similar to that used by the federal government. The provinces typically collect their own capital taxes.

(c) Business Profits and Capital Cost Allowances

Business profits that are subject to Canadian tax are calculated on a net basis, after the deduction of the expenses incurred to earn that income. Specific statutory capital cost allowances (CCA) permit the depreciation of capital property other than land. Separate CCA pools are maintained for various categories of assets. CCA is normally calculated on a declining balance basis from the undepreciated capital cost balance of the particular class.

For example, CCA rates are the following:

- Furniture and fixtures—20 percent
- Certain manufacturing equipment—25 percent
- Buildings—4 percent
- Automotive equipment and computers—30 percent

These particular capital cost allowances are calculated on a declining balance basis and are subject to a half-rate restriction in the year that an asset is acquired. The "put in use" requirement is a prerequisite in claiming the CCA.

A taxpayer may claim the CCA as to the cost of certain limited life licenses and leasehold improvements, claiming the amount on a straight-line basis over the prescribed life of the asset. Seventy-five percent of certain types of other intangible assets, including purchased goodwill, are included in a separate tax pool referred to eligible capital property and can be depreciated on a 7 percent declining balance basis.

(d) Interest and Taxes

Interest on money borrowed for the purpose of earning income from a business or property is deductible, subject to certain statutory provisions that may require the interest to be capitalized. In addition, Canada imposes a two to one thin capitalization requirement on loans provided by specified nonresident shareholders. Overriding rules stipulate that an expense must be incurred for the purpose of earning income and be "reasonable" in the circumstances in order to be deductible.

Corporate income taxes are calculated in Canada on a nonconsolidated tax basis. Special rules apply in the context of computing a corporation's taxable income and taxable capital where the taxpayer is "related," "affiliated," or "associated" with other persons or is part of a corporate group.

(e) Federal Part I and Provincial Corporate Income Taxes

A corporation is subject to federal income tax at the general rate of 38 percent, which is applied to the corporation's taxable income or its "taxable income earned in Canada." This tax is levied under Part I of the Canadian Income Tax Act (ITA). Canada imposes a corporate surtax, which in effect applies at the rate of 1.12 percent of taxable income on taxable income earned in Canada. Canada permits a provincial abatement in computing a corporation's federal income tax payable for a taxation year that is equal to 10 percent of the corporation's taxable income earned in the year in a province.

4.2 Taxation in Canada

Under the Income Tax Regulations (ITR), taxable income earned in the year in a province is determined generally by identifying those provinces in which the corporation has a permanent establishment. The amount is determined by allocating the corporation's taxable income or taxable income earned in Canada to those provinces by formula. The allocation formula is based on the gross revenues attributable to, and the salaries and wages paid by, each permanent establishment. In contrast with the United States, Canada does not apply a property factor in making this allocation. If a corporation does not have a permanent establishment in a province or provinces, the provincial abatement is not available to reduce the aforementioned tax.

Examples of the combined projected federal and provincial income tax rates for the next five years are set out in Exhibit 4.1 for the provinces selected.

Exhibit 4.1

PROJECTED FEDERAL AND PROVINCIAL INCOME TAX RATES

	Federal and Provincial			
	Selected Corporate Income Taxes on Business Income			
	Quebec	Ontario	Alberta	British Columbia
2000	38.13	43.95	44.62	45.62
2001	37.16	42.12	42.29	44.62
2002	35.16	38.62	37.62	42.62
2003	33.16	35.12	34.12	40.62
2004	31.16	31.62	30.12	38.62
2005	31.16	30.12	30.12	38.12

Special corporate income tax rates apply to both business and investment income earned by Canadian-controlled private corporations and to income from manufacturing and processing. The manufacturing and processing incentive is being phased out as federal income tax rates are reduced in accordance with measures enacted by Parliament.

(f) Federal Branch Tax (Part XIV Tax)

Canada imposes income taxation of branches through Part I of the Canadian ITA. In addition, Part XIV of the ITA imposes a 25 percent branch tax on nonresident corporations that carry on business in Canada. The statutory branch tax rate is 25 percent, but a reduced rate may apply under an income tax treaty (e.g., 5 percent rate between Canada and the United States).

A portion of the business profits may be exempt from branch tax. For example, the Canada–United States tax treaty provides for a Cdn. $500,000 exemption that is to be shared among related companies. The branch tax is imposed in each tax year regarding any increase in the cumulative adjusted taxable income earned in Canada by a nonresident corporation to the extent that such amounts have not been reinvested in specified Canadian property. The taxable income earned in Canada of a nonresident corporation includes income from businesses carried on in Canada and taxable capital gains from dispositions of taxable Canadian property (i.e., real property such as land).

(g) Corporate Capital Tax on Large Corporations (Part I.3 Tax)

Part I.3 of the Income Tax Act (ITA) subjects a corporation, whether resident or nonresident, to an annual Large Corporations Tax (LCT). The LCT is calculated for most corporations at the rate of 0.225 percent of the corporation's taxable capital employed in Canada for the year in excess of its capital deduction for the year. For a nonresident corporation, taxable capital employed in Canada for a taxation year is determined, in broad terms, as the total of the carrying values at the end of the year of all assets used or held by the corporation in the course of carrying on a business through a permanent establishment in Canada, less current indebtedness of the corporation. The current indebtedness portion does not include the current portion of bonds, debentures, mortgages, loans, and so forth relating to that business. A nonresident corporation is subject to the LCT for a taxation year only if it carried on business during the year through a permanent establishment in Canada.

The LCT, which was originally introduced as a minimum income tax, is not deductible in computing taxable income for either federal or provincial income tax purposes. Instead, the LCT may be reduced by the amount of any corporate surtax payable for the year or paid in any of the seven preceding and three following taxation years. The capital deduction for a taxation year is $10 million, less the portion of the capital deduction allocated to any other related corporation.

(h) Withholding Tax on Payments to Nonresidents (Part XIII Tax)

Canada imposes federal income tax on a withholding basis under Part XIII of the ITA. The withholding tax applies to amounts paid or credited by a person resident in Canada to a nonresident person on account of certain types of income, such as interest, dividends, rents, royalties, and management fees. The statutory rate of withholding is 25 percent applied to the gross amount paid or credited to the nonresident. Lower rates of withholding may be provided for various types of payments under an applicable income tax treaty.

It is conceivable that a particular type of income earned by a nonresident corporation may be subject to federal income tax under both Part I and Part XIII of the ITA. To avoid this result, the ITR provides that a nonresident person who carries on business in Canada is subject to federal income tax under Part XIII on all amounts otherwise taxable under that part except those amounts that may reasonably be attributed to a business carried on by that person through a permanent establishment in Canada. In certain circumstances, a nonresident person may be deemed to be resident in Canada for purposes of Part XIII, thus subjecting the

4.2 Taxation in Canada

nonresident person to Canadian nonresident withholding tax on particular payments made by one non-resident to another (i.e., interest). These circumstances are as follows:

- The nonresident person's business was carried on principally in Canada. The nonresident person manufactures or processes goods in Canada.
- The nonresident person operates an oil or gas well in Canada or extracts petroleum or natural gas from a natural accumulation in Canada.
- The nonresident person extracts minerals from a mineral resource in Canada.

An exception applies to interest paid on debt owing to an arm's length party where the debtor cannot be required, except in certain events of default, to repay more than 25 percent of the principal amount of the obligation within five years of the obligation's date of issuance.[1]

(i) Losses and Other Corporate Tax Attributes

A corporation's noncapital losses may generally be carried back and deducted in its three immediately preceding taxation years or carried forward and deducted in the seven taxation years following the taxation year in which the loss was incurred. Similarly, capital losses may be carried back three taxation years but may be carried forward indefinitely for deduction only against capital gains realized in these years.

These carryover rules are subject to a further set of restrictions when there has been either a direct or an indirect acquisition of control of the corporation. When there has been an acquisition of control, the corporation's capital losses automatically expire, as do any noncapital losses incurred by the corporation from property. Noncapital losses from carrying on a business continue to be available for deduction following an acquisition of control provided, in the relevant taxation year, that the corporation continues to carry on the business that created the losses for profit or with a reasonable expectation of profit. If this continuity condition is met, these noncapital losses may be deducted against profits from this business, and subject to certain limitations, from income from a similar business within the normal carryover period. Similar continuity rules apply to restrict the utilization of a corporation's undeducted scientific research and experimental development expenditures and any unclaimed investment tax credits.

(j) CCA Rules Upon Acquisition

Specific CCA rules apply when there has been an acquisition of control of a corporation. For example, when the fair market value of all the property included in a particular CCA class is less than the undepreciated capital cost balance of the class, the balance is written down to fair market value. The amount of the write-down is added to the corporation's noncapital loss balance.

---

[1] Pursuant to subparagraph 212(1)(b)(vii) of the ITA.

Similarly, in the case of nondepreciable capital property, there is a write-down of such property to its fair market value. The amount of the write-down is added to the corporation's capital losses. As noted previously, these losses expire on the acquisition of control if they cannot be carried back. To somewhat mitigate the harshness of these rules, a corporation may elect to have a deemed disposition of other capital property owned by it for the purpose of realizing gains that may be used to utilize the losses. The corporation will thereby have a higher tax basis in such assets to carry forward if an election is made.

(k) Acquisition of Control Rules

On an acquisition of control of a corporation, the corporation's taxation year is deemed to end at the commencement of the day on which the acquisition of control occurred. A special election is available to cause the taxation year to end immediately before the acquisition of control by filing a special designation. In addition, a special rule applies when the corporation's year-end would otherwise end within the seven days preceding the acquisition to extend the taxation year for that period.

The acquisition of control at year-end necessitates the filing of federal and provincial, income, capital, and other information returns that are normally associated with a year-end. The year-end rule also works in tandem with the other acquisition of control rules described earlier.

4.3 ALTERNATIVE BUSINESS STRUCTURES

Typically, the business structures used by nonresidents to carry on business in Canada are as described in the following sections.

(a) Direct Sales by Foreign Vendors to Canadian Customers

In this scenario, direct sales tax placed to customers from outside Canada and the vendors do not have a permanent establishment in Canada. Nonresident persons who carry on business in Canada are subject to tax on their taxable income earned in Canada. This taxation is subject, however, to the overriding provisions of an applicable tax treaty. Where a tax treaty applies, a nonresident is generally not subject to tax in Canada from carrying on business unless the business is carried on in Canada through a permanent establishment in Canada.

If a resident of a country with which Canada has an income tax treaty sells products or provides services in Canada, an analysis of the applicable income tax treaty should be completed to determine whether the nonresident vendor has a permanent establishment in Canada. Article V of the Canada–United States tax treaty, for example, deals with the concept of a permanent establishment. Generally, a corporation is only subject to Canadian tax if it has a permanent establishment in Canada and is carrying on a business in Canada through that permanent establishment.

Paragraph 1 of Article V of the Canada–United States tax treaty states that a permanent establishment means a fixed place of business through which the busi-

4.3 Alternative Business Structures

ness of a resident of a Contracting State is wholly or partly carried on. Paragraph 2 indicates that the term *permanent establishment* shall include a place of management, a branch, an office, a factory, and a workshop. Paragraph 5 applies to a person acting in a Contracting State on behalf of a resident of the other Contracting State, other than an independent agent of an independent status to whom paragraph 7 applies. Such a person is deemed to be a permanent establishment in the first-mentioned State if such person has, and habitually exercises in that State, an authority to conclude contracts in the name of the resident.

(b) Branch/Permanent Establishment in Canada

In the event that a nonresident carries on business in Canada through a branch, the nonresident would be subject to Canadian tax on its business profits allocable to its permanent establishment in Canada. A review of Article V of the Canada–United States tax treaty, for example, would have to be conducted to determine whether the nonresident has a permanent establishment in Canada. Some factors that would need to be considered in determining whether a nonresident has a permanent establishment in Canada are whether it employs individuals, leases property, whether contracts are executed in Canada, and so forth.

A nonresident carrying on business through a branch would be subject to federal and provincial income and capital taxes and to federal branch tax. One of the advantages of the branch structure is that losses of the branch may be available to offset against income in computing the nonresident's taxes in its jurisdiction of residence or domicile. The disadvantages of operating through a branch structure include the following:

- The applicable branch taxes are payable annually on after-tax profits not reinvested in the business
- The nonresident parent would be liable for all of the liabilities of the Canadian branch

If the Canadian operations are expected to be in a loss position, a nonresident investor may wish to carry on business in Canada through a branch in order to use the losses that arise in Canada to offset its taxable income from other sources. At a later date, the branch could be reorganized into a subsidiary on a tax-deferred rollover basis for Canadian tax purposes.

(c) Subsidiary Incorporated in Canada

A corporation that is incorporated in Canada would, by statutory definition, be deemed to be resident in Canada for Canadian income tax purposes irrespective of whether its central management and control resides in Canada.

The primary advantage of using a Canadian subsidiary to carry on business in Canada is that the corporation exists as a separate legal entity. Accordingly, the assets of its shareholders would not be exposed to creditors of the corporation. An exception to this creditor situation is a company that is formed in Nova Scotia as an unlimited liability company (ULC). A ULC is regarded as a corporation for

Canadian income tax purposes, but countries such as the United States treat the ULC as a disregarded entity, providing a flow-through of its results for tax purposes to the company's shareholder(s). A Canadian corporation would be taxable on its worldwide income and any initial operating losses of the corporation would generally not be available for consolidation in the nonresident's tax return. On the other hand, operating in the form of a subsidiary allows for the control of timing of dividends and the payment of withholding taxes.

4.4 TAX TREATMENT OF CAPITAL GAINS AND CAPITAL LOSSES

Canada imposes taxes on the disposition of capital property. Such capital property would generally include shares of private and public corporations for most investors. Capital property is defined for Canadian tax purposes as property, the disposition of which gives rise to a capital gain or a capital loss.

Not surprisingly, there is extensive jurisprudence on this capital property issue. The courts have looked to the primary and secondary intent of the holder and the holding period of the particular property. The distinction is important because only 50 percent of capital gains (net of capital losses) are taxable and capital losses may only be deducted against capital gains realized. The applicable period is the tax year, the three preceding years, or in any future year, subject to certain exceptions related to acquisitions of control of corporate taxpayers.

In addition, individuals who dispose of shares of a qualified small business corporation may be eligible to claim some or all of their cumulative $500,000 lifetime capital gains exemption to shelter the gain. Similarly, a disposition of shares of a qualified small business corporation may also give rise to a business investment loss, 50 percent of which (the allowable business investment loss) may, in certain circumstances, be deducted against other types of income.

4.5 TAX TREATMENT ON SALE OF GOODWILL AND OTHER INTANGIBLES

The proceeds from the sale of other intangible assets that are capital in nature (eligible capital property) are credited (at a 50 percent inclusion rate) to the taxpayer's cumulative eligible capital expenditure pool in respect of each business carried on by the taxpayer. Where there is a credit balance in this pool at the end of the year, this credit balance would be subject to tax as business income.

4.6 TAXATION OF DISPOSITIONS OF TAXABLE CANADIAN PROPERTY BY NONRESIDENTS

Gains arising from the disposition by nonresidents of taxable Canadian property are subject to Canadian tax, subject to the overriding application of an income tax treaty. Reporting requirements are specified by section 116. Taxable Canadian property is defined as property that meets the following criteria:

4.6 Taxation of Dispositions of Taxable Canadian Property

- Real property in Canada
- Property used or held by the taxpayer in carrying on a business in Canada, including eligible capital property, or inventory of such a business, other than:
  - property used in carrying on an insurance business
  - where the taxpayer is nonresident, ships and aircraft used principally in international traffic and related personal property, if the country in which the taxpayer is resident does not tax the gains of persons resident in Canada from dispositions of such property, principally in international traffic and related personal property

- If the taxpayer is an insurer, its designated insurance property for the year
- Unlisted shares of Canadian-resident corporations other than a nonresident-owned investment corporation, unless on the first day of the year the corporation owns taxable Canadian property, and other than a mutual fund corporation
- Unlisted shares of nonresident corporations if, at any time during the 60-month period that ends at that time, the value of the company's Canadian real and resource properties made up more than half the fair market value of all of its properties, and more than half of the fair market value of the share was derived directly or indirectly from such properties
- Listed shares that would be described in the previous two conditions if those paragraphs included listed shares, or shares of a mutual fund corporation, if at any time during the 60-month period that ends at that time the taxpayer and non-arm's length persons owned 25 percent or more of the issued shares of any class of the capital stock of the corporation
- Certain partnership interests, if at any time in the 60-month (currently 12-month) period that ends at the time, most of the partnerships value is attributable to Canadian property
- Capital interests in trusts (other than unit trusts) that are resident in Canada
- Units of unit trusts (other than mutual fund trusts) that are resident in Canada
- Units of a mutual fund trust if, at any time during the 60-month period that ends at that time, not less than 25 percent of the units of the trust belonged to the taxpayer and non-arm's length persons
- Interests in a nonresident trust if, at any time during the 60-month period that ends at that time, the trust met a test comparable to the one described in respect of a nonresident corporation previously
- Interests and options in property described, whether or not the property exists

If the taxpayer is an insurer, the property is designated insurance property for the year, notwithstanding the exemption from Canadian tax that may be available in an income tax treaty, such dispositions must nevertheless be reported to the Canada Customs and Revenue Agency (CCRA).

(a) Tax Clearance Certificate

A nonresident seller must obtain a tax clearance certificate for the sale or transfer of taxable Canadian property. The application for the clearance certificate can be made before the transfer, but must be made no later than 10 days after the transfer. In general, it may take the CCRA six to twelve weeks to process the request and issue the clearance certificate.

The information required with the application includes the following:

- Transferor name and address
- Transferee name and address
- Selling price (proceeds) and copy of purchase and sale agreement
- Cost base of the taxable Canadian property and computation of gain (or loss)

Valuation or appraisal reports substantiate the amount of the fair market value proceeds for non-arm's length transfers

- Valuation or appraisal reports substantiating the amount of the fair market value proceeds for non-arm's length transfers

(b) Deposit Procedure

In connection with obtaining a clearance certificate, where any gain is not treaty-exempt, the CCRA will not issue the certificate without a deposit for tax that may be payable by the transferor, by cash or letter of credit, up to a maximum of 25 percent of the gain. The transferor may recover all or a portion of such tax deposited by filing Canadian income tax returns. The tax/collateral provided to obtain the clearance certificate will be refunded or the security released if, on assessing the tax returns, the CCRA and the applicable provincial authorities conclude that the gain is treaty exempt.

If the clearance certificate is not applied for on a timely basis and the transferee acquires property for which an application should have been made, the transferee is liable for Canadian tax equal to 25 percent of the gross proceeds that were paid or deemed to be paid to the transferor. That amount must be withheld and remitted to the CCRA within 30 days after the month in which the acquisition occurred.[2]

4.7 ASSET PURCHASE TRANSACTIONS

The principal concern in a transaction in which a purchaser acquires a business directly is the allocation of the purchase price among various assets acquired (i.e., land, building, machinery and equipment and so forth). A seller would typically prefer to allocate as much of the proceeds as possible to land and goodwill. The

---

[2] Pursuant to subsection 116(5) of the ITA.

4.7 Asset Purchase Transactions

purpose is to include as much as possible at a 50 percent inclusion rate rather than the 100 percent inclusion rate, as would apply to recaptured depreciation on the sale of depreciable property or on the sale of inventory.

This preferred allocation of asset purchase costs from the seller's vantage point can be contrasted with the purchaser's preference to allocate the purchase price to property that can be depreciated for tax purposes. The purchaser would prefer to allocate more to assets with a high CCA rate, e.g., such as vehicles and computer equipment (30 percent declining balance), machinery and equipment (25 percent declining balance), and so forth. Seventy-five percent of the acquisition cost of goodwill can be amortized for tax purposes, based on a 7 percent declining balance rate.

(a) Double Taxation

An asset sale transaction may give rise to a double taxation concern from the seller's perspective. For example, if the business to be acquired is being carried on by a corporation, there will be a first level of taxation on the gains arising on the disposition of the assets. There will be a second level of taxation when the after-tax corporate proceeds are distributed to the shareholder or shareholders of the corporation. In such circumstances, a vendor may prefer a share sale to an asset sale transaction unless a premium will compensate for the additional tax burden. Further, if the seller is a nonresident of Canada, the full amount of any gain on a sale of the shares would potentially be exempt from Canadian tax, depending on the jurisdiction of residence of the seller.

When a transaction is structured as a purchase of assets, none of the seller's tax attributes generally flow through to the purchaser. That is, the purchaser has a cost base in the purchased assets that is equal to their purchase price. Exceptions to this rule, however, are available when the seller and the purchaser file specific elections. For example, an election[3] may be jointly filed if the acquiror acquires all or substantially all of the seller's accounts receivable as part of the purchase of a business. The election permits the acquiror to claim a bad debt allowance or write-off in the event that any of the purchased accounts receivable become uncollectible.

(b) Taxable Canadian Corporation

The parties can complete a transaction on a full or partial rollover basis if two requirements are met:

1. The purchaser is a taxable Canadian corporation, including a Canadian subsidiary owned by a nonresident person.
2. The consideration for the purchased assets includes shares of the acquiring entity.

---

[3] Pursuant to section 22 of the ITA.

In order for the transaction to be completed in this manner, both the acquiring corporation and the seller must jointly file an election in the prescribed form and manner and within a prescribed time period.[4] The amount elected by the transferor and the transferee is deemed to be the proceeds of disposition to the transferor, the cost to the transferor of the consideration received, and the cost to the transferee of the assets that it acquires. The amount elected cannot be less than the amount of any nonshare consideration and cannot be more than the fair market value of the transferred assets.

If an election under this provision is filed, the seller will defer tax until such time as the vendor disposes of the shares of the transferee corporation. At that time, the seller will realize either a capital gain or loss on the disposition of the shares of the transferee. This gain or loss determination has no effect on the transferee's tax position.

(c) International Issues

The seller may be able to reduce the amount of gain subject to tax if the seller is a Canadian corporation and the assets to be sold include shares of a "foreign affiliate" of the vendor. The seller may be able to reduce the amount of the gain that would be subject to tax regarding these shares by making a special election to treat all or a portion of the proceeds of disposition as a dividend[5] out of the affiliate's "exempt" or "taxable" surplus accounts. In general, such a deemed dividend must be included in the seller corporation's income, but the income is then deductible in computing its taxable income.

Activities can achieve tax-deferred transaction from the shares of a foreign affiliate that are disposed of to a foreign corporation in exchange for consideration that includes shares of the acquiring corporation.[6] In order for this rollover to be available, sufficient shares of the acquiring corporation must be issued to the seller so that the acquiring corporation qualifies as a foreign affiliate of the seller immediately following the disposition of the shares of the first mentioned affiliate.

4.8 SHARE PURCHASE TRANSACTIONS

A disposition of shares generally results in the realization of a capital gain or loss to the selling shareholders, subject to possible tax-deferred rollover treatment in certain circumstances. It may be possible, however, and depending on the circumstances, to structure a stock sale transaction that would provide a seller with either capital gains or deemed dividend treatment. For example, if the vendor is a Canadian resident individual, the effective tax rate on a capital gain will likely

---

[4] Pursuant to subsection 85(1) of the ITA and within the time prescribed in subsection 85(6). The prescribed election form is a T2057.
[5] Pursuant to subsection 93(1) of the ITA.
[6] Pursuant to subsection 85.1(3) of the ITA.

4.8 Share Purchase Transactions

approximate between 20 to 25 percent. In contrast, the tax rate on an actual or a deemed dividend may be as high as 33 percent.

(a) Nonresident Parties

Nonresident parties may prefer capital gains treatment if they are exempt from Canadian tax because of a bilateral tax treaty. These arrangements could be subject to Part XIII nonresident withholding tax. On the other hand, a seller that is a corporation resident in Canada may prefer dividend treatment where, because of the available inter-corporate dividend deduction, such a dividend would not be taxable.[7]

Such a "tax-free" inter-corporate dividend may be recharacterized as a part of the proceeds of disposition of the shares disposed of. This situation applies if the dividend exceeds the amount of the income earned or realized and on hand that is attributable to the shares pursuant to subsection 55(2) of the ITA. This is a capital gains avoidance provision.

(b) Seller's Perspective

From a Canadian tax perspective, a capital gain or loss normally arises for the seller when the acquiror acquires the target shares directly. A dividend[8] is deemed to be received by a selling shareholder when the target corporation purchases its own shares for cancellation. The selling shareholder can purchase its shares, for example, by using funds provided to it by the acquiring entity.

When a corporation acquires its shares from a selling shareholder, the corporation will be deemed to have paid, and the selling shareholder will be deemed to have received, a dividend to the extent that that amount so paid exceeds the paid-up capital[9] of the corporation's shares. Paid-up capital is equal to the legal stated capital of a corporation's shares subject to several specific adjustments prescribed in the ITA. The portion of the proceeds equal to the paid-up capital of the shares retains its character as proceeds for purposes of computing the gain or loss on the shares sold. Where the seller is a Canadian corporation, the selling corporation's loss, if any, must generally be reduced by all dividends or deemed dividends received on the shares disposed of.[10] Dividends received on any shares for which the shares sold were substituted must also be considered.

(c) Purchaser's Perspective

From a purchaser's perspective, where all of the shares of a Canadian target corporation are acquired, all of the tax attributes of the acquired corporation generally survive, subject to the application of the acquisition of control rules discussed elsewhere in this analysis. This means that the basis of the assets of the

---

[7] Pursuant to subsection 112(1) of the ITA.
[8] Pursuant to subsection 84(3) of the ITA.
[9] Defined in section 89 of the Act
[10] Pursuant to subsection 112(3) of the ITA.

target corporation is carried over. There is a limited ability to write-up the tax value of the assets.

The major exception regarding the write-up assets pertains to "eligible" nondepreciable capital property owned by the target corporation at the time that the assets were acquired. In order to utilize this write-up, referred to in Canadian tax parlance as the "88(1)(d) bump," it is necessary to wind-up the Canadian target into the acquiring corporation. The corporation itself must be a Canadian corporation or, as an alternative, amalgamate the target corporation and the acquiring corporation.

The cost base of eligible property may then be increased because of the 88(1)(d) bump, within prescribed limits, to an amount not exceeding its fair market value at the time that control of the target corporation was last acquired. The second limitation is that the amount of the bump cannot exceed the amount by which the adjusted cost base to the acquiring corporation of the shares of the target corporation exceed the tax basis of the target's assets net of its liabilities and reserves. Other adjustments in computing this bump may apply depending on the circumstances.

(d) Excessive Assets

The 88(1)(d) bump is particularly useful in situations where the target owns redundant or excessive assets that will be sold shortly after the target is acquired. For example, if the target corporation carries on more than one business, and the purchaser is only interested in one of the businesses, on a friendly takeover, the target could transfer the assets that will not be retained by the purchaser into a newly created subsidiary. This transfer would be completed before the takeover transaction and for tax purposes and would be completed on a tax-deferred rollover basis.

The purchaser would then acquire the shares of the target corporation and proceed to wind-up the target corporation and make a designation under paragraph 88(1)(d) of the ITA to bump up the adjusted cost base of the shares of the newly formed subsidiary. The shares of this newly formed subsidiary could then be sold with no tax or a reduced tax liability. This "buy, bump, and sell" strategy is an efficient means of bumping up the adjusted cost base of the shares on any foreign subsidiaries owned by the target corporation. These shares can be moved out from underneath the Canadian target corporation following the acquisition transaction to facilitate any international structuring by a foreign parent corporation.

The use of this bump strategy is subject to several extremely complex rules and requirements. The premise is that any of the property that is owned by the target corporation must not, as part of the same series of transactions or events, find its way back into the hands of the former target corporation shareholders.

4.9 PROFIT REPATRIATION, CROSS-BORDER PAID-UP CAPITAL, AND FINANCING ISSUES

Where a foreign corporation (Forco) acquires the shares of a Canadian corporation, the nonresident corporation usually should form a new Canadian subsidiary (Canco) to acquire the target corporation. If the acquisition is funded by having Forco first subscribe for shares of the capital of Canco, the paid-up capital of the shares of Canco will have full paid-up capital for Canadian tax purposes. This transaction will allow the future repatriation of this amount by way of paid-up capital reductions to occur without being subject to Canadian nonresident withholding tax.

In addition, if Canco funds the acquisition by issuing its own shares to Forco and by borrowing from Forco, the paid-up capital established through this initial capitalization will be useful in maximizing the amount of related-party debt that is not in excess of that allowable under the thin capitalization rules (see following discussion). Canco could be amalgamated with the Canadian target company after the Canadian target is purchased. This structure would be useful if there is the ability to bump-up the adjusted cost base of any of the property owned by the target. It then would be useful to match the interest expense on any borrowed money against the future income earned by the target corporation. The capital implications of such a merger should also be considered because the overall liability for such taxes may be increased as a consequence of the merger.

Depending on the jurisdiction of residence of the ultimate buyer, Canco could be either a normal corporation with limited liability or a Nova Scotia unlimited liability company (NS ULC). For Canadian tax purposes, an NS ULC is regarded as a corporation, but in the United States, for example, an NS ULC can be treated as a disregarded entity or a partnership.

4.10 SHARE-FOR-SHARE TRANSACTIONS

Section 85 of the ITA permits a seller to transfer property to a taxable Canadian corporation on a tax-deferred rollover basis. This rollover provision is commonly used in non-arm's length transactions (i.e., transfer of business or branch assets into a Canadian corporation). The rollover provision is also frequently used in arm's length takeover transactions. Property eligible for transfer under section 85 includes capital property, depreciable property, eligible capital property, and most types of inventory. This rollover provision can be used, for example, when a seller disposes of shares of a Canadian target corporation for shares of another taxable Canadian corporation.

The provisions of subsection 85(1) of the act, other than paragraph 85(1)(e.2) of the act, apply to that transfer of assets. The agreed amount as to the transfer will be deemed to be the proceeds of disposition to the transferor and the adjusted cost base to the transferee on the disposition and acquisition of the shares. This provision applies if the transferor and transferee jointly file an election pursuant to subsection 85(1) of the act as to the transfer of the target corporation shares. Time limits for the transaction are specified in subsection 85(6) or 85(7) of the Act, as the case may be.

(a) Compliance Issues

A seller may dispose of shares of one corporation to another corporation in exchange for shares of the acquiring corporation on a tax-deferred basis under section 85. Nevertheless, the process of preparing and filing the prescribed election forms can be a time-consuming and expensive exercise, particularly when many sellers are involved. Section 85.1 of the act may be used in these circumstances. A seller might not wish to recognize any portion of the gain or loss on the sale of the shares of the target corporation (the exchanged shares) until the seller ultimately disposes of its newly acquired shares of the purchaser corporation. Unlike a section 85 rollover, section 85.1 will apply automatically as long as the vendor treats the exchange of its shares as a rollover on the tax return.

(b) Selling Corporation's Perspective

The holder of such shares will be deemed, pursuant to subparagraph 85.1(1)(a)(i) of the act, to have disposed of the shares for proceeds of disposition equal to the adjusted cost base of the shares immediately before the exchange, unless the holder elects out. The holder will be deemed, by virtue of subparagraph 85.1(1)(a)(ii) of the act, to have acquired the newly issued shares of the acquiring corporation at a cost equal to the adjusted cost base of the target corporation shares immediately before the exchange. The following requirements must be satisfied in order for section 85.1 to be available to the seller:

- The shares being disposed of must be capital property to the seller.
- The shares being disposed of must be shares of a taxable Canadian corporation.
- The purchaser corporation must be a Canadian corporation.
- The seller must receive shares of any class of the purchaser corporation that are issued from treasury.
- The seller must not include any portion of the gain or loss on the exchanged shares in the seller's tax return for the year of the transaction.
- The seller and the purchaser corporation must deal at arm's length immediately before the exchange.
- Immediately after the exchange, the seller, or persons with whom the seller did not deal at arm's length, does not control the purchaser corporation.
- The seller and the purchaser corporation must not file an election under section 85 regarding the exchanged shares.
- The only consideration received by the seller for the exchanged shares are the shares of the purchaser corporation that are issued from the treasury of the seller. The purchaser corporation must not file an election under section 85 as to the exchanged shares.
- The only consideration received by the seller for the exchanged shares are the shares of the purchaser corporation that are issued from the treasury of the seller.

(c) Acquiring Corporation's Perspective

From the acquiring corporation's perspective, its cost of the shares of the target corporation is deemed, by virtue of paragraph 85.1(1)(b) of the ITA, to be the lesser of the fair market value and the paid-up capital of the target corporation's shares immediately before the exchange. In transactions involving more than one seller, the fact that one seller may not satisfy all of the required conditions described previously will not preclude the remaining sellers from using the section 85.1 rollover for their shares. Nor do all the sellers who qualify for the rollover need to take the same filing position regarding their shares.

A seller might receive both shares of the purchaser corporation and other consideration in exchange for the shares of the target corporation. In that event, a section 85.1 rollover may still be available, provided the seller can clearly establish which shares were sold entirely for treasury shares of the purchaser corporation and which shares were sold for other consideration. However, there are several precedents where the acquiror has purposely included a nominal amount of non-share consideration to ensure that section 85.1 will not automatically apply to what would otherwise be a share-for-share tax-deferred rollover transaction. Taxpayers would deliberately not apply rollover treatment in order to maximize the acquiring corporation's adjusted cost base in the shares of the target. This non-deferral could be important, for example, in order to maximize the amount of the 88(1)(d) bump described previously. Selling shareholders that want a rollover transaction in these circumstances would need to file a joint election with the acquiring corporation under subsection 85(1) of the ITA.

4.11 AMALGAMATION TRANSACTIONS

An amalgamation is the combination of two or more corporations to form a single corporation. Section 87 of the ITA provides a mechanism to amalgamate two or more Canadian corporations on a tax-deferred basis without the need to file any elections. Section 87 applies to essentially pool the tax attributes of each amalgamating corporation (the predecessor corporations) and to continue them in the new amalgamated corporation.

The assets and liabilities of each predecessor corporation are generally deemed to be acquired by the amalgamated corporation at their tax values. As a result, the predecessor corporations report no gains or losses. Similarly, tax accounts such as a corporation's loss carryovers normally flow through to the amalgamated company, subject to the acquisition of control rules previously described.

The rules in subsection 256(7) of the ITA prescribe several situations in which control of a corporation will be deemed to have been acquired as a consequence of an amalgamation transaction. The corporation formed on the amalgamation is deemed to be a new corporation for tax purposes, with its first taxation year commencing at the time of the amalgamation. The taxation years of each predecessor corporation are deemed to end at the time immediately before the amalgamation.

Each shareholder of a predecessor corporation who owned the predecessor corporation shares as capital property and received no consideration other than shares of the new corporation will obtain a rollover as to the disposition of the predecessor company shares. However, if a particular shareholder receives a combination of cash or other nonshare consideration and shares, the shareholder will be deemed to have disposed of its shares of the predecessor corporation at fair market value, thereby realizing a gain or loss, and to have acquired shares of the amalgamated corporation at that fair market value less the value of the nonshare consideration received.

Amalgamations are often used within a corporate group to rationalize business operations or as a method of applying tax losses of one company against the profits of another corporation in the group. The amalgamation can be a merger of a corporation with one or more of its wholly owned subsidiaries (a "short-form vertical amalgamation") or a merger of two or more sister corporations (a "horizontal amalgamation"). Further, a subsidiary of one corporation (the parent) may be merged with another corporation (X Co.), and shares of the parent may be issued to the shareholders of X Co. (a "triangular amalgamation"). Triangular amalgamations may be used to as a technique to effect a takeover and/or to squeeze out minority shareholders of a target corporation.

4.12 FOREIGN PURCHASERS

A rollover is currently available for share-for-share exchanges when the corporations involved are all residents of Canada or are all nonresidents. Currently, a cross-border share-for-share exchange does not qualify for rollover treatment; however, the supplemental information to the October 18, 2000, Federal Economic Statement indicated that the current Canadian government intends to develop a cross-border share-for-share exchange mechanism. This mechanism would be available both on the exchange of shares of a Canadian corporation for shares of a foreign corporation and on the exchange of shares of a foreign corporation for shares of a Canadian corporation. These new rules will not be effective until draft legislation has been released. At this time, such draft legislation is not expected until January 2002.

4.13 EXCHANGEABLE SHARE TRANSACTIONS

The fact that no rollover mechanism is currently available to exchange shares of a Canadian corporation for shares of a nonresident acquiror (Purchaseco) has led to the use of what are referred to as *exchangeable share* transactions. Using an exchangeable share transaction structure, the shareholders of a Canadian target corporation could exchange their target corporation shares for preferred exchangeable shares (the exchangeable shares) in a new Canadian corporation (Exchangeco). These exchangeable shares would, in turn, be essentially exchangeable for common shares of Purchaseco. The exchange provisions need to be carefully structured in order to avoid the application of taxes under Part VI.I of the ITA that may apply if Exchangeco redeems the exchangeable shares.

This structure is normally addressed through put and call arrangements. Part VI.I tax is a tax levied on dividends paid or deemed to be paid on taxable preferred and short-term preferred shares at either 25 percent, 40 percent or 66 percent, depending on the share type. The dividend payer and related parties may ultimately recover these taxes within prescribed limits in some circumstances through a taxable income deduction.

Purchaseco would then subscribe for common shares of Exchangeco from the treasury. Dividends on the exchangeable shares would be paid on the same basis as on the common shares of Purchaseco. The rights of the exchangeable share shareholders would be subject to various support agreements, and the holders of the exchangeable shares would, through a voting trust arrangement, be entitled to voting rights in respect of Purchaseco. In effect, the exchangeable shares are the economic equivalent of the common shares of Purchaseco but permit the shareholders of the Canadian target corporation to avoid realization of a gain until such time as the exchangeable shares are exchanged for shares of Purchaseco. Numerous recent U.S. public company acquisitions of Canadian corporations have been completed using this type of a transaction structure.

The advantage of an exchangeable share transaction to the existing shareholders of the target is that they can dispose of their shares, yet defer the resulting tax liability until their exchangeable shares are exchanged for shares of the Purchaseco. This transfer would likely occur at a time when they want cash for their exchangeable shares and consequently, they would sell their Purchaseco shares after exercising their exchangeable share exchange rights. While not legally owning stock of the Purchaseco, their exchangeable shares would be governed by a voting trust agreement (i.e., would have a right to appoint a trustee to vote such Purchaseco shares as if they were owned), and would have rights *pari-passu* with existing shareholders of the purchaser in the event of liquidation of the purchaser. Further, the target would be required to pay dividends on these shares equivalent to any dividends paid by the purchaser on common shares. The rights and value of such shares would therefore "track" the rights and value of the common shares of Purchaseco.

4.14 PROPOSED FIE RULES

The proposed Foreign Investment Entity (FIE) rules replace and expand existing rules that apply to offshore investment funds; however, the new rules cast a far wider net and establish alternative regimes: taxpayers must mark-to-market their investments in FIEs or, where certain conditions are met, may elect to pay tax on their share of the underlying income. The new system applies to a participating interest other than an exempt interest in a foreign entity (a defined expression) that is considered an FIE. Basically, an FIE is a nonresident entity, the investment property of which represents at least half of its assets. A complex set of measurement rules are proposed to determine if this test is met.

Disclosure in public documents may be affected by the new FIE rules. Senior management of foreign and Canadian corporations may be required to make representations to potential investors to permit them to determine whether the shares will be subject to FIE reporting and taxation. Historically, U.S. investors have tended to avoid shares of passive foreign investment corporations (PFICs) because of the onerous reporting and taxation aspects of those investments. It remains to be seen if Canadian investors will shun FIE investments; however, it is expected that, at a minimum, a potential investor in a foreign corporation or other entity will want to determine whether any incremental costs may apply under the FIE rules. The FIE proposals apply whether or not there is a tax-avoidance motive. Individuals (other than trusts) are exempt if resident in Canada for less than five years.

The Department of Finance requested comments on the draft legislation by September 1, 2000, and the new rules are slated to apply to taxation years that begin after 2000.

It is expected that the revised draft legislation will be released and that there may be significant changes to these rules before they are enacted.

4.15 FINANCING COSTS

Expenses may be incurred in connection with or in the course of borrowing money when this borrowed money was used to earn income from a business or property or in the course of issuing shares. Such expenses are deductible for tax purposes over a five-year period,[11] subject to proration in any short taxation year.

4.16 THIN CAPITALIZATION RULES

Under the Canadian thin capitalization rules, interest deductibility on debt owed by a Canadian corporation to a specified nonresident is limited based on such debt not exceeding two times the equity of the Canadian entity. For these purposes, debt is computed as the average of all calendar month amounts (where such month ends in the taxation year), each of which is the greatest total amount at any time in the calendar month of the corporation's debt owing to specified nonresidents. A specified nonresident person is a nonresident person who owns, alone or together with non-arm's length parties, 25 percent or more of the shares (i.e., either votes or value) of the corporation.

For these purposes, equity is computed as the total of the following three amounts:

1. The retained earnings of the corporation at the beginning of the taxation year on an unconsolidated basis (i.e., not including retained earnings of any other corporation). This retained earnings amount would not include any deficits (i.e., any deficit would be treated as a $NIL amount for these purposes).

---

[11] Pursuant to paragraph 20(1)(e) of the ITA.

4.16 Thin Capitalization Rules

2. The average of the contributed surplus at the beginning of each calendar month that ends in the taxation year where such contributed surplus was contributed by a specified nonresident shareholder of the corporation.
3. The average of the corporation's paid-up capital at the beginning of each calendar month that ends in the taxation year on shares held by specified nonresident shareholders of the corporation.

Any interest that is not deductible because of the application of the thin capitalization rules is still subject to Part XIII nonresident withholding tax when paid. Local bank debt, for example, with a parent guarantee is not subject to the thin capitalization rules.

CHAPTER 5

Taxation of Mergers and Acquisitions in Finland

Kirsi Hiltunen
Jaakko Sivonen
Ernst & Young Finland

5.1 Introduction
5.2 Tax Law
5.3 Tax Losses and Tax Credits under the Imputation System
5.4 Group Tax Relief
5.5 Share Acquisition (Excluding Exchanges of Shares)
5.6 Asset Acquisition (Excluding Tax-Free Spin-Offs or Contributions of Assets)
5.7 Mergers
    (a) Definition
    (b) Taxation of Tax-Free and Taxable Mergers
5.8 Divisions
    (a) Definition
    (b) Taxation of Tax-Free and Taxable Divisions
5.9 Tax-Free Transfer (Contribution) of Assets
    (a) Definition
    (b) Taxation of Tax-Free Transfer of Assets
5.10 Tax-Free and Taxable Exchanges of Shares
    (a) Definition
    (b) Taxation of Tax-Free and Taxable Exchange of Shares

5.1 INTRODUCTION

Finland's corporate taxation concerning mergers, divisions, spin-offs of assets, and exchanges of shares has been harmonized under the European Union (EU) Merger Directive (90/434/EEC). The same rules apply to purely domestic transactions.

The tax provisions concerning mergers, divisions, transfers of assets, and exchanges of shares are based on the principle of succession for the business. This means that the qualifying transactions generally do not cause realization of taxable income for the company undergoing the reorganization or for its shareholders. However, transfer taxes may be due in those situations. If the requirements for tax-neutral treatment are not met, the transaction may cause taxation at the corporate and the shareholder levels.

Share acquisition is probably the most common way to acquire an existing business in Finland. Nevertheless, the buyer's desire to get a step-up in asset base and eliminate past liabilities favor asset acquisitions.

Finland applies an imputation system on dividends, under which corporate tax is fully credited to resident shareholders. Another important feature in Finland is the group relief system, under which members of a qualifying group can transfer taxable profits to other corporate members, provided that the requirements of the relevant tax law are met. Finally, limitations are placed on availability of loss carry-forwards and tax carry-forwards when a company's ownership changes hands directly or indirectly. Tax treatment of corporate liquidations may offer some planning opportunities. These aspects affect the way business acquisitions and reorganizations are carried out in Finland.

The most important Finnish tax provisions concerning share and asset acquisitions, mergers, divisions, spin-offs of assets, and exchanges of shares are described in the this chapter from the point of view of a nonresident seller or buyer. However, the discussion does not attempt to cover all possible tax consequences or corporate law aspects that must be considered when planning for acquisitions and corporate reorganizations in Finland. Taxation of partnerships or other corporate bodies, such as cooperatives and branches, are not included because of the rareness of such entities in Finland.

5.2   TAX LAW

As far as tax law is concerned, reference must be made to the following acts, as amended; the Business Income Tax Act (Laki elinkeinotulon verottamisesta of 24.6.1968/360, EVL), the Act on Group Relief in Taxation (Laki konserniavustuksesta verotuksessa of 21.11.1986/825), the Act on Imputation Credit (Laki yhtiöveron hyvityksestä of 29.12.1988/1232), the Income Tax Act (Tuloverolaki of 30.12.1992/1535, TVL), and the Wealth Tax Act (Varallisuusverolaki 30.12.1992/1537, VVL). Furthermore, the Act on Fiscal Assessment (Laki verotusmenettelystä of 18.12.1995/1558, VML), the Transfer Tax Act (Varainsiirtoverolaki of 29.11.1996/931), and the Value-Added Tax Act (Arvonlisäverolaki of 30.12.1993/1501, ALV) contain relevant provisions.

5.3   TAX LOSSES AND TAX CREDITS UNDER THE IMPUTATION SYSTEM

Certain Finnish tax aspects have to be considered when planning for acquisitions and reorganizations in Finland. Therefore, the main features of tax losses and imputation tax credits are briefly discussed.

Tax losses may currently be carried forward for 10 tax years unless a qualifying ownership change occurs. There is no carryback. The losses can be netted

5.2 Tax Losses and Tax Credits under the Imputation System

against taxable income of the same income basket where the losses have occurred. A Finnish resident company may have three income baskets (i.e., business, personal, and farming).

An imputation system (*avoir fiscal*) for dividend distributions is applied to Finnish resident corporations and shareholders. The corporate tax rate in Finland has been 29 percent since tax year 2000. The taxable gross income of a shareholder consists of the dividends received and the imputation credit.

The imputation credit is 29/71 of the dividends distributed for tax year 2000. The amount of imputation credit corresponds with the corporate income tax rate of 29 percent. A resident shareholder can fully credit the corporate tax in his or her personal taxation. For example, if a company has an income of 100 in the corporation, the company has to pay income tax of 29 on that income.

The company may distribute dividends of 71 to its shareholders. At the shareholder level the net dividend of 71 and the imputation credit of 29 will be taxed as capital income or earned income, as the case may be. Under the imputation system, domestic dividends will be taxed once at the effective tax rate of the resident recipient.

A minimum tax on the dividend distribution in the form of compensatory tax ensures that corporations bear a full corporate tax on their profits. Tax-free income (e.g., foreign dividends) cannot be distributed to shareholders without taxation at the corporate level. If the compensatory tax were not levied, shareholders would receive an imputation credit for corporate tax that was not actually paid by the company.

The minimum tax is 29/71 of the company's dividend distribution for tax year 2000 or thereafter. If the company's tax on its taxable income is less than the minimum tax on its dividend distribution for the tax year in question, the company has to pay compensatory tax. On the other hand, the corporate tax on the company's taxable income may exceed the minimum tax based on the dividend distribution. In that event, the company may carry forward the excess for 10 years. The excess, termed *tax surplus*, will be considered in determining compensatory tax payable during those years.

On a shareholder level, the excess is generally refundable to an individual shareholder if the tax payable on the dividends is less than the imputation credit. The excess is not refundable for resident corporations. The shareholders may carry the excess only to future years to be set against their corporate taxes in those years. The excess imputation credit may generally be carried forward for 10 years.

The imputation system contains an exemption that allows for redistribution of tax-free foreign dividends by a Finnish company to its nonresident shareholders without the minimum tax in Finland, provided that certain requirements are met. The redistribution of foreign dividends by the Finnish entity can occur during 10 tax years after the tax year of receipt without the minimum tax, provided that a qualifying ownership change has not occurred.

The right to carry forward tax losses, tax surpluses, excess imputation credits, and dividend surpluses is generally forfeited if more than 50 percent of the shares in the company or in its immediate shareholder that owns 20 percent or more of its shares changes hands during the tax year when the tax loss or other tax attribute has been created. The same rule applies if the ownership change occurs afterwards; however, the tax authorities may, upon application, allow for usage of losses, tax surpluses, excess imputation credits, and dividend surpluses despite a qualifying ownership change.

5.4 GROUP TAX RELIEF

Finnish corporations that are part of a qualifying group can give group relief to each other when certain requirements are met. Group relief is tax deductible for the contributing company and taxable income for the recipient during the same tax year. The entries have to be made in the books of the contributor and recipient and not merely on their tax returns.

The requirements for tax-deductible group relief are as follows:

- The amount of tax-deductible group relief cannot exceed the taxable business profits of the contributor.
- The company together with its subsidiaries owns at least 90 percent of the votes of the participating entity so that the 90 percent ownership requirement of the votes is met among all participating entities.
- Both the contributor and the recipient are Finnish resident corporations or cooperatives.
- Ninety percent ownership of votes among the participating entities has lasted continuously for at least one tax year.
- Accounting periods of both the contributor and the recipient end at the same time, unless the Accounting Board has granted exemption.
- Neither participating entity is a bank, an insurance company nor a pension institution, as defined in the law.
- The contributor's board of directors has decided to grant group relief before the end of the tax year in question.

By using group relief, the profits of the Finnish target company can be netted against the interest expense of a Finnish holding company that has been used to acquire the shares in the target company. This netting technique is permissible provided that all the requirements for the tax-deductible group relief have been met. Therefore, the timing of the acquisition may change during the tax years, and the way the qualifying group has been set up can affect the time when the group relief becomes available.

5.5 SHARE ACQUISITION (EXCLUDING EXCHANGES OF SHARES)

When a Finnish company sells shares in a subsidiary or another entity, the sales price is fully taxable. The income amount is viewed as business income or, in some rare cases, personal income that is taxed at the prevailing corporate tax rate.

The length of the ownership period does not affect tax treatment. The seller deducts the remaining cost of the shares for tax purposes at the time of the sale. No separate capital gains taxation is levied for corporations. Effectively, the gain or loss is included in the business income basket or, in some cases, in the personal income basket of the seller.

If the seller is nonresident and does not have permanent establishment in Finland, Finland cannot tax the gain. The transaction is not taxable provided that the relevant tax treaty prevents Finland from taxing the transaction or provided that 50 percent or less of the assets of the target company comprises real estate.

Resident individuals will be taxed on capital gains, but the effective tax rate may be lower than 29 percent, which has been applied since 2000. When calculating the taxable gain, a resident individual may deduct 20 percent of the sales price as a deemed acquisition cost or 50 percent of the sales price if the shares have been owned for at least 10 years. When deducting the actual acquisition cost from the sales price, the resident can also deduct the related expenses. The resulting gain will be taxed at a flat rate of 29 percent, applicable since 2000.

The acquiring company may not usually deduct the acquisition cost of the shares before the shares are disposed of or before the target is liquidated; however, if the taxpayer is able to show that the fair market value of the shares in its subsidiary has substantially decreased, the subsidiary may in some cases write off for tax purposes an amount equal to the decrease. If the fair market value of the shares subsequently increases, the write-off may be added back to the company's taxable income.

The acquiring Finnish company may normally deduct the interest paid on the acquisition debt used to finance the acquisition of the target. Interest expense is deducted in the same income basket (i.e., business or personal income basket to which the asset belongs).

A transfer tax of 1.6 percent is levied on the purchase price of Finnish shares unless both the seller and the buyer of the Finnish target are nonresidents. Share transfers through the Helsinki Stock Exchange are exempt from transfer tax. Regarding availability of the losses and tax credits of the target company, see section 5.3.

5.6 ASSET ACQUISITION (EXCLUDING TAX-FREE SPIN-OFFS OR CONTRIBUTIONS OF ASSETS)

When a resident company sells a part or all of its business or individual assets, the sales price is fully taxable as business income or, in some cases, as personal income. The seller deducts the remaining cost for tax purposes according to the relevant tax provisions. The sales price for machinery and equipment is deducted from the depreciation base for similar assets, which reduces future depreciation.

If the seller disposes of its business premises or shares for such premises, the company may defer the taxable gain for two tax years immediately following the year of disposition. The two-year deferral is contingent on acquiring the company's business premises and taking them into use during that period. The seller must continue the business in order to defer taxation for business premises. If the seller realizes a loss on the business and assets sold, such a loss is tax deductible.

Any tax losses that the seller has remain with the seller. The seller can net the gains relating to a sale of the business or assets against the losses in the respective income baskets.

When a Finnish resident company or a permanent establishment of a foreign entity pays for the acquired business, and the price of this acquired business exceeds the fair market value of the assets, the difference is treated as tax-deductible goodwill. Goodwill can be amortized over the economic life of the asset, not exceeding 10 years. The buyer may appraise the acquired assets up to the fair market value of these assets in its books and records at the time of the acquisition. The buyer would then treat only the excess as tax-deductible goodwill.

Machinery and equipment can be depreciated at the maximum rate of 25 percent using the declining balance method. The buyer should consider such a step-up in basis. Buildings can be depreciated using the same method at the maximum rates of 4 percent, 7 percent, and 20 percent, depending on the purpose of the building.

If the acquired assets include shares in Finnish companies or real property situated in Finland, a transfer tax of 1.6 percent or 4 percent will be levied on their transfer value. Tax authorities may assess the transfer value if they deem that it does not correspond with the fair market value for such an asset.

According to Section 62 of the Value-Added Tax Act, a transfer of a business or a part of the business is value-added tax (VAT) exempt if the buyer continues the business and uses the assets and services for VAT-deductible purposes. Special rules govern transfers of real property.

5.7 MERGERS

(a) Definitions

A distinction must be made between tax-free mergers (Sections 52a and 52b of EVL) and taxable mergers that do not qualify under these provisions.

For the purposes of Section 52a, a tax-free merger means an operation whereby the following conditions are met:

1. One or more companies, on being dissolved without going into liquidation, transfer all their assets and liabilities *to another existing company* in exchange for the issue of new shares to the shareholders of the absorbed companies. If applicable, a cash payment is permissible, but this amount cannot exceed 10 percent of the nominal value, or, in absence of nominal value, of the value corresponding with the amount of paid-in capital for the new shares. The term *nominal value* is used in the Directive, literature, and in Finland's legislation and means the value that is stated on the shares.

5.7 Mergers

2. Two or more companies, on being dissolved without going into liquidation, transfer all their assets and liabilities to *a company that they form* in exchange for the issue of new shares to the shareholders of the absorbed companies. If applicable, a cash payment is permissible, but this amount cannot exceed 10 percent of the nominal value, or, in absence of nominal value, of the value corresponding with the amount of paid-in capital for the new shares.

3. A company, on being dissolved without going into liquidation, transfers all its assets and liabilities to the company holding all of the shares representing its capital.

When implementing the Merger Directive in Finland, the purpose was to cover all vertical and horizontal merger types, under two conditions: (1) the cash consideration does not exceed 10 percent of the nominal value of the new shares; (2) the absorbing company increases its share capital by issuing new shares. Other types of merger considerations are not allowed under Section 52a of EVL. Cross-border mergers are not possible because of a lack of relevant company law directives.

(b) Taxation of Tax-Free and Taxable Mergers

A merger is tax neutral if the requirements of the provisions of Section 52a and the principle of succession are met. A merger does not cause immediate tax consequences at the corporate or shareholder level, but there are certain exceptions.

In a tax-free merger, the absorbed company or companies are not deemed to be dissolved for tax purposes. The absorbing company continues to depreciate the assets and deduct the costs in the same way as the absorbed companies did. A merger gain or loss calculated for accounting purposes does not affect taxation of the absorbing entity. A tax-free step-up in the asset base is not possible.

The tax surpluses and other tax attributes under the imputation system, and tax losses of the absorbed company, are transferred to the recipient company if the recipient company or its owners have owned more than 50 percent of the shares in the absorbed entity from the beginning of the tax year during which the tax surpluses or losses were incurred. Tax authorities cannot grant special permission to use tax credits and losses if the 50 percent ownership requirement is violated in a merger.

The recipient and the absorbed company or companies are treated as separate taxpayers until the merger is complete. Because of the separate entity concept, the absorbed entities must file a corporate tax return for the tax year when the merger is completed; however, during the merger year, the total tax depreciation claimed by the receiving and absorbed entities may not exceed the amount that the combined entity would have been allowed to claim.

The succession principle also applies to the shareholders of the absorbed company. This implies that shares in the receiving company allocated to the shareholders in exchange for shares in the absorbed company are treated as if they were acquired at the same time and at the same purchase price as the shares in the transferring company. However, a cash consideration, if any, is subject to income taxation.

If the transaction does not qualify for tax-free treatment under Section 52a of EVL, the transaction is treated as a taxable liquidation for income tax purposes. The absorbed company is taxed on gains on its assets. The receiving company will receive a step-up in asset base. The shareholders will be subject to taxation.

For transfer tax purposes, a merger that is completed according to the merger rules under the relevant company law is tax-free. This means that no transfer tax is due on the issuance of new shares and on shares and real property that are transferred in a merger. However, a 1.6 percent transfer tax is levied on the cash consideration. Hence, a transaction may be free of transfer tax even though the transaction does not qualify as a tax-free merger.

5.8 DIVISIONS

(a) Definition

A distinction must be made between tax-free divisions (Sections 52c of EVL) and taxable divisions that do not qualify under this provision.

A division can be described as a transaction opposite to a merger. A tax-free division is a transaction where a company—on being dissolved without going into liquidation—transfers all of its assets and liabilities to two or more existing or new companies. The shareholders of the transferring company receive, in proportion to their ownership of shares in the transferring company, new shares issued by the recipient companies. Cash of up to 10 percent of the nominal value of the new shares is allowed.

According to income tax rules for tax-free division, the transferring company cannot continue to exist. Company law allows for such a partial division. Cross-border divisions are not possible because of an absence of relevant companies law.

(b) Taxation of Tax-Free and Taxable Divisions

The same principles that applied to the taxation of mergers are generally applicable to divisions as well. A division is tax neutral if the requirements of the provisions of Section 52c and the principle of succession are met. A division does not cause immediate tax consequences at the corporate or shareholder level with certain exceptions.

In a tax-free division, the transferring company is not deemed to be dissolved for tax purposes. The recipient companies continue to deduct the assets and costs in the same way as the transferring company did. A tax-free step-up in asset base is not possible.

The tax surpluses, including other tax attributes under the imputation system and tax losses of the dividing company, are transferred to the recipient company in proportion to what the recipient companies receive in terms of net assets from the dividing company. The net assets will be valued according to the Wealth Tax Act at the time the division takes effect.

5.9 Tax-Free Transfer (Contribution) of Assets

If the dividing entity has more than one income basket, the losses will be transferred to an entity that has a corresponding income basket. As a prerequisite for retention of tax attributes, the recipient companies or their owners must have owned more than 50 percent of the shares in the transferring entity from the beginning of the tax year during which the tax surpluses or losses were incurred.

The transferring company and the recipient companies are treated as separate taxpayers until the division is complete. Because of this separate taxpayer provision, the transferring entity must file a corporate tax return for the tax year during which the division is completed.

The business succession principle applies to the shareholders of the transferring company. This principle implies that shares in the receiving company that are allocated to the shareholders in exchange for shares in the dividing company are treated as if the shares were acquired at the same time and at the same purchase price as the shares in the dividing company. In a division, each shareholder receives shares in all recipient companies in the same proportion as he or she owned in the dividing entity.

The shareholder's existing cost has to be allocated to the new shares. The allocation is determined based on the ratio of net assets each company has received in the division, unless the ratio of fair market value of the shares would give a significantly different result. In the latter case, the ratio of market value of the shares is used to divide the shareholder's cost base among the new shares.

A cash consideration, if any, is subject to income taxation. If the cash compensation exceeds 10 percent of the nominal amount of the new shares, the division is treated as taxable for income tax purposes.

If the transaction does not qualify as tax-free under Section 52c of EVL, the transaction is treated as a taxable liquidation for income tax purposes. The transferring company is taxed on gains on its assets. The recipient companies will receive a step-up in asset base. The shareholders will be subject to taxation.

For transfer tax purposes, a division that is completed according to Section 52c of EVL and the relevant company law is tax-free. This means that no transfer tax is due on the issuance of new shares and on shares and real property that is being transferred in a division; however, a 1.6 percent transfer tax is levied on the cash consideration.

5.9 TAX-FREE TRANSFER (CONTRIBUTION) OF ASSETS

(a) Definition

In a tax-free transfer of assets, a company—without being liquidated—transfers all its assets and liabilities, or at least assets and liabilities of one branch of its business activity, to a new company or an existing company in exchange for new shares of the recipient company or companies. The new shares are received by the transferring company and not by its shareholders. In order to qualify under Section 52d of EVL, no cash compensation is permitted.

(b) Taxation of Tax-Free Transfer of Assets

The principle of business succession applies to the qualifying transfer of a branch of the business against new shares. Neither the contributor nor the recipient realize taxable income if they use the remaining book values. For income tax purposes, the transfer occurs at the remaining book values for taxation purposes. The recipient continues with the same asset base as if the contributor were using the same principles.

The tax surpluses and the losses of the transferring company cannot be transferred to the recipient company. The book value of the transferred assets reduced by the transferred liabilities relating to the branch of business constitutes the acquisition cost of the new shares for the contributing company.

If real property or securities are included in the transferred business, the recipient company is obliged to pay the transfer tax of 1.6 percent on shares and 4 percent on real property; however, the recipient may apply for a refund for the transfer tax or an exemption before the planned transaction is completed.

The provisions of EVL concerning the tax-free transfer of assets apply to transactions in which one or more recipient companies are located in another EU country. Finnish company law also recognizes such a transfer of assets; however, the tax exemption does not apply if the transferred assets do not remain effectively associated with a permanent establishment of the recipient company in Finland. Such a transaction is treated as taxable for the Finnish contributor of assets. In the latter case, the fair market price of the assets is included in its taxable income.

The Business Income Tax Act does not address inbound contributions of assets when a foreign entity contributes the business it has conducted through a Finnish branch to a Finnish corporation; however, Section 123a of the Income Tax Act provides that the losses of the branch will be transferred to the continuing Finnish company, provided that the requirements of the law are met.

The tax consequences of transactions that do not qualify as tax-free business transfers are explained in Section 5.6.

5.10 TAX-FREE AND TAXABLE EXCHANGES OF SHARES

(a) Definition

A distinction must be made between taxable and tax-free exchanges of shares. In a tax-free exchange of shares, a company acquires a sufficient number of shares in another company to give it the majority of the voting rights. As a consideration, the acquiring company issues new shares to the other company's shareholders. The majority of the voting rights, not the shares, is the crucial requirement. Based on Finnish case law, the shares may be acquired from several sellers and at different dates, but the purchases have to be connected together. The exchange is taxable for the shareholders if the acquisition does not reach the required control of the target.

(b) Taxation of Tax-Free and Taxable Exchange of Shares

The principle of succession is applied to a tax-free exchange of shares under Section 52f of EVL at the shareholder level. An exchange of shares is not deemed to be a disposal in a shareholder's income taxation. The acquisition cost of the new shares received in exchange corresponds to the acquisition cost of the shares handed over in exchange. The new shares are deemed to be acquired at the same time as the original shares.

Cash compensation may be used as consideration, but the cash compensation must not exceed 10 percent of the nominal value of the new shares issued by the acquiring company. If there is no nominal value, the cash compensation must not exceed 10 percent of the paid-in capital relating to the new shares in the recipient company.

A provision exists for discontinuing the capital gains deferral for income tax purposes. The deferral is cancelled if the person who received the new shares becomes a tax resident abroad according to Finnish domestic tax law or according to the relevant tax treaty within three years from the end of the tax year in which the exchange of shares took place. In such a case, the exempted amount is taxed in the tax year during which the person becomes a tax resident abroad.

For the acquiring company, the acquisition cost of the shares acquired in the exchange is the fair market value of the shares received. The target company may lose its losses and other tax attributes if more than 50 percent of its shares change hands, unless the tax authorities grant permission to use the losses despite the ownership change.

The provisions of EVL concerning tax-free exchange of shares apply to exchanges of shares in which one or more companies are situated in another EU country. If the transaction does not qualify as tax-free, the transaction is fully taxable for resident shareholders. The acquiring company is liable to pay the transfer tax of 1.6 percent of the Finnish shares received. The basis for the transfer tax is the fair market price of the shares acquired through the exchange of shares.

CHAPTER 6

Taxation of Mergers and Acquisitions in France

Jean-Marc Girard
Raphaël Coin
Gaël Beineix
International Tax Service, HSD Ernst & Young, Paris, France

6.1 **Tax Rates**
6.2 **Mergers**
  (a) Taxation of Companies in a Merger
  (b) Favorable Tax Regime
  (c) Merger Is Implemented at Fair Market Value
  (d) Merger Is Implemented at Book Value
  (e) Standard Regime
6.3 **Taxation of Shareholders in a Merger**
  (a) Shareholders of the Absorbed Company
  (b) Shareholders of the Absorbing Company
  (c) VAT
6.4 **International Mergers**
  (a) Territoriality Rules and Source of Income
  (b) VAT
  (c) Registration Taxes
6.5 **Foreign-Absorbing Company/French-Absorbed Company**
6.6 **Impact of the EU Merger Directive**
  (a) Scope of Application
  (b) Capital Gains
  (c) Provisions and Reserves
  (d) Losses
  (e) Cross Shareholding
  (f) Payment in Cash
  (g) Impact
6.7 **Contribution of Assets**
  (a) Eligibility for the Favorable Tax Regime
  (b) Taxation of Companies as Part of a Contribution of Assets
  (c) Registration Duties
  (d) Taxation of Shareholders

6.8 International Contribution of Assets
  (a) Contributions Made by French Companies to Foreign Companies
  (b) Contributions Made by Foreign Companies to French Companies
  (c) Contribution by a Foreign Company of its French Branch to a French Company

6.9 Divisions and Spin-Offs
  (a) Tax Consequences of a Spin-Off Under the Favorable Tax Regime
  (b) Tax Consequences of a Spin-Off Under Standard Regime

6.10 International Spin-Offs
  (a) Spin-Off of a French Subsidiary of a Foreign Company
  (b) Spin-Off of a Foreign Subsidiary of a French Company

6.11 Acquisitions
  (a) Acquisition of a Company Using a French Tax Consolidated Group
  (b) Limits on Interest Deduction
  (c) Thin Capitalization Rules
  (d) Rapid Merger Alternative
  (e) Tax Exposure of the Rapid Merger
  (f) Abuse of Law Theory
  (g) Abnormal Management Act
  (h) Financial Assistance Exposure
  (i) VAT on Acquisition of Shares

6.12 Treatment of Assets
  (a) Corporate Tax Consequences for Acquiring Company
  (b) Corporate Tax Consequences for the Seller
  (c) VAT and Securities Registration

6.13 International Acquisition of Shares
  (a) French-Acquiring Company/Foreign-Acquiring Company
  (b) VAT

6.14 Foreign-Acquiring Company/French-Acquired Company
  (a) Tax Consequences for the Buyer
  (b) Financing Costs Incurred in Connection with the Acquisition
  (c) Domestic Seller
  (d) Foreign Seller

6.15 International Acquisition of Assets
  (a) French-Acquiring Company/Foreign Assets
  (b) Foreign-Acquiring Company/Domestic Assets

6.16 International Acquisition of Assets: Tax Consequences for the Seller

6.17 Public Tender Offer

6.18 International Public Tender Offer

6.19 Hybrid Instruments
  (a) Inbound Financing
  (b) Outbound Financing

6.1 TAX RATES

The French standard corporate income tax rate is 33.33 percent, to which surtaxes of 6 percent and 3.3 percent are added for fiscal year 2001. Hence, the effective corporate income tax rate in France is 36.43 percent. For coming years, the effective corporate income tax rate will diminish, to 35.45 percent for fiscal year 2002. This rate comprises the standard corporate income tax rate of 33.33 percent plus the two surtaxes of 3 percent and 3.3 percent.

The surtaxes are computed on the corporate income tax liability, which is determined before the offsetting of the *avoir fiscal* and any tax credits. The French *avoir fiscal* mechanism represents a specific tax credit, the offsetting of which allows companies to avoid a double taxation of the profits at the level of the company and at the level of the shareholders. The *avoir fiscal* represents, for fiscal year 2001, 25 percent of the profits received. *Avoir fiscal* will be reduced for fiscal year 2000 to 15 percent. Several double taxation treaties entered into by France provide for a transfer of this *avoir fiscal* to foreign shareholders of French companies.

Corporate income tax is payable in four installments plus a final balancing payment. A specific reduced rate of 19 percent is applicable to long-term capital gains deriving from the disposal of certain assets held for more than two years. Before 1997, the sale of all fixed assets was eligible for this reduced rate; however, since then this reduced rate is applicable only to the following:

- Disposal of participation shares which, taken together, represent at least a 10 percent holding in the subsidiary
- Disposals of venture capital funds shares

More specifically, this reduced rate is applicable to income deriving from the license for the exploitation of patents or patentable inventions, as well as some other specific income. A surtax of 6 percent must be added to the reduced rate of 19 percent. Hence, the effective tax rate is 20.14 percent. The surtax for capital gains will be reduced to 3 percent for fiscal year 2002, reducing the effective tax rate to 19.57 percent.

Registration duty is payable in France upon the transfer of shares. The applicable transfer registration rate depends on the type of securities involved. The registration duty of shares of a corporation is 1 percent, capped at 20,000 French francs (FRF) or 3,049€. The registration rate is 4.80 percent for shares of French limited liability companies (LLCs). French LLCs include the SARL and/or the EURL, the latter being a sole ownership LLC.

There is no limitation on the amount, which is assessed on the transaction price or fair market value if higher. This disposition means that the 4.80 percent registration duty will be due upon the fair market value of the shares, or the transaction price, whichever is the highest. Transfer of real estate companies, and not transfer of mere real estate, is subject to a 4.80 percent rate; however, whatever the legal type of vehicle used, it is subject to a 4.80 percent rate.

The rate of value-added tax (VAT) for the fiscal year 2000 is 19.6 percent, but depending on the categories of goods, other rates may apply. Business *taxe professionnelle* and real estate *taxe foncière* can be cost effective in mergers and acquisitions operations because their liability may eventually impact the transaction price. The rate is fixed by each locality (i.e., cities, regions) for the companies that operate in that geographic area.

6.2 MERGERS

Under French domestic tax law, mergers encompass two types of transactions:

1. The absorption of one or more companies by another company, in which the second company alone continues to exist. The absorbed company is wound up without liquidation. The transfer of the assets and liabilities of the absorbed company or companies result in an increase in the share capital of the absorbing company. Where applicable, the successor corporation would then record a merger premium under "liabilities and shareholders' equity" in its balance sheet. The consideration for the transfer takes the form of an issue of shares of a Sociedad Anonima (SA), which are French corporations, or the shares of an SARL in the absorbing company which are issued to the shareholders of the absorbed company(ies).

2. The transfer by two or more companies of their assets and liabilities to a new company formed for that purpose

In both cases, the consideration for the transfer takes the form of an issue of shares (of an SA or an SARL), whether in the absorbing company or in the new company, to the shareholders in the old merged entities. The consideration may also include a payment of cash. The cash payment as a portion of the consideration cannot exceed 10 percent of the par value of the securities allocated.

Mergers by way of absorption correspond more closely to the needs of businesses and the reality of most merger situations. As such, this form of merger is much more common. In the case of a 100 percent wholly owned subsidiary, the merger does not result in an increase of capital.

(a) Taxation of Companies in a Merger

A favorable tax regime, in terms of registration duties, corporate income tax, and the tax treatment of share-for-share exchanges, applies to the merged entities. Such a merger must meet the following conditions:

- Absorbing and absorbed companies must both be liable to corporate income tax.
- If the consideration includes cash, the cash must not represent more than 10 percent of the total value of the consideration. If this ratio is exceeded, the transaction cannot benefit from the favorable regime for mergers under French tax and company law.

6.2 Mergers

The principal facets of mergers are corporate tax issues; however, registration duty, VAT, trade tax, and real estate tax are relevant as follows:

- *Registration duty:* A fixed duty of FRF 1,500 or 228.67€ is paid upon completion of the merger, whether the consideration for the merger consisted purely of shares or of another form of consideration. This stamp duty regime applies even if the merger does not qualify for the favorable merger regime and the merged entity is taxed under the standard corporate income tax regime for mergers.
- *VAT:* Contributions of stocks are, in principle, subject to VAT. The French Tax Authorities (FTA) allow the absorbed company not to invoice the absorbing company. Contributions of fixed assets are also exempt from VAT, provided that the absorbing company commits itself to proceed later to the eventual regular payments (i.e., proceed to the payment of the eventual VAT due by the absorbed company).
- *Trade tax/Real estate tax:* Under French Law, the trade tax and real estate tax are computed on the contributed assets on a rental basis, which cannot be below 80 percent of the previous year. Business tax is assessed on the rental value of the tangible assets owned or leased by the company and used by it, whereas the rental value of the lands and buildings is directly determined by the FTA. The rental value of the other tangible assets corresponds to their acquisition price or the amount of the rentals paid by the company. A retroactive clause in the merger agreement has no effect on those taxes when such clause provides that the merger will legally be effective at a date prior to the date of the merger operation. The choice of the date of the merger may then affect the overall liability depending on the date when those taxes are payable.

(b) Favorable Tax Regime

Assets contributed by the company being absorbed are contributed at their fair market value. These assets include all the assets, tangibles or intangibles, which are necessary for the company to carry out its activity, such as land, building, or patents, but in no circumstances inventory. These assets are recorded in the balance sheet of the absorbing company at this fair market value. All the unrealized capital gains are transferred and recorded in the accounts of the absorbing company. The principal benefit of the favorable tax regime consists in the exemption from taxation of the absorbed company. The absorbing company would otherwise be liable for this burden (Section 210A of the French Tax Code). We recommend that mergers be conducted at book value to prevent unrealized capital gains being taxed.

Capital gains arising from portfolio investment alone can benefit from the reduced taxation rate. All other capital gains are taxed at the standard corporate income tax rate. The parties to the merger can still benefit from the deferral regime if these provisions are applicable.

(c) Merger Is Implemented at Fair Market Value

A merger closes the accounting period and the trading activities of the absorbed company. In that context, operating profits made by this company are immediately taxed. Merger agreements can, however, include a retroactive clause that provides that the profits made during the financial year of the merger are attributed to the absorbing company.

The fair market value merger should have the following consequences for the absorbed company because the merger will be treated as an intermediary operation. The tax liability of the absorbed company will then be transferred to the absorbing company. The consequences of the merger are as follows:

- Reserves, equipment subsidies, and unrealized capital gains of the absorbed company are not taxed immediately. Instead, these items are transferred to the absorbing company.
- The absorbing company must take over the special reserve account of the absorbed company. The special reserve account is the reserve in which the long-term capital gains (taxed at a rate of 19 percent) are maintained.
- Assets contributed by the absorbed company become assets of the absorbing company. The value of the assets being transferred by the absorbed company to the absorbing company are stepped-up. France uses declining balance methods of depreciation. This method applies to the assets after the step-up.
- Capital gains realized upon the merger are taxed deferred.
- Inventory reflects unrealized profits on current assets. These unrealized profit amounts are determined when the absorbing company records those assets at their original cost. The asset amounts are taxed when the assets are ultimately disposed of. The company has a choice, however, and can use a different amount for asset values. Thus, the absorbing company may prefer to record the transferred current assets at some other value. Then, the company is taxed on the difference between original value and the value that the company selects.
- Nondepreciable assets (such as land, goodwill in most circumstances, and so on) are recorded in the absorbing company's books at their transfer value. The capital gains realized upon their ultimate sale are computed relative to their value in the book of the absorbed company.
- Assets are transferred at their fair market value, not at their original value. Capital gains are then computed on the basis of fair market value at the date of these transfers, not on the basis of their original value in the books of the absorbed company.

(d) Merger Is Implemented at Book Value

Mergers computed at book value, which have been officially permitted by the FTA,[1] can be made whenever the fair market value is close to the book value. We

---
[1] Administrative Guidelines 4 I 2 00, August 18, 2000.

recommend this mergers at book value method for internal reorganization operations. Unrealized capital gains will appear neither in the accounts nor in the tax computation. The whole merger is thus tax neutral.

(e) Standard Regime

The standard regime for mergers and acquisitions can be summarized as an immediate taxation of the operation. Such a standard regime can be advantageous if, for instance the absorbed company is in a loss-making position or has carried forward losses. Indeed, in such cases, the activity of the absorbed company is deemed to cease to exist. In such a situation, all provisions and unrealized capital gains are immediately taxable; however, these provisions and gains are offset against prior losses.

The absorbing company will not have to assume the absorbed company's special reserve and provisions. The consequences for the absorbing company are the following:

- The absorbing company cannot depreciate the contributed assets by the reducing balance method. The assets remain depreciable by the straight-line method, but obtain a step-up in value.
- The capital gains arise from the cancellation of the cross-shareholding. Thus, the shares of the two companies to the merger operation hold shares of each other. This cross-shareholding is taxable.

6.3 TAXATION OF SHAREHOLDERS IN A MERGER

(a) Shareholders of the Absorbed Company

The shareholders of the absorbed company become shareholders of the absorbing company through an exchange of shares. The shares of the absorbed company are canceled. These shares are replaced by new shares, which are issued by the absorbing company through its increase in share capital.

The potential capital gain arising from this share-for-share exchange is not taxable under Section 115-1 of the French Tax Code (FTC). This provision allows taxpayers not to treat the cessation of the business of the absorbed company as a liquidation. Accordingly, gains realized by the shareholders will not be treated as a liquidation premium. In such a case, no equalization tax is due. Equalization tax is levied on sums that have not been subject to corporate income tax at the standard rate. The shareholders are not subject to taxes on the distributed income under Section 159-2 of the FTC.

Gains arising from the share-for-share exchange are not taxable as income, but these gains are taxable as capital gains. Nevertheless, any gains can benefit from a deferral regime under Section 38-7 of the FTC.

A transaction may be taxable when cash is an element of the consideration as follows:

- If the amount of cash exceeds 10 percent of the nominal value of the shares received in exchange, the favorable tax regime or the tax deferral of the capital gains cannot apply.
- If the amount of cash is within this 10 percent threshold, the favorable tax regime applies, but the proportion of the capital gain that is linked to the cash element is immediately taxable.

When the exchanged shares are recorded on the balance sheet, the reduced capital gain rate applies. Shareholders can request application of the tax deferral regime even if the merger has taken place under the favorable tax regime of Section 210A of the FTC. Although shares received in exchange benefit from the tax deferral, these shares are recorded at their current value. For cross-shareholding, the merger results in a cancellation of the shares. Under the provisions of Section 210A-1 of the FTC, no capital gain tax is due on the canceled shares.

(b) Shareholders of the Absorbing Company

In principle, the merger does not affect the tax situation of the shareholders of the absorbing company because these shareholders do not participate in the capital increase of the company. The tax situation is impacted in the following two situations:

1. When there are cross-shareholdings and shares are canceled, section 210A-1 2 of the FTC provides that no capital gains tax should be assessed on those shares.
2. If the shareholders of the absorbing company are to benefit from the parent/subsidiary regime, the 10 percent holding requirement must be complied with after the merger.

(c) VAT

The transfer of second-hand immovable assets by persons who used these assets in their business is subject to VAT. Exemptions are granted for assets on which VAT was not reclaimed at the time of their acquisition, for instance, if these assets were used for VAT-exempt activities.

A total transfer of assets from one company to another can take place. In that event, a deferral of taxation is available. Deferral can apply if both the absorbing and absorbed companies are liable to VAT and the companies carry on taxable activities. The VAT tax exemption applies if the absorbing company undertakes to pay the VAT that would have been due if the absorbed company had continued to use the assets.

6.4 INTERNATIONAL MERGERS

(a) Territoriality Rules and Source of Income

The concept of residence is not clearly stated in France's General Tax Code. A company of whatever nationality is liable to corporate income tax only on

6.4 International Mergers

income arising in connection with its French-based activities. France's approach is different from taxation based on worldwide income, which applies in the United Kingdom, Ireland, and some other countries. In France, income is based on profits attributed to France according to the provisions of the relevant tax treaties.

Under domestic law, foreign companies are liable in France to corporate income tax on profits from the activity they carry out in France, unless a tax treaty provides otherwise. Therefore, a foreign company is liable to French corporate income tax on the following income items:

- Profits derived from a fixed place of business
- Profits derived from the activity of a dependent agent
- Profits derived from a complete commercial cycle, even in the absence of a permanent establishment in France
- Income derived from the direct ownership of real estate located in France
- Insurance premiums received from French sources.

In general, France's tax treaties provide that a non-French resident company is liable to corporate income tax on the following income items:

- Profits derived from a permanent establishment in France, as defined by the relevant tax treaty
- Income from real estate or other immovable assets located in France

According to the merger relief provisions, a French company is defined as a company that is incorporated in France under French company law and that has its head office in France.

A head office is not necessarily the registered office of the company, as stated in the Articles of Association. Instead, the head office is the place of effective management of the company. The place of effective management would normally be the place where directors' or shareholders' meetings are held, or where the accounting, legal, and financial activities are based.

(b) VAT

The dispositions of assets in an international merger are generally the same as domestic mergers when it comes to VAT. This treatment applies when both entities are subject to French VAT and do not perform activities that are exempt from VAT. The same rules apply if the foreign entity is absorbed by the French company.

(c) Registration Taxes

The favorable tax regime described in Section 6.2(b) applies without prior authorization from the FTA.

6.5 FOREIGN-ABSORBING COMPANY/FRENCH-ABSORBED COMPANY

The favorable tax regime will apply to both companies. Indeed, the FTC clearly provides that this special regime is available whatever the nationality of the company is, as long as it is liable to corporate income tax in France. The consent of the Ministry of Economy and Finances must nevertheless be sought before the transaction.

In order for the Ministry of Economy and Finances to grant consent, the FTA may require that the assets and liabilities of the absorbed company be transferred to a corporate body that is liable to French tax (e.g., a French holding). Thus, the assets and liabilities must be transferred to an entity that is able to fulfill the ongoing obligations of the absorbed company. The capital gains realized on the sale of nondepreciable assets must also be taxed in France. The unrealized capital gains deriving from the transfer of the depreciable assets must be transferred to the absorbing company. The merger should benefit from the tax treatment described previously if these conditions are met.

Transnational mergers are, however, difficult to achieve in practice for legal reasons. One of the possible answers may reside in the future creation of the European Company, which will be formally known as Societas Europeae (SE). An SE will, for tax purposes, be treated as any other multinational company according to the national fiscal legislation applicable at company level or branch level. There will be a fiscal advantage in creating a European Company by merger registered in one Member State but operating through branches in a variety of Member States. If the Member State where the head office is located taxes the worldwide income of the European Company, it will be possible, in the Member State where the head office is located, to offset losses from some permanent establishments against profits from other permanent establishments.

In practice, such offsetting is not often possible if the parent company is established as an independent entity operating through a variety of legally independent subsidiaries rather than as an SE; however, the SE will continue to be a taxpayer in the different Member States where the permanent establishments are located. The SE provisions may clearly amend the French territoriality principle if the SE's head office is located in France.

European Companies created by merger will be the first type of company to be able to benefit from the European Union (EU) Directive that eliminates double taxation of cross-frontier mergers; however, this EU Directive will require a technical amendment to the original directive to add SEs to the types of companies eligible under the directive. For VAT purposes, the same rules for when a foreign company absorbs a French company apply. The favorable tax regime, as described in the preceding section, applies as well to that operation without prior authorization from the FTA.

6.6 IMPACT OF THE EU MERGER DIRECTIVE

The EU Directive on Mergers, dated July 23, 2000, provides a relief regime for mergers involving companies that are resident of two different EU Member States. The regime provides for such mergers to be tax neutral as regards direct taxes. This directive has been, for the most part, implemented into French law. Therefore, most of the provisions described as follows are the same as those for French domestic mergers.

(a) Scope of Application

The EU Directive applies to all legal entities that are subject to corporate income tax:

- SA (Société Anonyme)
- SCA (Société en Commandite par Actions)
- SAS (Société par Actions Simplifiées)
- SARL (Société à Responsabilité Limité)

Corporate bodies that have elected corporate income tax treatment are outside the scope of application of the directive (e.g., partnerships that have elected to be taxed as a corporate entity).

Contrary to the position that the French FTA may have adopted in the past, a liquidation of a 10 percent French subsidiary into its EU sole shareholder should qualify for the application of the regime provided by the directive.

(b) Capital Gains

The EU Directive states that the difference between book and market values of the capital assets and liabilities transferred will not create a tax charge. French Law has been amended to extend the exemption to gains arising from the transfer of current assets and temporary investments.

(c) Provisions and Reserves

The EU Directive provides for a tax-exempt transfer of provisions and reserves from the absorbed to the absorbing company. The absorbing company assumes the rights and obligations of the absorbed company.

(d) Losses

The French tax authorities do not normally permit the transfer of premerger losses realized by the absorbed company. The EU Directive, however, provides for a transfer of premerger losses under domestic law.

(e) Cross Shareholding

The directive exempts companies from tax on any capital gains realized on the cancellation of cross shareholdings.

(f) Payment in Cash

The directive allows up to 10 percent of the consideration to be in cash, computed on the basis of the par value of the shares.

(g) Impact

Section 210C-1 of the FTC extends the merger relief provisions only to companies that are subject to French corporate income tax. However, in practice, the FTA will allow the merger regime to apply to transactions that result in the absorption by a French company of a foreign company, even if the foreign company is not taxed in France according to the French territoriality principle.

6.7 CONTRIBUTION OF ASSETS

A "contribution of assets" is an operation in which a company contributes both its assets and liabilities to another company, whether the entity is an existing company or a company created for this purpose. The consideration for this contribution is shares of the beneficiary company. Such a contribution of assets is termed a *partial merger*.

The contribution of assets method can be useful in the following circumstances:

- When the group wishes to effect an internal reorganization. A branch, for example, can be incorporated into a 100 percent wholly owned subsidiary.
- When cooperation with third-party companies is envisaged (e.g., in the context of a joint venture between two groups).
- When a company seeks to transfer one of its business lines to a competitor and wishes to retain a stake within the transferee company.

This type of merger can also benefit from the favorable tax regime available for mergers and spin-offs.

(a) Eligibility for the Favorable Tax Regime

All the companies involved in the transaction must be subject to corporate income tax to qualify for favorable tax treatment. Accordingly, the contribution of assets must relate to a full line of business (i.e., an autonomous business) as defined by French law pursuant to the transposition of the EU Directive of July 23, 1990. Moreover, the contributing company must commit itself to hold the shares received in exchange for a three-year period. If one of the companies does not qualify for one of these criteria, the company can seek the benefit of the favorable tax regime through the seeking of a ruling.[2] Such rulings, when granted, are, however, subject to conditions.

---

[2] The conditions to benefit from the granting of a ruling have been formally set out in the Administrative Guidelines 13 D 1 00 of June 27, 2000.

6.7 Contribution of Assets

The full line of business is defined as "all the assets and liabilities of a company's division which constitutes, from an organizational perspective, an autonomous activity, i.e. which can be operated as an independent business." Only the assets and liabilities of the line of business can be contributed under the contribution of assets provisions; no cash payment is allowed. In practice, the definition of the full line of business may be the first to consider.

All ownership rights in the assets contributed must be transferred to the beneficiary company; however, the following two exceptions exist:

1. Buildings used in the business can remain within the contributing company's assets as long as these buildings are put to the disposal of the beneficiary company.
2. The contributing company can retain ownership of commercial names or trademarks, provided the contributing company enters into a license agreement with the beneficiary company for at least a 10-year period.

(b) Taxation of Companies as Part of a Contribution of Assets

The favorable tax regime applies to corporate income tax, registration duties, and taxation of the shareholders. Section 210B of the FTC states that the favorable tax regime applicable to mergers can apply to contribution of full lines of business provided that the contributing company commits itself to the following activities:

- Hold the shares received in return for the contribution for at least three years.
- Compute the capital gains realized upon the transfer of the contributed assets on the basis of their original cost.

If these conditions are met, the favorable tax regime applies and its consequences are the following:

- Capital gains realized on nondepreciable elements can be deferred for tax purposes.
- Capital gains realized upon the transfer of depreciable elements can be spread over a five-year period. The depreciation period is 15 years in the case of buildings. A step-up in value is obtained in this manner. Goods are depreciated on a reevaluated basis.

The constraints remain the same as for a merger, as follows:

- The receiving company must assume the liabilities of the contributing company, as far as deferred capital gains and provisions are concerned.
- The current assets must be transferred in at book value.
- The brought-forward losses of the contributing company cannot be utilized, unless a ruling is obtained, which is rare.

The commitment to hold the shares for three years is not requested for minority shareholders who hold less than 5 percent of the share capital in order to ease the application of this favorable regime.

A contribution of assets is made at book value within the books of the contributing company. In the case of a subsequent sale of the assets contributed by the receiving company, a gain is recorded and thus taxed. Furthermore, when shares received in remuneration of the contribution are sold, and the value of these shares is equal to the fiscal value of the assets, a gain is recorded as well and taxed accordingly. To that extent, double taxation occurs because the gain is taxed upon the sale of the assets and upon the sale of the shares. The compatibility of this potential double taxation with the EU Merger Directive may be questionable.

In accordance with paragraph 1 of Section 210 of the FTC, contributions of shares representing more than 50 percent of the share capital of the company may be transferred. These shares that are contributed must represent a full line of business. Cash payments are permitted, but only to a limited extent. The cash payment can only represent a little amount. The contributing company is immediately taxed on the contribution gain represented by the cash payment.

Contributions bearing on 50 percent or less of the share capital of a company are not treated as contribution of a full line of business. In such a case, the favorable tax regime applies only upon granting of a ruling. Such participation does not constitute a full line of business for spin-off purposes. The FTA acknowledges that for companies listed on the stock exchange, this 50 percent capital threshold can be reduced to 30 percent. A taxpayer can request such a ruling if all of the previous conditions are not met.

A merger might come within the standard regime. For example, the contributing company does not want to commit itself to hold the shares for three years. In such a situation, a company can offset capital gains, for instance, by using its brought-forward tax losses.

(c) Registration Duties

Under the favorable tax regime, the transaction may be registered on payment of a fixed duty of FRF 1,500. This requirement applies to consideration expressed purely in shares, to consideration in the form of shares, and to other forms (e.g., the assumption of the contributed liabilities). This regime applies automatically when the contribution is about a full line of business, without the need to commit to hold the shares for three years.

Under the standard regime, a flat-rate registration duty of FRF 1,500 or 228.67€ is due when the conditions for the application of the favorable tax regime are not met. If the liabilities of the contributing company are assumed by the beneficiary company, this transfer will potentially give rise to another charge to registration duties.

(d) Taxation of Shareholders

The contributing company might decide to distribute the shares it received in remuneration of the contribution to its shareholders after the three-year period. If

6.8 International Contribution of Assets

so, this distribution is treated as a payment of dividends in kind. Under the favorable tax regime, such distributions can be exempt from taxation, but only if these distributions occur within the year after the contribution of assets (Section 115-2 FTC). However, because a three-year holding period is a condition of the favorable tax regime, this treatment is never applicable unless allowed under an exceptional ruling.

6.8 INTERNATIONAL CONTRIBUTION OF ASSETS

A favorable treatment of an international merger is possible, but company law conditions make it difficult to manage. As such, most international reorganizations are effectuated by the contribution of assets method. The following three major situations can be encountered:

- Contributions made by French companies to foreign companies
- Contributions made by foreign companies to French companies
- Contribution by a foreign company of its French branch to a French company

(a) Contributions Made by French Companies to Foreign Companies

The special regime set out at Section 210A and B of the FTC is applicable only to contributions made to foreign companies, and only if this operation has been agreed upon with the French tax authorities through the granting of a ruling (Section 210C-2 of the FTC). This ruling should be granted *de facto* under the dispositions of the EU Directive of July 23, 1990, in the absence of fraud or abuse. In practice, however, the FTA may ask to fulfill additional conditions, some of which may not be consistent with the EU Merger Directive, thus imposing a strict holding commitment.

Duty amounts need not be registered if the beneficiary company has its effective place of management or headquarters in France or another Member State of the EU. The prerequisite is that that entity is considered a corporation under the domestic law of the Member State for the purposes of registration duties.

(b) Contributions Made by Foreign Companies to French Companies

In principle, contributions made by a foreign company should not be taxable in France. This tax treatment, however, may vary depending on the applicable double taxation treaty signed by France with the country of residence of the foreign entity. The implementation of a substantial participation clause within the treaty may prove relevant.

(c) Contribution by a Foreign Company of its French Branch to a French Company

A foreign branch may seek to contribute its French branch to a French company. This situation occurs when a company may seek to convert its French permanent establishment into a French subsidiary. The contribution by a foreign company of its French branch to a French company may be viewed as the contribution of a full line of business within the meaning of Section 210B of the FTC. The overriding limitation is that the business can be considered as autonomous.

In principle, provided that the foreign company is subject to corporate income tax, contributions made by foreign companies should not need a ruling to be granted. Moreover, given the EU Directive of July 23, 1990, the ruling should be granted as a matter of course. In practice, however, the FTA may want to scrutinize the transaction and may require additional conditions to be fulfilled to approve the operation.

6.9 DIVISIONS AND SPIN-OFFS

A spin-off involves the termination of a company. This termination occurs only after the contribution of the company's assets to two or more companies, whether already existing or created for this purpose. Legally, a spin-off is assimilated to a merger, therefore its consequences are as follows:

- The company whose activities have been spun-off is wound up without liquidation.
- All this company's assets are transferred to the beneficiary companies.
- The shareholders in the company whose activities have been spun-off receive shares in the beneficiary companies.

A participation of 50 percent or less of the share capital of a company does not constitute a full line of business.

Before 1995, the favorable tax regime applied to spin-offs only upon granting of a ministerial ruling. The Finance Bill for 1995 withdrew this requirement provided that the following conditions are met:

- The company whose activities are being spun-off has at least two full lines of business (participation cannot be deemed to be a full line of business).
- The beneficiary companies receive one or more lines of business, with the corresponding assets and liabilities.
- Shareholders of the company whose activities are being spun-off commit to hold the shares received for at least three years. Minority shareholders, who hold less than 5 percent of the share capital, are exempted from this requirement.

(a) Tax Consequences of a Spin-Off Under the Favorable Tax Regime

Provided that the conditions described previously are met, or if a ruling has been granted, the spin-off benefits from the favorable tax regime for mergers, and the following results apply:

6.10 International Spin-Offs

- The fixed registration duty remains at FRF 1,500 or 228.67€.
- Tax deferral on capital gains are realized on nondepreciable assets.
- Spreading capital gains are realized on depreciable assets. This approach is similar to partial mergers.
- Tax deferral is provided for the exchange of shares.

(b) Tax Consequences of a Spin-Off Under Standard Regime

It is advisable that the company monitor closely the conditions stated previously for relief. The tax cost of a spin-off can be significant if these conditions are not met. For example:

- The company's profits and gains through corporate income tax and equalization tax are immediately taxed.
- The liquidation surplus for the shareholders is immediately taxed.
- Transfer duties are payable by the beneficiary companies on contributions in cash and other forms of consideration.

6.10 INTERNATIONAL SPIN-OFFS

Most of the tax consequences for international spin-offs are the same as for international mergers regarding direct and indirect taxes.

(a) Spin-off of a French Subsidiary of a Foreign Company

For a spin-off, when the beneficiary company is a foreign entity, the favorable tax regime, as described in the first section, is applicable only upon prior granting of a ruling. The favorable tax regime can apply without a prior ruling when the demerger is made between two French companies, regardless of the effective place of residence of their shareholders. The shareholders of the beneficiary companies can be resident abroad.

(b) Spin-Off of a Foreign Subsidiary of a French Company

The primary issues in the case at hand are the gains derived from the exchange of shares. Under French domestic tax law, a tax deferral may be granted, pursuant to the provisions of Section 38-7 *bis* of the FTC. However, these gain deferral provisions are granted only if the transaction is implemented under the French favorable tax regime. This situation may be impossible when two non-French subsidiaries are involved.

If the spin-off occurs between companies that are residents of EU Member States, there may be arguments under the Merger Directive to challenge the position described previously and benefit from a tax-neutral regime. In practice, the shareholders of the French company may approach the FTA to seek a benefit from a more definitive position.

6.11 ACQUISITIONS

French tax law makes a distinction between two types of securities:

1. Shares of corporations (such as SA).
2. Shares of LLCs (such as SARL).

As a general rule, two types of financing operation can be used to take over a company:

1. Payment in cash
2. A leveraged buy-out.

One of the major benefits provided by the French regime is that financing costs incurred by a company liable to corporate income tax are deductible from its taxable income. These amounts are deductible provided that the rules regarding the deductibility of loans made by shareholders to the company and the general principles of tax law are upheld.

Two situations can be contemplated:

1. An acquisition of a company within a tax consolidated group
2. An acquisition leading to a merger of the target company with the acquiring company.

(a) Acquisition of a Company Using a French Tax Consolidated Group

The tax consolidation regime allows profits to be offset against the losses realized by the other entities in the group. Therefore, in an acquisition context, this consolidation may allow the optimal tax deduction for the interest flows relating to the acquisition:

- The interest expense of the holding company will be offset by the profits of the target.
- Profits of the target can be distributed without deduction of the equalization tax.

It is not always possible for a group to opt for tax consolidation. Further, tax consolidation may have some adverse consequences. The parent company must hold, directly or indirectly, at least 95 percent of the share capital of the target company during the whole length of the fiscal year for consolidation to occur.

All the companies of the tax consolidated group must use the same accounting date. The taxpayer group must make an affirmative election to take advantage of the consolidated return provisions. The group must elect to benefit from tax consolidation benefits before the beginning of the period in question. The tax con-

6.11 Acquisitions

solidation regime will not be applicable during the period between the acquisition of the shares and the beginning of the next fiscal year. Thus, most of the costs incurred in connection with the acquisition may be lost.

(b) Limits on Interest Deduction

The consolidation regime has several advantages for domestic acquisitions. Consolidated groups should make sure that they do not fall into the provisions of Section 223B of the FTC. This section applies to the following:

- An acquiring company controlled directly or indirectly by the seller of the shares or directly or indirectly controlled by a company that also controls the seller. But Section 223B provides no definition of "control."
- As a result of the acquisition, the company whose shares are purchased becomes part of the acquiring company's tax consolidated group.

A portion (calculated on the basis of a formula provided by the FTA) of the interest charges incurred by the whole group is added back in when computing the group's consolidated income. The amount to be added back is determined by applying the ratio of the acquisition price of the newly consolidated company to the average amount of long-term debt shown in the balance sheet of all group companies.

The interest on borrowing will have to be added back to the consolidated taxable income for the 15 fiscal years following the acquisition of the shares unless the acquired company leaves the tax consolidated group. The amendment to Section 223B of the FTC does not apply when the company being purchased is already within the consolidated group at the time of the acquisition or the company is acquired by the seller from nonrelated parties in order to be resold. On the subsequent sale of the shares, the company is liable for corporate income tax on any capital gains arising from the disposal. The gross value of the shares recorded in the balance sheet is taken into account in determining the capital gain. Any provision for depreciation accumulated is added back and treated as long-term capital gain.

(c) Thin Capitalization Rules

Section 39 1 3° and 212 of the FTC provide for limitations on the interest deductions, which are allowed in connection with loans granted to a French company by a direct shareholder. The limitations are as follows:

- No interest can be deducted if the share capital is not fully paid up.
- The interest rate must not exceed the official rate published by the FTA.
- When the total debt-to-equity ratio exceeds 1.5:1, interest on the portion of the total amount of loans granted by direct majority shareholders or manager shareholders that exceeds 1.5:1 is not deductible. This limitation is not applicable when the direct shareholder qualifies for the parent subsidiary regime.

The only limitation that could be relevant is that of the maximum interest rate. The reference rate published by the FTA is the annual average of the effective rates applied by financial institutions for variable-rate loans granted to companies for an initial period exceeding two years. This rate was 5.61 percent for the first quarter of the year 2000.

(d) Rapid Merger Alternative

It is not always possible to operate Leveraged Buy Out (LBO) transactions from within a tax consolidation (e.g., because of limitations of debt creation rules, see previous discussion). In that context, merging the target company with the acquiring company may be contemplated as an alternative scenario. Because mergers imply a complete transfer of the assets, there is a *de facto* assumption of the liabilities of the companies, allowing the expenses incurred by the acquiring company to be offset against the profits of the target. This solution has two major advantages:

1. The holding company is able to service its debt, not only through the dividends paid by its new subsidiary, but also directly out of the retained profit reserves of the target.
2. The assets of the target, to which the acquiring company has full access, can be used to guarantee the banking loans, or the assets can be sold if the assets are not necessary for the activities of the company.

From a tax perspective, the merger results in a consolidation of the results of the holding company with those of the target, which allows the following:

- The holding company's financing costs can be offset against the taxable profits of the target.
- The reserves of the target can be assumed without any liability to deduct equalization tax.
- The assets of the target can be reevaluated on a tax-neutral basis, provided that the favorable tax regime rules set forth at Section 210A, and described previously, apply to the merger.

Depending on the activity of the target, a reverse merger can also be contemplated (i.e., the merger of the target with the holding company). This reverse merger can be advantageous when, for instance, the assets of the target consist principally of real estate, or if its activity is based on contracts involving strong personal links/relationships.

(e) Tax Exposure of the Rapid Merger

Although the tax effects of a merger under the consolidation taxation are the same as those under the rapid merger regime, the FTA is more likely to challenge rapid mergers. In practice, these transactions may be challenged as either one of the following:

6.11 Acquisitions

1. An abuse of law
2. An abnormal act of management

(f) Abuse of Law Theory

Section L64 of the French Procedural Tax Code allows the FTA to look through the taxpayer's own characterization of its transaction in order to determine whether the transactions are of a fictitious or tax-driven nature. If the abuse of law theory is sustained by the FTA during an audit, the penalties faced can amount up to 80 percent of the transaction value.

In the context of a rapid merger, the FTA would try to prove that the transactions were fictitious by challenging the following:

- The genuineness of the acquiring holding company. On this argument, in the *Régie Immobilière de Villeurbanne* case,[3] the Administrative Appeal Court held that the FTA could not challenge the genuineness of an acquiring holding company provided that the holding company was carrying on its activity in accordance with the laws and its Articles of Association.
- The genuineness of the merger, even though a merger may have many legal effects, which cannot be disregarded
- The genuineness of the legal and tax operation. Such a challenge would result in denying the existence of the legal personality of the holding company being denied. As we have seen, it is difficult to be called into question.

The FTA would then try to prove the fraud by the following devices:

- Challenging the economic goal of the operation, which is difficult to prove because a merger always occurs in the frame of an economic reorganization or with some other inherent economic motivation.
- Challenging the financial interest of the merger. This seems to be the most sensitive argument. In the case of a rapid merger, most of the financial benefit relates to the tax savings realized by merging the two companies and having the liabilities of the holding company borne by the target.

(g) Abnormal Management Act

The FTA could apply the Abnormal Management Act in order to reject the deduction of the interest expenses incurred in connection with the acquisition of the target. The following could apply at the level of the holding company:

1. The merger is clearly initiated in the interest of the holding company, and therefore the merger does not constitute an abnormal act of management. The operations directly preceding the merger must be monitored closely. In

---

[3] *Régie Immobilière de Villeurbanne*, CAA Lyon n°1408, May 26, 1992.

that context, the acquisition price could be challenged if it were below the book value of the shares acquired.

2. The financing of the acquisition could be challenged, at the level of the holding, on the ground that the holding company is thinly capitalized (see previous discussion developments about thin capitalization).

Under the abnormal act of management theory, as developed by French case law, a French entity can be denied a deduction for an expense that is deemed not to be incurred for business reasons (i.e., the expense is not justified and motivated by business reasons). Despite the lack of legal rules regarding thin capitalization, with the exception of those mentioned above, excessive debt to equity ratios situations are increasingly challenged in practice by the FTA through tax audits. In general, such reassessments are carried out on the grounds of an abnormal act of management.

(h) Financial Assistance Exposure

The rapid merger causes the assets of the two companies to be combined. In most cases, the acquiring company uses the assets of the target to service its debt. In that context, this combination of assets, which benefits directly to the shareholders of the acquiring company, must be monitored closely to make sure that it does not fall under the scope of Section 217-9 of the French Company Code. This section expressly forbids advances in cash or loans granted by a company to a third party in order to purchase its shares. Those dispositions, frequently referred to as "Financial Assistance" dispositions, are increasingly utilized when trying to challenge a rapid merger. If one of the shareholders of the acquiring company is a director of the target company at the time of the purchase, the tax authorities may construe this relationship as abuse of the company's assets exposure.

(i) VAT on Acquisition of Shares

Under French law, VAT is not deductible when incurred for the purposes of non-taxable transactions or transactions out of the scope of VAT. On the basis of this rule, VAT connected with the acquisition of shares is usually not deductible as no VAT applies to sales of shares.

The Administrative Tribunal of Poitiers rendered a ground-breaking decision on February 25, 1999, SA Rémy-Cointreau. The Administrative Tribunal held that a company could deduct input VAT borne on the costs when acquiring an interest in other companies, such as legal fees, commissions, and so forth, provided that the acquiring party was involved in the management of the target companies. The rationale of the Tribunal was that, in such a case, the involvement in the management of the target company meant that the shareholding could be considered as being part of the economic activity of the company within the scope of VAT. Thus, input VAT was deductible in application of Section 271 of the French Tax Code.

A few weeks before this decision, in the Versailles Administrative Court on February 11, 1999, SA Henri Azuelos had rendered an opposite decision in a similar case. In this case, the decision of the tribunal seemed, however, to be based on a factual issue rather than on a principle of non-deduction. No proof of the involvement of the management seems to have been presented. In a decision rendered on January 6, 2000, the Lille Administrative Tribunal applied to the European Community Court of Justice for a preliminary ruling to determine in particular whether VAT relating to acquisition costs on shareholdings is deductible.

6.12 TREATMENT OF ASSETS

Under French tax law, a business acquired as a going concern is viewed as a transfer of business, *tranfert de fonds de commerce.* This concept of *fonds de commerce* is not defined as such by French law. In our opinion, it should be viewed as the aggregate sum of both the tangible and intangible assets of this business.

(a) Corporate Tax Consequences for Acquiring Company

The base cost for tax purposes of an asset used in the acquiring company is the historic cost. The basis for depreciation is its acquisition value, as defined by Section 38 of Annex III of the FTC. The acquiring company is entitled to a tax deduction against future income for depreciation on fixed assets acquired with the business. Depreciation should be allowed on a straight-line basis over the useful life of the assets, and there are no prescribed depreciation rates. The declining balance method is not permitted because this method is generally permitted only for new assets.

As regards intangible property, goodwill and trademarks may not normally be amortized. Patents may be amortized because they have a useful life determinable in advance. Other intangible property can be amortized, provided its value diminishes through use or over time. Software is amortized over 12 months.

If the acquiring company pays a single global price for the acquisition of a going concern, then, according to French tax law, the tax basis of each asset acquired is historic cost. For acquisitions of real estate, the total price paid must be apportioned between the building and the land.

The FTA is entitled to adjust the prices of the assets purchased in the books of the acquiring company. For instance, if the acquiring company has entered an asset in its books at a value higher than its fair market value for tax relief purposes, the FTA can adjust that sum to correspond to fair market value. Under no circumstances can the acquiring company use the brought-forward tax losses of the acquired company. Financing expenses and interests related to the acquisition of the company are deductible for the acquiring company.

(b) Corporate Tax Consequences for the Seller

The tax consequences to the seller depend on the nature of the assets sold and the period of time the assets have been held by the selling company. The treatment of capital gains under domestic law is divided into two categories:

1. Short-term capital gains (or losses) are included in operating profits and taxed at the standard corporate income tax rate of 33.33 percent plus surtaxes.
2. Long-term capital gains, arising from shares held for more than two years, are taxed at the reduced corporate income tax rate of 19 percent plus surtaxes.

Since fiscal year 1997, capital gains arising from the following categories of shares are eligible to benefit from only the long-term capital gains regime:

- Participation shares, which are shares forming part of at least 10 percent of the capital of a subsidiary
- Venture capital fund shares

Short-term capital gains can be offset against short-term capital losses arising in the same fiscal year. If, after offsetting, a short-term capital loss remains, it is deductible from the current year profits. The excess losses can be carried forward under normal rules if the current year profits are insufficient. Similar rules apply to the long-term capital gains and losses, i.e., they are offset against each other. However, if this offsetting results in a long-term capital loss, the net long-term capital loss can only be carried forward against long-term capital gains arising in the next 10 years, or alternatively against the company's special long-term capital reserve.

(c) VAT and Securities Registration

The sale of the assets of a business, as opposed to the sale of a whole going concern, is subject to VAT. The sale of a going concern is subject to registration tax on the fair market value of the business, less the value of inventories. Inventories are subject to VAT. The registration duty applies at a rate of 4.80 percent. Even though the liability is borne by the purchaser, the liability generally impacts the acquisition price.

6.13 INTERNATIONAL ACQUISITION OF SHARES

(a) French Acquiring Company/Foreign Acquired Company

The situation of a French company purchasing a stake in a foreign entity is not fundamentally different from a French company purchasing shares in another French company. Dividends received from a foreign entity by a French company may be exempt pursuant to the French participation exemption regime. This regime provides, for fiscal year 2001, that dividends received from companies that are owned by at least 5 percent of the shares are exempt from taxation. Interest incurred for their acquisition should be deductible, under limitations described in the previous section (i.e., debt creation rules, financial assistance, and so forth).

No deductions are available if the foreign-acquired company has a loss or its value diminishes in the postacquisition period. The exception is a provision for

6.13 International Acquisition of Shares

booking subsidiary shares that could be deducted from long-term gains. Upon a subsequent future sale of the shares, the eventual resulting loss would be treated as a long-term capital loss.

French companies setting up branches or subsidiaries abroad can, in certain circumstances, apply to be allowed to set up a special tax-exempt provision in their accounts to provide for the losses incurred by the subsidiary or branch. The rules relating to this provision vary depending on whether the foreign activity is a sales establishment or service establishment.

The dispositions set forth at Section 209B of the FTC (French CFC regulations) may eventually impact the situation of the French corporate acquiror because the 209B regulations constitute an exception to the French territoriality principal. These regulations provide that any company is subject to corporate income tax in France when the company holds at least 25 percent of the shares of a company located in a country where the overall tax liability is less than one-third to the French liability. The liability is 22 percent or less. This income is taxed at the standard French corporate income tax rate on the profits derived from that company. Taxation is in proportion to the holding of the shares.

Furthermore, the profits (or losses) derived from the exploitation of a branch or a subsidiary in a "CFC country" cannot be mixed with the results of the French head office or parent company. The company must include CFC income in a different tax return. It could be questioned whether Section 209B of the FTC statute is contrary to the Rome Treaty and most of the double taxation treaties entered into by France. See Exhibits 6.1 to 6.3.

Exhibit 6.1

SALES ENTERPRISE

Investment Form	—Creation of an establishment —33.33% held subsidiary
Amount of the reserve	Losses incurred abroad during fiscal years following the investment, and for the four following years of the investment. Limited to the amount of the initial investment.
Reinstatement of the reserve	Up to the profits realized by the foreign establishment, for the fiscal years following the one in which the reserve has been deducted and at the latest during the fiscal year closed on the tenth year following the investment.

Exhibit 6.2

SERVICE ENTERPRISE

Investment Form	—Creation of an establishment —33.33% held subsidiary
Amount of the reserve	Losses incurred during the fiscal years closed after the investment and for the four following years, in the limit of the amount of the investment, the investment being limited to FRF 20 million or approximately ∊ 3.05 million.
Reinstatement of the reserve	Up to the profits realized by the foreign establishment, for the fiscal years following the one in which the reserve has been deducted and at the latest during the fiscal year closed on the tenth year following the investment.

Exhibit 6.3

INDUSTRIAL ENTERPRISE

Investment Form	—Creation of an establishment —10% held subsidiary
Amount of the reserve	50% of the sums invested in capital during the first five years of activity.
Reinstatement of the reserve	The global amount of the reserves bookcd must be reinstated by equal fractions within the results of the five fiscal years, starting from the sixth year following the investment.

(b) VAT

No VAT applies to sales of shares (see Section 6.12(c)).

6.14 FOREIGN-ACQUIRING COMPANY/FRENCH-ACQUIRED COMPANY

(a) Tax Consequences for the Buyer

French domestic law provides that a foreign resident company acquiring shares in a French company is subject to a 25 percent withholding tax. This withholding tax

6.14 Foreign-Acquiring Company/French-Acquired Company

rate may be reduced or eliminated under the terms of a double taxation treaty between France and the country of residence of the acquiring company. Alternately, the withholding tax can be reduced under the provisions of the EU Parent-Subsidiary Directive. This Directive applies if the foreign company holds at least 25 percent of the share capital of the French company.

Attention must also be paid to antiabuse provisions for intermediary holding, such as those set forth at Section 119 *ter* of the FTC (antidirective shopping clause) or at certain articles in double taxation treaties (antitreaty shopping clause). From a French perspective, those regulations allow the FTA to disregard the application of the favorable regime provided by the EU Directive, to the presence of an EU Member State based holding in between a French target and a non-EU Member State resident company. These provisions apply when the implementation of this holding was obviously tax driven.

Capital gains arising to the foreign company on the sale of shares in the French company are subject to French tax at a rate of 16 percent. These provisions apply if the foreign company has held a substantial interest of 25 percent or more in the French company at any time within the five years preceding the date of the sale; however, if the foreign company is a resident of a country that has signed a double taxation treaty with France, the treaty may exempt the capital gain in France.

(b) Financing Costs Incurred in Connection with the Acquisition

The foreign-acquiring company may aim to offset its interest expense relative to the financing of the acquisition against the profits of the French target company. If so, the acquiring company may consider creating a French subholding company. This French subholding company can borrow the funds directly and acquire the French target. It may then be possible for the two French companies to elect for the tax consolidation regime, but in no circumstances should the foreign group have owned the target before the acquisition. In such case, tax relief for interest expenses incurred on the financing loan may be restricted for a 15-year period.

It would also be possible that the French subholding company would consequently merge with the French target (see the previous section on rapid mergers). However, in order to prevent the FTA from challenging this operation on the grounds of abuse of law, certain conditions must be met, namely the following:

- The merging company must continue the business of the merged.
- The merging company must assume all the assets and liabilities pertaining to the merged company so that the merged company does not affect the merging company's activity.

The continuity of the activity of the merging company is important because it will otherwise lose the right to carry over its losses incurred before the merger (Section 221-5 of the FTC). There must be strong business reasons for this merged operation in order to minimize the risk of challenge by the FTA. Another alternative might be to achieve a *de facto* consolidation by transforming the target company into a partnership postacquisition, i.e., into a French SNC (Société en Nom Collectif) or an SCS (Société en Commandite Simple).

Interest paid by a French debtor to a non-French resident lender is generally exempt from withholding tax, assuming certain conditions are met. This regime, set forth at Section 131 of the FTC, is available provided that the following conditions are met:

- Interest paid derives from a loan agreement clearly stating the amount of the loan, the maturity date of this loan, and the remuneration of the lender.
- The lender has to be located outside of France.
- The borrower has to be a French company.

(c) Domestic Seller

The tax consequences of the sale of shares in a foreign company by a French company are the same as the sale of shares in a French company. Depending on the tax treaty, France should have the right to tax the capital gains arising from the sale of shares in the foreign company.

(d) Foreign Seller

Capital gains realized by a nonresident company on the sale of shares in a French company are normally taxed in France at a rate of 16 percent. This taxation presupposes that the foreign company held a substantial stake of 25 percent or more in the French company at any time during a period of five years before the disposal. If these requirements are not met, capital gains are taxed at the standard rate. If France has signed a double taxation treaty with the country in which the seller is resident, it is possible that those capital gains may even be exempt from taxation in France. No VAT applies to sales of shares. See Exhibit 6.4.

Exhibit 6.4

FOREIGN ACQUISITION PROCESS

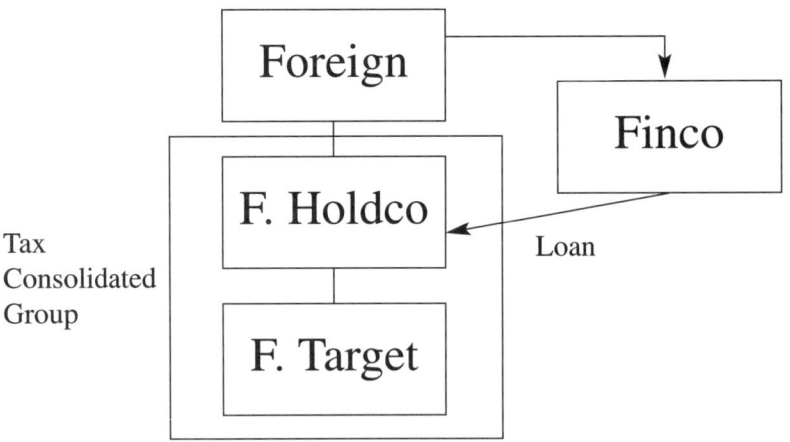

6.15 INTERNATIONAL ACQUISITION OF ASSETS

(a) French-Acquiring Company/Foreign Assets

Profits deriving from activities carried on by a French company outside of the French territory through the use of a branch are not liable to French corporate income tax because of the French principle of territoriality. Conversely, interest expenses on this type of acquisition should not be deductible in France. Losses realized by foreign branches are not deductible for French corporate income tax purposes. An exception exists, though, when the company has opted for the worldwide income or consolidated income regime after being granted a specific ruling. Only a few French groups have applied for this regime. Other delegation rules exist. (See developments on provisions for setting up an enterprise abroad.)

(b) Foreign-Acquiring Company/Domestic Assets

A foreign company that directly acquires a going concern from a French resident company is treated for corporate income tax purposes as conducting business in France through a branch. The foreign company would therefore be liable for French corporate income tax on the profits derived from that branch. The company's profits that do not derive from the branch are taxed separately. The foreign company is liable for withholding tax at a rate of 25 percent, which can be reduced by tax treaties, on the deemed distributed profits, unless the taxpayer can prove that no profits have been transferred away from France.

Withholding tax on branch profits (net of corporate income tax) is levied at a rate of 25 percent (or such lower rate as is provided by treaty). The company may obtain a repayment of the withholding tax if the head office distributes a dividend smaller than the total profits of the French branch within the 12 months after the year in which the profits were earned. It is also possible to avoid the payment of the withholding tax if the head office commits itself not to pay any dividends within this 12-month period.

If the foreign company establishes a subsidiary in France in order to acquire a French business as a going concern, the company will be subject to corporate income tax under normal conditions. Hence, the dividends paid to the foreign company by this subsidiary are subject to a withholding tax at a rate of 25 percent, or such lower rate as is provided by treaty. As mentioned previously, under the EU Parent-Subsidiary Directive, if the foreign company is resident in an EU Member State, dividends paid to it will be exempt from withholding tax, provided that the foreign company commits to hold 25 percent of the share capital for two years.

6.16 INTERNATIONAL ACQUISITION OF ASSETS: TAX CONSEQUENCES FOR THE SELLER

Most of the tax treaties signed by France with other countries provide that capital gains are taxed in the state in which they arise. Therefore, capital gains derived from the sale of assets located outside France should not be taxed in France as long as the gains represent a permanent establishment outside France. Even if the capital gains arise in a country with which France has not entered into a double taxation treaty, then, pursuant to the French territoriality rules, and assuming that the French CFC rules do not apply, the capital gains arising should not, in general, be taxed in France.

Under the double taxation treaties signed by France with other countries, France has the right to tax capital gains derived from the sale of immovable assets under a permanent establishment or for real estate property located in France. Sales of assets located outside France are not subject to French VAT. The sale by a non-French resident company of a business as a going concern or of an immovable asset located in France is subject to VAT in the same way as described in the preceding section for domestic transactions made by a French company.

The sale by a foreign company of assets or real estate in France is subject to the same treatment as for purely domestic transactions. Because of the territoriality principle, the sale of assets located outside France is not subject to registration duty in France unless the deed has been executed in France pursuant to Section 718 of the FTC.

6.17 PUBLIC TENDER OFFER

For takeover involving a share-for-share exchange, the specific provisions set out at Section 38-7 apply. For such a takeover, the taxation of the capital gains arising from this swap can be deferred, provided that the following conditions are met:

- No cash is paid in compensation for any loss in value due to the swap transaction.
- The exchanged shares are listed on a French stock exchange.
- The core exchange transaction is made in accordance with the legislation in force at the time of the operation.

Capital gains are viewed as occurring only upon a subsequent disposal of the exchanged shares, not upon the exchange itself. The conditions for the exchange are not to be considered as a disposal, and thus the benefits from the exemption of taxation are the following:

- A cash payment of up to 10 percent of the value of the total consideration is allowed, but any payment in excess of 10 percent is immediately taxed at the normal rate.
- The shares acquired need not be recorded in the balance sheet of the acquiring company at the same value as the company transferring them records in its own books. However, capital gains will be calculated on the transfer value of the shares.

6.19 Hybrid Instruments

- Tax deferral of capital gains is not possible if the shareholders of one of the party acquired the shares, which they will be exchanging in the following circumstances:

  — Through an increase in share capital
  — Which occurred less than three years before the exchange transaction
  — By an entity that is either held by or itself holds, directly or indirectly, more than 5 percent of the share capital of the other party to the transaction.

6.18 INTERNATIONAL PUBLIC TENDER OFFER

The deferral of taxation for takeover involving share-for-share exchanges should be available to international takeovers involving such exchange between a French company and a foreign company as long as both are listed on a French stock exchange. Capital gains arising from securities listed on a French stock exchange, and which are held by foreign residents, are not taxed in France, due to the provisions of Section 244 *bis* C of the FTC.

6.19 HYBRID INSTRUMENTS

Hybrid financing is commonly used to raise debt in France. In an inbound context (i.e., French borrower, non-French resident investor) these typically involve instruments which give rise to an interest deduction in France but benefit from equity characterization in the jurisdiction of the investor and therefore may be exempt therein.

(a) Inbound Financing

Among the instruments that may be used as hybrid instruments in a cross-border context are profit-sharing loans, *prêts participatifs* and several debt instruments that are convertible or exchangeable into shares in the issuer. Profit-sharing loans are governed by a law of July 13, 1978, and are legally treated as equity when calculating a company's indebtedness, but as debt (thus giving rise to a deduction) for tax purposes. These profit-sharing loans typically have a fixed or floating interest element and a second component in the return of the instrument that is based on the profits of the issuer. The interest payable is often capped. The characteristic of this kind of debt is that it is fully subordinated to the other debts of the company.

In a cross-border context, a profit-sharing loan may, in certain circumstances, be regarded as equity, thus benefiting from a favorable tax treatment in the investor's jurisdiction. A further advantage of a participating loan is that under French law and certain treaties entered into by France, interest may be payable totally free of withholding tax under specific conditions. On the other hand, several debt instruments exist in France with equity components. For example the following are available:

- Convertible bonds (*obligations convertibles en action* or OCAs)
- Bonds repayable only in shares (*obligation remboursables en action* or ORAs)
- Bonds with attached share warrants (*obligations avec bonds de souscriptions en actions* or OBSAs).

Of particular interest is the ORA, which is often used in a cross-border context. An ORA is a bond that at maturity is repaid in shares (typically a fresh issue of shares). Unlike the OCA, where convertibility is at the option of the holder, an ORA has no such option. Before the maturity of the instrument, the ORA is treated as debt for tax purposes, and the interest generated by this instrument is deductible, subject of course to the general limitations on interest deductibility.

The treatment of premium included in an ORA raises an issue (i.e., deductibility of the premium for the issuer is uncertain). On conversion of the bond into shares, from the bondholder's perspective, no taxable gain or loss is recognized at the time of the conversion. The gain or loss is taken into account in determining the bondholder's taxable income in the year in which the shares are subsequently disposed of. In other words, there is a rollover of the gain. From an international perspective, the ORA can be used as a hybrid instrument. It is possible to structure an ORA transaction between France and another jurisdiction such that the ORA is treated in the latter as an equity instrument, or in such a way that a tax deferral is available in the investor jurisdiction.

(b) Outbound Financing

In an outbound context, hybrid financing may involve the use of the French participation exemption regime, *régime des sociétés mères et filiales*. Structures do exist where the non-French resident borrower benefits from a deduction in its jurisdiction, and the French resident corporate investor receives dividends that are 95 percent tax exempt under the French participation regime available, provided the following conditions are met:

- The price of the shareholding must represent at least 5 percent of the share capital of the subsidiary.
- The shares must carry voting rights.
- The shares must either be subscribed on issue, or the parent company must commit to hold the shares for at least a two-year period.

At a more fundamental level, the investment should also satisfy the general civil law requirements for an equity investment. This focuses on contributions by shareholders, the existence of *affectio societatis*. *Affectio societatis* is the will of the shareholders to form a company and the participation of the shareholders in the company's profits and losses. As the features needed for an investment to

6.19 Hybrid Instruments

qualify as equity from a French legal perspective, it is often difficult to structure an investment that successfully combines debt treatment in the borrower jurisdiction with equity treatment in France. Other issues to consider in the outbound financing context include the French CFC rules (Section 209B of the FTC), the abuse of laws theory, and the French transfer pricing rules. See Exhibit 6.5.

Exhibit 6.5

OUTBOUND FINANCING

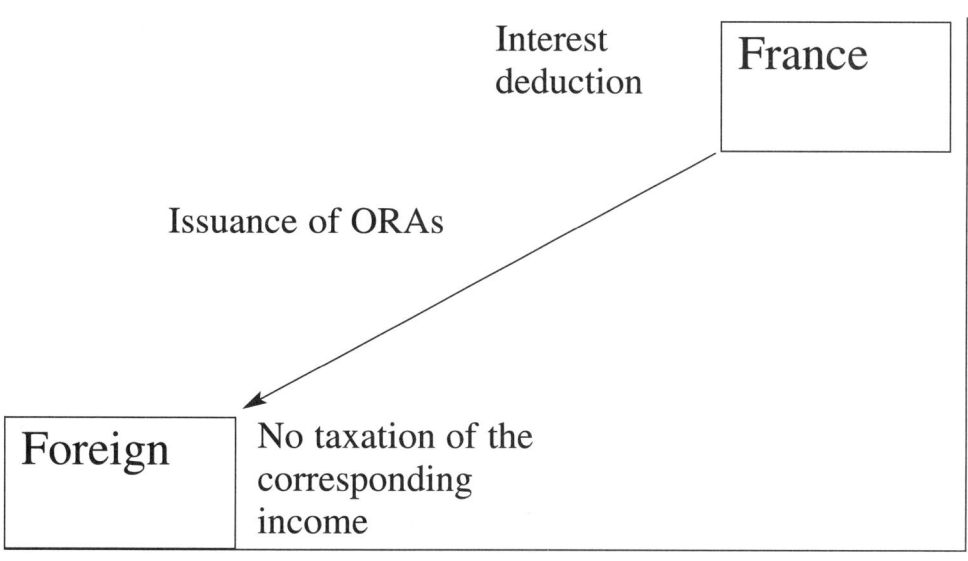

CHAPTER 7

Taxation of Mergers and Acquisitions in Germany

Dieter Endres
Stefan Ditsch
PricewaterhouseCoopers, Frankfurt

7.1 **The M & A Market in Germany**
    (a)   Economic Factors
    (b)   Old Economy Companies and New Market Companies
    (c)   Starting Over

7.2 **M & A Tax Consulting: The Key Issues**
    (a)   Planning the Acquisition of a German Business
    (b)   Tax Due Diligence Review
    (c)   Completing the Tax Due Diligence Review
    (d)   Role of the Tax Consultant

7.3 **Principal Taxes**
    (a)   Individual Income Tax
    (b)   Corporation Tax
    (c)   Solidarity Surcharge
    (d)   Trade Tax on Income
    (e)   Withholding Taxes
    (f)   Capital Taxes
    (g)   Value-Added Tax
    (h)   Real Estate Transfer Tax

7.4 **Highlights of the Tax Reform 2001**
    (a)   Key Features in the M & A Context
    (b)   Curtailing the Imputation System
    (c)   Capital Gains
    (d)   Impact of Tax Reform

7.5 **Revised Tax Consolidation Requirements (*Organschaft*)**

7.6 **Tightening of Thin Capitalization Rules**
    (a)   Tax Reform Provisions
    (b)   Thin Capitalization and Safe Harbors
    (c)   Holding Companies
    (d)   Thin Capitalization

7.7 **Effective Tax Relief for Financing Costs**
    (a)   Interest Deduction
    (b)   Dividend Issues

- (c) Foreign Dividends
- (d) Financing Tax Relief

7.8 Asset Step-Up
- (a) Goodwill
- (b) Intellectual Property
- (c) Noncompetition Payments
- (d) Asset Deal: Acquisition Costs/Purchase Price Allocation

7.9 Pooling of Profits and Losses

7.10 Avoiding or Minimizing Real Estate Transfer Tax

7.11 Safeguarding Existing Tax Attributes
- (a) Transfer of Shares
- (b) Merger of Companies
- (c) Partnerships
- (d) Other Aspects

7.12 Minimization of Withholding Taxes

7.13 Tax-Effective Exit Routes
- (a) Foreign Investors
- (b) Capital Gains

7.14 Tax Objectives of the Vendor

7.15 Sale of Shares in Companies
- (a) Reduction in the Level of "Significant" Investments
- (b) Changing the Definition of "Significant" Investment
- (c) Consequences of the Change in "Significant" Investment
- (d) Partnership Interest

7.16 Shares in Corporations

7.17 Considerations Applicable to All Sellers

7.18 Inbound Acquisitions into Germany
- (a) Assset Deal: Foreign Parent Acquires German Business
- (b) Foreign Partner Establishes German Partnership
- (c) Foreign Investor's German Subsidiary Acquires Assets

7.19 Partnership Acquisition
- (a) Partnership Taxation Principles
- (b) Partnership Acquisition vs. Asset Deal
- (c) Double-Dip Financing
- (d) Acquisition of a Partnership

7.20 Share Deals
- (a) Foreign Corporate Borrowing
- (b) Using a German Company for the Acquisition
- (c) Share Deal

7.21 Deferral Instruments

7.22 Reorganization and Demergers
- (a) Short-Term and Long-Term Interests
- (b) Tax-Free Reorganizations
- (c) Conversion of a Company to a Partnership
- (d) Merger Treatment
- (e) Anti-Abuse Regulations

7.1 The M & A Market in Germany

      (f)   EU Merger Directive
      (g)   Tax-Free Transfers

7.23 Joint Ventures and Merger of Equals
      (a)   Tax Planning for Business Combinations
      (b)   Domestic German and International Considerations
      (c)   Choosing a Location

7.24 Going Public
      (a)   Reasons for Going Public
      (b)   Reasons for Success of Offering
      (c)   Legal Structures
      (d)   Financing and Deduction of Financing Costs
      (e)   Inheritance and Gift Taxes

7.1 THE M & A MARKET IN GERMANY

The mergers and acquisitions (M & A) market in Germany had been booming during the 1997–2000 period. The boom in mergers and acquisitions is true in terms of both the size of transactions and the number of transactions. Some mergers and acquisitions have been among the largest ever completed anywhere. These included the following:

- The Daimler-Chrysler merger
- The Vodafone/Mannesmann deal
- The Hoechst/Rhone Poulenc (Aventis) merger
- Reckitt/Benckiser
- The recent takeover of Dresdner Bank by Allianz

Turmoil in the financial markets and uncertainty about the enactment of tax reform in Germany caused a temporary slowdown in M & A activity in 2000. The anticipated pro-business tax changes now are the law. The high-tech securities market has adjusted back from its euphoric peak. Thus, the signs are there for a sustained resurgence of M & A activity.

    The capital gains reform, in general, becomes effective in 2002. Thus, most taxpayers will not close their tax-sensitive transactions until 2002 to escape capital gains tax entirely or to achieve a reduced tax burden. The banks in particular, but also industrial multinational corporations (MNCs) with huge financing power, are monitoring the market for deal opportunities—both as prospective buyers and sellers.

      (a) Economic Factors

Moreover, the economic factors that have spurred the M & A boom in Germany and elsewhere are, if anything, accelerating. These factors include the following:

- The trend toward consolidation will continue. Size has always been important, but the European Union (EU) and globalization have set new standards in many industries for the critical mass needed to survive—let alone prosper. Moreover, capital needs in some industries have eliminated all but the largest competitors. For example, the world now has only two makers of intercontinental passenger planes, and even large automakers and banks have found themselves too small to continue on their own.
- The pace of change, including that competitors are growing via mergers and acquisitions, means that organic (internal) growth cannot generate the growth required to keep up. This is particularly true in entering foreign markets, where acquisitions are a standard way to enter with enough size and know-how to succeed.
- Merging with and acquiring other companies is an increasingly popular way to acquire technology, eliminate competitors, and enter new markets.
- In the high-tech industry, the impetus for a merger or acquisition can be to make the unified technology the industry standard.
- Synergy, efficiency, and elimination of duplicate costs are the drivers in many mergers and acquisitions. Combining duplicate branches, distribution centers and back-office operations often is the principal economic force behind a merger or takeover.

(b) Old Economy Companies and New Market Companies

These economic realities affect the "old economy" companies and the survivors of the "new market" companies of all sizes. Family-owned companies are particularly affected by these changes. Founder generations are faced with solving succession problems and dealing with raising the money and finding the expertise to keep up domestically and expand internationally. These companies are ripe candidates for mergers and acquisitions—as both the surviving and nonsurviving entities. Private equity funds are a growing source of funds for acquiring even large private companies. These funds are increasingly important investors.

Foreign investors considering investing in Germany can obtain the following advantages from an acquisition:

- A seamless penetration of the German market, including reduced startup costs
- A trained workforce in place that knows the German market
- Eventually—synergy

(c) Starting Over

There may be reasons for a foreign company to start from scratch in Germany. Although few corporate events offer as much potential for gain as a merger or acquisition, few corporate events also offer as much potential for loss. Examples abound of large and small combinations that have failed because of cultural differences, a poor business fit, overextension as a result of acquisition debt, and/or lack of due diligence, among others.

7.2 M & A TAX CONSULTING: THE KEY ISSUES

Tax planning should play a major role in structuring mergers and acquisitions. The slate is clean, so structures can be put in place at no tax cost that may be prohibitively expensive later on. These are major bottom-line opportunities. Tax awareness is particularly important in cross-border acquisitions because the form of the acquisition profoundly affects the tax efficiency of profit repatriation, financing arrangements, and exit strategies.

7.2 M & A TAX CONSULTING: THE KEY ISSUES

In general, parties undertake M & A transactions in order to add value, to achieve 1 + 1 = 3; however, many transactions fail to deliver the "1 + 1 = 3" goal and thus to achieve their full potential. These transactions may even destroy value or restrict a company's ability to react in a commercially sensible fashion to future developments. This situation could occur, for example, when the business is locked into a structure that cannot be changed for a certain period in time as a result of rulings it received.

Tax planning can create value if opportunities are identified, synergies are utilized, and, in particular, if the financing structure of a transaction is optimized. As the tax issues involved become more and more complex, cross-border transactions require international teams that are organized in such a manner as to cope with the time pressures involved in the transaction. At the same time, systems must be in place to ensure that the services are delivered in an efficient manner.

(a) Planning the Acquisition of a German Business

There are four tax issues in planning the acquisition of a German business:

1. Tax due diligence
2. Contractual work (tax clauses and indemnities)
3. Deal structuring
4. Negotiation support

(b) Tax Due Diligence Review

The first step in planning for the acquisition of a German business is a tax due diligence review to identify tax risks inherent in the business to be acquired. The concept here is that "You analyze the past but you buy the future." A due diligence review is designed to identify all inherent tax exposure items in order to avoid unpleasant surprises during the next tax audit. The report should describe the tax history and status of the target and should comment on future planning opportunities. In practice, the tax due diligence team needs to cooperate closely with the financial and legal teams in order to present an accurate and relevant analysis.

The outcome of the tax due diligence review and the projections about the future tax position are designed to reduce the risk of a bad investment decision.

The results are immediately reflected in the target valuation. These results form the basis for the final negotiation phase.

The tax risks of the target are generally assumed by the acquiror, so it is necessary that all critical matters are appropriately covered in the purchase agreement by guarantees or "hold-harmless" clauses. Standard tax clause wordings exist, but each transaction is unique and requires contractual provisions specific to the individual case, such as the consequences of hidden profit distributions, warranties as to the existence of loss carry-forwards or the amount of retained earnings, and so on. In any event, indemnities given by the seller can only supplement the implementation of tax due diligence procedures, but can never be a substitute for these procedures.

(c) Completing the Tax Due Diligence Review

The last, but obvious stage of the tax due diligence review is to identify tax-efficient acquisition and disposal structures that add value to the transactions. The tax planner has to address at least five objectives:

1. Optimizing the deduction of the acquiror's financing costs
2. Achieving a step-up of the book value of the underlying assets acquired to reflect the purchase price actually paid, with a resultant increase in the depreciation basis for following years
3. Minimizing transaction costs, such as the real estate transfer tax
4. Planning exit strategies to ensure that the investor achieves the maximum possible transaction gain
5. Minimizing the capital gain tax payable by the seller, if possible

Clearly, there is no one standard acquisition pattern. The strategy must be tailored to the needs of each specific case and depends on whether the sellers are individuals or corporations and on whether a foreign or German corporation or partnership is to be acquired. See following sections for a discussion of typical acquisition structures.

In summary, a thorough tax due diligence review, carefully drafted tax warranties, and a tax-effective acquisition pattern tailored to the individual needs of each case are key elements in a successful acquisition.

(d) Role of the Tax Consultant

The work of the tax consultant does not end with the parties' signatures on the purchase contract. The next step is postacquisition structuring in order to integrate the acquired business into the existing group in the most tax-efficient manner. Issues to be addressed include the following:

- Establishing tax consolidation (*Organschaft*)
- Transferring shareholdings
- Centralizing functions

- Adjusting finance
- Implementing transfer-pricing policies

A further step is to identify and, where necessary, adjust the tax rate drivers that underpin the global tax position. Acquisitions provide a real opportunity to reconsider elements of the previous tax policy, to overcome existing tax-related pitfalls, and thus to achieve a positive bottom-line impact. See Exhibit 7.1.

Exhibit 7.1

M & A TAX CONSULTING

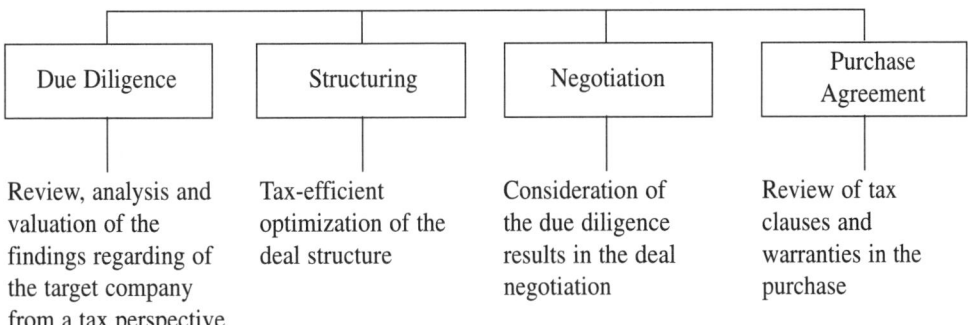

7.3 PRINCIPAL TAXES

Under the German constitution, the German federal government is empowered to enact tax statutes that are, wholly or partially, either collected or spent by the 16 states. The states have the right to enact tax statutes only if the federal government either has not exercised its legislative power or has allocated the power to promulgate certain tax statutes. Additionally, the municipalities, as self-administered public organizations, have limited rights to enact statutes that set the levy of local taxes. The primary taxes to consider when planning German M & A transactions are described as follows.

(a) Individual Income Tax

Income tax (*Einkommensteuer*) is levied on natural persons. The determination of taxable income reflects the ability to pay, taking into account the personal circumstances of the taxpayer. Natural persons are fully liable to German taxes if they maintain either a place of residence or their habitual abode in Germany. Nationality is irrelevant. The rates rise progressively to a top rate of 48.5 percent (from 2001 onwards).

Members of certain churches and religious communities are subject to church tax. Church tax is levied by the states on behalf of the religious communities (e.g., Roman Catholic, Protestant, etc.) entitled to the revenue as a surcharge on the income tax of the taxpayers of generally 8 percent or 9 percent.

(b) Corporation Tax

Corporation tax (*Koerperschaftsteuer*) is assessed on corporate taxpayers (GmbH, AG, KGaA). A corporation with either its management or seat in Germany is deemed to be resident and to be unlimitedly liable to German tax. From 2001 onward, the German corporation tax rate is subject to a flat rate of 25 percent, irrespective of whether the taxpayer is a resident or a nonresident corporation having German branch income and regardless of the corporation's dividend policy. Hence, the German effective tax rate of a foreign investor will no longer be reduced when profits are repatriated from Germany, as was the case under the previous split-rate system. See Exhibit 7.2.

Exhibit 7.2

CORPORATION TAX RATES

	Year 2000	From 2001 onwards
Retained earnings	40%	25%
Distributed earnings	30%	25%

Corporations with noncalendar year-end will only be entitled to the lower 25 percent rate as from business year 2000/2001.

(c) Solidarity Surcharge

Germany imposes a 5.5 percent solidarity surcharge (*Solidaritätszuschlag*) in addition to the regular income corporation tax. Both resident and nonresident taxpayers are subject to the solidarity surcharge. The solidarity surcharge is calculated based on the corporation and income tax liability, increasing the corporation tax burden to, effectively, 26.38 percent and the top tax rate of income tax from 48.5 percent to 51.17 percent. The surcharge is intended to cover costs following the German reunification and is therefore seen as temporary. The present plan is to abolish the solidarity surcharge, perhaps in stages, within the next five years.

(d) Trade Tax on Income

Trade tax (*Gewerbeertragsteuer*) is a municipal levy intended to cover additional costs of local authorities from the presence of businesses in their area. The trade tax is computed on taxable income as determined for corporation tax purposes, adjusted for various items. The most important adjustment is the add-back of 50 percent of interest on long-term loans that has been deducted on the corporate tax return as a business expense. The adjusted income is subject to a 5 percent trade tax, which is then increased by a local multiplier set by each municipality. Local multipliers range from 300 percent to approximately 500 percent, resulting in tax rates of from 15 percent to 25 percent (e.g., Berlin 17.1 percent, Cologne 18.4 percent, Frankfurt 20 percent, Hamburg 19 percent, Munich 18.1 percent). The trade

7.3 Principal Taxes

tax liability is deductible, not only from its own base of assessment, but also for corporation tax purposes.

(e) Withholding Taxes

Dividend distributions made in 2001 for a financial year ending before December 31, 2001, are subject to a 25 percent withholding tax. Thereafter, distributed profits are subject to only a 20 percent withholding tax. This rate is reduced to 0 percent for distributions made to EU resident companies according to the EU Parent-Subsidiary Directive, which requires 10 percent minimum shareholding for at least 12 months. The withholding tax can also be reduced under a double tax treaty (e.g., 5 percent to 15 percent under the US–German Treaty).

Interest payments in general are not subject to withholding tax in Germany under German statutory law. However, there are exceptions if, for example, the interest yield is profit related, the loan is secured by German real estate, or the loan is secured by a ship registered in a German ship register. Because the exemption is regulated under German domestic law and not by treaty regulations, loans from non-treaty countries (e.g., tax havens) do not have a disadvantage from a withholding tax perspective.

The withholding tax on royalties is currently 25 percent but will be reduced to 20 percent; however, under most German double tax treaties, the withholding tax is in general reduced to 0 percent.

(f) Capital Taxes

There are no taxes on forming a company or stamp duties under current German law. Germany previously had a net assets tax and a trade tax on capital. After the abolition of the net assets tax and the trade tax on capital, land tax is the only remaining tax levied at recurring intervals on the assets of a business. The land tax is assessed at varying local rates (usually between 1 and 2 percent annually) on the taxable value of land owned and is paid in favor of the local authority where the land is situated. These taxable values are calculated under a specific formula and are often significantly lower than the current market values.

Inheritance and gift tax is levied as a one-time charge on the transfer of ownership in assets by way of inheritance or gift. The rates vary between 7 percent and 50 percent of the value of the transfer and depend on the closeness of kinship between donor and the beneficiary as well as on the overall amount.

(g) Value-Added Tax

Transaction and consumption taxes are charged on the spending of income or assets. In addition, customs duties are imposed on the import of goods into Germany.

German value-added tax (VAT) is levied on the EU system under statutory provisions drawn up in accordance with the relevant EU directives. This tax is levied on the domestic supply of goods and services by a business, on certain items seen as its own consumption, and on the import of goods as well as on their acquisition from another EU member state (Sec. 1 UStG). Share deals are in principle exempt from VAT. The VAT is ultimately borne by the final consumer, but the taxpayer is the business performing the supply. In principle, VAT is not a cost factor for its taxpayers because the taxpayers can deduct the VAT charged to them by their suppliers from the amounts payable. These amounts are paid to the tax office for the charges that businesses have made to their customers. The standard VAT rate is currently 16 percent.

(h) Real Estate Transfer Tax

A real estate transfer tax of 3.5 percent of the transaction price is levied on all transfers of ownership of real estate. This tax is also levied when more than 95 percent of the shares in a company owning real estate are transferred or are united in a single hand (just as an explanation: it applies also in the case of individuals). The taxable value is calculated under a special formula because no specific sales price is established for the real estate individually. Similarly, this tax is due when 95 percent or more of the capital shares in a land-owning partnership change hands over a five-year period. Real estate transfer tax is part of the costs of acquisition of real estate and is therefore to be capitalized. This real estate transfer tax is immediately deductible as a business expense where levied as to a reconstruction or when partnership shares change hands, because neither of these two instances are acquisitions in the accounting sense.

7.4 HIGHLIGHTS OF THE TAX REFORM 2001

(a) Key Features in the M & A Context

German tax reform reduced effective tax rates. The benefits achieved with the tax reform 2001 marks the first fundamental reform measures for many years. The German Bundestag, the Parliament, adopted the tax reform for 2001 on July 6, 2000, based on the results of the mediation procedure achieved on July 4, 2000. On July 14, 2000, the German Bundesrat, the Council of States, also approved the Act of the Reduction of Tax Rates and the Reform of Taxation of Business Income. See Exhibit 7.3.

The tax reform package included significant tax cuts for both corporations and individuals and was a radical overhaul of the tax regimes, applying to dividends and capital gains. The German tax reform is consistent with recent tax reforms in other countries in its attempt to reduce tax rates and simultaneously increase the tax base of corporations and individuals.

(b) Curtailing the Imputation System

The split-rate system for corporation tax (30 percent on distributed profits and 40 percent on retained earnings) has been replaced by a uniform rate of 25 percent.

7.4 Highlights of the Tax Reform 2001

This 25 percent rate replaces the 40 percent flat corporate income tax rate, which currently applies for a branch or partnership interest of a foreign corporate investor. The top individual income tax rates will be lowered in steps to ultimately 42 percent in 2005.

Exhibit 7.3

GERMAN TAX REFORM 2001

German tax rates (2001)	
Income tax—top rate	48.5%
Corporation tax	25.0%
Solidarity levy	5.5%
Trade tax	13 to 20%
Land tax	1 to 2%
Inheritance and gift tax	7 to 50%
VAT	16% / 7%/ 0
Real estate transfer tax	3.5%
Combined tax burden (assuming 18 % trade tax)	
German branch	39.6%
Corporation (without dividend withholding taxes)	39.6%
With 5% dividend withholding tax (e.g. to U.S.)	42.6%

The most fundamental tax change relates to the taxation of corporations and their shareholders. The previous imputation tax system has been replaced by a so-called half-income tax system. Under the new provisions, the double taxation of distributed profits inherent in a classical corporation tax system will be avoided.

The final burden on the corporation is 25 percent of its profits, the corporation tax rate. Germany taxes individual shareholders on one-half of dividends actually received through the "dividend received deduction" mechanism. Correspondingly, only 50 percent of the expenses relating to the income described previously are tax deductible. Corporate shareholders will not be taxed on any dividends received as a "dividend exemption."

(c) Capital Gains

From an M & A perspective, the most important changes that took place affected the taxation of capital gains. Following the principles for the taxation of dividends, the government introduced a full capital gains exemption for corporate shareholders selling shares in German or foreign corporations. The government applies the half-income scheme for the taxation of capital gains for individuals.

Under the new legislation, the exemption will generally apply to capital gains recognized from 2002 onward. Moreover, the Council of States (*Bundesrat*) has passed another resolution calling on the federal government to supplement the reform with an additional law providing further tax relief, in particular to small and medium-sized entities (so-called *Steuerergänzungsgesetz* dated December 1, 2000). As part of this process, the so-called half-average tax rate, which was abolished in 1999, has been reintroduced for certain capital gains realized by entrepreneurs retiring from their partnership or sole proprietorship business. See Exhibit 7.4.

Exhibit 7.4

TAX RATES

	2000	2001	2003	2005
Individual income tax (maximum)	51%	48.5%	47%	42%
Corporation tax for German resident corporations	40% (repatriation)		25%	
	30% (distribution)			
Corporation tax for German non-resident corporations (German branches of foreign corporations)	40%		25%	
Solidarity surcharge	5.5%			
Trade tax	13–20%			

(d) Impact of Tax Reform

In summary, the 2001 Tax Reform Act has created a new M & A tax planning world. The changes of this tax reform package, in particular with respect to the taxation of capital gains, has an important influence on the strategies of those selling businesses. The new framework would do the following:

- Provide a preferential capital gains tax regime (full or partial) and therefore reduce the attractiveness of an asset deal.
- Eliminate former asset step-up models (e.g., internal asset deal model or the conversion model).
- Initiate a trend to organize business ventures as corporate entities in order to benefit from the aforementioned capital gains tax regime.

In general, the government took from the buyer and gave to the seller. Therefore, the timing of transactions will become a major issue to structure deals from a tax perspective in order to benefit from the new regime. The detailed consequences of the tax reform on structuring transactions in Germany will be discussed in following sections.

7.5 REVISED TAX CONSOLIDATION REQUIREMENTS (*ORGANSCHAFT*)

A German domestic business (corporation or partnership—parent), as controlling shareholder, rather than receiving dividends from the German subsidiary, can elect to have the subsidiary's income taxed to the parent rather than in the subsidiary (so-called *Organschaft,* Section 14 and 17 CTA). In order to achieve tax consolidation between a German subsidiary and its domestic parent company (or other business entity) for trade tax and VAT purposes, the legislation requires the subsidiary to be financially, economically, and organizationally integrated with its parent company.

The subsidiary meets the financial, economic, and organizational requirements by undertaking the following:

- *Financial integration:* If the parent company controls more than 50 percent of the voting rights of the subsidiary. Under previous law the minimum shareholding level could be met either by a direct or indirect holding but not by a combination of both. This "cumulation prohibition" has been dropped in the 2001 Tax Reform Act.
- *Organizational integration:* If the will of the dominant enterprise is carried out in the management of the controlled company, e.g., by identity of management in the parent company and in the subsidiary, strict group management guidelines, or via a management and control agreement *Beherrschungsvertrag* under German corporate law.
- *Economic integration:* If the parent company is engaged in a trade or business or carries on management functions. Where the parent company is merely a holding company, business integration is deemed to require as a minimum that the parent holds investments in at least two active companies. It is not necessary that both are members of the *Organschaft.* In particular, one of the companies could be a foreign company. However, it must be apparent that the parent is managing its investments as opposed to playing a passive role.

As a result of the tax reform, for German corporate tax purposes, the subsidiary must demonstrate financial integration with nothing more; however, so far it is still mandatory that the subsidiaries conclude a profit and loss pooling agreement. It should be noted that the *Organschaft* rules are currently under review by a working group of the German Ministry of Finance, so changes are expected this year.

7.6 TIGHTENING OF THIN CAPITALIZATION RULES

Germany limits shareholder debt financing by loan capital. These limits are set by statutory and other restrictions on the tax deductibility of interest. After various unsuccessful attempts, the government enacted shareholder debt financing regulations in 1993 (Section 8a CTA). The basic rule is that interest and similar payments by a German company to its shareholders are hidden distributions of profit where the following occurs:

- The charges are made by a more-than-25 percent shareholder, by a related party, or by a third party with recourse. This recourse structure covers, in particular, back-to-back financing and guarantees.
- The shareholder or other entity receiving the interest payment is not itself subject to German income or corporation tax. This relationship includes foreign companies holding their German shares through a German permanent establishment or partnership, and therefore filing corporation tax returns as limited—nonresident—taxpayers.
- Where specified debt-equity ratios are exceeded. The specified debt is the total amount owing to the shareholders covered by these rules. Equity is based on the balance sheet at the beginning of the year, including profits and capital reserves/minus book value of investments in case of operating companies.

(a) Tax Reform Provisions

The government has used the tax reform to tighten the thin capitalization rules despite the overall effect of the tax reform of significantly reducing the tax advantages of financing a German operation through loan as opposed to equity capital. The formal wording of Section 8a CTA has been amended to take account of the abolition of the imputation system. In substance, the freedom of the German management to finance its operations through shareholder or related-party loans has been reduced by lowering the debt-equity ratio from 3:1 to 1.5:1. For holding companies, the reduction has been from 9:1 to 3:1. The safe haven for loan interest based on factors such as gross revenue or profits has been abolished altogether. See Exhibit 7.5

Exhibit 7.5

PERMISSIBLE EQUITY STRUCTURES

Debt-to-equity ratios	until 2000	after tax reform 2001
German holding company	9:1	3:1
German operating company	3:1	1.5:1
profit based or other non-fixed interest remuneration	0.5:1	0

(b) Thin Capitalization and Safe Harbors

Where shareholder loans, as defined earlier, exceed the applicable safe harbor, interest payable on the excess is disallowed for corporation tax purposes. The

7.6 Tightening of Thin Capitalization Rules

excess is treated as a deemed distribution. The thin capitalization rules do not apply for trade tax purposes. The 50 percent trade tax disallowance of interest applies whether a company is thinly capitalized or not.

The 3:1 and 1.5:1 ratios applicable to fixed interest financing are safe havens, rather than absolute limitations. This means that the tax authorities cannot automatically treat interest paid as a hidden distribution because ratios have been exceeded. The company has the opportunity to document that it could have obtained the financing on the same conditions from third parties.

(c) Holding Companies

Holding companies' 3:1 debt-equity ratio is a significant advantage. A holding company qualifies for the higher ratio if its main activity is owning and financing investments in other companies (but not in partnerships). Alternatively, the holding company can have investments in other companies that make up more than 75 percent of its gross assets, based on its balance sheet at the end of the previous business year. Such a holding company can incur significantly more debt from its foreign shareholders than could an operating subsidiary, which it can then distribute among its subsidiaries as needed. The subsidiaries are not subject to the debt-equity ratios because they have borrowed from a German company rather than from the foreign parent directly.

(d) Thin Capitalization

Loans from third parties do not in general come within the scope of the thin capitalization rules of Section 8a CTA; however, loans are deemed to be shareholder loans if the third party (e.g., the bank) has recourse to the shareholder or a back-to-back financing arrangement (i.e., the shareholder loan is routed to the German company through a bank) is in place. The German tax authorities generally have the view that a loan taken up by the German subsidiary is always backed by the parent company and therefore has to be included in the shareholder loan calculation. This issue needs to be discussed as to specific cases on "third-party test" if the thin capitalization limits are exceeded. However, based on an administrative ruling, loans from a German bank or the German branch of a foreign bank to a German subsidiary do not fall under the rules of Section 8a CTA, where these loans are guaranteed by an affiliated group company, assuming that no back-to-back loan is in place.

Many inbound investors set up a domestic holding company or consider escaping the rules altogether by having a partnership structure in order to allow for a maximum gearing under the new limitations. Further planning may include debt pushdown strategies. A German holding company may purchase other German or non-German group companies for debt, making use of the interest deduction within the given debt-equity safe harbors, to shelter other German operating income from being taxed. There are no thin capitalization rules for partnerships under current law; however, the financing of a German partnership requires careful planning as well.

7.7 EFFECTIVE TAX RELIEF FOR FINANCING COSTS

Two of the most important decisions in any acquisition are

- Whether debt or equity is used at the level of the acquiror/acquisition vehicle
- Where debt is placed

The decision is typically based on the following considerations of the tax arbitrage and the tax capacity in the respective jurisdictions. Given the 40 percent tax burden in Germany, any inbound investor would be inclined to finance acquisitions with debt if the interest could be deducted against German income. This can be achieved by undertaking the following:

- Establishing an acquisition vehicle in Germany
- Funding the acquisition vehicle with loan capital
- Offsetting operating profits of the target company against the interest expenses of the acquisition vehicle

(a) Interest Deduction

Interest charged to a German subsidiary by its foreign parent or a related party is generally a tax-deductible expense as long as the related-party debt falls within the limits of the German debt-equity rules (Sec. 8a CTA); however, such interest will often fall under the definition of "long-term" within the trade tax rules, with the result that only one-half of the interest is deductible expense for trade tax.

As a rule, interest can be paid abroad free of any withholding tax. Thus, where a foreign shareholder or related party grants a loan to the German subsidiary, the total tax burden will correspond to the taxes levied abroad on the interest income together with German trade tax on one-half of the interest amount. This burden contrasts with equity finance for which no interest can be charged or deducted, which thus—put simply—substitutes foreign taxation with German taxation. Loan finance is thus generally preferable in those cases where the German overall effective burden is higher than that of the foreign company.

(b) Dividend Issues

German tax law changed the taxation of dividends. The following issues need to be monitored carefully when a German acquires domestic or foreign target companies due to the changes in taxation of dividends. Under the new regime, intercorporate dividends are in general tax-exempt, irrespective of shareholding and holding periods. Under Section 3c paragraph 1 ITA, expenses in connection with tax-exempt income are generally deductible only insofar as they exceed the exempt income. Therefore, under current rules, a domestic corporate shareholder of a German company generally cannot deduct any costs or expenses that are directly connected with such tax-free dividend income. Planning tools to avoid this lack of expense deduction include the following:

7.7 Effective Tax Relief for Financing Costs

- *Tax consolidation:* A fiscal unity (*Organschaft*) allows a full deduction for the financing costs, for example, since the transfer of the profit is not regarded as a dividend. An *Organschaft* requires a majority of the voting rights in the controlled company.
- *Ballooning:* Costs in connection with tax-exempt income should be deductible to the extent that the costs exceed the relevant tax-free dividend or capital gain received in the same year. As such, the timing of the incidence of income and expense should be planned so that they fall in different periods.

(c) Foreign Dividends

Foreign dividends received by German corporations will, under the new German tax system, be free from German tax regardless of any double tax treaty. This general exemption is independent of the level of shareholding, the activities of the foreign company, or the extent of the holding period. In contrast to the rules applicable to domestic-source dividends, the nondeductible, directly related costs are defined as being a flat percentage of 5 percent of the relevant dividend (Section 8b paragraph 5 CTA). Consequently, all financing and stewardship costs exceeding this amount will therefore be deductible. If there are no such costs, 5 percent of the dividend effectively becomes taxable income. Interestingly, this 5 percent rule does not apply to the tax-free gain on the sale of the foreign investment.

When a German company owns both domestic and foreign shareholdings, but cannot form an *Organschaft,* its overall German tax situation will benefit to the extent its domestic holdings are financed out of its own equity. This would leave its loan capital as the financing source for those investments abroad. In individual cases, it might even be worth looking at forming an intermediary foreign holding company as an acquisition vehicle for a domestic investment as a means of avoiding most of the impact of the disallowance of the directly connected expenses. However, since Section 3 (1) ITA treats German-source income different from foreign-source income, it has been criticized by tax professionals and lobby groups. The Ministry of Finance is now reconsidering the issue, and it would not be a surprise if changes to Section 3c 1 ITA, or even its entire abolition, were to result.

(d) Financing Tax Relief

Following the abolition of capital taxes in Germany and the reduction under the 2001 Tax Reform Act of the German corporation tax rates, the foreign investor may need to reconsider the traditional recommendation of financing a German operation with loan capital to the maximum possible extent. Tax differentials in favor of foreign countries have progressively diminished. This change has correspondingly reduced the attraction of charging expense to a German subsidiary unless one can be sure that the rate at which corresponding income would be taxed abroad is and will remain lower.

7.8 ASSET STEP-UP

The acquiror has two ways of achieving an assets step-up: (1) an asset deal or (2) the acquisition of an interest in a partnership. In the case of the acquisition of a partnership, the acquiror is permitted to allocate hidden reserves to the respective assets in supplementary tax balance sheets and to claim the tax depreciation on these amounts. Hidden reserves are the difference between fair market value and book value of the asset. These amounts supplement to the acquiror's share of the profit or loss as shown by the financial statements.

Regarding the allocation of the hidden reserves to the respective assets, the goal should be to allocate as much as appropriate to the values of assets that have a shorter lifetime (e.g., inventory). The other tangible and intangible assets should be reviewed under the same approach, keeping in mind that land and shareholdings are normally not depreciable and buildings have a rather long depreciation period. Because know-how, patents, and so on have been created by the company itself and are normally expensed for tax purposes, these assets need to be identified and an amortization period, normally based on the lifetime/cycles of the intellectual property, should be determined. See Exhibit 7.6.

Exhibit 7.6

ACQUISITION COSTS

Expenses:

    Consulting fees, severance payments, covenant not to compete, inventory, and so forth.

Short-term amortization period

    Know how, car fleet, and so forth.

Medium-term amortization period

    Machinery, patents, and so on.

Long-term amortization period

    Goodwill, brand name, buildings, and so on.

Not depreciable or only in the case of sale or extraordinary write-down

    land, shareholdings, and so on.

(a) Goodwill

Under German tax law, goodwill can be amortized over 15 years. It is the general rule that first tangible assets and other intangible assets have to be stepped up to fair market value. The additional amount is then allocated to and amortized as goodwill; however, in the case of a pure share deal, the hidden reserves (including goodwill) are reflected in the higher outside value of the company. The step-up cannot therefore be utilized because shares in a company are generally not amortizable.

(b) Intellectual Property

In the high-tech environment of today, intellectual property is typically an asset that needs to be identified because intellectual property is normally amortizable over a shorter lifetime than goodwill. The taxpayer should make sure that intellectual property is migrated to the most effective location from a business, tax, and legal point of view. Germany is not a typical jurisdiction for license companies because the royalty income is taxed at standard rates. The decision is often made to transfer the intellectual property to a lower taxing jurisdiction. From a tax point of view, in these cases the taxpayer should ensure that a treaty location is chosen in order to reduce the statutory withholding tax rate on royalties and the risk of constituting a permanent establishment.

(c) Noncompetition Payments

A payment for a covenant not to compete is tax deductible only if an agreement expressly specifies the details regarding term, penalties, and so on. The tax authorities will often challenge such a payment as a deduction over the term of the agreement but will rather include the payment in the goodwill position if not specifically agreed upon in the agreement, e.g., regarding the term, scope, penalties.

(d) Asset Deal: Acquisition Costs/Purchase Price Allocation

The acquisition of shares in a company results in a step-up of the outside value but not in a step-up in the values of the underlying assets. Before the 2001 Tax Reform, a tax-neutral step-up could be achieved at least for corporate tax purposes by converting a company into a partnership. This scheme was sacrificed by the government when introducing the new capital gains taxation regime. Of course, tax planners are thinking about devices to come up with asset step-ups in share deals even after the introduction of the new law. Yet none of these ideas are risk-free or have yet been tested by tax audit. These devices include for example, downstream mergers or the hybrid character of a KGaA.

7.9 POOLING OF PROFITS AND LOSSES

The acquisition pattern for a German investment typically includes the interposition of a German acquisition vehicle in order to push debt into Germany. The taxpayer has to take measures to pool these expenses with the profits of the target company and/or with those of any other German subsidiaries to effectively utilize the financing costs incurred by the holding company.

Under the old imputation tax credit regime, the blending of tax rate could be achieved for corporation tax purposes through dividend distributions. In this case, the corporation tax paid by the targets/subsidiaries was refunded to the parent company if the NOLs covered the dividend and its imputation tax credit. Under the old regime, this saving technique did not work for trade tax purposes because there was already an exemption system for dividends. This technique now no longer works for corporation tax either, because domestic dividends are now exempt. As a result, the directly related financing costs would generally not be deductible by the parent company. This problem can be solved by implementing an *Organschaft,* a tax pooling within Germany in order to offset financing costs of the holding company against the operating profits of the target.

In the case of an acquisition, the following issues need to be planned carefully:

- The integration criteria need to be in place from the beginning of the financial year of the subsidiary. If it is not possible to change the financial year, there is normally a tax consolidation leakage for an interim period until the criteria can be met. The change of the financial year generally needs to be approved by the tax authorities if an interim financial year is chosen. The new tax year needs to be supported by business reasons, such as adjusting to the financial year of the parent company.
- There may be no other activities in the vehicle than the holding of the target company. In that event, an investment of a second company needs to be transferred to the parent company in order to qualify for the economic integration test. This second company does not have to be part of the *Organschaft* and can be, for example, a foreign company.
- The profits of a subsidiary are automatically transferred to the parent company under the profit and loss pooling agreement. The profits must be actually paid over or converted into a loan in the course of the following financial year for the *Organschaft* to be acceptable for tax purposes. This issue needs to be kept in mind if, for example, tax planning schemes, such as "check the box" rules, are used where the parent company is treated as a transparent entity for U.S. tax purposes. In this case, measures have to be taken to qualify the profit transfer as stock dividend to avoid adverse U.S. tax consequences.

7.10 AVOIDING OR MINIMIZING REAL ESTATE TRANSFER TAX

Real estate transfer tax is the only transaction tax of overall planning importance to most companies. Its primary object of minimizing real estate transfer tax is the purchase of real estate including the buildings standing thereon. Tax minimization encompasses other transactions of similar economic effect, such as the grant or sale of a long-lease for a premium or the purchase of buildings standing on a site owned by someone else.

Real estate transfer tax is imposed on changes in the ownership of companies or partnerships that own German real estate. Real estate transfer tax is levied when at least 95 percent of the partnership shares change hands over a five-year period. Changes in indirect or ultimate ownership are sufficient for this tax to fall due; however, the converse does not apply. That is, the transfer of 95 percent of the shares in a partnership held by one group company to, say, its own parent within a wholly owned group structure would still trigger this tax.

The transfer of shares in a company that owns German real estate triggers the real estate transfer tax when either 95 percent of the shares change hands or when 95 percent of the shares fall for the first time directly or indirectly under common ownership. By contrast to the rules for partnerships, there is no five-year or any other period within which a series of transfers are treated collectively. Thus it is feasible to transfer 100 percent of the shares in a company without raising a charge to the tax—the transfer must merely be made under separate agreements with different parties.

The Real Estate Transfer Tax Act provides relief to the taxpayer from a multiple charge to this tax when ultimate ownership of the real estate is transferred under various titles. Thus the government provides relief when the entire share capital of a company owning real estate falls to a single owner, who then assumes the direct ownership in the real estate by merging the acquired company into its own business. On the other hand, there is no corresponding relief for multiple instances of taxation on multiple transactions of the same type. Thus, the acquisition of 95 percent or more of the share capital in a company owning real estate by a subsidiary company followed by a sale of the 100 percent investment in the subsidiary within the group will lead to the tax being charged twice.

7.11 SAFEGUARDING EXISTING TAX ATTRIBUTES

Both an asset and a share deal can jeopardize existing tax attributes of the target business. The most obvious example is the preservation of loss carryforwards in case of a share deal. A corporation is allowed a one-year carryback limited to DM 1 million or about 571,292 € only for corporate tax purposes and an unlimited carryforward. However, the use of NOLs may be restricted under specific loss limitation rules.

(a) Transfer of Shares

Section 8 paragraph 4 CTA introduces a restriction on loss relief in the case of a direct or indirect transfer of more than 50 percent of a company's shares. Section 8 denies loss relief in cases where the profitable business is seen as having a different "identity" from that which originally made the loss. The avowed purpose of this restriction was to curb the purchase and sale of companies whose only asset was a tax loss; however, present practice seems to show that many laudable and genuine attempts to save failing businesses can be penalized. It is important to emphasize that the definition of "common business identity" is restrictive rather than exhaustive. In general, loss relief is denied where both the following conditions are fulfilled:

- More than 50 percent of the shares in the company change hands.
- The company continues or resumes its business with mainly new assets.

Transfer of more than 50 percent of the shares does not have to occur as a single act; however, if it does not, the individual share transfers should be seen as occurring within the same temporal context. This is assumed wherever the ownership of more than 50 percent of the issued share capital is transferred during the course of a five-year period.

The business will be deemed to have continued or resumed "mainly" with new assets whenever new assets of more than the gross assets (balance sheet assets total) at the time the shares were transferred are contributed to the company by the shareholders or are acquired from the proceeds of (related or third-party) finance. As with the transfer of the shares, an increase can occur during the five-year period. Intangible assets as well as hidden reserves (e.g. off-balance sheet goodwill or appreciation in value of real estate) should be taken into account in this respect, even where the relevant items cannot be taken up in the financial statements. Once a company has lost its "economic identity" under this definition, it has no way of reviving the loss relief that has been cancelled.

An injection of assets solely for the purpose of restoring solvency is not harmful. The additional assets must benefit that business from which the loss arose. The business must be carried on a similar scale for a further five years. Any denial of the right to carry forward losses applies to the entire remaining loss and carries forward at the time the denial takes effect. Conversely, losses utilized in the period between the times that the first and second of the two conditions were met will not be retroactively cancelled.

(b) Merger of Companies

In principle, a respective set of rules applies for the merger of a company that has loss carryforward (Sec. 12 Paragraph 3 RTA)

(c) Partnerships

A partnership has to own NOLs for trade tax, but not for corporation tax; however, a change of ownership usually leads to annulment of that part of the trade tax NOL represented by investment from new partners.

(d) Other aspects

Other special tax rules like special depreciation allowances, tax-exempt subsidies, and incentives can be endangered if the respective requirements to apply them are not checked. This is relevant to all forms of the special tax regime and needs to be pursued in respect of all other incentives and subsidies granted by federal, state, or municipal authorities.

7.12 MINIMIZATION OF WITHHOLDING TAXES

Interest payments in general are not subject to German withholding tax. This interest has the additional advantage of reducing the tax base in Germany. The

7.12 Minimization of Withholding Taxes

debt financing of German investments is a straight-forward way of optimizing the withholding tax planning in Germany.

Hybrid finance instruments, i.e., finance instruments that qualify as debt instruments in one jurisdiction but are characterized as equity under the tax law of the other country, can possibly provide a tax deduction in Germany based on the benefits abroad of an equity investment; however, the statutory withholding tax rate that is attached to profit-related loan instruments (normally the case for hybrids) will not be reduced under some significant treaties like the U.S. treaty. Hybrid financial instruments also have a negative aspect because profit-related instruments do not qualify for a safe harbor under the German thin capitalization rules.

The statutory rate in Germany for withholding tax from dividend distributions is 20 percent; however, in an international context, this withholding tax rate is generally reduced by treaties, especially in Europe by the EU Parent-Subsidiary Directive. Within the EU, dividend distributions in general are not subject to withholding tax if a shareholding of at least 10 percent and a 12-month holding period is met. In contrast, the withholding tax under the treaties is normally reduced to 5 to 15 percent.

In order to counteract any treaty (or directive) shopping, an exemption from German taxation or reduction in German taxation does not apply when specific situations apply. Nonapplication applies when the income that is otherwise subject to tax is received by an interposed corporation in a country that is an EU Member State or has a double tax treaty with Germany, and where the following occurs:

- The shareholders of the interposed corporation would not have been entitled to German tax relief if they had received the income in question directly.
- There are no business or other good reasons for the existence or incorporation of the interposed company.
- The interposed company does not carry out any business activities of its own.

German tax authorities are believed to apply these anti-treaty shopping rules not only for withholding taxes but to all claims under a treaty; however, in practice, the German tax authorities principally apply these provisions to withholding tax on dividends and royalties. No official guidance is available, but the German tax authorities appear to look through an ownership chain until they find a claimant who does not fail the Section 50d Income Tax Act test based on the criteria listed earlier. The treaty entitlement (if there is a treaty) then applies.

The partnership/branch route can be a viable option to reduce withholding tax because under current German tax law no branch profits tax exists. Because the corporation tax rate is now a uniform rate of 25 percent, these alternatives are now advantageous when no EU parent company provides for a 0 percent withholding tax.

7.13 TAX-EFFECTIVE EXIT ROUTES

With respect to exit taxation, what is "highway of exit taxation"? Several routes potentially apply when implementing a deal structure. It is important for strategic investors to have flexibility to reorganize the business or to restructure the business for an initial public offering (IPO) or other form of divestment but also for private equity investors who usually need to foresee an exit strategy in their basic planning.

(a) Foreign Investors

Foreign investors who are resident in a treaty jurisdiction and who hold an investment in a German company are protected from German capital gains taxation under the rules of most German treaties (see Article 13 OECD Treaty), which grant the right to tax only to the jurisdiction of the shareholder. Special exceptions sometimes apply to real estate companies, e.g., Double Tax Treaty [DTT] United States, Canada and other special cases.

The foreign investor may hold more than 1 percent of the shares in a German company and there may be no protection under the treaty. In that event, the capital gain is taxed in Germany at standard income/corporation tax rates plus the solidarity surcharge. Therefore, the interposition of legal corporate entities, which are tax resident in treaty countries, is a route to protect later proceeds from capital gains tax in Germany.

(b) Capital Gains

The law stipulates that the tax exemption for capital gains of corporate entities under Section 8b CTA should also apply to foreign corporations that hold an investment in Germany, not only through a German branch but directly. If this interpretation is confirmed by the German tax authorities, it will not be necessary to interpose treaty jurisdictions because corporate investors in nontreaty countries, (i.e., tax havens) would be shielded from German taxation on capital gains tax by German statute law.

In the case of the sale of a German partnership, the double tax treaty leaves the tax authorities with the right to tax an eventual gain with the jurisdiction where the permanent establishment is located (Article 7 and 23 OECD Treaty), i.e., Germany. However, if the assets of the partnership include investments in companies, the foreign partners should also benefit from the new tax regime, i.e., the respective part of the capital gain should be tax-exempt in the case for corporate and taxable assets to only one-half for individual investors.

7.14 TAX OBJECTIVES OF THE VENDOR

The general principle for the seller is to maximize its proceeds from the sale, (i.e., to reduce the costs of the transaction where taxes are in general the most important factor). Following the recent changes to capital gains taxation, there is

7.15 Sale of Shares in Companies

generally a clear argument from a tax point of view to sell shares of a company rather than to offer an asset deal, giving the acquiror the benefit of a direct step-up of the target company's assets. A seller would therefore offer an asset deal if the purchaser would compensate the seller for the additional tax burden. Otherwise, an asset deal is likely to be a viable option only if the seller, or the selling company, has NOLs that can be utilized. An asset deal is more complex than a share deal from a legal perspective because all the assets, liabilities, contracts, and employees have to be transferred under individual succession principles.

7.15 SALE OF SHARES IN COMPANIES

Apart from the special case of shares issued in the course of corporate reconstructions, capital gains realized by natural persons on the sale of shares held in German or foreign companies are taxable only when the shareholding could be seen as speculative or when the shareholding ranked as a significant investment. Gains on the sale of securities are seen as speculative when the sale is no later than one year from the date of purchase. A taxable gain on the sale of a significant investment is deemed to have arisen under the redrafted Section 17 (1) ITA. This situation arises whenever the taxpayer sells shares of a company in which the shareholder directly or indirectly held 1 percent or more of the issued share capital at any time during the immediately preceding five years. However, only one-half of the gain realized is actually charged as tax under the half-income method, if taxable at all.

(a) Reduction in the Level of "Significant" Investments

The reduction in the level of "significant" investments (from 10 percent or more to 1 percent or less) greatly increases the scope of taxation of long-term gains from the sale of shares by private individuals. This will now become the rule for smaller companies. This widening of the exposure to taxation takes place because the lower tax burden on retained earnings would tempt shareholders to accumulate corporate earnings with a view to subsequent realization through tax-free capital gains. When closing this loophole, the government has accepted further restrictions on the fundamental exemption from taxation of value increases of privately held assets.

The German government imposes the reduced level of "significant" investments for the first time in the year 2002, assuming that the company that issued the shares has a calendar year-end. If, however, the company's year-end is different from the calendar year, the date from which the new rules will be applied is advanced accordingly. Gains from the sale of 1 percent holdings in German companies with a business year ending on June 30, 2002, will, for example, be taxable from July 2002 onward. The position regarding investments in foreign companies is, at the time of this writing, still unclear because the act contains preconditions that a foreign company cannot meet. Indeed, it is possible that the new rules will be retroactively applied to foreign investments from January 1, 2001.

(b) Changing the Definition of "Significant" Investment

The extension of the definition of a "significant" investment from one of 10 percent to one of 1 percent will move into the tax net many individual investments previously held in the belief that any subsequent sale would be without income tax consequences. In retrospect, previously irrelevant value appreciation within the private sphere will have potentially serious tax consequences.

Taxable capital gains realized by private individuals from the sale of a "significant" holding are changed with one-half of taxable income under Section 3 No. 40c ITA. This one-half provision applies so as to not burden natural persons as shareholders with greater tax obligations on the sale of their shares than they would have borne had they taxed dividends under the half-income method. This one-half provision applies to short-term gains from speculation (Sec. 23 ITA) and to gains on the sale of shares held as business assets by sole traders or partnerships.

On the other hand, losses, write-downs, and costs of disposal are deductible only as to one-half (Section 3c (2) ITA). As an exception, any extraordinary write-downs previously deducted from taxable income will be recaptured in full, whether by write-back to reflect a subsequent increase in value or as part of the capital gain on sale. Certain types of shares issued in the course of corporate reconstruction will qualify for only half-income taxation on disposal after a waiting period of seven years.

(c) Consequences of the Change in "Significant" Investment

The change in the law means that private persons wishing to sell shares from a "significant" investment under the previous definition (at least 10 percent) will be in a more favorable tax position if they can defer the realization of a capital gain until the advent of the half-income method in 2002. Conversely, it will be to their advantage to realize capital losses before December 31, 2001.

(d) Partnership Interest

Up to the end of 1998, gains from the sale of businesses, business units, partnership shares, and significant investments in corporations were taxed at reduced rates in the hands of natural persons, under certain conditions and within certain limits. The government abolished these partnership provisions as of January 1, 1999, for both systematic and revenue-raising reasons. The government replaced the partnership provisions that sought to relieve the harsh effects of taxing the entire accumulated hidden reserves in the year of realization. The government almost entirely eliminated that year's highest rate by means of a calculation emulating a spread of the gain over a five-year period.

After its debate on the Tax Reduction Bill on July 14, 2000, the *Bundesrat* formally requested the government to reintroduce the original system of favorable taxation, at least within limits and for the benefit of those about to retire. The government complied with this request in a supplementary act to the Tax Reduction Act. Under the new rules, profits from the sale of businesses or partnership shares will, on application, be taxed in the hands of a natural person who is older than 55 or who is a permanent invalid, at half the rate of income tax.

This half-rate of income tax would apply to taxable income consisting of the total of the entire actual taxable income for that year, together with tax-free income items such as those taken into account when determining the overall tax rate; however, the rate to be applied to these profits on disposal must be at least the lowest rate of income tax. The new rules are restricted to the first DM 10 million or approximately 5,113 million ϵ of taxable gain and may only be applied to any one taxpayer once in his or her lifetime starting from the 2001 year of assessment (Sec. 34 (3)ITA).

7.16 SHARES IN CORPORATIONS

Capital gains are not taken as taxable income when the gain arises from the sale of shares in a domestic or foreign corporation held by a domestic corporation or as an asset of the German permanent establishment of a foreign corporation. Special provisions are expected to apply to banks and financial services companies regarding their current profits from trading in securities. There are no minimum levels of shareholding and no business activity restrictions.

The tax exemption applies from the year 2002; however, if the company in which the shares were held has a noncalendar year-end, the initial application of Section 8B (2) CTA will be delayed accordingly. The converse of this fundamental exemption of capital gains on the sale of shares from taxation is, of course, that corresponding losses or write-downs will no longer be deductible. Thus, other things being equal, a German corporation planning on selling its investments will have an interest in closing negotiations so as to be able to realize losses (or write-downs) in 2001 and gains not before 2002.

The sale of partnership shares is generally subject to corporation tax but, based on a 1998 Supreme Tax Court decision, the sale of partnership shares is not subject to trade tax. However, the capital gain realized on the sale of the interest in the partnership should not be subject to corporation tax insofar as the gain relates to an appreciation in value of investments in companies held by partnerships.

7.17 CONSIDERATIONS APPLICABLE TO ALL SELLERS

The capital gains treatment is not lost where the investment is indirectly held through a partnership (Sec. 8b (6) CTA). Under an anti-abuse provision, the tax exemption or half-income method for capital gains from the sale of shares issued by a subsidiary will not be granted during the first seven years after the reconstruction in exchange for a tax-free contribution of a business unit. This provision tends to put companies with multiple business lines or branches at a disadvantage over corporate groups As such, German corporations might consider enhancing their freedom of action for the future by reconstituting their individual business units and partnership holdings as subsidiaries. This can be done free of tax as asset dropdowns under the Reconstruction Tax Act.

7.18 INBOUND ACQUISITIONS INTO GERMANY

This remaining portion of the chapter describes acquisition alternatives concerning the acquisition of a German Target GmbH by a foreign investor (US/UK). Here we provide a general overview about the German tax issues but do not provide a full listing of all possible alternatives. Every case needs to be considered in light of the individual facts and circumstances.

It is assumed that Target GmbH is held by its German parent D-GmbH. The German transaction is part of a worldwide deal. In order to push debt down to Germany and for various other reasons, the parties conclude a separate sales contract between D-GmbH and the purchaser.

(a) Asset Deal: Foreign Parent Acquires German Business

In the first scenario, the foreign parent company acquires the assets of target GmbH, resulting in a German branch of the foreign headquarters. See Exhibit 7.7.

Exhibit 7.7

ASSET DEAL THROUGH A GERMAN BRANCH

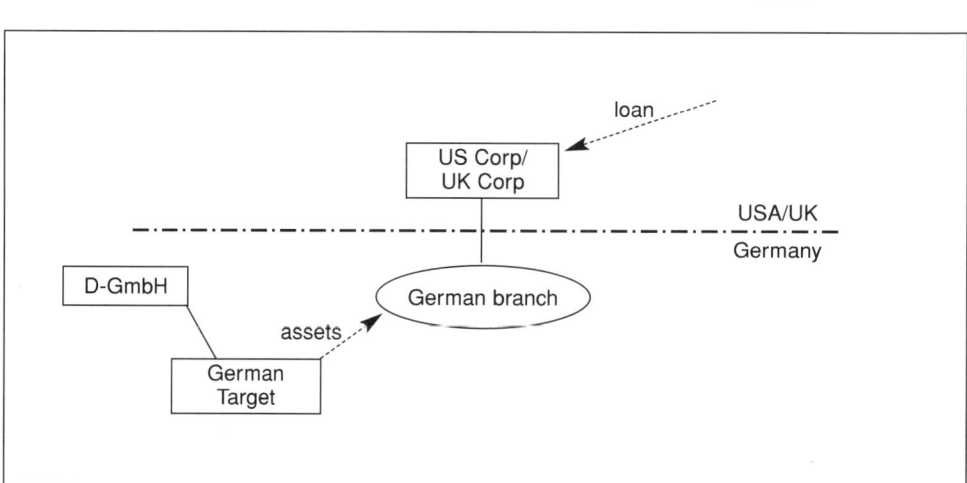

Interest payments incurred by the foreign investor in connection with the acquisition in Germany are tax deductible for German tax purposes. These interest payments might also be deductible for foreign tax purposes. Furthermore, no debt-equity ratio has to be considered because there are no formal thin capitalization provisions for branches. Because there is no branch profits tax under German tax law, profits can be repatriated without withholding tax. Moreover, the purchase price can be transformed into depreciable assets in Germany. However, capital gains from the future disposal of the tangible and intangible assets will be taxable in Germany.

7.18 Inbound Acquisitions into Germany

From the perspective of the seller, an asset deal will not be the preferred route under new law because the sales of shares would be tax exempt. In contrast, the sale of the assets is subject to standard tax rates. Therefore, such a deal structure is only likely to be realistic in somewhat unusual circumstances, such as where the seller has higher and otherwise not immediately useful NOLs, or where the German target company was formed by a business unit within the past seven years.

Step-up:	Yes
Debt Pushdown:	Yes
Thin Cap Rules:	No
Double-Dip:	Yes
Withholding tax on branch profits:	No
Exit:	Taxable in Germany

(b) Foreign Partner Establishes German Partnership

In the next alternative, a foreign investor set up a German partnership with a second partner in the group purchasing the target's assets. See Exhibit 7.8.

Exhibit 7.8

ASSET DEAL THROUGH A GERMAN PARTNERSHIP

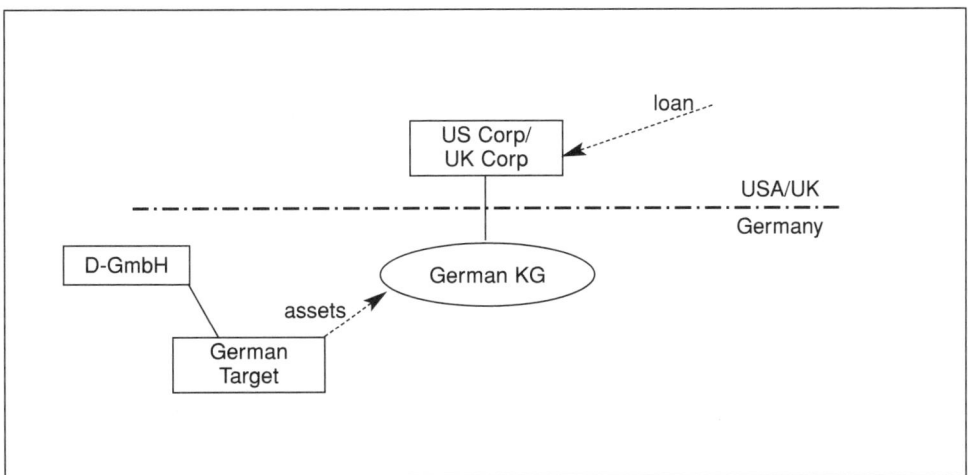

The interest expenses are deductible in Germany, both in the case where the loan is given directly to the partnership or where it is taken up by the partner to finance its partnership investment via an equity contribution. Both routes should also result in a double-dip because the interest expenses could also be deductible for foreign tax purposes. Under current law, there are no thin capitalization rules for partnerships. As in the first scenario, the asset deal will result in a step-up of the asset values. However, a later disposal of the partnership will be taxable in Germany from the standpoint of corporation tax only.

(c) Foreign Investor's German Subsidiary Acquires Assets

In the next alternative, a German subsidiary of the foreign investor acquires the target's assets. See Exhibit 7.9

Exhibit 7.9

ASSET DEAL THROUGH A GERMAN CORPORATION

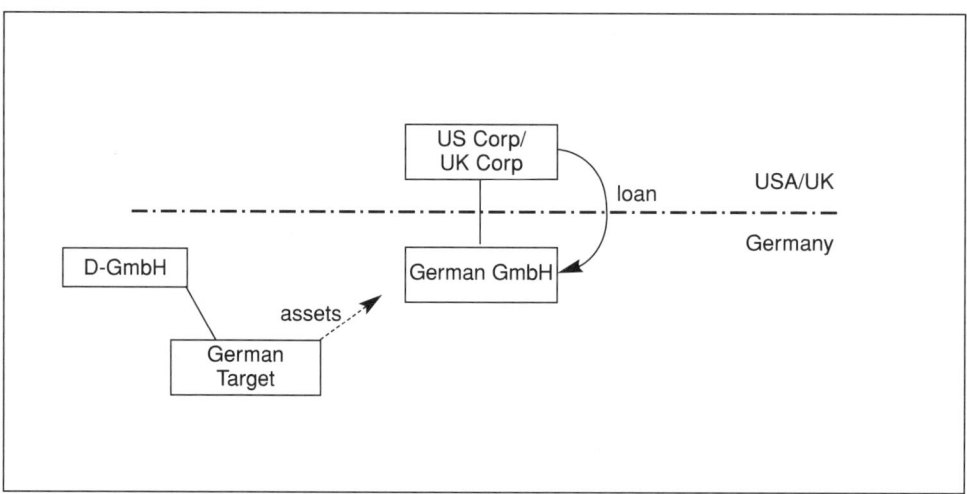

Germany allows a deduction of interest payments in connection with the acquisition in Germany and permits a transformation of the purchase price into depreciable assets. German corporation thin capitalization rules apply to the German GmbH, which require a 1.5:1 debt-equity ratio. Capital gains resulting from the future disposal of the acquired assets by German GmbH will be taxable in Germany; however, the disposal of GmbH's shares are not taxable. A U.S. investor can take additional advantage of the structure by using the "check-the-box" rules regarding the German GmbH.

Step-up:	Yes
Debt pushdown:	Yes
Thin cap rules:	Yes (1.5:1 debt-equity ratio)
Withholding tax on dividends:	US: 5% / UK: 0%
Exit:	Not taxable in Germany

7.19 PARTNERSHIP ACQUISITION

This section provides an overview of the German tax considerations regarding the acquisition of a partnership.

(a) Partnership Taxation Principles

Income earned by a foreign corporation directly investing in a German partnership is taxed under German law as though that corporation had maintained a German permanent establishment. The foreign corporation's partnership share is regarded as its German branch. After the 2001 Tax Reform, the corporate tax rate for a partner investing through a partnership has been reduced from 40 percent to the same 25 percent that also applies for German corporate entities. The overall tax burden is roughly 40 percent including trade tax and solidarity surcharge; however, there is no branch profits tax under current German law on profit distributions to its partners.

From a corporate tax point of view, the partnership is a conduit; however, the partnership is a taxpayer for trade tax purposes. This means that the partnership will first pay trade tax and then will be responsible for determining the taxable income to be allocated to each partner. The partnership is not responsible for making the actual corporate tax payments for each partner.

The partner in partnership in Germany is subject to special tax procedures. Expenses incurred by the partner in connection with its interest in the partnership are deductible. Such deductibles include, for example, costs of financing the investment or goodwill write-offs if the partnership interest was acquired for more than its nominal value. On the other hand, income allocated to the partnership to the partner (including loans, royalties, management charges and so forth) is treated as a profit distribution. These expenditures are only deductible in the financial accounts drawn up for the purposes of computing each partner's profit share. This additional set of income information must be reported by the partnership in its return of taxable income allocated to the partners in so-called supplementary balance sheets.

(b) Partnership Acquisition vs. Asset Deal

The seller generally prefers to sell the shares of the corporation because of the advantageous capital gains tax regime. A seven-year holding period applies. A reorganization of a partnership or a business into a corporate entity is typically not a viable option if a sale is currently planned because of this holding period. However, in comparing an assets deal with a sale of a partnership interest, in principle, a seller should be interested in organizing the assets to be sold in a partnership format.

The sale of interest in a partnership is not subject to trade tax under the current law. In order to avoid the trade tax burden, deals have been structured in which the respective business assets have been distributed in a partnership and then later sold; however, because the tax authorities are aware of this deal structure, they will try to challenge the deal if the timing of the dropdown and the subsequent sale is too aggressive (i.e., because there is no period of grace) and there is no business reason for the drop-down.

(c) Double-Dip Financing

In cross-border deals, the special partnership taxation concepts permit the financing of costs in connection with the partnership investment. This process opens the opportunity for "double-dipping" (i.e., paying once, deducting twice) as to the respective expenses. Expenses incurred at the partnership level in the foreign jurisdiction are treated as expenses in the partner's domestic tax return and reduce the taxable income deriving from the partnership for German tax purposes. The typical issues to deal with from a foreign tax perspective are the following:

- "Dual consolidated loss" rules provide that a taxpayer can use the same loss/expenses twice.
- Foreign tax credit issues: Due to the additional interest deduction in Germany, the respective foreign-source income carries only reduced foreign tax credits, which can eventually lead to a tax uplift. The tax paid in country A is "lifted up" to the tax rate in country B in the foreign jurisdiction.
- The other country applies the same concept or strictly disallows domestic expenses connected with foreign-source income.

Therefore, such a double-dip structure needs to be carefully reviewed from the point of view of foreign statutes. Double-dip structures may require detailed calculation as to the income impact and foreign tax credit position, (e.g., for U.S. and UK investors). However, these double-dip structures can be quite advantageous and significantly improve the return on the investment if the fact pattern fits.

(d) Acquisition of a Partnership

The foreign company borrows money and acquires a direct interest in the partnership. See Exhibit 7.10.

The acquisition of a partnership interest is treated as an asset deal for German tax purposes for both corporate tax and trade tax purposes. For financial statement purposes, the interest in the partnership will be sold (i.e., only the outside value in the partnership interest will increase), but book values of the underlying assets of the partnership will not be stepped-up to their fair market values. For financial reporting purposes, the depreciation of the assets in the accounts of the partnership will be only partial. A goodwill amortization would be captured only in consolidated financial statements.

7.20 Share Deals

Exhibit 7.10

ACQUISITION OF A PARTNERSHIP

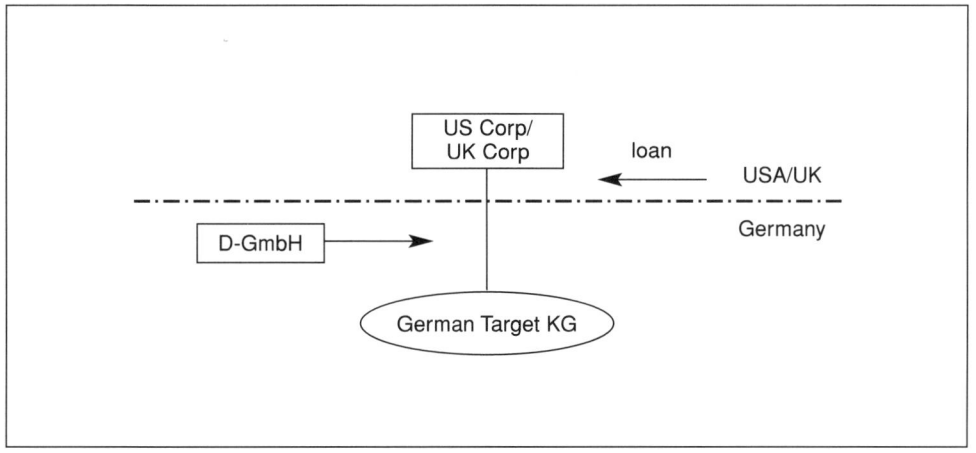

Partnerships under current law are not subject to thin capitalization rules. As such, the financing cost can generally be deducted without statutory limits, and these costs can perhaps be double-dipped. This alternative is advantageous from a financing perspective. However, capital gains from the future disposal of the acquired assets will be taxable in Germany for corporation tax purposes.

Step-up:	Yes
Debt Pushdown:	Yes
Thin Cap Rules:	No
Double-Dip:	Yes
Withholding tax on branch profits:	No
Exit:	Taxable in Germany

7.20 SHARE DEALS

(a) Foreign Corporate Borrowing

In the first alternative, the foreign company borrows and acquires the shares in the German target company. See Exhibit 7.11.

This loan-acquisition alternative is straight-forward, but it is not attractive from a pure tax point of view. In this alternative, the interest is deductible in the foreign jurisdiction, but not in Germany. The acquisition of the shares does not allow a step-up of the underlying assets. The advantage of this structure is the favorable exit route because the capital gain resulting from the sale of the shares would not be taxable in Germany.

Exhibit 7.11

FOREIGN COMPANY BORROWING

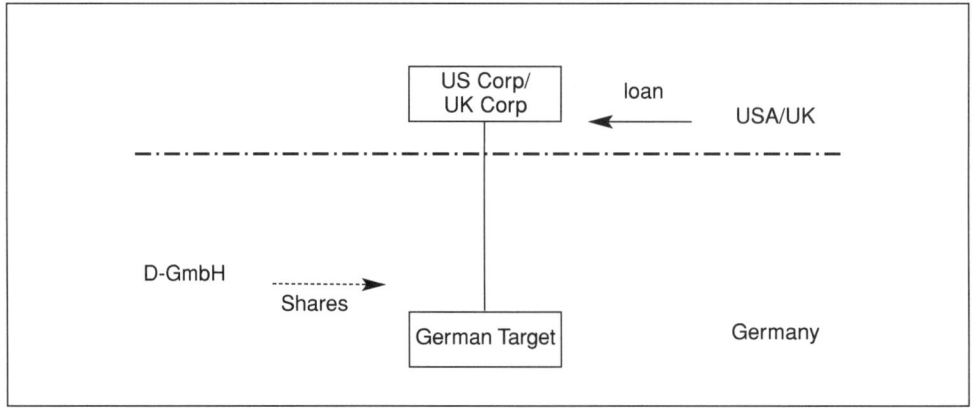

Step-up:	No
Debt Pushdown:	No
Thin Cap Rules:	N/A
Withholding Tax on Dividends:	US: 5% / UK: 0%
Exit:	Not taxable in Germany

(b) Using a German Company for the Acquisition

As a second alternative, the taxpayer should consider using a German company to acquire shares in the German target company. See Exhibit 7.12.

Because the foreign parent acquires the shares, the purchase price cannot be transformed into depreciable assets in Germany. Thin capitalization rules apply to the German GmbH. The debt-equity ratio is 1.5:1, but, in determining the equity, the book value of the investment in target has to be deducted (often leaving no room at all for gearing, or leveraging with debt).

Under the U.S. "check-the-box" rules, it should be possible to eliminate the interest income if the acquisition vehicle is treated as a disregarded hybrid entity. Operating profits of the German target can be offset by interest expenses of the fiscal unity parent, German GmbH (so-called *Organschaft*). An *Organschaft* arrangement is essential to avoid nondeductibility of finance expenses. If the acquisition vehicle is not an operating company, a second subsidiary needs to be added to fulfill the economic integration criteria for *Organschaft* purposes. This would also be helpful for German thin capitalization purposes, i.e., to qualify as a holding company. Under the tax reform 2001, future capital gains from the disposal of the shares in the German Target will be tax exempt for the acquisition vehicle, German GmbH, in Germany.

Exhibit 7.12

USING A GERMAN COMPANY

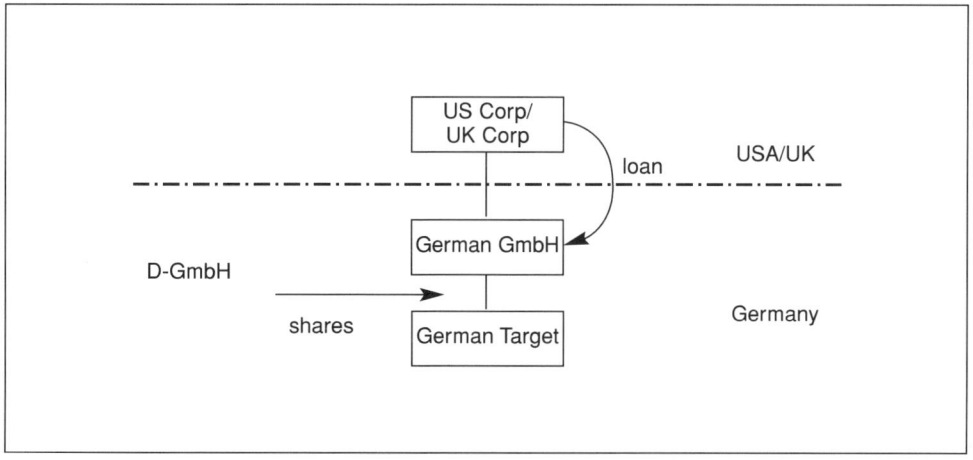

(c) Share Deal

A share deal is likely to be the preferred route for the seller because the capital gain resulting from the sales of the shares of target GmbH is tax exempt.

Step-up:	No
Debt Pushdown:	Yes
Thin Cap Rules:	Yes
Income Consolidation:	Yes
Withholding Tax on Dividends:	US: 5% / UK: 0%
Exit:	Not taxable in Germany

The acquisition vehicle holds shares in two companies in order to improve the thin capitalization position, thus becoming a holding company for thin capitalization purposes. See Exhibit 7.13.

Under the new legislation, capital gains from the future disposal of shares in the German target and the German GmbH by German holding GmbH will be tax exempt in Germany. The sales of the shares in the holding company would not be subject to German income taxation. By establishing a German fiscal unity between the German holding company and its subsidiaries, an offset of operating profits of German GmbH and German Target with interest expense by the fiscal unity parent, German Holding GmbH (so-called *Organschaft*) is possible. Moreover, an increased debt-equity ratio of 3:1 applies to the German holding company without any book value deductions when determining the equity of German Holding GmbH. As in any share deal, the purchase price cannot be transformed into depreciable assets in Germany.

Exhibit 7.13

SHARE DEAL THROUGH A GERMAN HOLDING COMPANY

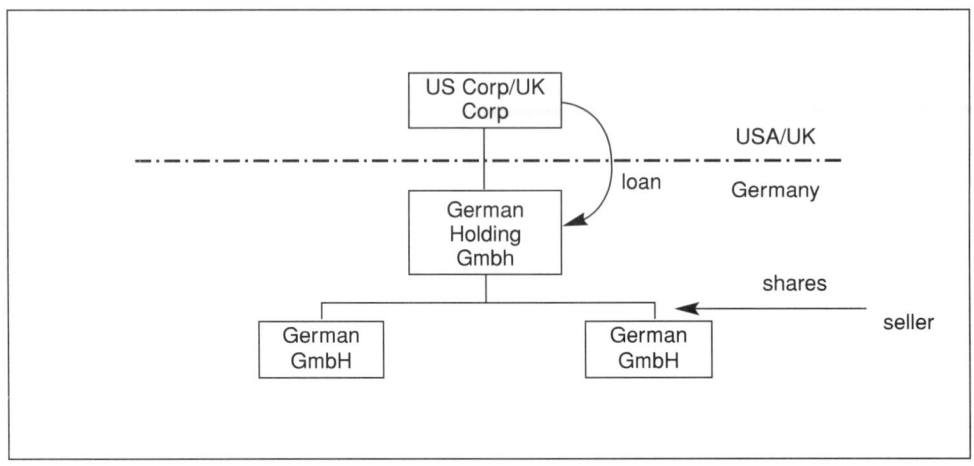

Step-up:	No
Debt Pushdown:	Yes
Thin Cap Rules:	Yes (but holding privilege 3:1 debt-equity ratio)
Income Consolidation:	Yes
Withholding Tax on dividends:	US: 5% / UK: 0%
Exit:	not taxable in Germany

In the last acquisition pattern described here, a German partnership (with two group partners) acts as an acquisition vehicle in a share deal. See Exhibit 7.14.

A double deduction of interest payments may be achievable by using this structure as under some of the previous alternatives. Interest payments on loans borrowed the by US/UK corporation are tax deductible in the US/UK. These interest payments are tax deductible in Germany because they relate to the investment in German KG. Furthermore, profit pooling is possible between German KG and German Target, e.g., through active business in German KG or by adding a second investment German GmbH to German KG.

Because the investment is through a German partnership, no thin capitalization limitations apply. Another benefit of this structure is that there are no withholding taxes on profit repatriations, which is less important for UK shareholders as a result of the EU Parent-Subsidiary Directive. No German corporation tax or trade tax will be triggered in case of disposal of the investment in German Target as German Target is owned indirectly by a corporate shareholder. It makes no difference whether the shareholder is domestic or foreign.

7.21 Deferral Instruments

Exhibit 7.14

SHARE DEAL THROUGH GERMAN PARTNERSHIP

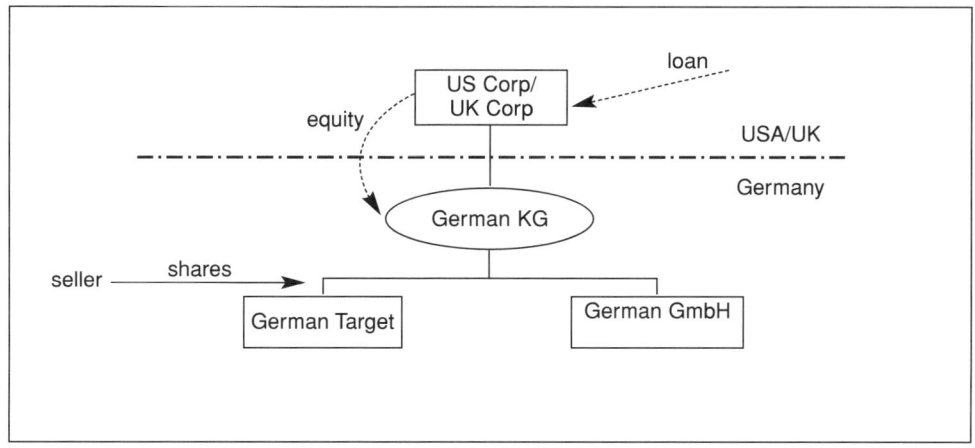

Step-up:	No
Debt Pushdown:	Yes
Thin Cap Rules:	No
Double-Dip:	Yes
Withholding tax on p/s profits:	No
Exit:	Not taxable in Germany

7.21 DEFERRAL INSTRUMENTS

Tax reform will have a positive affect on private equity and M & A transactions. From the seller's perspective, the tax changes are going to have a major impact on strategies. Therefore, the objective of a vendor will typically be to realize its capital gain tax-free in 2002. Nobody wants to lose this benefit by acting too quickly. Those presently conducting sales negotiations will try to defer the actual transfer of the shares until 2002.

Various schemes are intended to ensure now that the transaction will in fact take place in 2002. For example, consider the following:

- Granting isolated or combined put and call options
- Concluding temporary joint venture contracts whereby the potential buyer initially becomes a joint venturer through a capital increase
- Issuing convertible bonds where specified shares are granted at the end of the term
- Entering into sale and repurchase arrangements
- Using stock-lending schemes

- Buying business lease instruments where in a first step the business is leased to the potential buyer and an option is granted to the buyer for the purchase of the shares at a later point of time
- Converting a target company to a KGaA (partnership limited by shares) whereby the seller acquires a minor interest but becomes the general partner and the shares are sold in 2002
- Working with short business years in order to accelerate the start of the capital gains exemption regime
- and combinations of the above

Care is necessary when attempting any of these schemes. The tax authorities will be looking for grounds to contend that, in "economic substance," transfers took place in 2001.

Germany intends to enact a Takeover Bill in the near future. After the first "takeover war" between Mannesmann and Vodafone, the Federal Ministry of Finance presented a first draft of the Takeover Bill that should replace the nonbinding Takeover Code, an instrument of voluntary self-regulation. The Takeover Bill will include regulations as to mandatory and voluntary cash and exchange offers. The Takeover Bill will include rules as to the duty of neutrality for the board of the target company and specify what defense measures are allowable. Furthermore, the German Government intends to take the opportunity of the Takeover Act to add a squeeze-out rule into the German Public Companies' Act.

7.22 REORGANIZATION AND DEMERGERS

Historical group structures are often unsuited to take advantage of new situations resulting from international competition. Modernizing the existing structure involves a sizable capital gains tax cost being incurred. If so, management may decide to forgo the long-term benefits to avoid the short-term pain.

(a) Short-Term and Long-Term Interests

German tax law has long since recognized this clash of interests between short-term and long-term benefits. As a result, German tax law has removed many of the potential tax barriers that otherwise would have hindered necessary or desirable group internal reorganizations through the provisions of the Reorganization Tax Act (RTA). The RTA provisions apply especially to domestic mergers and to conversions of other business enterprises into limited companies.

These reorganization arrangements may be accomplished at existing book values subject to the overriding proviso that Germany has not restricted the right ultimately to tax the capital gain realized on a subsequent third-party sale. Furthermore, the partial transformation of the EU Mergers Directive and other directives into German national law has opened new possibilities for tax-free contributions of businesses located abroad and for tax-free share exchanges. The tax

7.22 Reorganization and Demergers

burden on such transactions, which previously was often prohibitive, may in many cases be deferred indefinitely.

(b) Tax Free Rorganizations

In particular, the following reorganizations may be carried out free of tax:

- Conversion of a partnership into a corporation and vice versa
- Mergers and demergers of German companies
- Dropdown of a division into a new subsidiary
- Transfer of individual assets within a partnership
- Exchange of shares of EU companies and drop-down of branches in EU countries in exchange for shares in EU companies

The new capital gains regimes introduced under Tax Reform 2001 in addition to the rules of the RTA provide additional flexibility for intra-group reorganizations.

(c) Conversion of a Company to a Partnership

The conversion of a company into a partnership after acquisition of the company's shares was a commonly used procedure before the Tax Reform 2001. This conversion would achieve a tax-neutral step-up of the book values of the underlying assets of the target company. The statute has abolished these step-up rules so that the route from a partnership into a corporate entity (rather than vice versa) will probably be seen more often in the future because the new capital gains regime favors shareholders in corporate entities.

(d) Merger Treatment

Typically, a merger of companies transfers the tax attributes of the merged entity to the absorbing company (e.g., NOLs, holding periods). In general a merger loss or a merger gain is not taxable; however, a merger loss can have a negative side effect for financial statement purposes. The merger loss reduces distributable reserves or earnings and therefore restricts the possibility of making dividend distributions.

Spin-offs

In the past, business philosophy often encouraged conglomerates to set up conglomerates to spread risks. The trend is now increasingly to concentrate on the core business. Noncore business activities are either being sold, transferred to a joint venture, or maintained separately. A noncore business activity may not be ready for an immediate sale. In that event, the noncore business may be transferred to a separate company by means of a spin-off or split-up.

Section 15 RTA permits a tax-neutral spin-off if the business transferred and the business retained both qualified as "business units" (*Teilbetriebe*) before the spin-off occurs. An investment in a partnership or a 100 percent shareholding in a company are deemed in legal terms to constitute a *Teilbetrieb*.

(e) Anti-Abuse Regulations

Anti-abuse regulations prohibit spin-offs that are set up solely for a subsequent sale of the shareholding. This transaction is deemed to be for the subsequent sale if shares in either of the companies involved in the spin-off are sold with period of five years after the demerger and these represent in value 20 percent or more of the value of the shares in the company before the spin-off occurred. This provision effectively prevents a tax-neutral spin-off of a business unit of a company whose shares are listed and traded on an ongoing basis on a stock exchange. In Section 16 PTA, the legislature has now incorporated into the tax code the earlier regulations on the tax-neutral spin-off or split-up of business activities into a partnership.

NOLs

Certain tax provisions, such as those relating to the merger of companies, permit the transfer of tax attributes. For example, this provision permits tax loss carry-forwards to be moved from one company to another. Other provisions, such as those relating to a dropdown according to Section 20 RTA, leave the tax attributes where they are. Specifically, the tax loss carryforward applies to a company that is dropping down its business or a business unit into a new company in exchange for shares. A dropdown or transfer of individual assets that do not qualify as a business unit is a taxable event. The difference between the asset's fair market value and book value is subject to standard tax rates.

(f) EU Merger Directive

German tax law incorporated the EU Merger Directive in 1992. Section 23 RTA provides that shares of an EU company or net assets of an EU branch can be contributed at book values (i.e., without realization of a taxable gain) in exchange for shares in another EU company. The book value transfer applies if the company that receives the contribution holds the majority of the shares after the contribution.

The shareholder of the EU company whose shares are contributed may be either a corporate or individual taxpayer and may be resident outside the EU. The EU Merger Directive has therefore been used (e.g., by U.S.-based multinational companies to establish their European holding company structures). A practical problem sometimes arises in terms of the contribution being reflected at book value. Some jurisdictions, (e.g., the UK), do not apply the strict "book value" concept. The U.K. requires that the shares contributed should be capitalized at fair market value. Therefore, such a reorganization should be carried out only on the basis of a binding ruling.

(g) Tax-Free Transfers

The scope of tax-free transfers of assets between partners and their partnerships has been extended somewhat in order to facilitate the restructuring of partnerships. The previous, even more liberal, rules were severely limited by the Tax

7.23 Joint Ventures and Merger of Equals   7-41

Reform Act from 1999 to 2002. That measure permits tax-free transfers of assets only among different unincorporated businesses belonging to the same taxpayer. From January 1, 2001, onward, assets may now be transferred tax free among different entities if the ultimate taxation of the hidden reserves contained in the assets is not endangered. Specifically, the following tax-free transfers will be possible from January 1, 2001, onward:

- Transfers of business assets from a partner to the partnership and vice versa
- Transfers of assets from a partnership to the collective ownership of one or more of the individual partners and vice versa
- Transfers of assets used in the partnership from one partner to another partner in the same partnership

Such transfers are not tax free, however, to the extent that a corporation is a partner in the partnership and the transfer of the asset leads to a direct or indirect increase in the corporation's partnership share. This restriction is intended to prevent abuse of the enhanced flexibility in reorganizing partnerships.

Generally speaking, the German tax provisions that regulate reorganizations, combined with the advantageous capital gains regime, permit a reasonable degree of flexibility when planning business reorganizations. However, there are issues, such as the loss limitation rules and possible real estate transfer tax exposure, that need to be carefully reviewed in each specific case.

7.23 JOINT VENTURES AND MERGER OF EQUALS

As international business relations intensify, mergers, joint ventures, and other forms of strategic alliances between multinational and national corporations are becoming increasingly popular. To put matters into context, the term *joint venture* is used here to denote a business owned and managed jointly by two otherwise independent multinational corporations. In contrast to a *merger of equals,* which is all-embracing (and involves a combination of all of the business operations), the joint venture arrangement is limited to a specific project and leaves the partners with some other business activities outside the joint venture. A joint venture could therefore be seen as a "treaty of friendship," whereas a merger can be compared more to a "marriage." The following comments focus on combined equity investments, rather than contractual agreements, which are sometimes considered for a looser combination of businesses activities.

(a) Tax Planning for Business Combinations

Tax planning in connection with business combinations is usually directed at three broad areas:

1. Eliminating or reducing tax costs (e.g., capital gains taxes, capital and other transfer taxes) in connection with the combination of the businesses

2. Optimizing the annual ongoing overall tax burden on the income actually earned and distributed to the business partners/shareholders

3. Advance planning to avoid or limit the realization of a future taxable gain, should it be decided later to dissolve or wind up the combination. This issue is obviously more important in the context of a joint venture, although there have been cases where, after a relatively short period of time, consideration has been given to winding up mergers of equals.

(b) Domestic German and International Considerations

Parties have been able to arrange mergers and joint ventures in a purely German context, for the most part, without triggering major income tax costs, under the rules of the German RTA. However, combinations between a German partner and a partner from a foreign jurisdiction have in the past often led to debates, often with political overtones. The most prominent acquisition/merger during the last few years was undoubtedly the Daimler/Chrysler merger, where tax issues and economic realities ultimately resulted in Germany being selected as the "home" for the combined top company.

The choice of a U.S. holding company would have led to both the loss of German imputation tax credits and to capital gains tax problems for German shareholders. In contrast, these tax problems generally did not arise for U.S. shareholders in the scenario adopted. A cross-border business combination does, of course, involve many complex issues, with many more tax and nontax (i.e., pooling of interest) considerations.

The question is which is the best location for the seat of the combined business operations, be it established as a result of a merger or an equity joint venture? This often becomes a political battle, in which tax issues are put forward as the reason for the choice rather than actually being the reason for the choice. The decision about the location is often determined by nontax considerations, such as possible future public share offerings, employee representation on supervisory boards, product liability, company flexibility, or even a general appreciation of the openness of the investment climate.

Only if nontax considerations do not dictate the choice of the location will tax issues play a significant role. As a rule, foreign non-German partners often have a preference for their own jurisdiction or one of the jurisdictions that has the reputation of being suitable for such combinations (e.g., the Benelux countries). The following comments concentrate on the German tax regime and its (new and old) flexibility, so that it should not surprise the reader that there are cogent arguments for locating and operating the business venture within a German entity.

(c) Choosing a Location

The following comments provide an overview of the major tax attributes that multinational companies (MNCs) seek when choosing a location to combine or hold investments and how Germany measures up against these criteria. As an

7.23 Joint Ventures and Merger of Equals

example, the combination of a U.S. and a German MNC are chosen, assuming that the German operations are sizable and profitable.

Choice of entity

Before discussing tax issues in detail, more general comments about available options in terms of the choice of legal form for the business entity may be helpful. In the case of a joint venture, the GmbH and partnership legal forms are possible alternatives, whereas in a merger of equals scenario, a partnership is unlikely to be considered because it cannot be listed on a stock exchange. Under German tax law, a KGaA (partnership limited by shares) could be an option within a German context, but generally this structure will not be accepted in an international deal.

Flexible tax environment for reorganizations

German reorganization tax rules are flexible in terms of tax-neutral reorganizations, such as transfers, dropdowns, and spin-offs of both legal entities or business units. The capital gains regime, which permits tax-exempt sales of shares in both foreign and domestic subsidiaries on entering into and winding up such structures, constitutes an argument in favor of a German vehicle.

Tax exemption for dividends

German Tax Reform 2001 has introduced a general tax exemption for dividends received by a German company, irrespective of the size of the shareholding, the activities of the foreign company, or the holding period. This general tax exemption applies when a partnership is the joint venture vehicle. If individuals were partners, the half-income system, (i.e., taxation of only one-half of the dividend income) would be applicable for both German-source and foreign-source dividend income.

Exit taxation

The German capital gains regime, in combination with the wide tax treaty network, offers attractive opportunities from a tax viewpoint to exit from the common venture vehicle and for the management of the joint venture vehicle to streamline its operations after the combination of the businesses.

Deductibility of financing and other costs

Financing and other expenses are generally tax-deductible in Germany. In the case of a German joint venture or merged entity in corporate form, expenses equivalent to 5 percent of tax-exempt foreign dividends received are deemed to be directly related to this income and, therefore, will in effect be taxed in Germany; however, any expense in excess of this percentage remains fully deductible. For example, in the case of financing costs in connection with the acquisition of a foreign shareholding, the excess can be used to offset German-source income otherwise taxable at approximately 40 percent.

The German thin capitalization rules have to be considered in the case of ownership of at least 25 percent of a German company's shares by nonresidents. Interest on loans to a German company from a nonresident shareholder or related party are not deductible in arriving at taxable income. These interest amounts are reclassified as a constructive dividend if the loans exceed certain safe harbor debt-equity ratios. The German Tax Reform 2001 has resulted in a reduction in the safe haven ratio for holding companies from 9:1 to 3:1, but this change has to be seen in the context of a tax burden, which has been reduced from about 50 percent to about 40 percent.

In the case of a joint venture, the partnership structure has the advantage that expenses are tax deductible for German purposes under German partnership taxation principles. Such expenses include financing costs and other expenses e.g., management costs, and administrative expenses. Furthermore, the thin capitalization rules would not apply in this structure.

Withholding tax aspects

Germany has entered into tax treaties with more than 85 countries. Therefore, Germany surpasses by far locations such as the Netherlands and Luxembourg in terms of treaty coverage. This wide treaty network is particularly important for withholding taxes because the treaties reduce or eliminate local withholding taxes on dividends, interest, or royalties. For example, in the case of dividends, the U.S.–German treaty provides for a reduction to 5 percent for corporate shareholders with a 10 percent shareholding (15 percent in other cases).

As an EU member country, Germany can also take advantage of the EU Parent-Subsidiary Directive, i.e., dividends paid from EU subsidiaries to a German parent can be paid free of any withholding taxes.

A partnership may be viewed with mixed feelings in this respect. On the one hand, a German partnership is not subject to a branch profits tax, i.e., there are no additional tax charges on profit repatriations. Conversely, dividends from a foreign subsidiary typically do not qualify for the lower treaty withholding tax rate for inter-corporate shareholdings or for the application of the EU Parent-Subsidiary Directive because in these cases direct share ownership between corporations is generally required.

In the case of the combination of German and U.S. business operations, there is normally a withholding tax leakage because interposing a vehicle generally creates an additional layer of withholding tax for one of the partners.

Group taxation provisions

The German government has ensured through the provisions of Tax Reform 2001 that consolidation of taxable income and losses under the German group taxation (*Organschaft*) rules has become easier.

Unrestricted loss carryforward

Losses incurred by foreign branches and corporations usually do not qualify for German tax relief. However, losses suffered by German holding companies (e.g., as a result of financing costs) can be carried forward for an unlimited period.

Limited anti-avoidance legislation

The tax planner needs to consider carefully the impact of anti-abuse provisions that may restrict or counteract the benefits of a holding company structure. Particular attention needs to be paid to the general substance requirements and the anti-treaty shopping provisions in German statutory law and tax treaties.

Controlled Foreign Corporation (CFC) rules:

The German Controlled Foreign Corporation (CFC) provisions are still a major challenge to a German outbound investment tax planner. The tax planner must consider these provisions, especially for multi-tier holding companies; however, new rules, which have already been proposed, should ease the situation.

No duties on share transfers, no taxes on formation, no capital taxes

There are no capital taxes or stamp duties and few transaction or excise taxes, VAT apart, that are of any real significance to most businesses. Taxes on insurance premiums and on sales and deemed sales of real estate are the two main exceptions.

Based on the tax aspects listed previously, it is not possible to come to a clear conclusion about whether such a combination vehicle should be located in Germany or abroad or whether it should be a corporate versus a partnership entity. A decision is likely to depend on the relative weighting given to each factor by the respective partners; however, the abolition of the imputation tax credit system of corporation tax, coupled with the exemption for corporations from taxation on capital gains on the sale of shares, will make it much easier for German companies to join international joint ventures and/or business combinations.

7.24 GOING PUBLIC

There is a visible trend on the German market toward transforming family-owned or closely held enterprises into companies limited by shares (Aktiengesellschaft/AG) or into a commercial partnership limited by shares (Kommanditgesellschaft auf Aktien/KGaA), particularly when a stock exchange listing is the goal.

(a) Reasons for Going Public

Some of the more important reasons for going public are as follows:

- Obtaining new capital to finance future growth
- Fungibility of the shares
- Sale of the company in installments
- Qualified management
- Capital market discipline and transparency

Many venture capitalists are currently searching for appropriate candidates for a listing on a German stock exchange, but before a company can be listed, the corporate or group structure must be in place. Therefore, the decision about whether and where the operating company, the holding company, or the business division should be "listed" must be taken at the beginning of the process. This issue is of special relevance if a multilevel group has international mutual dependence. It is also important to decide which group company needs the cash from the listing, e.g., for repayment of debt or financing of investments.

(b) Reasons for Success of Offering

The success of a listing depends on the equity story and on the preparation, structuring, execution, and timing of the listing. Tax questions are certainly not top priority items when going public, but complete disregard for their impact usually leads to irrevocable disadvantages. As to tax issues, some of the main concerns are the following:

- Tax-neutral reorganization into an AG or KGaA
- Utilization of NOLs
- Tax treatment of capital gains arising from the IPO
- Tax deductibility of capital procurement costs
- Exit taxation of investors

An additional tax issue as to the listing of a family-owned business is that it increases significantly the basis for inheritance tax as compared to a nonlisted company or partnership or other business form. Going public therefore not only requires a detailed analysis of the tax situation of the company and its shareholders but also has to include inheritance tax planning.

(c) Legal Structures

In going public, the commercial enterprise needs to avoid lawsuits, which, in Germany, is likely to mean the legal form of a corporation (AG) or a commercial partnership limited by shares (KGaA). The share capital of an AG can be divided into DM 5 shares (2 Euro, respectively). Shares can be transferred to another person without notarization.

7.24 Going Public

The taxation treatment of a company limited by shares is the same as that for a limited liability company (*Gesellschaft mit beschränkter Haftung,* GmbH). However, many more company law rules have to be observed in the case of an AG.

A commercial partnership limited by shares (KGaA) is characterized by the special position of the general partner. The limited equity holders (*Kommanditaktionäre*) have a position akin to that of lenders. They are excluded from management decisions but do have limited rights to share in profits and to information and control. Only the capital of the limited partner is listed on the stock exchange and is subject to the rules as established under the German Stock Corporation Act. If the general shareholder is a German resident, then the taxation of the commercial partnership takes place in two stages: (1) the proportional income of the general partner is taxed under the rules of the income tax law, and (2) the income of the partnership is subject to corporation tax, levied on the KGaA. Dividends paid to limited partners are taxable by the recipients.

Under the provisions of the German Reorganization Tax Act, it is generally possible to transform a German partnership or a GmbH into an AG or KGaA without giving rise to an income tax charge. The conversion of a GmbH into an AG does not generally affect the tax attributes of the corporate entity (e.g., in terms of capital gains taxation). The conversion of a partnership into a corporate vehicle "taints" the shares of the company for seven years. A capital gain realized on their disposal is only tax exempt, respectively subject to the half-income tax treatment, on the expiration of the seven-year period. Therefore, if there is any intention for the business to go public, the business should be organized from the beginning as a separate corporate entity rather than a partnership or a business unit/division within a company. In the case of the dropdown of a business unit, the seven-year holding period after a dropdown also applies. In the case of a split-up/spin-off of the division, a five-year holding period applies.

The transformation of a partnership or a GmbH into a KGaA or AG does not trigger stamp duties or capital transfer taxes. Capital taxes were abolished in Germany many years ago.

(d) Financing and the Deduction of Financing Costs

The raising of new capital to finance the company's future growth is certainly one of the main motives for going public. It is difficult for young growth companies to achieve the required equity capitalization or to obtain credit on the German capital market. Fortunately, a trend is now developing under which more and more growth companies are being financed by venture capital companies, which expect high yields in terms of future profits, but are in the meantime able to dispense with debt security requirements.

In contrast to capital raised in the form of equity from the stock exchange, venture capital is debt for the company. The interest is fully deductible for corporation tax purposes and deductible to the extent of one-half for trade tax purposes. By contrast, dividends on equity stock stem from taxed profits. These payments are not tax deductible for the paying company, but the receipts are either tax-exempt at the level of a German resident corporate shareholder or subject to the half-income tax regime in the case of an individual recipient.

The equity capital procurement costs should also be considered. The costs for placement, including selling commissions, are usually between 4.5 percent and 5.5 percent of the total volume of the issue. Additionally, consulting fees and printing costs will arise.

Transformation costs, consulting fees, and printing costs, as well as capital procurement costs, are deductible expenses for accounting and tax purposes. Under German law, these costs cannot be capitalized but must be expensed. Furthermore, it is not permissible to set off these expenses against the share premium. Although there are undoubted advantages of having wholly tax-deductible expenses, the incidence of these costs in any one year may seriously depress earnings. Careful timing of their placement may make it possible to spread this burden over two years.

(e) Inheritance and Gift Taxes

Another important issue to be considered when going public is the inheritance/gift tax aspects. Partnerships are valued for these purposes at the amounts shown in their balance sheets. Unlisted companies are usually valued under a formula based partly on the average taxable income over the past three years and partly on the net assets value as shown in the last balance sheet. The value for listed companies is the stock exchange value. High-growth companies in particular can therefore often have a stock exchange value many times higher than that on which an inheritance or gift tax would otherwise have been based. Therefore, the tried and tested rule is that the membership rights should first be given away as a gift (anticipated succession of the donor), then the legal transformation of the enterprise should be carried out and, finally, the listing should be applied for.

CHAPTER 8

Taxation of Mergers and Acquisitions in Ireland

Dermot P. Clarke
David J. Rorke
Tax Partner and Tax Director, Ernst & Young Ireland

8.1 Introduction
8.2 Irish Taxes that Affect Merger and Acquisition Activity
  (a) Corporation Tax
  (b) Corporation Tax Phased Reduction
  (c) Dividend Treatment
  (d) Capital Expenditure
  (e) Capital Gains Tax
  (f) Stamp Duty
  (g) Capital Duty
  (h) Dividend Withholding Tax
  (i) Value-Added Tax
  (j) International Withholding
  (k) Tax Incentives
  (l) Losses
  (m) Reorganizations
  (n) Groups
  (o) Other Tax Issues
8.3 Structuring of Transactions
  (a) Share Sale
  (b) Drop-Down
  (c) Reconstruction
  (d) Anti-Avoidance Provisions
8.4 Asset Sale
  (a) Stamp Duties
  (b) Value-Added Tax
  (c) Losses
  (d) Capital Gains
  (e) Basis Issues
  (f) Commercial Issues
  (g) Acquisition Costs

8.5 Financial Structures
  (a) Group Relief and Declining Tax Rates
  (b) Treaty Considerations
8.6 Outbound Investment
8.7 Mergers
8.8 Legal Structures
  (a) Partnerships
  (b) Joint Venture Company
  (c) Branch of a Foreign-Registered Company
  (d) Exit Strategies
8.9 Conclusion

8.1 INTRODUCTION

Merger and acquisition activity is an increasingly important aspect of the business landscape in Ireland today. The strong growth in the Irish economy in recent years has resulted in a higher level of merger and acquisition activity. This merger and acquisition activity reflects both inward investments by foreign multinationals and outward investment by large Irish businesses.

This analysis of mergers and acquisitions in Ireland examines the following:

- Consideration of those taxes that impact on merger and acquisition activity in Ireland
- Structuring mergers and acquisitions and in particular the distinction between asset sales and share sales in the context of inward investment into Ireland and domestic Irish merger and acquisition activity
- Aspects peculiar to outbound investment from Ireland

8.2 IRISH TAXES THAT AFFECT MERGER AND ACQUISITION ACTIVITY

The principal taxes affecting merger and acquisition activity in Ireland are as follows:

- Corporation tax
- Capital gains tax
- Dividend withholding tax
- Stamp duty
- Capital duty
- Value-added tax

8.2 Irish Taxes that Affect Merger and Acquisition Activity

(a) Corporation Tax

The place of tax residence of a company generally determines its exposure to Irish corporation tax. The principal test of tax residence in Ireland is the location of the place of central management and control of the company. If central management and control is located in Ireland, then the company is considered to be an Irish tax resident.

A new rule applied to tax residence in Ireland beginning February 11, 1999. Any company incorporated in Ireland is regarded as an Irish tax resident subject to certain exceptions. These exceptions principally apply in the following situations:

- Where the Irish company is under the control of persons resident in a tax treaty country
- Where the Irish company is under the control of a quoted company
- Where the Irish company in question also carries on a trade in Ireland or is related to a company that carries on a trade in Ireland

These exceptions were principally introduced into the tax code to cater to situations involving the *bona fide* use of Irish incorporated non-Irish resident companies to facilitate planning structures for inward investment into Ireland.

(b) Corporation Tax Phased Reduction

Corporation tax in Ireland on profits from active trading activities currently stands at 24 percent. This tax rate will, however, decline on a phased basis to a 12.5 percent rate beginning with January 1, 2003 (see Exhibit 8.1). The corporate tax rate is 25 percent for passive income such as investment income, rental income, and so forth. This tax rate applies to dividends received by Irish companies from subsidiaries located in overseas jurisdictions.

Exhibit 8.1

CORPORATION TAX REDUCTION PHASES

Year	Tax rate
Calendar year 2000	24%
Calendar year 2001	20%
Calendar year 2002	16%
Calendar year 2003	12.5%

A company that is tax resident in Ireland is liable to Irish corporation tax on its worldwide income and capital gains. In the case of a company that is not a tax resident in Ireland, but that is carrying on a trade in Ireland through a branch or agency, liability to Irish corporation tax arises as to any income or capital gains attributable to the branch activity. A nonresident company is also liable to Irish capital gains tax on specified Irish assets. The specified assets are land and buildings in Ireland, minerals or mineral rights, and shares deriving their value from Irish land or minerals.

(c) Dividend Treatment

No corporation tax applies when an Irish resident company receives dividends from another Irish resident company. Dividends received by an Irish resident company from companies resident in other jurisdictions are liable to tax at the higher corporation tax rate of 25 percent. Credit is available for withholding tax and underlying tax, depending on the terms of the tax treaties in force between Ireland and the jurisdictions in question.

Irish domestic law provides credit for the underlying tax, which is paid at lower tier levels in the foreign group, whether this is in one country or different countries. This provision applies to dividends received from "25 percent subsidiaries." To be a "25 percent subsidiary" at least 25 percent of voting rights must be held by the parent company. The 25 percent participation threshold must apply through the tiers of the foreign group.

An Irish resident company might receive dividends from companies resident in other jurisdictions with which Ireland does not have a tax treaty. Irish domestic law provides for unilateral credit relief in that event. Unilateral relief operates by reducing Irish tax on the dividend by any withholding tax paid in the foreign jurisdiction on the dividend and by an appropriate part of the foreign tax on the income underlying the dividend.

(d) Capital Expenditure

Specific rules in the Irish tax code apply to capital expenditure on the purchase of assets. The principal deduction is capital allowances (tax depreciation) on plant and machinery and on certain industrial buildings. In the case of plant and machinery, allowances are currently provided on a straight-line basis over seven years (at 15 percent for six years with 10 percent in the seventh year). However, in the 2001 budget statement, the Minister for Finance indicated that allowances would be given on a straight-line basis over five years in the case of expenditures made on or after January 1, 2001. In the case of industrial buildings, allowances are provided on a straight-line basis at the 4 percent rate for 25 years. A deduction is available for the cost of purchasing patent rights. This deduction is claimed on a straight-line basis over 17 years. No deduction is available for the purchase of goodwill or similar intangibles, such as brands and so on.

(e) Capital Gains Tax

The current rate of capital gains tax in Ireland is 20 percent. This tax applies to gains that arise on the disposal of chargeable assets. These assets include real property, certain debts, goodwill, and stocks and securities.

An allowance is made for the effect of inflation between the date of acquisition of the asset and the date of disposal in calculating capital gains that have arisen. Accordingly, tax is levied only on real gains. Indexation is not, however, available in the case of the disposal of an asset acquired within the previous 12 months.

(f) Stamp Duty

Stamp duty is a tax levied on legal documents and is effectively a transfer tax. Stamp duty applies at the rate of 1 percent on the transfer of stocks or securities and at rates of up to 6 percent on the transfers of other property, e.g., real property and so on. Stamp duty may be avoided where assets are capable of transfer by delivery. For example, movable assets transfer by delivery and do not require a legal document to effect a conveyance of title.

(g) Capital Duty

Capital duty arises at a rate of 1 percent on the value of assets contributed for shares in Irish incorporated limited liability companies (LLCs). The capital duty applies to contributions in exchange for the issuance of shares in Irish incorporated LLCs. In contrast, no capital duty arises in the case of an Irish incorporated unlimited liability company. The exposure to capital duty may be reduced by injecting funds in the form of a capital contribution as opposed to a subscription for shares. A capital contribution may, however, have adverse implications in relation to base cost for a future disposal.

(h) Dividend Withholding Tax

Dividend withholding tax applies to dividends and other distributions paid by Irish tax resident companies. The dividend withholding tax applies at the standard rate of income tax in force at the time of the payment of the dividend or other distribution (currently 22 percent). There are, however, the following exceptions to the application of dividend withholding tax:

- When an Irish resident subsidiary company makes a distribution to its parent company that is resident in another European Union (EU) Member State, then dividend withholding tax is not imposed because of the provisions of the EU Parent-Subsidiary directive. The directive requires that the parent company control at least 25 percent of the voting rights in the subsidiary.
- There is an exemption from dividend withholding tax when the recipient of the dividend is a company not resident in Ireland, which is resident in a tax treaty country and which is not under the control of Irish resident persons.
- Dividend withholding tax does not apply when the recipient of the dividend is a company not resident in Ireland, where the company is ultimately controlled by persons who are resident for tax purposes in a tax treaty country or in an EU Member State. In addition, the recipient company must not be under the control of persons who are not so resident.

- Dividend withholding tax does not apply when the recipient of the dividend is a nonresident company, the principal class of shares of which are substantially and regularly traded on a recognized stock exchange in a treaty country or in an EU Member State. This exemption also applies when the recipient company is a 75% subsidiary of a company whose shares are so traded.

The recipient company must file certain declarations in order to qualify for an exemption.

(i) Value-Added Tax

The value-added tax (VAT) may apply to the purchase of business assets at rates of 12.5 percent or 21 percent, depending on the assets involved. This purchase results in a cashflow disadvantage rather than a permanent cost when the purchaser is registered for VAT. In certain circumstances, the transfer of ownership of goods in connection with the transfer of a business or part of a business to another VAT-registered person is treated as not being a supply of goods. The result is that no VAT is charged on the transfer.

(j) International Withholding

When interest is paid by an Irish company to a nonresident, this interest is subject to a withholding tax at the standard rate of income tax (currently 22 percent). This withholding tax does not apply, however, when the interest is paid to a company resident in the EU or in a tax treaty country. In order to qualify for this exemption, the interest must be paid in the course of a trade or business carried on by the company. The exception will not apply when the interest is paid in connection with a trade or business carried on by the recipient in Ireland through a branch or agency.

Circumstances may arise where interest or royalties are payable to a company resident in a nontax treaty country. Taxpayers should consider using a conduit company resident in a country that has a tax treaty with both Ireland and the country of residence of the recipient of the interest or royalties. In this way, the payments of interest or royalties may be made without deduction of withholding tax. The Netherlands and Cyprus are commonly used for this purpose.

(k) Tax Incentives

A company carrying on manufacturing activities in Ireland before July 23, 1998, is liable to tax at a special corporation tax rate of 10 percent on profits from its manufacturing operations until December 31, 2010. Companies that commenced manufacturing operations after July 23, 1998 can avail of the special 10 percent rate until December 31, 2002. After that date, the companies will be liable to tax at the rate of 12.5 percent applicable to trading profits.

Other tax incentives available in Ireland include an allowance for research and development expenditure (R & D) carried out in Ireland. An exemption from tax is also available for income arising from patent royalties when the research and similar activities leading to the invention, which was covered by the patent, were carried out in Ireland.

(l) Losses

Trading losses that arise can be set against all other profits of the company in the current accounting period or in the preceding accounting period of equal length. These losses may also be carried forward without limit for set-off against profits of the same trade. Restrictions exist when the losses arise as to a trade liable at the special 10 percent rate of tax. In this case, such losses may be set against income taxable at the 10 percent rate only in the preceding accounting period or carried forward against future trading profits. Certain restrictions exist in relation to the availability of losses when a change in ownership occurs.

(m) Reorganizations

Ireland has various provisions that relieve the taxpayer from capital gains tax, stamp duty, and capital duty in order to facilitate reorganizations. In the case of capital gains tax, a share-for-share exchange ("paper for paper") is not regarded as giving rise to a disposal of the original shares for capital gains tax purposes. This share exchange is subject to certain conditions being met.

The share exchange facilitates an acquiring company obtaining control of an existing company and results in the vendors of the existing company postponing a charge to capital gains tax. The new shares received by the vendors are deemed to take the place of the existing shares held by them. These new shares are regarded as being acquired at the cost and on the date on which the original shares were acquired, (i.e. the new shares retain the original basis of the old shares).

The stamp duty code provides relief from stamp duty as to certain transfers arising in the context of corporate reconstructions and reorganizations. Relief from duty is available when transfers of assets between associated companies take place where the companies have a 90 percent direct or indirect relationship. Relief from capital duty is available as to certain amalgamations and reconstructions that involve the issue of new shares in one company to the shareholders of another company. Conditions apply to the relief, including *inter alia,* a requirement for a 75 percent relationship to exist.

(n) Groups

Unlike certain other jurisdictions, it is not possible in Ireland to file a consolidated tax return for a group of Irish companies. Irish legislation requires each entity within a group to file a separate return.

Provision is made in the Irish legislation for "group relief" for trading losses and for certain other losses. These losses can be surrendered between the company incurring the loss and other companies in the group that have taxable profits. For these purposes, a group is regarded as consisting of an Irish resident parent company and all its Irish resident 75 percent subsidiaries. Group relief is also available in a situation when two Irish resident companies are 75 percent subsidiaries of an EU parent company.

Another form of group relief (consortium relief) is available when a consortium owns a company. A company is so regarded if all of its ordinary share capital is directly owned between them by five or fewer companies and the company in question is not a 75 percent subsidiary of any of the consortium members. In these circumstances, losses incurred by the company owned by the consortium may be surrendered proportionately to the consortium members.

(o) Other Tax Issues

At present, there is no controlled foreign corporation legislation within Ireland. Similarly, no thin capitalization provisions currently exist. There is no general transfer pricing legislation, but certain specific provisions may need to be addressed in particular circumstances.

The Irish Revenue operates no ruling system in relation to proposed transactions or schemes. In certain circumstances, however, the Irish Revenue may be prepared to give an opinion provided the Irish Revenue is satisfied that the proposed transaction is for *bona fide* commercial purposes. Such an opinion is not binding upon the Irish Revenue because they always reserve the right to review the situation in light of the actual fact pattern that emerges.

8.3 STRUCTURING OF TRANSACTIONS

A major decision in relation to a proposed merger or acquisition is whether the deal is to be structured as an asset purchase or a share purchase. Both types of transaction have relative advantages and disadvantages for the seller and the purchaser. These advantages/disadvantages are often mutually exclusive to both parties. Each transaction has to be considered on its own merits but, in general terms, it may be stated that sellers normally prefer a share deal while purchasers in general would prefer an asset deal.

(a) Share Sale

It is probably fair to say that a share sale is more common than an asset sale in mergers and acquisitions. From the seller's perspective, a share sale offers the advantage of a clean break with the business being disposed of, without the necessity of having to tidy up residual issues that would exist when a business is disposed of by way of an asset sale from an existing entity.

A share sale is not all bad news from the purchaser's perspective, however. Some advantages that accrue to a purchaser in a share sale scenario are that trading losses in the entity being acquired can survive the transfer (this topic is considered further as follows), whereas capital gains tax losses can also be passed on to the purchaser. A further advantage is that no VAT applies to a share sale.

Stamp duty at 1 percent will apply on the sale of shares in an Irish incorporated company unless the transaction can be structured in such a way that this lia-

8.3 Structuring of Transactions

bility can be eliminated (e.g., paper for paper). A disadvantage for the purchaser in relation to a share sale is that no step-up in basis is achieved for the assets of the company, either for capital gains tax or capital allowances (tax depreciation) purposes.

A share sale raises the prospect of the purchaser inheriting existing tax or other liabilities of the target company. Typically, the purchaser seeks to ensure that extensive tax warranties and indemnities are contained in the share purchase agreement. In contrast, on occasion, liabilities may surface later that are not adequately covered by the warranties and indemnities. A dropdown may apply in a situation where the purchaser has concerns about potential liabilities in the target company.

(b) Dropdown

The seller may choose to organize affairs so that the business that the purchaser wants to acquire is transferred from the existing company to a new 75 percent subsidiary of the existing company (Newco). When a purchaser wishes to acquire a target company but is concerned about the possible existence of liabilities in that company, the purchaser then purchases Newco instead of the existing company. Certain tax consequences arise in a dropdown situation.

It is critical to ensure that no binding contract or agreement is in place between the seller and purchaser before the dropdown is effected. The existence of such a binding contract or agreement would result in the transfer from the existing company to Newco not qualifying for certain reliefs provided for in Irish tax legislation. These reliefs include the following:

- The transfer of tax losses to Newco, subject to certain conditions. The transfer of assets qualifying for tax depreciation to Newco at written-down value results in no recapture of tax allowances previously granted.
- In a dropdown situation, where assets are transferred from the existing company to Newco, no capital gains tax arises on the initial transfer to Newco (as they are regarded as a transfer within a group); however, once the existing company sells Newco, Newco leaves the existing capital gains tax group and any deferred capital gains are crystallized in Newco. Newco is treated as disposing and reacquiring the assets at market value. This provision applies to assets that were previously transferred from its former parent.
- Normally, in a dropdown situation, the tax liability arising as to these gains is recovered from the vendor under the terms of the tax deed of indemnity. This tax deed of indemnity is included in the share purchase agreement.

Stamp duty will apply to the transfer of the assets from the existing company to Newco. The associated company's relief is not available because Newco and the existing company cease to be associated within a period of two years from the transfer.

(c) Reconstruction

It may be possible to structure an effective dropdown under specific provisions relating to reorganizations and reconstructions. Under this structure, there is no capital gains tax liability on the transfer of assets from an existing company to a new company where that new company issues shares to the shareholders of the existing company. A reconstruction may also qualify for relief from stamp duty and capital duty subject to certain conditions.

(d) Anti-Avoidance Provisions

Certain anti-avoidance provisions may result in existing trading losses or capital gains tax losses not being available to the purchaser. This situation applies when the company being acquired has existing trading losses or capital gains tax losses. These anti-avoidance provisions deny the benefit of trading losses where the following situations apply:

- A major change occurs in the nature or conduct of the trade within a period of three years either before or after the sale.
- The scale of trading activities has become small or negligible and, before any considerable revival of the trade, there is a change in the ownership of the company.

The legislation provides that a "major change in the nature or conduct of a trade" includes the following:

- A major change in the type of property dealt in the trade
- A major change in customers, outlets, or markets of the trade or services or facilities provided in the trade
- A major change in customers, outlets, or markets of the trade

Ireland initiated anti-avoidance provisions to deal with capital gains tax loss buying. These anti-avoidance provisions apply to companies with unused capital gains tax losses that are subsequently bought by other companies solely with the intention of sheltering capital gains tax within that other group. The purpose of the anti-avoidance provisions is to ensure that such capital gains tax losses cannot be used subsequently by a group that has had no previous connection with the company in which the capital losses were generated. Thus, the capital gains tax losses are regarded as "pre-entry losses."

8.4 ASSET SALE

An asset sale has advantages and disadvantages for both the vendor and the purchaser, as it does in the case of a share sale. The purchaser will receive a step-up in basis for both capital gains tax and capital allowances (tax depreciation) pur-

8.4 Asset Sale

poses. The amount that can be claimed cannot exceed the original cost incurred by the vendor in the case of tax depreciation for industrial buildings.

(a) Stamp Duties

Stamp duty at rates of up to 6 percent can be incurred by the purchaser on the acquisition of the assets in an asset sale situation. The taxpayer may reduce the duty cost by transferring certain assets by delivery, e.g., inventory and movable plant and machinery. Stamp duty is charged solely by reference to the gross value of the chargeable assets being acquired, i.e. amounts netted off in arriving at the purchase price, such as business liabilities being assumed by the purchaser, are adjusted.

(b) Value-Added Tax

Another issue that arises for the purchaser in an asset sale situation is that VAT at rates of up to 21 percent may arise on the sale. If the purchaser is registered for VAT then this does not result in a cost but may have adverse cashflow implications. The sale may be exempted from VAT if the sale can be regarded as the disposal of a going concern.

(c) Losses

An asset sale results in certain implications arising for the seller. Normally, the disposal of the business results in a cessation of the seller's trade, with the result that any unused losses expire. There are restrictions in relation to the use of losses incurred on the business being disposed of being set against profits from another trade that continues to be carried on by the seller.

(d) Capital Gains

In an asset sale situation, the seller may be able to avoid capital gains tax by electing to defer the gain by investing the proceeds of the disposal in new qualifying assets. This capital gains tax rollover relief (tax deferral) is available, provided the reinvestment takes place within a period of three years after the disposal of the business. Normally, in an asset sale situation, capital gains would typically arise on assets such as real property and intangibles such as goodwill. In the absence of rollover relief, such gains are taxed at the capital gains tax rate of 20 percent.

The shareholders in the seller will also potentially be exposed to a "double charge" to capital gains tax. The shareholders may be subject to capital gains tax on the disposal of their shares of the seller upon a liquidation of the seller. The shareholders of the selling company will therefore have to consider how to distribute the after-tax capital gain arising from the asset sale.

(e) Basis Issues

An asset disposal by the seller results in the clawback of capital allowances (tax depreciation) previously obtained by the vendor. On occasion, the purchaser may agree to treat the assets as being transferred at their tax written-down value, but this is unusual.

A major issue that arises in the case of an asset sale is the allocation of the purchase price between the various classes of assets involved. Again, the vendor and the purchaser have differing objectives in relation to this exercise. The purchaser's objective is to attribute as much consideration as possible to assets on which a tax deduction will be obtained, e.g., inventory and plant and equipment qualifying for tax depreciation. The vendor seeks to allocate consideration to assets where a lower rate of capital gains tax of 20 percent may apply or where tax deferral is possible (i.e., claim rollover relief). Again, this is a situation where the final outcome depends on the negotiations between the vendor and purchaser.

(f) Commercial Issues

Other commercial issues arise in the case of an asset sale. These issues principally relate to dealing with the customers and suppliers of the business being disposed of and advising the customers and suppliers of the changed circumstances. This may necessitate negotiations with customers or suppliers who are perceived as being crucial to the ongoing health of the business being disposed of. Similar commercial issues also arise in a share sale scenario involving the transfer of a business to a Newco followed by the subsequent disposal of the Newco.

(g) Acquisition Costs

Fees to advisors involved in the acquisition process are more than an insignificant cost of an acquisition. Such costs are not tax deductible under the Irish taxation system in the case of a successful acquisition. These amounts must be treated as a part of the capital cost of making the acquisition. An argument can be advanced in certain circumstances for a tax deduction of the costs associated with an abortive acquisition, but this is somewhat of a gray area.

8.5 FINANCIAL STRUCTURES

A common approach when a share sale is involved is to set up a special-purpose acquisition vehicle to acquire the target company. This structure would normally involve setting up an Irish holding company that would borrow funds to make the acquisition.

Under Irish legislation, a deduction can be claimed for interest paid on money borrowed by a company to acquire shares of a trading company or shares of a holding company of trading companies. Similarly, a deduction can be claimed for on-lend of money to a trading company or a holding company of trading companies, which is used for the purposes of the trade or business of the company or of a connected company. However, it is necessary for the investing company to have a participation of at least 5 percent in the company and for there to be at least one director of the investing company to be on the board of the company or of a connected company.

8.5 Financial Structures

(a) Group Relief and Declining Tax Rates

Relief is given for the interest paid by the investing company by way of group relief to shelter the profits of the target company from tax. The structural conditions set out previously are somewhat restrictive, but certain concessions have been agreed to in the past with the Irish Revenue authorities that result in structures becoming slightly more flexible. A case in point is the legislative requirement that the acquisition vehicle or a directly owned subsidiary of the acquisition vehicle must make the purchase of the target. The Irish Revenue gave concessions enabling several layers of holding companies to be put in place above the target, thereby facilitating the structuring of debts in connection with the acquisition with different types of debt (i.e., senior, mezzanine, and junior) being placed in different layers of the structure.

One consequence of falling tax rates in Ireland is that in the case of inward investment foreign companies may seek to retain the acquisition debt in a country with a higher tax rate if this is more efficient in group tax terms. Ireland does not have thin capitalization rules or debt-equity requirements. This explains the preponderance of debt financing rather than equity financing in relation to acquisitions. The principal advantage of debt financing is that the interest on the debt is normally tax deductible, whereas dividends are not.

(b) Treaty Considerations

One complication that can arise in relation to debt financing is that under Irish domestic legislation, interest paid to a nonresident parent company or affiliated company may be recharacterized as a distribution. This will result in the interest being recharacterized as a dividend and thus not tax deductible; however, in the case of tax treaties that Ireland negotiated before 1976 (the date of introduction of corporation tax in Ireland), it is possible to elect to override this provision in the domestic legislation and obtain a tax deduction for such interest. A list of the countries with which Ireland has tax treaties negotiated before 1976 and where such an election can be made is as follows:

Belgium	Japan
Canada	Luxembourg
Cyprus	Netherlands
France	Norway
Germany	Pakistan
Italy	Zambia

In more recent treaties, interest paid by a resident of Ireland to a resident of the treaty partner country may, under the nondiscrimination article of the treaty in question, be deductible in computing taxable profits on the same basis as if it were paid to an Irish resident. A list of such treaties is as follows:

Czech Republic	Malaysia
Denmark	Mexico
Estonia	New Zealand
Finland	Portugal
Hungary	Russia
Israel	Slovakia
Korea	South Africa
Latvia	Spain
Lithuania	United States

Some Irish double taxation treaties do not afford protection from distribution treatment under Irish domestic legislation or, alternatively, are capable of differing interpretations as to whether distribution treatment is avoided. A list of such treaties is as follows:

Australia	Sweden
Austria	Switzerland
Poland	United Kingdom

8.6 OUTBOUND INVESTMENT

Most of the tax issues arising in relation to outbound investment depend on the jurisdiction in which the investment is being made. Nevertheless, certain Irish tax considerations also arise. In particular, given falling Irish corporation tax rates, it is often desirable to locate the acquisition vehicle and the acquisition debt in the same tax jurisdiction as the target in order to shelter the target company's future profits with the interest on the debt.

Another Irish issue that arises in relation to outbound investment is that dividends received from overseas subsidiaries of an Irish company are liable to Irish corporation tax at the higher rate of 25 percent, subject to credit for withholding tax and underlying tax. The treatment depends on the terms of the tax treaty between Ireland and the foreign jurisdiction concerned. Irish domestic legislation also provides for unilateral double taxation relief when there is no taxation treaty between Ireland and the foreign jurisdiction in question.

In structuring outbound investment from Ireland, consideration may also be given to the use of an offshore holding company in a favorable tax jurisdiction that provides a participation exemption (e.g., the Netherlands). Careful planning in this regard can result in dividends from the target company being exempt from tax at holding company level and a capital gains tax participation exemption being obtained.

Many outbound acquisitions (particularly in the high-tech/e-commerce area) are made by Irish companies that benefit from the 10 percent rate of corporation tax. Such companies generally prefer to acquire assets so that valuable intellectual property can be exploited from Ireland, with the related income benefiting from low rates of tax. The overseas vendor may, however, prefer a share sale to avoid a capital gains tax charge at vendor company level. It is important to consider tax structuring at an early stage so that going forward global taxes can be minimized.

8.7 MERGERS

The discussion so far has principally concerned acquisitions either within Ireland or by Irish companies in other jurisdictions. Mergers are not a common feature in Ireland because there are no legal mechanisms in Irish company law providing for the merger of one company into another or for a demerger of an existing company. Notwithstanding the absence of such a legal mechanism, some concessions have been obtained from the Irish Revenue Commissioners in relation to stamp duty issues arising on what are effectively demergers that take place under the operation of law in foreign jurisdictions.

8.8 LEGAL STRUCTURES

The previous analysis mainly deals with either asset or share acquisitions by an Irish resident acquiror. It may be appropriate to adopt other structures, some of which are discussed as follows.

(a) Partnerships

Under Irish law, a partnership is not regarded as a separate legal entity for legal and tax purposes. Instead, a partnership is regarded as a fiscally transparent entity. The profits of a partnership are not assessed on the partnership, but are instead assessed separately on the partners who are deemed to carry on a separate trade. Partnerships involving companies are not uncommon, and again the partnership profits are assessed separately on the companies involved.

(b) Joint Venture Company

An investor considering taking a stake in a joint venture company will have to consider issues similar to those involved in making an acquisition, such as obtaining tax relief for debt on borrowings, the taxation treatment of dividends received from the joint venture company, and so forth. In joint venture situations, it is usual that there will be a shareholder's agreement governing the running of the joint venture company and the relationship between the joint venture parties. Such an agreement also usually deals with exit mechanisms for the parties and so forth.

(c) Branch of a Foreign-Registered Company

Irish assets might be acquired by a foreign company and operated as an Irish branch of that foreign company as an alternative structure. In the early stages of development of the Irish business, when losses may arise, this structure has the advantage that relief should be obtained for the losses in the head office jurisdiction. A branch also has the advantage that remittances to the head office are not subject to any withholding tax.

This can be contrasted with the situation of an Irish subsidiary, where depending on the residence of the foreign parent and the tax treaty position, dividend withholding tax may be an issue.

In a branch situation, the branch will not be able to avail itself of Irish tax treaties. Instead, regard will have to be made to the treaty network of the jurisdiction in which the head office is tax resident.

(d) Exit Strategies

In the past, the most common exit strategy in Ireland was to arrange for a sale of shares. The current capital gains tax rate is only 20 percent, causing such a course of action to be a simple exit mechanism.

A foreign resident owner of Irish shares is not subject to Irish capital gains tax on a disposal of the shares unless the shares derive their value or the greater part of their value from Irish real property or mineral rights ("specified assets").

In a situation when a foreign owner of an Irish resident subsidiary is contemplating a sale of the assets of the Irish subsidiary, then consideration might be given to transferring the tax residence of the Irish subsidiary to a jurisdiction with which Ireland has a tax treaty. Such a transfer of residence to a treaty jurisdiction does not give rise to an exit charge for capital gains tax purposes. It may be possible to exploit these provisions in relation to an asset sale if matters can be structured so that the newly non-Irish resident subsidiary is not within the charge to Irish tax as a branch.

8.9 CONCLUSION

The previous commentary focuses on the acquisition of an existing Irish business by either an Irish or foreign purchaser or the acquisition of a foreign business by what will already be a substantial Irish company. It may be appropriate, however, to consider Ireland as an intermediate entity in a cross-border acquisition. The corporate tax of 12.5 percent will apply to all trading profits from January 1, 2003.

CHAPTER 9

Taxation of Mergers and Acquisitions in Italy

Robert Lazzarone
Franco Carlo Papa
Ernst & Young Italy

9.1 **Direct Taxation**
    (a) Tax Neutrality Principle
    (b) Substitute Tax
    (c) Transfer of Subjective Economic Positions of the Divided Company
    (d) Tax Treatment of Losses
    (e) Tax Treatment Applicable Merger Funds
    (f) Income Tax Return
9.2 **Indirect Taxation**
    (a) Value-Added Tax and Registration Duties
    (b) Value-Added Tax Return
    (c) Other Taxes
9.3 **Sale of Going Concerns and Substantial Participation**
    (a) Standard Tax Regime Applicable to the Sale of a Going Concern
    (b) Standard Tax Regime Applicable to the Sale of Substantial Participation
    (c) Substitute Tax Applicable to the Sale of Substantial Participation
    (d) Value-Added Tax and Registration Duties
9.4 **Capital Contributions**
    (a) Standard Tax Regime Applicable to the Going Concern
    (b) Substitute Tax Applicable to the Contribution of a Going Concern
    (c) Indirect Taxation
9.5 **Exchange of Shares**
9.6 **Anti-Avoidance Provisions**
    (a) Fictional Interposition
    (b) Anti-Avoidance Provisions
    (c) Tax Rulings

9.1 DIRECT TAXATION

(a) Tax Neutrality Principle

Mergers and demergers in Italy are neutral for income tax purposes under Sections 123 and 123 *bis* of the Presidential Decree No. 917 of December 22, 1986 (T.U.I.R.). Accordingly, these mergers and demergers do not give rise to any taxable capital gain or deductible capital loss. The business assets maintain their historical tax values. However, the taxpayer can transfer the higher assets' values without realizing any immediately taxable gain on the sale under Legislative Decree No. 358 of October 8, 1997.

(b) Substitute Tax

A substitute optional taxation regime provides for the application of a reduced 27 percent rate. This amount applies to the negative merger or demerger difference under Legislative Decree No. 358/97. The merger or demerger difference is the difference between the net worth of the merged, or split, company and the book value of the transferred or written-off shares in these companies. The taxpayer can step up the basis of the assets of the merged company for income tax purposes if the taxpayer pays the substitute tax on such difference.

Such substitute tax is a definitive tax liability and the substitute tax is not deductible for income tax purposes. Italy lowered the substitute tax from 27 percent to 19 percent under Section 6 of Law No. 432/2000 and Legislative Decree 358/97. The procedure for Section 6 and Section 2 reflects the substitute tax payments under paragraph 1 of Legislative Decree 358/97.

Under the former procedure, the taxpayer can pay the tax in one to five installments under Section 2. Pursuant to the new procedure, the taxpayer is no longer allowed to elect such deferred payment. The payment takes place exclusively in one installment. The tax must be paid within the term provided for the payment of the corporate tax. This timing relates to the fiscal year when the capital gain was realized or when the merger was carried on.

The substitute taxation regime does not apply in case of winding up of the company. Moreover, a partial or an entire restatement of the tax basis may be available at no additional cost. This restatement takes place if the merger follows an acquisition and if taxpayers can prove that sellers have fully paid their Italian income tax on a resulting gain.

(c) Transfer of Subjective Economic Positions of the Divided Company

Specific rules are provided for the transfer of the subjective economic positions of the divided company. In this respect, Section 123 *bis,* paragraph 2 of T.U.I.R. states that:

> *From the effective date of the split-up the subjective economic positions of the split company and the related operational obligations shall be attributed to the receiving companies and in the case of a partial split-up, to the company itself in proportion to the respective portions of accounting net worth transferred or retained.*

9.1 Direct Taxation

Such provision does not apply when some items are connected with elements of the divided property. In this case, the items shall follow said elements and their owners.

(d) Tax Treatment of Losses

Pursuant to Section 123, paragraph 5, the losses that a merged company incurs can be used to reduce the income of the combined company as only to the portion determined as follows:

- The portion of losses available cannot exceed the net worth reflected in the last balance sheet. The amount is lower if the balance sheet is drawn up at the time the merger is established. This amount is to be determined without taking into account any contributions to capital made during the 24-month period before the date of this balance sheet.
- The profit and loss account for the company, the losses of which are to be carried forward, shows revenues and expenses, for the fiscal year before the merger, revenues from sale of goods, and rendering of services. The amounts reflect expenditure for costs related to employees and related social contributions that are higher than 40 percent of the average of the two previous fiscal years.

Tax losses can be carried forward. However, some of the shares could be even partially owned by the merging company. In that event, the losses cannot be carried forward for an amount equal to any write-down of said shares made by the merging company. The amount of the merger difference is used to write up the transferred assets. The same rules apply in the case of a demerger, as stated by Section 123 *bis* of T.U.I.R.

(e) Tax Treatment Applicable to Merger Funds

Following the merger, the merging company prepares financial statements for the merged company's funds. The merged business should distinguish between taxed and nontaxed funds. Taxed funds (so-called free funds) have been already taxed in the hands of the merged company. As a result, the merging company can distribute the funds to its shareholders without any further taxation.

As to nontaxed funds (so-called *fondi in sospensione d'imposta*), these funds can be divided into the following categories:

- *Taxable funds such as extraordinary income funds:* In the event that the merging company does not reflect these funds in its financial statements, these extraordinary income funds will increase its taxable income.
- *Funds taxable only in case of distribution, such as gain revaluation funds:* The merging company must enter these distribution funds in its financial statements. The merging company must reflect these funds to the extent that the positive merger difference or capital increase is higher than the aggregate capital of the companies (including the merging entity) involved in the merger. These funds increase the merging company's taxable income in case of distribution to the shareholders.

(f) Income Tax Return

As to income tax returns, the ordinary rules apply in case the parties anticipate the merger's effects or deferred to the beginning of the fiscal period. In this case, the merging company should file only one income tax return because at that moment, the companies had already merged. In the event that the merger occurred in the course of the fiscal period, the merger amounts should be divided as follows:

- *Fiscal period before the merger:* The merging company should file the tax returns for each merged company within four months from the date the merger was effected, as stated by Section 11 of Presidential Decree No. 600 of September 29, 1973;
- *Fiscal period subsequent to the merger:* The merging company should file the tax returns in compliance with ordinary rules.

9.2 INDIRECT TAXATION

(a) Value-Added Tax and Registration Duties

Mergers and demergers do not trigger the application of the value-added tax (VAT) as stated by Section 2, paragraph 3, letter f of Presidential Decree No. 633 of October 26, 1972. Moreover, the merging company can benefit from tax facilities applicable to the merged company as to the import of goods and services that are exempt from VAT. Presidential Decree No. 131 of April 24, 1986 provides for the application of a registration tax equal to ITL 250,000 or 129.11€ to both the resolution and the merger deed.

(b) Value-Added Tax Return

As a general rule, the merging company should file the ordinary returns for VAT purposes. After the merger, the VAT credit or debt of the merged companies may be transferred to the merging company. The VAT credit/debt can be transferred during the fiscal year. In that situation, the merging company should file a prospectus about the sales of goods and services rendered by the merged company in the portion of the year previous to the merger; however, if the merger occurred between January 1 and the due date for filing the income tax return, the merging company should file the VAT return for the previous fiscal year.

(c) Other Taxes

Both mergers and demergers are subject to the application of the local tax on Increased Value of Immovable Goods (INVIM). This tax ranges on a progressive basis between 3 percent and 30 percent. INVIM is levied on the increase of the property value. This amount is calculated as the difference between the acquisi-

9.3 Sale of Going Concerns and Substantial Participation

tion cost and the market value of the property on December 31, 1992. In such calculation, the acquisition cost may be increased by the cost incurred for the improvement of the property. INVIM applies only if the transfer occurs not later than January 1, 2003. Moreover, INVIM applies to property owned for a 10-year period, even if the property is not sold.

9.3 SALE OF GOING CONCERNS AND SUBSTANTIAL PARTICIPATION

(a) Standard Tax Regime Applicable to the Sale of a Going Concern

As part of the sale of a going concern, the seller can choose in addition to the optional substitute taxation between two different capital gain taxation regimes. Pursuant to Section 54 of T.U.I.R., the capital gains from the sale may be included for their entire amount in the year in which the gains were realized or in equal installments in the current and following fiscal years, not to exceed the fourth year. The first option may be more tax convenient in case the seller has suffered losses for the current year or has losses carried forward from the previous years.

The seller of a going concern may opt for the application of the 19 percent substitute tax on capital gains realized on the sale, as stated by Section 1 of Legislative Decree 358/97 and as amended by Section 6 of Law No. 432/2000. In order to benefit from the application of such substitute tax, the seller must have owned the going concern for at least three years. The seller may not use the net operating losses to offset the substitute tax due if the taxpayer elects to use the optional substitute taxation regime.

(b) Standard Tax Regime Applicable to the Sale of Substantial Participation

As regards the standard taxation regime of the capital gains realized on sale of substantial participation, a participation can be defined as "substantial" if it meets the requirements set by Section 2359 of the Civil Code. According to Section 2359, a company is deemed to control another company if it meets the following criteria:

- The company has the voting majority in the ordinary shareholders' meeting.
- The company has sufficient voting rights to exert a dominant influence.
- The company is able to exert a dominant influence because of its contractual relationship with the other company.

Companies are considered to be related if one of them exerts a significant influence on the other. A "significant influence" is presumed if a company has at least one-fifth of the voting rights, or one-tenth of the voting rights if the company is listed.

(c) Substitute Tax Applicable to the Sale of Substantial Participation

The seller of a substantial participation in controlled or related companies, as defined earlier, may elect for the application of the 19 percent substitute tax on capital gains realized on the sale. Moreover, in order to benefit from the application of the substitute taxation regime, the substantial participations in controlled or associated companies must have been reflected in the seller's last three financial statements as fixed financial assets.

(d) Value-Added Tax and Registration Duties

According to Section 2, paragraph 3 of Presidential Decree No. 633 of October 26, 1972, the sale of a going concern is not subject to VAT. The acquiring company can benefit from the tax facilities applicable to the merged company with respect to import goods and services exempt from VAT provided that, as specified by the Minister of Finance in Circular No.16/E of January 15, 1996, the following requirements are met:

- The seller transfers all its credit to the acquiring company.
- The acquiring company performs the same activity as the seller.

A 3 percent registration duty generally applies to the sale of a going concern; however, if the going concern consists of assets subject to different tax rates, the corresponding rate is levied on each asset.

Pursuant to Section 10 of Presidential Decree 633/72, the transactions connected to the selling of shares are exempt from VAT. The exemption decreases the percentage of the VAT deductible by the acquiring company in compliance with the pro-rata principle. The registration duty is normally due in a fixed amount of ITL 250,000 or 129.11∈, provided that the sale is exempt from the special stock exchange transfer tax, otherwise applicable in an amount of ITL 140 each ITL 100,000. The sale of a going concern is subject to the application of INVIM as previously described.

9.4 CAPITAL CONTRIBUTIONS

(a) Standard Tax Regime Applicable to the Going Concern

Under the standard tax regime, the capital gain arising from the contribution of a going concern may be taxed in two different ways. The transferor may decide to include capital gain in the taxable base of the fiscal year in which it was realized. In this case, capital gain would be subject to the ordinary income tax at a 36 percent rate. On the other hand, Section 54 of T.U.I.R. allows the taxpayer to defer the payment in the following years, not to exceed the fourth year, provided that the going concern has been owned for at least three years.

9.5 Exchange of Shares

(b) Substitute Tax Applicable to the Contribution of a Going Concern

Section 4, paragraph 1 of Legislative Decree 358/97 provides a preferential tax treatment applicable to an Italian transferor contributing a going concern to an Italian corporation in exchange for shares on a tax-free basis. The company to which the going concern is contributed can elect to retain the historical tax value of the assets received. The shareholding attributed to the transferor will retain the same value as the contributed assets. In order to benefit from such preferential tax treatment, the transferor must have owned the going concern for at least three years. Such preferential treatment applies to the following situations:

- Transactions carried out between Italian-resident entities
- Transactions performed between an Italian resident and a foreign entity, provided that the contributed going concern is located in Italy

Section 4, paragraph 2 states that, in the event that the transferor has owned the going concern for at least three years, the transferor or the transferee can elect for a 19 percent substitute tax to apply to the gain realized on the contribution. The preferential tax treatment provided for the contribution of a going concern applies to the contribution of substantial participation as described.

(c) Indirect Taxation

Pursuant to Section 2, paragraph 3 of Presidential Decree No. 633 of October 26, 1972, the sale of a going concern is not subject to VAT. Accordingly, a registration duty, in the fixed amount of ITL 250,000 or 129.11ϵ, is due as stated by Presidential Decree No.131/86. The tax on stock exchange contracts applies to contribution of participations regardless of their entity, at the fixed amount of 140 ITL for each 100,000 ITL.

9.5 EXCHANGE OF SHARES

Through the exchange of shares, a company can purchase (or integrate) a majority shareholding in another company by assigning its own shares to the shareholders of the entity. According to Section 5, paragraph 1 of Legislative Decree 358/97, the exchange of shares is neutral for income tax purposes, provided that the following criteria exist:

- The cost of exchanged shares or stocks is attributed to the shares received in exchange.
- No compensation in cash is paid.

Pursuant to Section 5, any cash that may be received is taxable at the recipient level. Section 5, paragraph 2 states that the exchange of shares is treated as neutral for income tax purposes. Such an amount is made through capital contributions into companies. Under this method, the transferor acquires control of a company in accordance with Article 2359, subsection 1, No. 1 of the Civil Code. In this case, the shares (or quotas) received should be valued on the basis of the corresponding portion of the net equity of the transferee as a result of the capital contribution. If the receiving company enters a higher value in its books, the company will give rise to a capital gain taxable according to the ordinary or substitute tax regime.

9.6 ANTI-AVOIDANCE PROVISIONS

(a) Fictional Interposition

The concept of fictitious interposition applies as stated in Section 37 of Presidential Decree No. 600 of September 29, 1973. Section 7, paragraph 3 of Legislative Decree 358/97 introduced specific rules aimed at identifying potentially elusive transactions. In particular, Section 37, paragraph 3 of Presidential Decree No. 600 of September 29, 1973 sets forth a specific anti-avoidance provision concerning persons owning income through interposed persons. Pursuant to Section 37, in case of assessment, the taxpayer can be taxed on income accrued by another person, if it is demonstrated that the latter person was interposed by the taxpayer in order to avoid taxation. The provision applies only in the event that the interposition can be deemed as fictitious on the ground of serious, exact, and consistent presumptions as proved by the Tax Inspectors.

(b) Anti-Avoidance Provisions

General anti-avoidance provisions are contained in Section 37 *bis* of Presidential Decree No. 600 of September 29, 1973. Legislative Decree No. 358/97 inserted Section 37 *bis* into Presidential Decree No. 600 of September 29, 1973, which governs the assessment of income taxes. The anti-avoidance provision is applicable only to the following operations:

- Company transformations
- Mergers
- Demergers
- Voluntary winding up
- Distribution of sums to stockholders drawn from entries of net assets other than those formed consisting of profits
- Capital contribution or transfer of going concerns and company/corporate rentals
- Assignments of credits or tax surpluses
- Intra-community operations foreseen by Directive No. 434/1990
- Caluations of determined assets

The Legislative Decree extends the range of transactions governed by Italian anti-abuse provisions. The Tax Authorities can consider related transactions. By virtue

9.6 Anti-Avoidance Provisions

of the aforementioned powers, Tax Authorities may combine related transactions in order to determine whether the anti-abuse provisions should operate. Accordingly, transactions that are not specifically covered by the anti-abuse provisions may fall within the purview of these rules if related to qualifying transactions.

(c) Tax Rulings

In order to prevent the Tax Inspectors from assessing the application of the anti-avoidance provisions contained in Presidential Decree No. 600/73, the taxpayer can apply for a ruling on the fairness of the transactions that it intends to perform. The ruling is not binding on the Tax Authorities; however, the procedure shifts the burden of proof from the taxpayer to the Tax Authorities. The Tax Authorities must send to the taxpayer a request for clarification of an apparent nonconformity before issuing an anti-avoidance assessment. The taxpayer has, therefore, the opportunity to justify him or herself. The taxpayer may avoid an assessment procedure and any possible subsequent litigation whenever this defense is deemed plausible and acceptable.

A new tax ruling procedure was introduced by Law No. 212 of July 27, 2000 (the so-called Taxpayer Code). In accordance with this procedure, the taxpayer submits a written request to the Tax Authorities. The Tax Authorities provide "objective uncertainty" of the tax law, including a detailed description of the facts involved, the proposed steps to be taken and, if possible, a solution. The Tax Authorities must reply within 120 days. The Tax Authorities' opinion is valid only for the case on which the ruling is requested and only for the single taxpayer. Failure to reply within 120 days implies that the taxpayer can assume that the Tax Authorities agree with the proposed solution.

The Taxpayer Code has established, at each regional Department of Revenue, the taxpayer Guarantor (the so-called *Garante*). Law 212/2000 allows the *Garante* to ask tax offices for clarification and to oblige them to respond within 30 days. In case the Tax Authorities' acts are found to be defective, the *Garante* shall require the competent tax office to render them void. The *Garante* is also empowered to proceed on the taxpayer's (or any other individual's) request or notice relating to administrative defects or malpractices that may damage the fiduciary relation with the taxpayers.

CHAPTER 10

Taxation of Mergers and Acquisitions in Japan

Kan Hayashi
Al Zencak
PricewaterhouseCoopers, Tokyo

10.1 Introduction
    (a) Common Forms of Business Entity
    (b) Foreign Ownership Restrictions
    (c) Corporate Tax
    (d) Withholding Tax
    (e) Taxation of Dividends
    (f) Tax Losses
    (g) Thin Capitalization
    (h) Other Taxes
10.2 Sale of Shares or Assets
10.3 Structuring a Share Deal
    (a) Profit on Sale of Shares
    (b) Distribution of Profits
    (c) Acquisition Structure (Form and Location of Acquisition Company)
    (d) Funding Costs
    (e) Acquisition Expenses
    (f) Government Approval
    (g) Preservation of Tax Losses
    (h) Repatriation of Profits
10.4 Structuring an Asset Deal
    (a) Seller's Perspective
    (b) Valuation of Goodwill in Related Party Transfers
    (c) Calculation of FMV
    (d) Buyer's Perspective
    (e) Funding Cost
    (f) Acquisition Costs
    (g) Cost Basis Step-Up/Treatment of Goodwill
    (h) Consumption Tax
10.5 Share-for-Share Exchanges or Transfers
10.6 Tax-Free Corporate Reorganization Rules
    (a) Introduction
    (b) 100 Percent Direct or Indirect Ownership in Subsidiary

    (c) More Than 50 Percent Direct or Indirect Ownership in Transferee Corporation
    (d) Joint Business Reorganization (50 Percent or Less Ownership)
    (e) Investment in Kind
    (f) Post-Establishment Transfer
    (g) Merger
    (h) Restriction of Using Built-In Losses
    (i) Basis Allocation Rule
10.7 **Exit Strategies**
    (a) Sales of Shares
    (b) IPO
    (c) Profit Repatriation
10.8 **Outline of Tax Reform Other Than for Corporate Reorganizations**
    (a) Taxation for Finance
    (b) Consolidated Tax Return System
10.9 **Conclusion: Preparation for the Deal**
    (a) Foreign Exchange Control Laws
    (b) Japanese Commercial Code (JCC)
    (c) Japanese Anti-Monopoly Law/Consolidated Tax Filing
    (d) Japan's Ministry of Finance

10.1 INTRODUCTION

Companies incorporated in Japan are subject to Japanese tax on their worldwide income. A branch of a foreign company is subject to tax in Japan only on its income that is attributable to the Japanese branch.

Japanese corporations are entitled to claim a tax credit against their corporate and inhabitants taxes for foreign tax paid. Such foreign tax includes withholding tax and the underlying tax as to dividends from a foreign subsidiary, down to a second-tier subsidiary.

A tax haven is defined as a territory that imposes a corporate tax of 25 percent or less. Undistributed profits of a foreign subsidiary that is located in a tax haven are included in the taxable income of the Japanese parent unless the parent satisfies specified conditions for exemption from the rules. A foreign tax credit is available for any foreign taxes that are paid by a tax haven foreign subsidiary.

Capital gains and losses are treated as ordinary income or losses and taxed accordingly. However, a rollover provision is available for deferring the gains realized from the sale of real property, where the proceeds are reinvested in certain specific fixed assets.

Significant changes in the Japanese Commercial Code (JCC) and corporate tax laws have taken place regarding stock-for-stock exchanges and tax-free reorganizations—mergers in order to facilitate M & A and corporate restructurings.

10.1 Introduction

(a) Common Forms of Business Entity

Exhibit 10.1 shows the most common business entities in Japan prescribed under the JCC:

Exhibit 10.1

COMMON BUSINESS ENTITIES

Name of entity or legal form	Description	Japanese tax features
Japanese branch	Standard form for foreign companies operating in Japan	Japanese corporate tax payable on profit; no withholding tax on the remittance of branch profits
Kabushiki Kaisha (KK)	Standard company form	Japanese corporate tax payable on profit; withholding tax on dividends
Yugen Kaisha (YK)	"Small company" business company form	Basically same as KK, although it may be possible for U.S. investors to treat a YK as fiscally transparent for U.S. tax purposes
Tokumei Kumiai (TK; Undisclosed Association) under Commercial Code	Under a TK contract, parties agree that one (undisclosed party) of them shall make a contribution toward the business of the other (Operator) and that they shall allocate any profits or losses arising from such business.	Distributions made by a Japanese operator to investors in TK may be deductible for Japanese tax purposes. Distribution to non-Japanese resident investors (undisclosed party) may or may not be subject to Japanese taxation depending on the number of undisclosed parties (10 or more), existence of PE in Japan and the tax treaty concerned.

(b) Foreign Ownership Restrictions

Generally, a foreign company is permitted to own 100 percent of a Japanese company, subject to certain reporting procedures. The Japanese government has relaxed its foreign ownership policy. As a result, it is now easier for foreign investors to acquire Japanese companies directly.

(c) Corporate Tax

Japanese corporations and branches are subject to the following taxes:

- National corporate tax
- Local inhabitants tax
- Business enterprise tax

The current combined effective rate of tax (national and local) is approximately 42.05 percent after taking into account the tax deductibility of the business enterprise tax.

(d) Withholding Tax

Withholding tax applies to the following types of income:

- Japanese-source dividends
- Interest
- Royalties
- Service fees
- Rent received by a foreign corporation

Withholding tax is imposed at the rate of 20 percent under Japanese domestic law. Japan has an extensive tax treaty network, so that lower tax rates may be available, depending on the particular treaty that applies. A service fee that is not sourced in Japan and remittances of branch profits are not subject to withholding tax.

(e) Taxation of Dividends

Dividends net of attributable financing costs received by a Japanese company (ParentKK) from another Japanese company (SubKK) may be excluded from the taxable income of ParentKK provided that ParentKK owns 25 percent or more of SubKK. If ParentKK owns less than 25 percent of SubKK, only 80 percent of the dividends from SubKK net of attributable financing costs may be excluded from the taxable income of ParentKK. There is also a special rule relating to minor shareholding and investment trust that must be considered.

Exclusion from taxable income is not permitted for dividends on shares that were acquired within one month before the year-end of the company paying the dividend concerned and sold within two months after the same year-end.

The Japanese income tax that is withheld by the Japanese dividend paying company at 20 percent is generally recoverable by the recipient either as a credit against its taxable profits or as a refund if the recipient is in a tax loss position. There may be situations where the credit is not available and the recipient can only report the withheld tax as a deduction against income.

(f) Tax Losses

Tax losses may be carried forward in Japan for up to five years. Currently, losses may not be carried back except, for example, for tax losses incurred by small and medium-sized corporations. A small or medium-sized corporation is a corporation whose capital is ¥100 million or less and 50 percent or more of its stock is not held by a "large company," including a foreign company, in the first five years of operation. Such losses may be carried back one year upon application by the taxpayer.

10.1 Introduction

A company may be permitted to carryforward losses that are incurred during the first five years after the date of incorporation for seven years if it meets certain requirements.

A change in ownership of shares in a company or a change in the nature of a company's business does not give rise to the expiration or limitations on the use of tax losses in Japan. "Latent" tax losses (e.g., the difference between the Japanese tax book value of assets and their actual market value) are generally not realized until a taxable event, such as a sale of the assets or a transfer of assets pursuant to a merger.

(g) Thin Capitalization

Interest arising from debts due to foreign controlling shareholders which are either Japanese nonresidents or foreign corporations holding 50 percent or more of shares of a domestic corporation, is not tax deductible if the debt exceeds three times the net equity of the Japanese company. The excess interest is permanently disallowed as a deduction. The disallowed interest deduction cannot be carried back or forward. However, the excess interest may still be subject to Japanese withholding tax for interest.

Third-party debt that is guaranteed by an affiliate is not subject to the thin capitalization rules. The thin capitalization rules provide a comparable company ratio exception, which is determined based on standards similar to those that should be used under a transfer-pricing context. Under this exception, it is permissible to use a ratio that is higher than 3 to 1 if such ratio is also used by a specific Japanese corporation of similar size conducting similar business activities. The tax authorities take a very strict position on the comparability exception.

Interest expense that is incurred for debt that is used to acquire shares in a domestic entity is not allowed as a deduction because the dividend is generally tax-free. Funding costs to acquire foreign shares is, in principle, tax deductible, but subject to an adjustment in determining the foreign tax credit applicable to the relevant foreign-sourced dividend income.

(h) Other Taxes

Japanese consumption tax (currently 5 percent) applies to goods sold and services rendered in Japan, excluding shares or securities but including goodwill. Export and certain services invoiced to nonresidents are zero-rated. Such consumption tax may be recoverable by the payers depending on their consumption tax recovery position. Typically, this consumption tax would not be recoverable for an individual who is not registered for consumption tax purposes. The consumption tax may be only partially recoverable for a company in the financial sector, but it may be fully recoverable for manufacturing or other service companies.

The security transfer tax has been abolished. Stamp duty is payable on taxable documents, with the maximum of ¥600,000 per document.

10.2 SALE OF SHARES OR ASSETS

In many situations, the buyer or seller will have conflicting interests regarding whether to structure the transaction as a sale of shares or assets. Important considerations may include the following:

- The extent to which gain or loss will be recognized by the seller on the disposition
- The buyer's willingness to increase the purchase price to achieve structuring objectives
- The seller's after-tax investment return (in addition, many buyers want to purchase only selected assets or businesses.)

Because of Japan's relatively high individual and corporate tax rates, a sale followed by a liquidation or distribution of after-tax proceeds to the seller may have a significant impact, depending on the circumstances, on the acquisition price and the structure of the transaction.

A seller of a profitable business is more likely to be interested in selling shares because this may mitigate the consequences of possible double taxation on gains at both the corporate and shareholder levels. However, where the target company has operating loss carryforwards that are available to shelter gains on appreciated assets, a seller may prefer to dispose of assets if the seller can sell the assets at a higher value because the gain could be offset by the loss carryforwards.

If the transaction is structured as a sale of shares, the seller will be subject to income tax. If the transaction is structured as a sale of assets, the target will be required to allocate the sales price among the assets to calculate the amount of the gain or loss to be recognized.

10.3 STRUCTURING A SHARE DEAL

(a) Profit on Sale of Shares

The gain that is realized on the sale of shares is included as income and taxed at the normal tax rates. Neither stamp duty nor transfer duty is payable on the transfer of shares. Consumption tax does not apply to the sale of shares.

Gains derived by Japanese corporate sellers on the disposition of shares is taxed at the current combined effective corporate income tax rate of approximately 42.05 percent. Gains derived by a foreign seller on the disposition of shares of a Japanese company may not be subject to Japanese tax, depending on the facts and applicable tax treaty.

Gains derived by individual sellers on the disposition of shares are taxable at the combined national and local individual tax rates of 26 percent. Individual sellers who have losses in the same income category may deduct such losses against share gains in the same year. Individual sellers may not generally carry

10.3 Structuring a Share Deal

forward losses. If the target is a publicly traded company, an individual seller who realizes a gain on the sale of shares may elect to be taxed at a rate of 1.05 percent on the sale proceeds. The election to be taxed at a rate of 1.05 percent is effective until March 31, 2003.

(b) Distribution of Profits

Capital gains may be distributed as dividends to the shareholders without any restrictions [see 10.1(d) and 10.1(e)].

(c) Acquisition Structure (Form and Location of Acquisition Company)

Generally, an acquisition of a Japanese company is achieved through a direct acquisition by a foreign investor. When a buyer intends to exit in subsequent years, it may wish to use an appropriate holding company in the United States, the Netherlands, Switzerland, or Germany. The Japanese tax treaties with these countries provide exemptions from Japanese tax on gains from the sale of shares in a Japanese corporation.

An acquisition of the target's shares will permit the survival of any Japanese corporate tax attributes of the target, including net operating loss carryforwards. However, when a premium is paid to acquire shares, the goodwill arising from the purchase of shares is not amortizable to the buyer for Japanese tax purposes.

The target's tax basis in its assets remains unchanged in connection with a share purchase, as there is no change in the tax attributes of the target. Further, there would not necessarily be any costs from the transfer of employees, which tend to be normal features of asset purchases. On the other hand, subsequent decisions made by the acquiror regarding personnel issues may be constrained by the target's existing work rules, severance, and retirement plans.

(d) Funding Costs

Interest incurred by a Japanese company on funds that are used to acquire shares in another Japanese corporation is tax deductible. However, to the extent a deduction is taken for interest that is attributable to the debt that is used to acquire the stock on which the dividends are paid, the dividends cannot be excluded from taxable income. For this purpose, interest attributable to such shareholdings includes interest expense, other than interest on bonds and interest paid on bank loans of three years or more.

(e) Acquisition Expenses

Acquisition costs incurred by a Japanese company regarding the acquisition of shares in another Japanese corporation are not tax deductible in Japan. Such costs may be capitalized and deductible for tax purposes when the shares are sold.

(f) Government Approval

No approval is required for a share acquisition, but such acquisition may be subject to anti-trust clearance and other approvals for operational license, depending on the nature of business concerned.

(g) Preservation of Tax Losses

Tax losses, unabsorbed tax depreciation, and tax incentives stay with the target company after a share deal. If a company with tax losses is merged with another company, such tax losses may be carried over to that other company and used, subject to the net operating loss carryforward rules; however, it may be possible to step up the cost basis of the assets transferred to enable the other company to claim additional depreciation or amortization on the increased cost basis in the case of a "disqualified" reorganization or asset sale. (For a more detailed analysis of these two issues, please see section 10.6, Tax-free Reorganizations.)

(h) Repatriation of Profits

For repatriation of profits, consider the withholding tax implications relating to the payment of dividends, royalties, and interest. The payment of royalties and interest are subject to the Japanese transfer pricing regulations (and thin capitalization rules for interest).

10.4 STRUCTURING AN ASSET DEAL

(a) Seller's Perspective

A business may be transferred from one entity in Japan to another by way of a sale of the assets and liabilities of the business (Business Transfer) at fair market value for Japanese tax purposes (JFMV). The transferor company will record a profit or loss for Japanese tax purposes based on the difference between the proceeds received for the transfer and the book value of the business that is transferred. The transferee company will generally record the assets and liabilities at the JFMV. The difference between the transfer price and the JFMV of the assets and liabilities in the business transfer would generally be treated as goodwill for Japanese tax purposes.

A payment received by the transferor company for goodwill would be included in its taxable profit, but any accumulated net operating losses of the transferor could offset the taxable profit. The transferee company would record the goodwill in its accounts and amortize the goodwill for tax purposes on a straight-line basis over a period of five years.

In the absence of real estate or marketable securities or goodwill it may be possible to structure the business transfer so that most of the business assets are transferred at net book value without the recognition of taxable gain.

10.4 Structuring an Asset Deal

The disposition of assets by the target will result in a gain taxable at the combined national and local corporate tax rate of 42.05 percent. The amount of the target's gain or loss will be equal to the difference between the amount received for the assets and the target's adjusted tax basis in the assets. There is no distinction under Japanese corporate tax law between capital gains and ordinary income. In many cases, the tax and accounting basis in the assets is the same because there is a close degree of book and tax conformity.

(b) Valuation of Goodwill in Related Party Transfers

Under the Japanese tax laws, the Inheritance Tax Law provides a method for calculating goodwill directly, not as a gap between the total business value and net book value. In practice, this inheritance tax method is often used for corporate income tax purposes as well. This method is used to calculate the "excess earning" power that is represented by the excess portion of 50 percent of the average historical taxable income over a designated return on total assets (currently 3.5 percent). This method gives a low value for goodwill, where the total tangible assets used for business concerned are not small, but it could give some value for software or venture business due to smaller tangible assets.

For the valuation of total business value, other methods such as the market approach, comparables, and their combination are often accepted by the tax authorities. The use of the discounted cashflow (DCF) method to determine the value of a business is less common to the Japanese tax authorities, but it could be accepted if the DCF was computed by an independent professional firm. Because the calculation of goodwill involves the determination of the excess earning power, it is often difficult to justify the existence of goodwill as to a loss-making company. Furthermore, because the valuation of goodwill often involves subjective factors, the issue is often subject to dispute with the Japanese tax authorities.

(c) Calculation of FMV

The basis for calculating the FMV of certain assets is summarized as follows. Other methods may be used if these methods give an unreasonable result:

- *Land and buildings:* Appraisal value determined by an authorized real estate appraiser. Otherwise, a value publicized by the government for purposes of the fixed assets tax or similar tax, known as *Rosenka*.
- *Depreciable assets:* Value determined by applying depreciation rates specified for Japanese tax purposes
- *Retirement reserves:* Most Japanese companies provide accrued retirement allowances up to the tax-deductible limit that approximates 20 percent (currently 27 percent for 2001 and 23 percent for 2002 under tentative measures) of the full liability on a voluntary retirement base; however, Japan Generally Accepted Accounting Principles (GAAP) has recently implemented a similar principle used under FAS 87, which may differ from the deductible amount calculated based on the Japanese tax rules.

The seller of assets is required to collect Japanese consumption tax (currently 5 percent) from the buyer in connection with a sale of assets.

(d) Buyer's Perspective

Asset purchases in Japan may be more cumbersome and costly to the acquiror than share purchases because of transaction taxes and filing procedures applicable to such acquisitions.

The transaction may be structured as an acquisition of specific assets or businesses if the target has assets the acquiror does not want to purchase, or contingent or unrecorded liabilities. Although the rules are changing, Japanese accounting procedures do not yet require extensive financial statement disclosures and permit, in certain situations, the recording of assets and liabilities off-balance sheet in the financial statements of nonconsolidated subsidiaries. Accordingly, emphasis on preacquisition financial and legal due diligence is necessary.

An acquiror may prefer to acquire assets, for example, where the target does not have attractive tax attributes, such as operating loss carryovers, or where the acquiror expects to be able to recover a significant portion of the Japanese consumption taxes imposed on the purchase. In addition, an acquiror may also decide to acquire assets when there is an intention to integrate those assets into its existing business.

Under an asset deal, if a buyer does not have a presence in Japan, it could form a domestic corporation (e.g., a KK) that would take over the business operation of the target company.

(e) Funding Cost

The debt-equity ratio of the KK could be structured so that it is within the scope of the conditions stated under thin capitalization rules (discussed earlier) to maximize the interest deduction. Because the Japanese national and local tax rates are relatively high, the use of debt financing should reduce the Japanese tax to the KK.

(f) Acquisition Costs

The cost of acquisition—including professional fees, taxes, and charges—should, to the extent identifiable, be added to the cost of the relevant assets that are acquired. The tax treatment of these costs should then correspond with the tax treatment of the underlying assets (i.e., depreciable, amortizable or tax deductible when the assets are finally sold).

(g) Cost Basis Step-Up/Treatment of Goodwill

The acquiror's basis in the target's assets for Japanese tax purposes determines the amount of allowable depreciation and the cost of goods sold that may be deducted to determine the acquiror's taxable income after the acquisition. The acquiror will

10.5 Share-for-Share Exchanges or Transfer

take a cost basis in an asset acquisition. Therefore, the acquiror will be required to allocate the purchase price among the assets acquired to calculate future depreciation deductions to be taken by the acquiror.

If the target's FMV, including any goodwill arising from the asset acquisition, exceeds the adjusted tax basis of its assets, an asset acquisition allows the acquiror to record the assets at their respective FMV and obtain tax deductions for depreciation and amortization.

(h) Consumption Tax

Japanese consumption tax is imposed on the transfer of assets (including goodwill) included in a business transfer; however, consumption tax that is paid by the transferee can be recovered, depending on the transferee's tax position.

10.5 SHARE-FOR-SHARE EXCHANGES OR TRANSFER

Under a stock-for-stock exchange, the issued and outstanding shares that are held by shareholders of a company that will become a wholly owned subsidiary (BCo) will be transferred to a company that will become the 100 percent parent company of BCo (ACo) (known as *Kabushi Kokan*). ACo will issue new shares to BCo's shareholders, which become shareholders of ACo.

Another option is a stock-for-stock transfer (known as *Kabushi Iten*). Under this option, shares of a company that will become a wholly owned subsidiary (BCo) that are held by BCo's shareholders will be transferred to another newly established company (ACo). ACo will issue new shares to BCo's shareholders so that ACo will become the 100 percent parent company of BCo. This approach is often used to create a common holding company of more than two entities.

The capital gain that would be realized by the shareholders of BCo on the transfer of BCo's shares pursuant to a stock-for-stock exchange or transfer for tax purposes is deferred, provided the following conditions are satisfied:

- ACo records the shares obtained from the former BCo's shareholders at an amount that is equal to or less than the total book value of the shares that were held by the BCo shareholders before to the stock-for-stock exchange.
- The total amount of shares that the BCo shareholders should receive as a result of the stock-for-stock exchanges should be at least 95 percent of the consideration that is received.

The book value of the BCo shares that must be recorded by ACo is the book value of the net assets of BCo immediately before the stock-for-stock exchanges if the number of shareholders in BCo has 50 or more stakeholders.

When cash or other assets are granted to the BCo shareholders at the time of the stock-for-stock exchange, gain or loss is equal to the amount of the cash or other property received less the book value of the shares transferred that is allocable to the cash or other property received.

10.6 TAX-FREE CORPORATE REORGANIZATION RULES

(a) Introduction

The corporate reorganization rules are effective for corporate reorganizations completed on and after April 1, 2001. Under the new corporate reorganization rules, assets and liabilities can be transferred at book value provided that certain conditions are met. As a result, the capital gain or loss that would be realized on the transfer will be deferred. However, if cash or assets, other than shares, are paid to the transferor or the merged company as consideration, the assets must be transferred at their FMV.

The new corporate reorganization rules apply to the following types of corporate reorganizations:

- Qualified corporate spin-offs and split-ups
- Qualified investment (contribution) in kind
- Qualified post-establishment transfers
- Qualified mergers

The following conditions for qualified reorganizations are *generally* common to each type of reorganization listed previously.

(b) 100 Percent Direct or Indirect Ownership in Subsidiary

A transfer of a business unit to a new or existing wholly owned subsidiary in return solely for shares/stock in the subsidiary can be accomplished on a tax-free basis. No other tests need be satisfied. In a split-up, the transfer can be accomplished on a tax-free basis even if the shares are issued to the shareholder who owns 100 percent of the transferor.

(c) More Than 50 Percent Direct or Indirect Ownership in Transferee Corporation

Tax-free transfers of a business unit to a less than 100 percent owned subsidiary can be accomplished if the transferor owns more than 50 percent, directly or indirectly, in the transferee corporation and the following conditions are satisfied:

- *Transfer of business unit:* It is expected that about 80 percent or more of the employees in the transferred business unit immediately before the reorganization will continue to be engaged in the transferred business at the transferee corporation.
- *Continuing business requirement:* The business that is transferred will continue to be operated by the transferee corporation after the transfer.
- *Assets transfer requirement:* The principal part of the business assets and liabilities used in the transferred business unit will be transferred to the transferee corporation.

(d) Joint Business Reorganization (50 Percent or Less Ownership)

The transfer of a business unit to a transferee corporation—50 percent or less of whose shares are owned by the transferor before the transfer—or the transfer of business units jointly made by unrelated parties can be accomplished on a tax-free basis under the following circumstances:

- The aforementioned conditions for transfers to a more than 50 percent owned subsidiary are satisfied.
- *Continuing shareholding requirement:* In general, more than 80% of the former shareholders of the transferor corporation must continue to hold the shares of the transferee corporation.
- *Business relevancy requirement:* The business transferred by the transferor and one of the businesses of the transferee must be "relevant" to each other.
- *Comparable business size requirement:* The ratio of either sales, number of employees, or another appropriate measure of the transferred business unit and the transferee's relevant business must be no greater than 5:1. However, if this condition cannot be met, this condition will still be satisfied if the transferor corporation sends at least one of its management-level persons to management of the transferee corporation. A management-level person would be a director, managing director, or similar person who is working in company management.

(e) Investment in Kind

An investment in kind, or contribution to capital, which generally meets the previous conditions, can be accomplished on a tax-free basis.

(f) Post-Establishment Transfer

Under a post-establishment transfer, the transferor corporation first incorporates a new corporation via a cash contribution, and the transferee corporation then uses the cash to purchase the transferred assets. This transaction can be accomplished tax-free if the following conditions are satisfied:

- The transferor company held all of the outstanding shares of the transferee company throughout the period up to and including the asset transfer.
- The transferor company expects to continue to hold the shares of the transferee company.
- The assignment of assets was planned at the time of the establishment of the subsidiary, and the assets were actually transferred within six months from the establishment of the subsidiary.
- The amount of cash paid to the transferor company is approximately the same as the amount contributed by the transferor company to the transferee company.

(g) Merger

In general, a tax-free merger can be accomplished if the aforementioned conditions are satisfied. No step-up in basis is allowed in a tax-free merger under the new rules.

Under the new tax rules, net operating losses (NOLs) of an acquired company are allowed to be transferred to an acquiror, subject to certain conditions. NOLs that arose before the loss company became a group member are generally not allowed to be used unless the merger took place five years since the loss company was acquired or such merger of the group companies satisfies the "Joint Business Test." On the other hand, the use of NOLs is not restricted in a qualified merger under a joint business reorganization between unrelated parties. In the case of spin-offs, split-ups (except for split-ups that can be regarded as merger equivalent), or contributions in kind, the NOLs remain with the transferor corporation.

Even if the Joint Business Test is not satisfied, the NOL that is incurred after the loss company became a group member of the acquiring company can be utilized in the case of a qualified merger.

(h) Restriction of Using Built-In Losses

In a qualified merger under the joint business reorganization, all of the built-in losses can be used when realized by the acquiring company. In a qualified merger within a group, a deduction of built-in losses is subject to and restricted by rules similar to those applicable to NOLs.

(i) Basis Allocation Rule

The new law provides that the shareholder's tax basis in a transferred corporation in the case of qualified split-ups is determined by allocating the basis in the transferring corporation in accordance with a ratio of the net asset value of the transferred business over the net asset value of the transferring corporation.

10.7 EXIT STRATEGIES

(a) Sales of Shares

Capital gains derived by a foreign corporation from the transfer of shares in a Japanese corporation are subject to Japanese corporate tax at the regular rates if the foreign corporation transferred at least 5 percent of the shares in the Japanese corporation in an accounting period and the foreign corporation owned at least 25 percent of the shares in the Japanese corporation at any time during the three-year period before the end of the accounting period in which the transfer was made (quasi-business transfer), However, the gain is specifically exempt from Japanese tax under certain tax treaties. For example, resident corporations of the Netherlands, Switzerland, the United States, and Germany are exempt under tax

10.9 Conclusion: Preparation for the Deal

treaties from Japanese tax on capital gains derived from the transfer of shares in a Japanese corporation, unless the gains are attributable to a fixed place of business (P/E) in Japan of the shareholder (i.e., if the shareholder held the shares through its Japanese branch).

(b) IPO

No special major tax laws or regulations are applicable to capital gains arising from an initial public offering (IPO) in Japan.

(c) Profit Repatriation

Generally, it is tax effective for the target to remit payments overseas to the acquiror or its affiliates in the form of tax-deductible payments, such as interest, royalties, cost of goods sold, or payment for services, rather than in the form of dividends that are not tax deductible in Japan. However, such payments are generally subject to scrutiny for transfer pricing purposes. In addition, the recipient should ensure that the services provided do not result in it having a PE in Japan.

10.8 OUTLINE OF TAX REFORM OTHER THAN FOR CORPORATE REORGANIZATIONS

(a) Taxation for Finance

Under the 1999 tax reform, the election to be taxed based on 1.05 percent of the sales proceeds from the sale of stock was to be abolished on and after April 1, 2001. Under the 2001 tax reform, this election is extended for an additional two years and will be abolished on and after April 1, 2003.

Nontaxation of interest for Japanese government-registered international bonds held by nonresidents or foreign corporations will be applicable to those instruments acquired via overseas financial institutions that are approved by the Bank of Japan and the tax office director, such as global custodians.

(b) Consolidated Tax Return System

The consolidated tax return system was not introduced in the tax reform in 2001; however, it is scheduled to be included in the 2002 tax reform. A technical review has started with respect to this provision.

10.9 CONCLUSION: PREPARATION FOR THE DEAL

Japan has many different kinds of taxes and regulations that are applicable to merger and acquisition deals. Thus, it is important for a party to any merger or acquisition to ensure that these taxes and regulations are being complied with.

(a) Foreign Exchange Control Laws

Japan's Foreign Exchange Control Law provides that foreign investors, including Japanese companies in which 50 percent or more of the shares are held by non-residents, or companies incorporated under foreign laws, must report all inward direct investment to the appropriate authorities within 15 days of making the investment. This is not for an approval process but only for reporting purposes.

(b) Japanese Commercial Code (JCC)

Formation of a company by way of contribution of assets in kind is generally subject to review by an inspector, who is appointed by the court (*Kensayaku*) under the JCC. Likewise, the JCC provides restrictions on the ability of acquirors to purchase business assets through a newly formed Japanese company. Business asset acquisitions that involve a newly formed Japanese company could be subject to the same court-appointed inspector requirement. These procedures may take time and delay the implementation of asset acquisitions; however, a corporate spin-off by virtue of the JCC from April 1, 2001 is not subject to such a review, although it has to comply with other conditions (i.e., less cumbersome).

(c) Japanese Anti-Monopoly Law/Consolidated Tax Filing

The recent changes to Japan's Anti-Monopoly Law no longer prohibit the use of holding companies in Japan. Because the Japanese tax rules do not currently provide for consolidated tax reporting, however, no particular tax incentives are associated with the use of domestic holding companies by foreign investors. The Ministry of Finance has considered the implementation of a consolidated tax filing system for many years and is expected to implement such a system in the 2002 tax reform.

(d) Japan's Ministry of Finance

Japan's Ministry of Finance has broad discretionary authority over many aspects of Japan's financial markets and the interpretation of laws relevant to financial institutions. As a result, tax planning techniques that may be reasonable and appropriate for nonfinancial services entities may not be possible for financial institutions without prior Ministry of Finance approval.

CHAPTER 11

Taxation of Merger and Acquisitions in Kazakhstan

Aigoul Kenjebayeva
Joseph Luke
Abai Shaikenov
Salans, Hertzfeld & Heilbronn, Kazakhstan

11.1 Introduction
    (a) Empirical Experience
    (b) Chapter Focus
11.2 Overview of Kazakhstan Tax and Legal System
    (a) Corporate Taxes
    (b) Tax Rates
    (c) International Tax Considerations
    (d) Value-Added Tax
    (e) Excise Taxes
11.3 Currency Control
    (a) Availability for Using Foreign Currency
    (b) Current and Capital Movements
11.4 Corporate Law
    (a) General Partnerships
    (b) Limited Partnerships
    (c) Production Cooperative
    (d) Closed Joint Stock Company and LLC
11.5 Securities Law
    (a) Issuable Securities
    (b) National Securities Commission
    (c) Disclosure to the National Securities Commission
    (d) Acquisition of Securities
11.6 Anti-Monopoly Provisions
    (a) Role of State Agencies
    (b) Halting of Production
11.7 Restrictions on Foreign Ownership of Domestic Businesses
11.8 Analysis of Mergers and Acquisitions
11.9 Legal Form
    (a) Types of Entities Usually Used for Acquisition of Assets
    (b) Types of Legal Contracts

11.10 Corporate Income Tax Consequences to the Seller
    (a) Revaluation
    (b) Below-Market Price Transfers
11.11 Value-Added Tax Consequences to the Seller
11.12 Transfer Pricing Regulations
11.13 Barter Operations
11.14 Taxation on the Sale of an Enterprise
11.15 Corporate Income Tax Consequences to the Buyer
11.16 Value-Added Tax Consequences to the Buyer
11.17 Tax Consequences of the Purchase of a Business as an Enterprise
11.18 Acquisition of Shares
    (a) Legal Form
    (b) Tax Consequences
11.19 Mergers
    (a) Legal Forms
    (b) Tax Consequences
11.20 Divisions
11.21 Carryover of Tax Attributes
11.22 Consolidation
11.23 Financing
11.24 Repatriation of Capital and Profits
11.25 Conclusion

11.1 INTRODUCTION

Since gaining independence from the Soviet Union in 1991, the Republic of Kazakhstan has been in the process of establishing its own legislation system. Kazakhstan has adopted a significant number of laws and regulations related to business development. The most recent laws on joint stock and limited liability companies were adopted in 1998, and the most recent tax code in 1995.

(a) Empirical Experience

Since 1991, Kazakhstan experience in the field of mergers and acquisitions has grown, mostly as to acquisitions, as one company acquired the assets or stock of another company. Thousands of state enterprises were acquired in the course of privatization, which is still ongoing. In 2000, the most noteworthy examples of acquisitions were the following:

- One of the largest Kazakhstan banks acquired 50 percent of the stock of the national air company and obtained the management rights to the other 50 percent as repayment for debt.
- A Canadian oil company, which owns an oil field in Kazakhstan, has acquired more than 88 percent of the stock of the refinery plant in exchange for stock and cash.

- One of the largest Kazakhstan private pension funds has merged with a smaller pension fund previously owned by the Kazakhstan trade union.

While Kazakhstan's practice in mergers and acquisitions grows, the taxation of mergers and acquisitions remains vague. At the end of 2000, the Kazakhstan legislature was reviewing drafts of the new tax code, part of which should be put into effect in 2001 and the remaining part in 2002. The new tax code is at least the third major change in the Kazakhstan tax legislation in 10 years. Among the expected changes will be new provisions that address some of the areas regulating application of taxes to legal entities, including the payment of taxes by liquidating and reorganizing legal entities.

(b) Chapter Focus

This chapter is devoted to a discussion of the tax aspects of corporate mergers and acquisitions in Kazakhstan. Obviously, the decision for companies to merge or for one company to acquire another must be based on several factors in which tax consequences are not the only legal issue that must be examined, although these tax consequences may be important. After this introductory section is a brief description of the existing legal landscape in Kazakhstan, emphasizing those areas that are important for commercial activity. Later we describe the tax consequences of acquiring assets, stocks, or a business for both the seller and the purchaser. Finally, we examine the taxation aspects of restructuring, either through mergers or consolidations or through spin-offs or divisions. The chapter ends with some miscellaneous observations and a conclusion.

Kazakhstan legislation has not created a legal structure exactly identical to a western corporation. The closest structure would be a "joint stock company," which, in many of its features, is similar to a corporation.

11.2 OVERVIEW OF KAZAKHSTAN TAX AND LEGAL SYSTEM

(a) Corporate Taxes

Taxes in Kazakhstan are paid in accordance with the Law of the Republic of Kazakhstan (RK) dated April 24, 1995, "On Taxes and Other Mandatory Payments to the Budget," as amended (the Tax Code). The Tax Code regulates the following activities:

- Payment of income tax
- Value-added tax (VAT)
- Excise tax
- Social tax
- Land tax
- Tax on vehicles
- Tax property
- Fee for registration of the issuance of shares
- Special taxes and mandatory payments applicable to subsoil users.

All persons, residents and nonresidents, who have taxable income in a fiscal year, must pay income tax. For tax purposes, taxable income is the positive difference between the total aggregate income and allowable expenses related to receipt of such income. Notably, the Tax Code establishes limits for such allowable expenses; for instance, expenses for travel and representation are deducted only up to the limit determined by the government.

(b) Tax Rates

The basic income tax rate for resident legal entities is 30 percent, but a lower income rate of 20 percent is available for those legal entities registered in special economic zones. The income tax rate is 10 percent for those legal entities that use land in their main business activity. Resident legal entities involved in certain specified "priority" sectors of the economy receive reduced tax rates where these entities have concluded investment contracts with the government. Subsoil users receiving income beyond 20 percent of gross receipts also must pay tax on excess profits.

A legal entity pays income tax separately from its participants or shareholders. But income received by a simple partnership, such as a consortium, is distributed among the participating entities, and the participants pay income tax at the applicable rate. A simple partnership working under a subsoil use contract is taxed as a single entity.

(c) International Tax Considerations

A foreign entity is considered a resident taxpayer if the entity has a permanent establishment in Kazakhstan. A permanent establishment includes the following:

- A fixed place of a taxpayer's activities through which the taxpayer conducts business fully or in part
- A construction, assembly, or collection site
- An installation or other structure used in exploration for natural resources
- The provision of services

The income taxation on nonresidents, such as a branch or representative office of a foreign company, is withheld by Kazakhstan. The withholding tax is imposed on Kazakhstan-source payment at the applicable rates. These witholding rates are the following:

- 5 percent for insurance payments and telecommunication and transportation services
- 15 percent for dividends and interest
- 20 percent for certain other kinds of income

11.9 LEGAL FORM

(a) Types of Entities Usually Used for Acquisition of Assets

The practice of acquiring assets is not well studied and analyzed in Kazakhstan. There has been comparatively small activity in this area, leading to lack of publicly available sources of information. Our survey is based mainly on our impression of the market.

In most cases, foreign companies interested in acquisition of assets acquire these assets through subsidiaries organized under the laws of Kazakhstan. Branches as well as representative offices are considered permanent establishments of foreign companies. Net profits received by these branch or representative entities are subject to an additional 15 percent income tax beyond the normal 30 percent tax rate. This tax structure may discourage the foreign investor from structuring a deal through branches or representative offices.

In cases of acquisitions through joint stock companies, if the book value of the assets to be transferred constitutes at least 25 percent of the corporation's total assets, the selling corporation is required to have the approval of the General Shareholders Meeting before the disposition of the assets or stock. In like manner, any company purchasing assets that represent at least 25 percent of the value of the company must have approval of its shareholders.

(b) Types of Legal Contracts

Assets may be purchased through cash or in exchange for other assets or goods. In case of a sale of fixed assets for cash, the taxable amount would be determined as the difference between the cash proceeds of sale and the cost of such assets less the amount of amortization. The cost of such assets includes expenses related to their acquisition, construction, assembly, and installation, as well as other expenses that increase their value, except those expenditures can be deducted.

The legislation does not regulate cash consideration where the amounts are paid in portions during an extended period of time (e.g., overriding royalty). In such circumstances, the most probable outcome would be that the tax authorities would require the valuation of such consideration and the tax authorities would tax this amount in the usual way. It is also most probable that the amount of consideration would be taxed without regard to its net present value.

The actual transaction is usually conducted through a sale and purchase contract, unless the assets are purchased as an enterprise. In that case, the acquisition must be executed through a contract for the sale of an enterprise.

The sale of an enterprise may include the sale of buildings, equipment, materials, products, and land, but also debts, claims, and other obligations to third parties. As such, the Civil Code of Kazakhstan establishes special presale obligations on behalf of the seller, which include informing creditors and satisfying demands of those creditors that do not agree with the transfer of their debts to the new owners.

In addition, after transfer of the enterprise from the seller to the buyer, the two parties continue to be jointly liable on the debts included in the transferred prop-

(d) Value-Added Tax

Value-added tax (VAT) is the increment of value created in the process of manufacture and circulation of goods, works, or services and includes import of goods into Kazakhstan. VAT is determined as the difference between the amount of the VAT assessed for goods sold, works performed, or services rendered and the amount of the VAT payable for goods acquired, works performed, or services rendered.

The VAT payer is always the seller of goods, works, and services. However, in a case where the seller is a foreign company without a registered tax presence in Kazakhstan, the relevant VAT is to be collected by withholding. Here the relevant VAT is to be collected and transferred to the budget by the resident buyers or by the nonresident buyers who have a permanent establishment in Kazakhstan.

Generally, the VAT rate is 20 percent of the taxable turnover. VAT at the rate of 10 percent applies to turnover connected with disposal and importation of different food products. Kazakhstan imposes no VAT on certain activities. VAT at the rate of 0 percent applies to the following:

- Export of goods
- International transportation
- Sale of textile, sewing, and tanning for shoes by Kazakhstan residents
- Sale of refined precious metals of one's own production by Kazakhstan residents

(e) Excise Taxes

Excise taxes are paid on goods produced in, or imported into the territory of Kazakhstan. These excise taxes are listed in the Kazakhstan Tax Code and are imposed on the gambling business. Excisable goods are not subject to excise tax if the goods are exported and the producer furnishes proof of exportation. Excise taxpayers include all individuals and legal entities, residents or nonresidents, that do the following:

- Producing excisable goods
- Importing excisable goods
- Conduct gambling business in the territory of Kazakhstan

Subsoil users in Kazakhstan pay taxes in accordance with conditions defined by their subsoil use contracts. The tax regime provided by a subsoil use contract is stabilized for the term of the contract. There are two models of payment of tax depending on the type of the subsoil use contract. According to the first model, a subsoil user pays all types of taxes and mandatory fees. According to the second model, production sharing, a subsoil user transfers a part of the mined resources to Kazakhstan and pays income tax, VAT, bonuses, royalties, social tax, and certain mandatory fees. Additionally, subsoil users, except those who work under production-sharing agreements, pay an excess profit tax at rates ranging from 4 to 30 percent of the net income.

11.3 CURRENCY CONTROL

The framework for currency transactions in Kazakhstan, including rights and obligations of entities dealing with currency and liability for noncompliance with the currency regulations, is established by the Law of the Republic of Kazakhstan. The applicable law is "On Currency Regulation," dated December 24, 1996, as amended, and in several regulations of the National Bank of the Republic of Kazakstan. Currency law distinguishes between Kazakhstan nonresidents and residents. All legal entities established in Kazakhstan are residents of Kazakhstan. Branches and representation offices of foreign companies are nonresidents.

(a) Availability for Using Foreign Currency

Resident and nonresident entities may open bank accounts in Kazakhstan in either *Tenge,* Kazakhstan's local currency, or in foreign currency. In order to open bank accounts, both residents and nonresidents must be registered with the local tax agency and obtain a taxpayer's identification number. All payments between Kazakhstan residents must be transacted only in *Tenge.* Payments between residents and nonresidents may be made in any currency agreed upon by the parties.

Kazakhstan residents are subject to certain limitations on currency transactions. The most significant of these limitations is that Kazakhstan residents may obtain foreign currency in Kazakhstan's internal market only for purposes of payments to nonresidents and for repayment of foreign currency loans. Thus, resident legal entities may not purchase foreign currency as a protection from inflation risks. Purchased foreign currency must be disposed of within 30 banking days from the purchase date. Resident legal entities may withdraw cash in foreign currency only for payments of salaries to nonresident employees and for expenses for business travels.

(b) Current and Capital Movements

Currency law distinguishes between "current" foreign currency operations and foreign currency operations "which are connected with the movement of capital." Transactions connected with movement of capital include the following:

- Investment
- Transfer of currency as a payment for ownership
- Other rights to immovable property; payments connected with crediting export-import operations which last for more than 180 days
- Obtaining loans for more than 180 days

Transactions connected with movement of capital from nonresidents of Kazakhstan in the amount of more than US $100,000 must be registered with the National Bank of Kazakhstan. The following activities require licensing by the National Bank of Kazakhstan:

- The retail sale or rendering of services for foreign currency in cash
- The residents' opening accounts in foreign banks and financial organizations
- Transactions connected with movement of capital, which provide transfer of foreign currency to nonresidents

Noncompliance with any of the requirements of the currency law is sanctionable in the amount equalling the transaction value. The officials of an entity not in compliance may also be penalized through administrative fines and criminal penalties.

11.4 CORPORATE LAW

The Civil Code of the Republic of Kazakhstan contains a complete list of structures that are recognized as legal entities in Kazakhstan. Commercial enterprises may be created in the following forms:

- In the form of a state enterprise
- A business company, namely, general partnership, limited partnership, limited liability company (LLC), additional liability company
- A joint stock company (JSC)
- A production cooperative

(a) General Partnerships

A general partnership is an entity in which participants bear joint and several liability for the partnership obligations in case the property of the partnership is insufficient. A general partnership must have charter capital of no less than 25 times the monthly calculation index (as of December 30, 2000, approximately US $125).

The highest managing body of a general partnership is the general partners' meeting, in which each partner has one vote unless otherwise agreed in the founders' agreement. The general partners' meeting elects executive bodies that manage day-to-day activities of the partnership. A partner may transfer its participation interest in the partnership only with the consent of the other partners. An entering partner becomes fully liable for all existing debts of the partnership even though these debts were incurred before entry into the partnership. Partners continue to bear full liability for activities of the partnership for two years after the partnership has wound up.

(b) Limited Partnerships

A limited partnership is an entity that includes, besides one or more partners who bear joint and several liability, one or more participants (investors) whose liability is limited by the amount of their contribution to the assets of the partnership. The charter capital of a limited partnership may not be less than 50 times the monthly calculation index (as of December 30, 2000, approximately US $250).

Investors may not participate in the partnership's management in order to have protection from joint and several liability. An investor's participation interest in a limited partnership is freely transferable.

An additional liability company is one in which participants are liable for the obligations of the company in the amount proportional to their contributions in the event that the company's property is insufficient to cover its debts. In other aspects, an additional liability company is similar to an LLC.

(c) Production Cooperative

A production cooperative is a legal entity established by Kazakhstan citizens who personally participate in its activities and contribute their property to operation of the cooperative. Members of the production cooperative bear subsidiary liability for the obligations of the cooperative in the amount specified by the founders' agreement.

(d) Closed Joint Stock Company and LLC

The most common forms of legal entities selected by investors are the LLC and the closed joint stock company (CJSC). Both the LLC and the CJSC provide limited liability for their participants and stockholders. However, liability may be imputed to stockholders beyond the value of their capital contributions when a stockholder is responsible for causing the bankruptcy of the company.

The minimum amount for charter capital of LLCs or CJSCs is 100 times the monthly calculation index (as of December 30, 2000, approximately US $500). The number of participants in either form of a company may not exceed 100. Otherwise, such companies must be reorganized or liquidated. The highest governing body of the LLC and CJSC is the general stockholders' meeting, which has certain exclusive rights, such as the right to elect managing and supervisory bodies of the company, to approve financial documentation, to reorganize or liquidate the company, and so on. Generally, each stockholder has the number of votes at the general participants' meeting that correspond to its proportion of the total participation interest.

Participants in an LLC and shareholders in a closed joint stock company have similar rights to one another. These rights include the following:

- The right to participate in the company's management
- The right to receive profits from the company's activities
- The right to receive information on the company's activities, including examination of financial documents
- The right to challenge decisions taken by general meetings of shareholders/participants of the company in the court
- The right to receive part of the remaining property of the company in the event of its liquidation

For both closed JSCs and LLCs, Kazakhstan legislation restrains the right of a shareholder/participant to alienate shares/participating interest to third persons. Both a participant and a shareholder of a reorganizing company have the right to request the redemption of their shares/participating interest if the participant or shareholder has voted against the reorganization or has not participated in the general meeting of participants/shareholders that took a decision to reorganize.

The difference between closed and open joint stock companies is fundamentally one relating to issuance, acquisition and alienation of the stock, the number of shareholders allowed, and the minimum amount of authorized capital required. As between the two types of JJCs, the open JSC is more complex and costly because of the requirements regarding corporate governance, mandatory registration of shares, and the amount of the authorized capital. An open JSC must have a reserve capital of no less than 15 percent of its total authorized capital. Stock of open JSCs may be acquired and traded freely. An open JSC must have authorized capital of not less than 5,000 times the monthly calculation index (as of December 31, 2000, approximately US $25,000).

All legal entities, including LLCs and JSCs, are separate taxable entities independent of their stockholders under Kazakhstan legislation. The earnings of an LLC and a JSC in Kazakhstan are subject to taxation at two different levels: at the corporate level on the company's "taxable income," and a second time, at the participants' level when the company distributes profits to the participants *pro rata* with their contributions.

11.5 SECURITIES LAW

Issuance, registration, trading on securities, and activities of the professional participants of the securities market are regulated by the laws dated March 5, 1997. These laws are termed "On the Market of Securities" and "On Registration of Transactions with Securities in the Republic of Kazakhstan." The following securities may be traded in Kazakhstan:

- Shares
- Bonds
- Warrants
- Debentures issued by Kazakhstan companies
- Securities of foreign issuers, turnover of which is permitted in Kazakhstan
- Mortgage deeds
- Bills of lading
- Other documents specified by legislation

There are two kinds of securities in Kazakhstan:

- Those securities that have uniform characteristics and requisites within one issuance, turnover of which is regulated by identical conditions of issuance (issuable securities)
- All other securities

The law establishes requirements only for issuable securities.

(a) Issuable Securities

A company must either obtain a national identification number for the issuance or register the issuance (whichever is applicable) with the authorized government agency in order to trade on the issuable securities. Transactions with issuable securities may be performed only if such securities provide a national identification number or were registered. Securities with registered issuance may be freely traded. In contrast, securities having a national identification number may be distributed only among founders of the corporation, predetermined persons, or qualified investors.

(b) National Securities Commission

An issuer must disclose certain material information to the National Securities Commission in order to obtain a national identification number or register securities. Registration of the securities' issuance may be denied only if information submitted to the National Securities Commission does not conform to legislation or to the prospectus. The issuer must pay a registration fee to the state treasury for each issuance. The amount of the fee is 0.1 percent of the value of securities for the initial issue and 0.5 percent for subsequent issues.

Upon successful registration of the issuance, a corporation publishes information about the issuance in public newspapers. Such information should be timely updated in order to reflect material changes in the company's position. Every six months during distribution of an issue, the issuer is obligated to submit a report on the results of the distribution to the state agency until the distribution is complete.

(c) Disclosure to the National Securities Commission

A company that registered the issuance of securities must submit to the National Securities Commission within 20 days after the end of each quarter. The company must publish quarterly balance sheets and income statements, together with information on the status of securities distribution. A company can register a second issue of securities only after distributing all securities of the previous issuance and filing a statement on distribution of securities with the National Securities commission.

The issuer and the underwriter are responsible for submitting correct information on the issuance to the general public. The law prohibits misleading statements in reports and public information and insider trading. For the purpose of this rule, "insiders" include directors of the issuer and professional participants of the securities market, where these directors of the issuer and professional participants of the stock market have an agreement with the issuer, auditors, and state officials who have controlling authority over the issuer.

The law prohibits the intended concealing of information regarding securities and the securities market, which must be disclosed to the public in accordance with the law. Licensed broker and dealer companies may not conclude transactions with securities if concluding such transactions contradicts clients' interests.

The law imposes administrative fines and criminal sanctions, including imprisonment, for violation of the aforementioned requirements.

(d) Acquisition of Securities

Certain acquisitions of securities must be reported to the National Securities Commission. If a person independently or jointly with affiliated persons intends to acquire 30 percent or more of the voting shares of an open corporation having more than 500 shareholders, the person must notify the company and the National Securities Commission of this intention. The corporation may not directly stop such purchase, but may itself buy shares or offer them to other third parties at a price higher than offered by the person attempting to purchase the 30 percent or more of the shares.

The acquiror must offer to purchase from the other shareholders all the remaining stock of the corporation at a price that is no less than the average price of shares acquired by that person within six months before the offer. The acquiror must do so within 30 days of the acquisition of 30 percent or more shares of an open corporation. Such offer must be published in certain media and contain information about the acquiror, its affiliated persons, the quantity of shares it owns, and the offered purchase price. The acquiror is obligated to purchase all tendered shares within 30 days of the offer publication. Otherwise, the acquiror must dispose of all shares constituting more than 29 percent of the corporation shares.

11.6 ANTI-MONOPOLY PROVISIONS

Anti-monopoly protection is provided by the laws "On Unfair Competition" (dated June 9, 1998) and "On the Development of Competition and the Limitation of Monopolistic Activity" (dated June 11, 1991). These anti-monopoly provisions establish the general rules for maintaining free competition on the market. The law "On Natural Monopolies" regulates certain commodity and service markets, including oil and gas pipeline systems, airports, and so forth where the creation of competitive conditions is impossible or economically inexpedient because of the technical peculiarities of producing and providing these types of goods or services.

(a) Role of State Agencies

State agencies are prohibited from any conduct that limits independence of entrepreneurs or creates unfair advantages to some of the entrepreneurs while the state agency discriminates against other entrepreneurs, or otherwise limits competition. The court may deem invalid documents issued by state agencies in violation of this rule. The law prohibits any action that might eliminate or limit competition.

The law probihits some actions, which are expressly forbidden:

- Fixing or dividing of the market among competitors
- Horizontal mergers of market competitors resulting in a substantial limit or elimination of competition in that market
- The unauthorized use or disclosure of commercial secrets
- Deliberate dissemination of false information of a competitor's goods or services
- Tying arrangements
- Copying a competitor's product in a way that could mislead the consumer
- Illegal use of a trade name or other commercial name of an entrepreneur which could mislead customers

In order to stop prohibited activities, the authorized state agency can issue a binding demand to the violators to cease unfair competition. If violations do not stop, the authorized state agency can file a suit with the court to suppress the unfair competition, redress its consequences, collect the income received from unfair competition to the state treasury, and recover losses incurred by competitors and consumers as the result of unfair competition.

(b) Halting of Production

The antitrust law precludes market competitors that have a predominant position in the market from certain specified activities:

- Decreasing or halting production with the intent of increasing the price of the goods or creating an artificial market deficit
- Creating artificial obstruction to entry into the market
- Setting prices in violation of procedures created by normative acts
- Including in a contract such terms that are not reasonably related to the object of the contract

The antitrust law prohibits companies that are natural monopolies from doing the following:

- Pursuing other activities
- Possessing property intended for nonmonopoly activities
- Possessing stock of other commercial enterprises
- Alienating fixed assets without the consent of the authorized government agency
- Eestablishing prices or tariffs higher than determined by the authorized government body

11.7 RESTRICTIONS ON FOREIGN OWNERSHIP OF DOMESTIC BUSINESSES

The law does not generally prohibit foreign ownership of domestic businesses. However, the law restricts foreign ownership in banking, insurance, and real estate.

In banking, the total registered charter capital of all banks with foreign ownership may not exceed 50 percent of the total registered charter capital of all banks in Kazakhstan, except as otherwise permitted by the National Bank of Kazakhstan. Nonresidents of Kazakhstan may own 5 or more percent of the Kazakhstan bank's shares only if such nonresidents have a minimum rating from one of the rating agencies determined by the National Bank. Additionally, nonresidents may not directly or indirectly possess or manage more than 25 percent of a Kazakhstan bank's shares unless this is approved by the National Bank.

The insurance law prohibits the operation of a foreign insurance company or reinsurance companies in Kazakhstan because the law prohibits such direct insurers. Foreign insurance companies may act as reinsurers in Kazakhstan through their branches and representation offices. The total registered charter capital of insurance/reinsurance companies with foreign ownership may not exceed 25 percent of the total registered charter capital of all insurance/reinsurance companies registered in Kazakhstan, except as otherwise permitted by the National Bank.

A foreign legal entity or individual may lease any type of land; however, ownership is highly restricted. Foreigners may own or lease land designated for industries and construction, but owning agricultural land is strictly prohibited.

11.8 ANALYSIS OF MERGERS AND ACQUISITIONS

Kazakhstan legislation lists and defines merger and acquisition terms, including the following as possible reorganizations of a corporation:

- Consolidations
- Merger
- Spin-offs
- Divisions

Kazakhstan legislation allows a corporation to transform itself from an open JSC to a closed JSC, to an LLC or to a sole proprietorship. In addition, the Special Part of the Civil Code provides for business acquisition through a "contract for the sale of an enterprise." In practice, all the methods of acquisition allowed by legislation have been used.

The first part of this section provides information on the acquisition of a business, first through the acquisition of assets, followed by acquisition of a company through the purchase of shares, and then as a purchase of an enterprise. The second part of this section is devoted to the consequences of mergers, spin-offs, and divisions.

erty that were transferred without the consent of the creditor, under Article 496 of the Civil Code. The right of ownership is transferred to the buyer only after state registration of this right in the appropriate governmental agency in accordance with the Civil Code.

Kazakhstan adopted a finance leasing law in mid-2000 that allows for the possibility of acquiring assets through a lease. Such a lease can provide for the transfer of ownership rights to the asset at the end of the lease, with or without an additional final payment. This type of acquisition is becoming increasingly popular. Under the new law, the Contract of Financial Leasing, like the agreement for the sale of an enterprise, enters into force only after state registration of the contract in the proper agency.

11.10 CORPORATE INCOME TAX CONSEQUENCES TO THE SELLER

The sale of an asset produces a taxable gain for the seller. The gain is equal to the positive difference between the amount for which the seller sold the asset and the current book value of the asset. This sales amount may reflect the cost of the asset and all relevant expenses attendant in its acquisition, realization, and production plus any possible depreciation.

(a) Revaluation

Revaluating book value of the assets may reduce taxable gain. In general, the reevaluation is conducted by applying the book value of the "cost increase index." This index is either determined by the appropriate governmental agency or calculated based on the real market values of the assets.

In the first type of revaluation, the new value is to be assigned at the beginning of the tax year. Such revaluation does not create any tax obligation on behalf of the company owning the asset. In the second case, reevaluation above the cost increase index, as determined by the governmental agency, is taxed as income at the rate of 15 percent, which must be paid within 30 days of the valuation. Thus, it is possible to increase the book value by paying the 15 percent tax before realizing the sale of the assets, the income tax for which would normally be 30 percent.

(b) Below Market Price Transfers

When assets are transferred gratis or at below-market price, the negative difference between the income from the sale of the assets and their book value is treated as income of the seller. This difference is included in the aggregate annual income. The loss from the acquisition is considered as income subject to the deduction of expenses like insurance payments, paid taxes and fines, uncollectable debts, and other expenses.

Losses on the disposal of assets may be deductible in some cases. For instance, the taxpayer can deduct the disposal of a building that has been used in commercial activities for more than three years. Like other business activity losses, this disposal loss may be carried forward up to three years. The taxpayer can compensate losses on sales of securities with the income received from transactions with other securities during the same tax period. Kazakhstan permits a five-year capital loss period. If such losses were not compensated in the year of occurrence, these losses may be carried forward for a period of up to five years.

11.11 VALUED-ADDED TAX CONSEQUENCES TO THE SELLER

The sale of assets may be subject to corporate income tax and value-added tax (VAT). A 20 percent VAT applies to domestic sales of goods and services (e.g., for most fixed assets and inventory). Outbound export sales of fixed assets, inventory, and intangibles do not attract VAT, subject to certain conditions. These conditions relate to obligations of Kazakhstan under international agreements to which it is a party.

The VAT is paid, where applicable, on acquisition of assets. Normally, the VAT becomes creditable when the assets are entered into the buyer's books. Therefore, as a general rule, the VAT on subsequent sale of the assets is not to be reduced by any VAT paid earlier on the asset. However, the Tax Code provides a list of turnovers that are exempt from VAT, including, among others, sale of buildings, land, securities, and shares in the foundation capital of a legal entity.

The VAT is generally capitalized as an increment of the book value of an asset for this kind of activities. In this case, a portion of the VAT is amortized accordingly, as the asset is amortized. That portion of the VAT left is creditable in the event that the asset is sold before the asset is fully amortized. In case of a sale below the market price, the difference between the amount of VAT that is subject to set-off and the amount that is actually accrued should be deducted from the set-off amount.

11.12 TRANSFER PRICING REGULATIONS

Kazakhstan introduced transfer pricing regulations for the first time at the end of 1998. Under these transfer pricing rules, the tax authorities were vested with a right to control the prices used by the parties in cases when the transaction takes place between related parties. The transfer pricing rules also apply to barter operations and where the prices used by the taxpayer deviate from the market value of identical goods by more than 20 percent. The term *related parties* is defined as one company, that is a party to the transaction, owning at least 33 percent in the property of the other.

Kazakhstan was in the process of adopting a new law on transfer pricing at the time that this chapter was being prepared. The new provision would enlarge the scope of operations that is subject to state control, to include the following transactions:

11.14 Taxation on the Sale of an Enterprise

- Where one of the companies enjoys tax exemptions
- Where one of the parties has been registered in a designated tax haven
- Where one of the parties has recorded a loss for the last two tax periods

Moreover, the new transfer pricing law is much stricter than its predecessor. Now, export-import operations with a price deviation of at least 10 percent from the market price are subject to state control. In addition, the list of parties considered "related" has changed to include companies that participate directly or indirectly (in management, control, or capital) in the other company with at least a 10 percent share. Other qualifications of "related parties" are rather detailed and include a wide range of companies, including certain trust management arrangements.

11.13 BARTER OPERATIONS

The barter exchange is treated as a cash sale of the assets under the current tax rules. Identical goods are defined as goods having complete similarity to one another. No income is accrued in a barter of identical goods and, thus, there is no tax liability; however, for an equivalent exchange, which implies exchange of assets that are not identical but have equivalent cost, the income is calculated based on the cost of the received assets. It is important to note that, for VAT-exempt assets, the turnover for barter is determined based on the cost of the assets that have the highest cumulative price of realization, subject to the condition that such turnover may not be lower than actually sustained expenses.

11.14 TAXATION ON THE SALE OF AN ENTERPRISE

Unfortunately, the Tax Code does not provide clear regulation of the treatment of the sale of an enterprise as a whole. In general, such a sale is treated as a sale of tangible and intangible assets. The taxpayer and the tax authorities apply the principles described earlier.

Nevertheless, a problem can arise with the allocation of price between individual assets. The existing legislative acts do not provide any guidance on this issue. The most developed approach would be to apportion the selling price using the ratio between the selling price and the book value of the assets. The debts for taxes on the acquired property are not transferred to the buyer because under the Tax Code the payer of all taxes is the seller. However, a transfer of other debts and liabilities of the enterprise is also not defined by the tax legislation or by any official clarifications of the tax authorities.

From the VAT perspective, the sale of an enterprise as a whole is an exempt turnover. Therefore, there is no need to apportion the prices because the taxable turnover is exempt from VAT for all purposes.

11.15 CORPORATE INCOME TAX CONSEQUENCES TO THE BUYER

As a general rule, the buyer's tax basis will be the cost of acquisition, the purchase price, and all attendant costs of acquiring the asset or business. Acquisition costs are not deductible, however. The taxpayer may amortize the book value of the assets at a rate determined by the Tax Code.

Kazakhstan adopted new rules on amortization at the beginning of 2000. Before the introduction of these amortization rules, all assets were divided into eight categories, with specific marginal amortization rates established for each category. At present, the categories have been changed, providing much more detail and giving the companies opportunities to amortize their assets in a way more suited to the actual needs of the enterprise.

Moreover, under the new amortization rules, the taxpayer may choose to calculate amortization separately for each asset, not as part of its amortization category, which was the prior obligatory method. In addition, for newly operated machinery and equipment, the taxpayer may calculate amortization deductions in accordance with an "increased" rate, which is determined by the Tax Code separately for each type of equipment. Rapid amortization is subject to the condition that the equipment is to be used in business activities for at least three years.

11.16 VALUE ADDED TAX CONSEQUENCES TO THE BUYER

The amount of the taxable turnover for the purposes of VAT is determined on the basis of the value of sold assets. This process takes into consideration the price excluding VAT, but is not less than the actual cost of acquisition of the assets. VAT paid for the assets may be offset against received VAT. The amount of VAT is capitalized as an increment of the cost of the assets for the VAT-exempt turnover. Acquisitions of securities are treated as financial services, which are VAT-exempt under the Tax Code, and, therefore, do not attract VAT.

Outbound sales are generally not subject to VAT, but several exceptions exist because of international agreements concerning the VAT that Kazakhstan has concluded. One of the most important is the Agreement between the Governments of Country Members of Confederation of Independent States (CIS) "On Harmonized Principles of the Tax Policy." In accordance with this agreement, mutual payments between residents of these countries are conducted with VAT included. This means that export out of Kazakhstan is performed with 20 percent VAT and import with set-off of the VAT indicated in the invoice. Kazakhstan also has agreements on principles of indirect taxation with Kyrgyzstan, Azerbaijan, Moldova, Ukraine, and Belarus. Export from the territory of Kazakhstan under these agreements is conducted at a zero rate for VAT, and for import into Kazakhstan, a 20 percent VAT is applied.

11.17 TAX CONSEQUENCES OF THE PURCHASE OF A BUSINESS AS AN ENTERPRISE

The buyer acquires the assets in the aggregate in a purchase of an enterprise. The buyer incurs no tax liability in the purchase; however, the tax regulations do not specify whether the buyer takes book value of the assets as shown in the balance sheets of the company purchased or as based on the fair market value of the goods. Usually, in the accounting practice in Kazakhstan, the taxable basis is determined based on the fair market value of assets calculated at the time of the purchase.

Kazakhstan tax legislation recognizes goodwill. Goodwill is defined as the ability of the enterprise to receive income through its prestige, business reputation, and contacts. The value of goodwill is determined as the difference between assets and liabilities of the purchased enterprise.

Goodwill may be amortized, but the amortization of goodwill is not clearly regulated in the tax legislation. The only reference to goodwill is found in a letter from the Ministry of Finance, dated September 8, 1997, which states that goodwill is an intangible asset and "bad will" (negative goodwill) should be accrued as the deferred income pertaining to future periods. The most widely accepted accounting practice suggests amortizing goodwill for the whole period of its activity, with a maximum of 40 years.

11.18 ACQUISITION OF SHARES

(a) Legal Form

Sales of shares normally take place under a purchase-and-sale contract. The tax implications of the puchase-and-sale contract depend on whether the company is an open or closed JSC. In a transaction between a purchaser that is a Kazakhstan legal entity and a non-Kazakhstan legal entity or individual, the Kazakhstan legal entity may have to withhold the appropriate income tax and remit the tax to the treasurer for the seller.

(b) Tax Consequences

The sale of shares is a straightforward transaction. The seller of the stock of a company is required to pay income taxes on the difference between the selling price and the acquisition price. The buyer bears no tax consequences for the sale. The tax basis of the stock is its acquisition price. The purchase of shares of an open JSC is a nontaxable event.

Losses incurred on sales of securities are not deductible. Such losses can be used to offset the income gained upon the sale of other securities. Sales of securities are defined as "financial operations" for the purposes of Kazakhstan tax law and as such, according to the general exemption for financial operations, are not subject to VAT.

11.19 MERGERS

(a) Legal Forms

Combining companies in Kazakhstan is performed either through consolidations or affiliations. Kazakhstan's statutory definition of *consolidation* is the creation of a new company by the transfer to it of all assets, rights, and obligations of two or more other companies according to a transfer agreement with the subsequent termination of the activities of those companies. One company is united with another and the target corporation terminates its existence.

(b) Tax Consequences

The transfer of assets and liabilities under any form of reorganization is not a recognized taxable event under Kazakhstan legislation. Thus, the tax basis of the assets transferred is their book value as recorded in the Act of Transfer, basically preconsolidation or premerger balance sheets. Further, in either context—affiliation or consolidation—no new tax liabilities are created, although the existing tax liabilities and rights are passed through to the new company. These tax liabilities include any tax penalties, late payment interest, and the reclaiming of overpaid or overassessed taxes (existing up to the formal completion of the reorganization).

The purchaser must issue shares in the new company that result from the transaction. The emission fee (0.1 percent securities tax levied on initial emissions, 0.5 percent on subsequent emissions) applies to these new shares. Shareholders in receipt of new stock in exchange for those of the terminated corporation are not liable for taxes on the exchange.

11.20 DIVISIONS

Kazakhstan legislation states that companies may divide (split-up) or create spin-offs. In a split-up, the company terminates its activity by transferring all its property, rights, and obligations to newly created companies, with a subsequent exchange of shares of the old company for shares of the new companies. In a spin-off, an existing company creates one or more new companies and transfers to it or them some part of its assets, rights and liabilities. Both the split-up and the spin-off are nontaxable events.

In a split-up, the tax liabilities of the original company are allocated among the newly formed companies on a pro-rated basis, in accordance with the predivision balance sheets. If it is impossible to determine the successor companies' respective portions of the original company's tax liabilities, the tax authority may apply to the court to make the successor companies jointly and severally liable for any tax arrears, penalties, and late payment interest of the original company.

In a spin-off, the tax liabilities of the original company remain with the latter and are not passed to the newly formed company or companies unless the distributing company has become unable to meet such liabilities as the result of the spin-off. In this case, the tax authorities may apply to the court to make the new company or companies jointly and severally liable for the original tax liabilities extant at the time of the spin-off.

The cost basis in the assets acquired by the successor company or companies is determined by the book value of these assets as indicated in the predivision balance sheet. The original company's shareholders who receive shares of stock of the new company or companies in a spin-off or split-up do not bear any tax liability.

11.21 CARRYOVER OF TAX ATTRIBUTES

The concept of carryover of tax attributes is the most undeveloped issue in Kazakkstan in the general taxation of mergers and acquisitions. There are no specific rules for the carryforward of net operating losses or VAT credits of the target company or for restrictions on their use.

In practice, carryover of tax attributes is performed under the general rules of tax law and heavily depends on the type of merger used in the particular transaction. In the acquisition of assets transaction, as a rule, no tax liabilities are carried over to the resulting company, but will remain with the preexisting company. In the acquisition of shares, the tax liabilities of the original company are carried over to the resulting company or companies.

11.22. CONSOLIDATION

In Kazakhstan, consolidation is one of the following:

- A combination of two or more corporations for the creation of a new one
- A combination of business or assets of two or more corporations or individuals for the achievement of certain aims through a simple partnership or consortium

Consolidation is a combination of two or more corporations for the creation of a new entity. Consolidation is a process in which capital, assets, rights, and liabilities of two or more companies are unified into a single new corporation. The previously existing corporations cease to exist in this type of consolidation. Such consolidation may take place only if the consolidation is approved by vote of the qualified majority stockholders of the combining corporations at the general stockholders' meeting. Because all rights and liabilities of the combining corporations are transferred to the newly created corporation, this new corporation bears tax liabilities for the "old" corporations from the time of its registration.

A combination of business or assets of two or more entities for the achievement of certain aims is called a *simple partnership* if the structure is created with participation of a physical person or a *consortium* if the structure is created by legal entities. A consortium is created under an agreement on joint activities. Among other clauses, an agreement on joint activities must contain clauses about the following:

- The amount and kinds of the property intended for the joint use
- The procedure for taking decisions
- Profit distribution
- The management of day-to-day business of the simple partnership

Participants of a simple partnership or consortium bear joint and several liability for the obligations of the simple partnership/consortium, unless otherwise determined by the agreement on joint activities. Unlike in previously described consolidation, no new legal entity is created upon combination of business or assets of two or more corporations. Therefore, participants in a consortium are independent entities and as such, may participate in other consortiums or associations.

For tax purposes, a consortium is not treated as a single entity. Therefore, its participants bear all tax liabilities arising from the activities of the consortium. Generally, one of the participants, an operator of the consortium, is obliged to prepare a consolidated financial statement of a consortium, and to notify the other participants of the amount of tax and time for its payment. Each participant of the consortium reflects assets, liabilities, and interest arising from the activities of the consortium in its books, preparing individual and consolidated financial statements. Therefore, for calculation of tax payment, a participant adds income and deductions arising from the consortium to income and deductions arising from nonconsortium activities.

A consortium of subsoil users, who operate under a single subsoil use contract, is an exception from the general rule on the tax treatment of a consortium. Such a consortium of subsoil users is recognized as a single taxpayer and must pay all taxes and other mandatory payments to the treasury, according to conditions fixed by the subsoil use contract. Also, income and deductions of a consortium of subsoil users may not be consolidated with any other income and deductions arisen from nonconsortium activity of such subsoil users.

11.23 FINANCING

Methods of financing acquisitions may be as simple as using one's own capital or a straightforward loan arrangement. A company may also issue a security in the form of additional stock or bonds. Additional securities must be registered with the state authorities and a government fee of 0.5 percent of the nominal value of the issue of securities.

11.24 REPATRIATION OF CAPITAL AND PROFITS

Presently, there are no restrictions on the repatriation of capital and profits for foreign companies. However, Kazakhstan residents, such as subsidiaries, are subject to certain limitations on currency transactions. The most significant currency limitations are that Kazakhstan entities must obtain permission of the National Bank of Kazakhstan in order to open bank accounts abroad. Kazakhstan entities must obtain consent from the National Bank for certain capital-movement transactions that transfer hard-currency assets, whether cash or securities valued in hard currency, from residents to nonresidents.

In the past, the National Bank required the mandatory exchange of a certain percentage of the hard-currency export receipts of resident legal entities. Kazakhstan repealed the mandatory exchange provisions, but the National Bank retains the right to regulate the flow of capital from the country, including reinstitution of mandatory currency exchange.

11.25 CONCLUSION

The laws on taxation the authors depict in this chapter show that certain issues have yet to be resolved. Nevertheless, it is hoped that this description has presented the reader with a basic understanding of this aspect of mergers and acquisitions.

Kazakhstan's history as a sovereign nation is still extremely short. Throughout this brief period, the country has sought to develop national law that supports a free market economy. This process is one of evolution as experience in commerce and taxation increases. Initial legislation, drafted against the national backdrop of a constituent of the former USSR with a command economy, has given way to legislation more suitable to the present conditions of a market economy. As might be inferred from the foregoing chapter, this dynamic process continues.

CHAPTER 12

Taxation of Mergers and Acquisitions in Korea

Kyun (Ken) Cook
Ernst & Young, Seoul

12.1 Acquisition of Assets Compared with Shares
12.2 Tax Burden on Assets or Business Transfers
12.3 Tax Burden on Share Transfer
12.4 Other Important Tax Considerations
12.5 Investment Vehicles Commonly Available
12.6 Conclusion

Korea declared a financial moratorium and requested a bailout from the International Monetary Fund (IMF) in 1997. During this period, Korea has seen record sales of businesses, nonperforming loans, and commercial real estate. In 1999, alone, the foreign direct investments into Korea amounted to a record 15 billion U.S. dollars. For the 11 months ending November 30, 2000, the total foreign direct investment was 14 billion U.S. dollars. Korea has never experienced so much merger and acquisition activity in the prior years, both in size and number. This chapter examines the major tax issues surrounding acquisition of Korean businesses.

12.1 ACQUISITION OF ASSETS COMPARED WITH SHARES

It is always a contentious issue to reach an agreement between a potential buyer and a potential seller regarding which deal structure to use. This decision is particularly serious in Korea mainly because of the sharply contradicting tax and accounting positions of the parties to the transaction. In general, Korean sellers prefer a transfer of shares because this structure results in a significantly lower tax burden than does a transfer of assets or business. However, foreign buyers generally prefer a transfer of assets because of the concern about accounting transparency and contingent liabilities, which the foreign investor may inherit by acquiring shares. These issues are further explored in the following sections.

12.2 TAX BURDEN ON ASSETS OR BUSINESS TRANSFERS

A sale of assets or business that consists of real estate could be detrimental to a Korean company because of the high combined corporate income tax and capital gains tax. Capital gains arising from a sale of assets or business are subject to the corporate income tax at the rate of 30.8 percent. In addition, capital gains from real estate are taxed again at 16.5 percent, called *special capital gains tax,* resulting in a combined tax rate of 47.3 percent. The special capital gains tax is payable even if the taxpayer corporation is in a loss position for corporate income tax purposes. Furthermore, to the shareholders of a Korean company, dividends on the distribution of remaining capital gains are taxed at a personal level. This tax on dividends is only partially recoverable through the Korean dividend tax credit.

In an effort to assist Korean companies in their restructuring of business, a temporary relief from capital gains tax is provided to a sale of real estate if certain conditions are met. One of the conditions is that the proceeds from the sale must be used to repay debts from financial institutions or that the real estate is disposed of as a part of a formal restructuring of business. Up to December 31, 2000, the capital gains tax was completely exempted if the sale proceeds were used to repay debts from financial institutions. The capital gains tax is reduced by 50 percent if the real estate is disposed of as a part of a formal restructuring of business.

The temporary tax exemption was set to expire at the end of December 31, 2000. However, the temporary tax exemption was extended for another year with a reduced rate of exemption based on the tax revision bill, which is to be effective as of January 2001. As per the revised tax law, it is proposed that the capital gains tax exemption rate be reduced from 100 percent to 75 percent for the sale of real estate in order to repay debts from financial institutions.

To the buyer of assets or business, the transaction tax costs are also higher than those in an arrangement in which shares are obtained. Certain assets that are required to be registered with the provincial authorities, such as real estate and vehicles, are subject to the acquisition tax and the registration tax. The acquisition tax is imposed at the rate of 2.2 percent. The registration tax applies at varying rates depending on the type of assets (e.g., 3.6 percent for real estate and 5 percent for passenger vehicles.)

A foreign buyer must establish an entity in Korea before buying assets or business. The issuance of new shares by the new Korean entity is subject to a registration of capital. The capital registration tax is assessed at 0.48 percent on the par value of shares. The capital registration tax rate is increased by three times if the corporation is established in the Seoul Metropolitan area and has been in existence less than five years. The new Korean entity is subject to value-added tax (VAT) at the rate of 10 percent if the acquisition is classified as an individual asset transfer as opposed to a whole business transfer. The VAT paid, however, is refundable, and, thus, is not a true cost to the new Korean entity.

12.3 TAX BURDEN ON SHARE TRANSFER

Korean shareholders generally prefer selling shares to selling assets or business because of the large tax burden to the seller of assets or business. There is no capital gains tax for a sale of listed shares, unless the seller is a major shareholder. The shareholders are subject to a low capital gains tax at 22 percent for a sale of nonlisted shares. The rate is reduced to 11 percent if the shares are of a small- or medium-sized company. In addition to the capital gains tax, the seller is subject to securities transaction tax at the rate of 0.3 percent for listed shares traded through the Korean Stock Exchange and 0.5 percent for all other trades.

The buyer of shares is normally not subject to any transaction tax except for the following situations. If a buyer acquires shares of a nonlisted company, and if the shareholder acquires 51 percent or more of its equity, the shareholder would be subject to deemed acquisition tax at the rate of 2.2 percent on the book value of underlying assets that are required to be registered with provincial authorities. Also, if the buyer acquires new shares of a Korean company instead of existing shares, the Korean company would be subject to capital registration tax at 0.48 percent or 1.44 percent.

12.4 OTHER IMPORTANT TAX CONSIDERATIONS

The potential tax burden on the sale of shares is significantly less than that on the sale of assets or business to Korean shareholders. Therefore, Korean shareholders normally insist on selling shares in most M & A negotiations being undertaken in this country.

The tax burden to a buyer is larger with an acquisition of assets or business compared with an acquisition of shares, although the tax is at a much smaller magnitude. Despite the tax burden to the foreign buyer of assets or business, most foreign buyers seem to favor an assets or business purchase over a purchase of shares, principally because of their concern with inheriting potential contingent liabilities. This approach is not surprising considering the current economic crisis, which partly is caused by the lack of accounting transparency.

Although a buyer would end up bearing a little larger tax cost by choosing an asset or a business transfer, there are other compensating benefits. For example, if the purchase price contains a significant amount of goodwill, such goodwill can be booked in the new Korean company that acquired the assets or business and amortized over five years or longer for tax purposes. Another example is that the acquisition financing can be done through the new Korean company so that the related interest expense can be used to reduce the taxable income generated from the acquired business.

These benefits are not available to the buyer if the buyer acquires shares instead of assets or business. In an assets or business purchase arrangement, however, any tax loss carryforward balance accumulated in a target company cannot be transferred to the new Korean company, whereas a transfer of such loss is possible under a share deal. Consequently, if a loss carryforward balance in a target company is the major consideration for the buyer, it needs to evaluate a share deal more carefully. For tax purposes, the NOL can be carried forward for five years.

12.5 INVESTMENT VEHICLES COMMONLY AVAILABLE

A foreign buyer needs to establish a new Korean company to acquire assets or business. The most commonly used company types are Chusik Hoesa (CH) and Yuhan Hoesa (YH). Between those two types, CH is the normal stock corporation and is mostly perferred. YH is similar to a limited liability company (LLC) in the United States, and is not allowed to go public or issue corporate bonds. YH, however, is the only *non per se* entity in Korea eligible for the "check-the-box" regulation for U.S. tax purposes.

A holding company structure within Korea is allowed to hold investment in the equity of Korean subsidiaries, but with severe limitations. Up to December 31, 2000, dividends received by a holding company were fully taxed again unless the holding company is qualified under the Fair Trade Act (FTA). For a qualified holding company, a dividend-received deduction (DRD) is allowed at 60 or 90 percent, depending on the equity holding threshold. Under the tax revision bill to be effective in January 2001, the DRD ratio is to be increased to 100 percent for a wholly owned subsidiary. The equity threshold is 80 percent for nonlisted companies and 30 percent for listed companies.

The FTA qualification requirements are stringent. For example, a qualified holding company cannot have a debt equity ratio exceeding 1 to 1. According to the tax revision bill to be effective in January 2001, the DRD will also be available to nonqualified holding companies at the rate of 30 percent or 50 percent, depending on the equity holding threshold and the type of corporation. However, the use of a domestic holding company as an investment vehicle is rare at present because of the aforementioned limitations.

12.6 CONCLUSION

A decision on the choice of acquisition structure and the type of investment vehicle is a complicated one requiring a comprehensive study of local tax and business requirements as well as the foreign investor's tax and investment goals for the international businesses. This chapter has attempted to identify the major local tax issues related to an acquisition of a Korean target by a foreign investor.

CHAPTER 13

Taxation of Mergers and Acquisitions in Mexico

Jaime Gonzales-Bendiksen*
Baker & McKenzie, Monterrey

13.1 **Introduction**
13.2 **Mergers**
    (a) Merger Definition
    (b) Classification
    (c) Procedure
    (d) Effective Date of Mergers
    (e) Effects
13.3 **Split-Offs**
    (a) Definition
    (b) Classification
    (c) Procedure
    (d) Effective Date of Split-Offs
    (e) Effects
13.4 **Tax Aspects of Mergers**
    (a) Definition
    (b) Taxation Exemption
    (c) Land Transfer Taxes
    (d) Tax Attributes
    (e) Other Tax Implications
    (f) Examples
    (g) Which Company Should Survive/Disappear?
    (h) Allocation and Timing of Expenses
    (i) Tax Liability
13.5 **Tax Aspects of Split-Offs**
    (a) Definition
    (b) Taxation Exemption
    (c) Land Transfer Taxes
    (d) Tax Attributes
    (e) Other Tax Implications

---

*The authors wish to thank Danae Liñan-Mendoza, Ricardo Morales-Barron, Ernesto Silvas-Medina, and Gerardo Prado-Hernández for their assistance in creating this chapter.

(f) Examples
(g) Tax Liability
13.6 Acquisitions
(a) Stock Versus Assets
(b) Tax Basis for Purchaser
(c) Tax Liability
(d) Assets and Going Concern
(e) Taxation of Seller
13.7 Who Should the Purchaser Be?
(a) Stock
(b) Assets
(c) Value-Added Tax (VAT)
13.8 Conclusion
Appendix 13A Average Cost per Share

13.1 INTRODUCTION

In Mexico, the General Law of Commercial Companies, Chapter 9, deals with the following types of mergers and acquisitions for commercial companies:

- Mergers
- Changes of business forms
- Split-offs

13.2 MERGERS

(a) Merger Definition

There is no statutory definition of a merger in Mexico. A merger can be defined as the event in which the following occurs:

- Two or more entities integrate all of their assets, liabilities, and net worth into one of them, with the other or others ceasing to exist.
- Two or more entities integrate into a new entity that is created as a result of the merger, with all other participating entities ceasing to exist.

Commentators, such as professor Rodríguez y Rodríguez, define a merger in the following terms:

> *It consists in the legal union between several social organizations which jointly concentrate themselves, so that one legal organization replaces several organizations.*

Another commentator, Jorge Barrera Graf, defines a merger as a complex, contractual, *"sui generis,"* corporate act, developed in various and successive steps,

13.2 Mergers

whose effects consist in the universal transfer or succession of assets and liabilities from the merged or disappearing company or companies to the surviving or merging company.

This merger process involves the transfer and acceptance of those partners or stockholders of the merged companies into the merging company. The merger and acceptance is generally accomplished through a capital increase as well as the extinction of one or more commercial companies by its/their integration or its/their incorporation or absorption, as referred to as follows.

There is no uniform opinion regarding the nature of the merger. A merger has been characterized as an incorporation agreement, as a universal succession among existent companies (*intervivos*), as a special type of assignment, and as a way of dissolving, restructuring, or transforming commercial companies.

(b) Classification

Based on the text of the applicable provisions as well as on opinions of Mexican commentators, mergers can be classified as follows:

By integration

A merger by incorporation is carried out by incorporating a new commercial company, into which one or more other commercial companies merge or integrate, and as a result, they are extinguished.

By incorporation or absorption

A merger by absorption assumes the existence of two or more commercial companies, one of which will survive, while the other companies cease to exist once they universally transfer their assets, liabilities, and capital to the surviving company.

(c) Procedure

The following procedure should be followed in order to carry out a merger between commercial companies:

1. The first step is a proposal of the merger, made to the stockholders by the Board of Directors or administrator of the commercial companies involved. This item is not a requirement established by the law, unless the bylaws of such companies require their management bodies to make this type of proposal.

2. Thereafter, a merger agreement should be executed between or among the commercial companies participating in the merger. This agreement must set forth at least the following requirements:

    - The type of merger to be implemented
    - The precise determination of which commercial companies will disappear and which will survive

- The percentage of interest participation in the capital of the surviving company that the stockholders or partners of the disappearing company or companies will hold after the merger
- The moment or timing on which the merger shall become effective among the participants as well as before third parties, as well as those transactions that the commercial companies should carry out before the merger becomes effective
- The manner whereby the liabilities of the commercial companies involved in the merger shall be guaranteed or extinguished
- Provisions dealing with the labor implications for the disappearing company or companies
- Any other matters that should be dealt with in accordance with the bylaws of the commercial companies involved in the merger

3. Concurrent with or following the merger agreement, each of the companies entering into such undertaking must hold a general extraordinary shareholders' meeting, in case of stock corporations, which requires a qualified voting majority to adopt such a resolution, or its equivalent for other types of commercial companies. The shareholder meeting approves the merger agreement and the corresponding implementing resolutions.

4. The minutes of the aforementioned shareholders' or partners' meetings must be formalized in a public instrument before a notary public or public broker, along with the merger agreement. This public instrument must be recorded at the Public Registry of Property and Commerce of those jurisdictions corresponding to the corporate domicile of the companies involved in the merger.

5. At the same time, the merger resolutions adopted by the shareholders' or partners' meetings of each of the commercial companies involved in the merger, along with their last balance sheet (typically prepared specifically for purposes of the merger) and the method to be applied to extinguish the liabilities of the disappearing companies, must be published in the Official Gazette of the State corresponding to the corporate domicile of the commercial companies involved in the merger.

(d) Effective Date of Mergers

A merger is effective to third parties three months after the minutes of all of the companies involved, embodying the merger resolutions, are recorded in the Public Registry of Property and Commerce of their corresponding corporate domicile. During this three-month period, the creditors of the companies involved in the merger may judicially oppose such a merger, in which case the effects of the merger may be suspended until final judicial resolution is obtained with no further legal recourse. As an exception, the merger may become effective upon registering the merger resolutions in the Public Registry of Property and Commerce, when any one of the following takes place:

13.3 Split-Offs

- The companies involved in the merger agree to pay all of their debts.
- All their creditors consent to the merger.
- These companies deposit in a bank the amount of their debt

When the companies elect to pay all of their debts, all term obligations are deemed to become due and payable.

(e) Effects

Vis-à-vis the creditors and debtors

The main effect of mergers, with respect to the creditors and debtors of the companies involved, is the change of the company before which they will validly enforce their rights and obligations, depending on the type of merger in place. That is, a merger results in a creditor or debtor substitution.

In addition, as mentioned previously, during the three-month period after the merger, the creditors of the companies involved in the merger have the right to judicially oppose the merger through a court procedure. The filing of an opposition claim by creditors suspends the effects of the merger until a judgment with no further recourse declares that the opposition has no grounds.

Vis-à-vis the companies participating in the merger

The effects of a merger, with respect to the disappearing companies, is the loss of their corporate existence, without formally requiring a process of dissolution and liquidation. All of the assets, liabilities, and net worth of the merged companies are transferred to the company surviving the merger or to the new company resulting from the merger.

Vis-à-vis the shareholders or partners of the companies

The main effects of a merger between or among two or more companies with respect to their shareholders or partners is that the shareholders or partners of the disappearing company or companies are entitled, by law, to become members of the surviving or the new company resulting from the merger.

13.3 SPLIT-OFFS

(a) Definition

From a corporate standpoint, a split-off takes place in two situations:

1. When one entity decides to extinguish itself and divides all or a part of its assets, liabilities, and net worth into two or more parts, which are contributed in blocks to other newly incorporated companies.

2. When one company, without extinguishing itself, contributes in block part of its assets, liabilities, and net worth to one or more newly incorporated companies.

(b) Classification

Similar to mergers, split-offs may be classified by incorporation or by absorption.

By incorporation

The split-off by incorporation occurs when the distributing company divides its assets, liabilities, and net worth, totally or partly, into two or more newly incorporated companies, after which the company is extinguished. The steps to be taken for the incorporation of the new companies depends on the assets, liabilities, and net worth to be transferred by the distributing company because the capital stock of the newly incorporated companies is determined according to their value.

By absorption

On the other hand, a split-off by absorption, or partial split-off, takes place when the distributing company contributes part of its assets, liabilities, and net worth to another company or companies, newly incorporated for such purpose, with the distributing company keeping the remaining part of its assets, liabilities, and net worth and continuing to be a legal entity with corporate existence.

(c) Procedure

Split-offs must follow the procedure set forth:

1. The split-off must be approved in a shareholders' or partners' meeting, depending on the type of commercial company involved, by the majority vote specified in their corresponding bylaws.
2. The shares or equity quotas of the distributing company must be fully paid-in.
3. As with mergers, in a split-off the partners or shareholders of the distributing company must participate in the new company or companies in the same proportion they held in the capital stock of the distributing company.
4. The resolutions approving the split-off must set forth the following information:

    - The description of the form, term, and mechanisms for the transfer of the assets, liabilities, and equity
    - The description and identification of the portion of the assets, liabilities, and net worth corresponding to the distributing company, if such is the case, and/or to the new company or companies

13.3 Split-Offs

- The audited financial statements of the distributing company, corresponding to its last fiscal year
- The obligations that the distributing company and/or the new company or companies assumes as a result of the split-off
- The draft bylaws for the new company or companies resulting from the splitoff

5. The resolutions approving the split-off must be incorporated into a public document before a notary public or a public broker and registered with the Public Registry of Property and Commerce. In addition, an excerpt of the split-off resolutions and of a balance sheet showing the effects of the split-off must be published in the Official Gazette of the State where the companies have their corporate domicile and in one newspaper of broad circulation corresponding to the corporate address of the distributing company.

6. In the event the distributing company ceases to exist as a result of the split-off, once the split-off becomes effective, registration of the distributing company with the Public Registry of Property and Commerce should be cancelled.

(d) Effective Date of Split-Offs

The split-off will become effective 45 calendar days from registration of the split-off resolutions with the Public Registry of Commerce or from publication of the split-off resolution excerpt, whichever occurs later. During this 45-day period, the creditors and a partner or shareholder or group of partners or shareholders representing at least 20 percent of the capital stock of the distributing company may challenge the split-off. In this case, the effects of the split-off are suspended until a judgment with no further recourse is issued, dismissing the motion for suspension.

(e) Effects

Vis-à-vis creditors and debtors

The principal effect of split-offs, as with mergers, as to the creditors and debtors of the distributing company, is the possible change of the company before which the creditors will validly enforce their rights and obligations. This change depends on the specific assets and liabilities transferred to the new company or companies. That is, a split-off, too, may result in a creditor or debtor substitution.

Vis-à-vis the companies involved

Regarding the distributing company, the effect of the split-off is that it ceases to exist, without the need for a formal liquidation procedure. In that case, the distributing company transfers its overall assets, liabilities, and net worth to the new companies. On the other hand, the distributing company will remain in existence when it transfers only part of its assets, liabilities, and net worth to the new company or companies. In the latter scenario, the distributing company will reduce its capital stock in the proportion in which it transferred net worth to the new company or companies and will cancel the shares or equity quota certificates representing such reduction in its capital stock.

Vis-à-vis the new company or companies

As to the new company or companies, the main effect of the split-off is the following:

1. The coming into being of such companies,
2. The transfer, to this or these companies, of all or part of the assets, liabilities, and net worth of the distributing company.

Via-à-vis the partners or shareholders

The most important effect of the split-off in connection with the partners or shareholders is that they will become shareholders or partners of the new company or companies in proportion to their holdings in the distributing company.

Another important effect of the split-off regarding the shareholders or partners of the distributing company is when the shareholders represent less than 20 percent of the capital stock of the distributing company and are against the split-off. In that situation, the shareholders have the right to withdraw from the company and obtain the reimbursement of their shares or equity quotas (appraisal right). The shareholders must request the appraisal rights within 15 days after the date of the meeting approving the split-off. The effects of the split-off will be suspended until the corresponding judgment is handed down. Partners or shareholders who have cast their vote against the split-off are entitled to withdraw their contributions to the company.

13.4 TAX ASPECTS OF MERGERS[1]

(a) Definition

Mexican tax provisions do not expressly define mergers. A merger meets the following criteria:

- The event where two or more entities integrate all of their assets, liabilities, and net worth into one of them, with the other or others ceasing to exist.

---

[1] By Jaime González-Bendiksen, partner, Baker & McKenzie, Guadalajara, Juarez, Monterrey, Tijuana.

13.4 Tax Aspects of Mergers

- The event where two or more entities integrate into a new entity that is created as a result of the merger, with all other participating entities ceasing to exist.

(b) Taxation Exemption

Gains from transfers of property as a result of mergers are, in principle, taxable, including gains derived by the stockholders as a result of the corresponding exchange of stock. However, upon compliance with most simple requirements, transfers as a result of mergers qualify for nonrecognition treatment and, as such, are tax free. The specific requirements are as follows:

- The surviving entity or the new entity resulting from the merger files the short-year tax return of the disappearing entity. This return must include the following:
  - For income tax purposes, all taxable income and allowable deductions
  - For value-added tax purposes, the value of all taxable and exempt acts or activities, as well as all creditable tax
  - For assets tax purposes, the value of all assets or liabilities, in all events from the beginning of the tax year through the date of the merger

- The surviving entity or the new entity resulting from the merger files the information returns of the disappearing entity.
- The surviving entity or the new entity resulting from the merger files a notice of the merger, within the month following the merger, setting forth the names of the entities merged and the date of the merger.

The law sets forth no limitation. As such, this tax-free treatment applies to the following: transfers of goods between or among the entities participating in the merger and to the exchange, by the shareholders, of shares of the disappearing entity for shares of the surviving or new entity. Up to the year 2000, the recognition of tax-free mergers applied to mergers taking place outside of Mexico as well. As a result, the merger provisions applied to international mergers between Mexican entities and foreign entities and to mergers between foreign entities. Beginning in 2001, however, the benefit is restricted to mergers of entities incorporated in Mexico. Losses suffered by the stockholders as a result of taxable or nontaxable mergers are not deductible.

(c) Land Transfer Taxes

The tax-free status for mergers applies to federal taxes only (i.e., income tax, assets tax, and value-added tax), not to state or municipal taxes. Therefore, where real property is involved, typically land transfer taxes, which are not federal, will apply. The rates vary by state, but can generally be said to be in the vicinity of 2 percent.

(d) Tax Attributes

The tax attributes in the disappearing entities carry over to the surviving entity or the new entity resulting from the merger. Thus, no valuations are necessary. Specifically in order to determine the gain on future sales the following items provide for a carryover:

- Land
- Securities representing the ownership of goods
- Securities whose yields are not considered interest
- Gold or silver coins formerly used as domestic or foreign currency and so-called troy ounces

These assets carry the basis they had in the disappearing entity and are considered acquired by the receiving entity on the dates they were acquired by the transferor.

- Depreciable or amortizable assets are considered acquired on the date acquired by the transferor and carry the depreciated value of the transferor.
- The basis in stock received by the surviving or the new entity as part of the assets is the average cost per share the disappearing entity had on the date of the merger.[2]
- The stockholders also receive a carryover in the tax basis of the stock issued by the surviving entity or the new entity in exchange for the stock of the disappearing entity, which is the average cost per share that the disappearing company had as of the date of the merger.[3] The stock of the new entity is deemed acquired on the date of the merger.
- Corporate taxpayers are required to carry a record of the capital contributions made by the stockholders in a so-called capital contributions account (CUCA). This account is transferred to the surviving entity in a merger. However, when the absorbing entity owns stock of the disappearing entity before the merger, the balance of the CUCA that carries is reduced in proportion to the portion that such stock represents with respect to the overall stock of the disappearing entity.
- Corporate taxpayers may reduce their corporate tax rate from 35 percent to 30 percent by reinvesting the profits (i.e., by not paying out dividends). The 5 percent difference is paid when the profits are paid out. To keep track of the reinvested profits, these taxpayers must carry an account called a *reinvested net after-tax profits account* (CUFINRE).[4] This account carries to the entity surviving a merger.
- After-tax profits are subject to a 5 percent withholding tax when paid to non-residents or individuals. On the other hand, distribution of profits that have not

---

[2] The average cost per share is discussed in Appendix 13A.
[3] The average cost per share is discussed in Appendix 13A.
[4] The CUFINRE account is discussed in Appendix 13A.

13.4 Tax Aspects of Mergers

been taxed at the corporate level triggers a 53.85 percent tax for the distributing entity, not the stockholders. In order to keep track of the former, corporate taxpayers must carry a so-called *net after-tax profits account* (CUFIN).[5] This account, too, is transferred to the surviving entity under a merger.
- The right of the disappearing entities to credit input value-added tax (VAT) against their output VAT or to file for a refund is transferred to the surviving entity or to the new entity resulting from the merger. Note that VAT is generally borne by the end consumer. All other enterprises participating in the production and distribution chain are entitled to recover the VAT they pay on their inputs against the VAT they collect from their customers on their output, or to file for a refund.

Exceptions to this rule are as follows:

- Inventory, which carries no tax basis. The reason is that, unlike other countries, Mexico allows immediate expensing of inventory, as opposed to the cumbersome inventory control and valuation methods (LIFO, FIFO, straight-line, declining balances, and so forth).
- As a most important exception, Mexican law provides that net operating losses cannot be transferred as a result of a merger. This provision has been ruled by the Mexican Supreme Court to be unconstitutional. When the entity suffering the losses is the surviving entity, it can continue to use its losses, but only against income from the same line of business that generated the loss.
- No mention is made in the law regarding foreign tax credits of the disappearing entity. It thus appears that any foreign tax credits that remain unused after the merger are lost.
- Assets tax taxpayers typically enjoy a tax holiday for the preoperational period, the year in which activities commence, and the two following years. The exemption, however, is lost when the exempted entity either merges into or absorbs through merger another entity. The loss of exempted status is effective from the tax year after the merger. New entities resulting from a merger do not enjoy this four-year exemption either.
- Moreover, taxpayers are entitled to credit, against their assets tax liability, the excess of income tax over assets tax in the past three years, and to secure a refund of assets taxes paid, against the excess of income taxes over assets taxes in the following 10 years. These rights are not transferred as a result of the merger.

(e) Other Tax Implications

Estimated tax payments

Taxpayers must make, in July, an adjustment to their estimated tax payments for the first six months of the year, in order to "true" them up. This is done by calcu-

---
[5] The CUFIN account is discussed in Appendix 13A.

lating an approximation to book profits for the first six months and applying a 30 percent tax rate (which, as mentioned earlier, is used when deferring the balance of 5 percent of the rate as a result of reinvesting the tax year's profits) to the result. The taxable income (with certain adjustments) for the first six months is then calculated and the result under the preceding sentence subtracted. The 35 percent corporate tax rate is applied to this result. The sum of both of these results is paid in August. When a short year occurs as a result of a merger, the following rules regarding the adjustment apply for the disappearing entity:

- When the short year lasts less than seven months, no adjustment takes place.
- When the short year lasts up to the seventh month, the adjustment takes place during this month, for the first six months, except if the tax return for the short year is filed within the month following the close of the short year.
- When the short year lasts longer than eight months, the adjustment for the first six months should be done according to the regular rules.

Tax consolidation

Mexico recognizes consolidation for tax purposes. Special effects arise whenever one of the entities of the group ceases to be controlled by the holding company. No such effects arise in the event of mergers between two controlled entities or upstream mergers of a controlled entity into the holding company.

Value-added tax

Value-added tax taxpayers must make estimated tax payments monthly or quarterly, depending on certain income thresholds. Entities surviving a merger continue to make estimated tax payments with the frequency they did before the merger. New entities resulting from a merger make estimated tax payments, during the year of the merger, within the same periods as did the entity that contributed the largest amount of assets to the merger. Thereafter, these new entities must make their estimated tax payments according to the general rules.

Certified financial statements

Taxpayers meeting specific statutory thresholds are required to have their financial statements certified for tax purposes. From a merger standpoint, the results for both the surviving entity or the new entity resulting from the merger and the disappearing entity, corresponding to the year of the merger, should be certified by an external auditor registered with the tax administration. The surviving or new entity should also have its results for the immediately succeeding year certified.

13.4 Tax Aspects of Mergers

Cancellation of federal taxpayer registration

The surviving entity or the new entity resulting from the merger must file, together with the tax return for the short year of the disappearing entity, a notice of cancellation of the tax registration of such entities.

Short year

The tax year of the entities disappearing as a result of a merger ends on the date of the merger.

(f) Examples

Examples of mergers include the following:

- Typical mergers to consolidate the operations and results of one or more entities of the group
- Joint venture mergers to join forces with unrelated target entities
- The company can be merged into another entity of the group instead of liquidating a given entity. Mergers involve a much more simple process than the complicated and sometimes painful liquidations.

(g) Which Company Should Survive/Disappear?

Several financial and other considerations dictate which entity should survive and which entity should disappear in a merger. From a tax standpoint, two main points mentioned previously must be considered: the fact that net operating losses cannot be transferred as a result of a merger and the fact that land transfer taxes will be incurred when real property is transferred under a merger. These two factors typically dictate that the entity with the losses or owning the real property should survive.

Licenses or permits typically have no bearing on this decision because they normally are transferred as a result of the merger. Nonetheless, each individual license or permit should be analyzed to determine if any restrictions exist, such as foreign ownership or limitation of benefits as under transfer pricing advance pricing agreements with the tax authorities. Distributing contracts entered into by each entity to be merged should also be scrutinized to ensure that they include no termination or acceleration provisions, or to plan accordingly. Labor is typically not an issue because work contracts can easily be transferred under a merger through an employer substitution.

(h) Allocation and Timing of Expenses

Expenses in carrying out a merger may be of a certain consideration. Allocation and timing are thus two important strategy components. Where one of the entities has net operating losses, it might not make sense to have it incur the merger expenses and simply increase its losses. It might be better, from a tax standpoint, to have the party in a profitable position incur and deduct the expenses.

Another consideration is employee profit sharing. Employers are required to share 10 percent of their taxable income (with certain adjustments) with their employees. Thus, when one of the entities to the merger has employees and the other does not, it might be wise to have the entity with the employees incur the expenses, in order to reduce its profits and thus reduce its 10 percent employee profit sharing.

Where the entity to whom it would make more sense to allocate the expenses is to be disappearing as a result of the merger, it would be advisable to incur most, if not all, expenses before the merger and allocate them to the disappearing entity. Allocations should be reasonable and not outright arbitrary.

(i) Tax Liability

Tax provisions mention nothing regarding the liability of the surviving entity or the new entity for the tax obligations of the disappearing entity. Nonetheless, corporate rules do provide that the entity surviving the merger or the new entity created as a result of the merger acquires all of the rights and obligations of the disappearing entity. It is thus clear that the surviving or new entity is directly liable for all tax obligations of the disappearing entity.

13.5 TAX ASPECTS OF SPLIT-OFFS

Split-offs may also be used in acquiring stock or assets or coupled with mergers.

(a) Definition

Unlike for mergers, Mexico's tax provisions do set forth a definition of split-offs, quite similar to the definition used for corporate purposes, mentioned earlier. Split-offs are defined as those events:

- Where one company residing in Mexico transfers part of its assets, liabilities, and net worth to one or more new companies residing in Mexico and incorporated to that effect, without disappearing.
- Where one distributing entity residing in Mexico transfers all of its assets, liabilities, and net worth to two or more new entities residing in Mexico, incorporated to that effect, and disappears.

The entity transferring the assets, liabilities, and capital will hereinafter be referred to as the *distributing entity*. The new entity arising as a result of the split-off and to whom the assets, liability, and capital are transferred will, indiscriminately, be referred to as the *new entity* or the *new entities*.

(b) Taxation Exemption

In principle, gains from transfers of goods as a result of split-offs are taxable the same as any other transfer; however, where given requirements are met, a split-off may be treated as a tax-free nonevent. The specific requirements are as follows:

13.5 Tax Aspects of Split-Offs

- A continuity of interest requirement, to the effect that at least 51 percent of the owners of voting stock of the distributing entity and of the new entity remain unchanged for one year before and one year after the date notice of the split-off is given to the tax authorities. Stock with limited voting rights and certain preferred shares are not considered voting stock for these purposes.
- The holding periods do not apply with respect to publicly traded stock, traded through stock exchanges or recognized markets listed under so-called miscellaneous resolutions issued by the Ministry of Finance and Public Credit. The restrictions do not apply to transfers as a result of death, liquidation, judicial adjudication, or donation between spouses, ascendants, or descendants or in donations of amounts not exceeding three minimum wages. Where successive split-offs take place, or a merger following a split-off, without the two-year period having expired, the period must be computed from the date notice of the last of these events is given to the tax administration.
- When the distributing entity is to disappear as a result of the split-off, the entity should first appoint one of the new entities to file the short-year tax return and the information returns of the distributing entity. When this appointment is not made, the tax administration may demand compliance with these filings from any of the new entities. The short-year return must include: for income tax purposes, all taxable income and allowable deductions; for VAT purposes, the value of all taxable and exempt acts or activities as well as all creditable tax; and for assets tax purposes, the value of all assets or liabilities, in all events from the beginning of the tax year through the date of the split-off.
- The distributing entity, if any, or the new entity indicated in the split-off should file a notice of the split-off with the tax administration, within one month from the date of the split-off, setting forth the names of the parties to the split-off and the date thereof.

Because of the statutory definition mentioned previously, tax-free split-offs are available only for entities residing in Mexico.

(c) Land Transfer Taxes

As with mergers, a tax-free split-off typically does not avoid local land transfer taxes.

(d) Tax Attributes

The tax attributes in the distributing entity generally carry ratably to the new entity. No valuations are thus necessary. Specifically:

- In order to determine the gain on future sales, land, securities representing the ownership of goods, securities whose yields are not considered interest, gold or silver coins formerly used as domestic or foreign currency, and so-called

troy ounces, carry the basis they had in the distributing entity. These assets are considered acquired by the new entity on the dates they were acquired by the distributing entity.
- Depreciable or amortizable assets are considered acquired on the date they were acquired by the distributing entity and carry the depreciated value of this entity.
- The basis in stock received by the new entity as part of the assets is the average cost per share the disappearing entity had on the date of the split-off.[6]
- The stockholders also receive a carryover in the tax basis of the stock issued by the new entity in exchange for the stock of the distributing entity, which is the average cost per share that the distributing entity had as of the date of the split-off.[7] The stock of the new entity is deemed acquired on the date of the split-off.
- Corporate taxpayers are required to carry a record of the capital contributions made by the stockholders in a so-called capital contributions account or "CUCA." This account is transferred to the new entity ratably to the proportion in which the net worth of the distributing entity is divided between/among this entity, if it survives, and/or, the new entity or entities resulting from the split-off.
- Corporate taxpayers may reduce their corporate tax rate from 35 percent to 30 percent, by reinvesting the profits (i.e., by not paying out dividends.) The 5 percent difference is paid at the time when the profits are paid out. To keep track of the reinvested profits, these taxpayers must carry an account called reinvested net after-tax profits account or "CUFINRE."[8] This account carries to the new entity in the same proportion mentioned in the preceding point.
- After-tax profits are subject to a 5 percent withholding tax when paid to non-residents or individuals. On the other hand, distribution of profits that have not been taxed at the corporate level triggers a 53.85 percent tax for the distributing entity, not the stockholders. In order to keep track of the former, corporate taxpayers must carry a so-called net-after tax profits account or "CUFIN."[9] This account, too, is transferred to the new entity, as indicated previously.
- An interesting feature is that, contrary to mergers, in split-offs both the distributing entity and the new entity are entitled, ratably to the proportion in which the net worth of the distributing entity was divided, to use the net operating losses of the distributing entity.
- Regarding assets tax, as indicated earlier, taxpayers are entitled to credit, against their assets tax liability, the excess of income tax over assets tax in the past three years, and to secure a refund of assets taxes paid, against the excess of income taxes over assets taxes in the following 10 years. These rights are transferred to the new entity, to the proportion in which the assets (minus allowable liabilities for assets tax purposes) are divided as a result of the split-off.

---

[6] The average cost per share is described in Appendix 13A.
[7] The average cost per share is described in Appendix 13A.
[8] The CUFINRE account is described in Appendix 13A.
[9] The CUFIN account is described in Appendix 13A.

13.5 Tax Aspects of Split-Offs

Exceptions to this rule are as follows:

- Inventory, which, as indicated earlier, carries no basis for tax purposes.
- As to foreign tax credits, where the distributing entity survives, the entity keeps the entire right to use these credits. Conversely, where the distributing entity ceases to exist as a result of the split-off, the right to foreign tax credits is divided among the new entities in proportion to their share of the net worth of the distributing entity.
- Contrary to mergers, in split-offs the right of the distributing entity to credit input VAT against their output VAT or to file for a refund remains with this entity. Where the distributing entity disappears as a result of the split-off, then the new entity designated to that effect in the split-off must file the corresponding VAT returns for the distributing entity and file for refunds, if any, also on behalf of the distributing entity.

(e) Other Tax Implications

Capital redemptions

Capital redemptions are deemed dividends and may be subject to certain taxes when the amount of the redemption exceeds the amount of the capital contributions made by the stockholders (carried by each entity in a capital contributions account, CUCA) or when the entity suffering the redemption has retained earnings. Split-offs are expressly not considered a capital redemption for these purposes provided the sum of the net worth of the surviving entity, if any, and of the new entities resulting from the split-off is equal to the net worth of the distributing entity before the split-off. Further, the new shares issued as a result of the split-off are exchanged to the stockholders of the distributing entity.

Assets tax

The assets tax holiday, mentioned in the mergers section, does not apply to new entities resulting from a split-off; however, the distributing entity may continue with its exemption, if it continues to exist.

Estimated tax payments

Taxpayers are required to make estimated tax payments throughout the year, on account of income tax, assets tax, and VAT. The following special rules apply as a result of split-offs.

Regarding income tax:

- The new entity must begin making estimated tax payments from the month of the split-off. Because calculation of estimated tax payments is based on the prior year's ratio of taxable income (before allowance for the past year's net

operating losses) over gross income (with certain adjustments), in calculating the estimated tax payments for the first tax year, the new entity should use the ratio corresponding to the distributing entity.
- Taxpayers must make estimated tax payments monthly or quarterly, depending on certain income thresholds. Distributing entities will continue to make estimated tax payments with the frequency they did before the split-off. The new entity, however, will, for the year of the split-off, make estimated tax payments within the same periods as the distributing entity. Thereafter, the new entity will make estimated tax payments according to the general rules.
- The distributing entity may credit, in calculating future estimated tax payments for the year, all estimated tax payments made earlier during the same year. The new entity is not entitled to any credit of these earlier payments.
- The distributing entity may have to make the six-month adjustment to its estimated tax payments for the short year, in accordance with the rules discussed previously for mergers.

Regarding assets tax:

- During the year of the split-off and the following tax year, the amount of estimated tax payment for the corresponding period is computed as follows: The assets tax for the last 12-month tax year of the distributing entity is divided between/among this entity and/or the new entities, in proportion to their share of the assets (minus allowable deductions) of the distributing entity as of the date of the split-off. For these purposes, the 12-month tax is adjusted for inflation by multiplying. Assets are multiplied by the factor resulting from dividing the national consumer price index for the month preceding the last month of the tax year preceding the split-off by the index for the month preceding the last month of the tax year immediately preceding the aforementioned 12-month year.
- The distributing entity is entitled, in computing its estimated tax payments, to credit the amount of the estimated tax payments made during the year and before the split-off. The new entity is not entitled to credit any such payments.
- In computing the assets tax for the year, a taxpayer may elect to apply the assets tax that would have resulted in the fourth preceding tax year, adjusted for inflation, without any reduction, instead of the assets tax calculated under regular rules. If the distributing entity made this election, both this entity and the new entity must continue this election, with the following variations. For the year of the split-off, they must consider, instead of the tax that would have applied under normal rules in the fourth immediately preceding tax year, the tax that would have applied for the distributing entity in the penultimate tax year preceding the split-off, using the ratio mentioned previously.
- For the year after the split-off, they must use the tax that would have applied in the year immediately preceding the split-off. As from the third tax year after the split-off, each entity shall consider the assets tax that would have applied, in its specific case, for the immediately preceding penultimate tax

13.5 Tax Aspects of Split-Offs

year. If the distributing entity did not exercise this option before to the split-off, this entity, as well as the new entity resulting from the split-off, may elect to do so, following the rules mentioned in the preceding sentences.

Regarding value-added tax:

- The distributing entity will continue to make estimated tax payments with the frequency it did before the split-off. The new entity will, for the year of the split-off, make estimated tax payments within the same periods as the distributing entity. Thereafter, the new entity will make estimated tax payments according to the general rules.

Certified financial statements

Taxpayers meeting specific statutory thresholds are required to have their financial statements certified for tax purposes. In the event of split-offs, the results for both the distributing entity and for the new entity, corresponding to the year of the split-off and the subsequent year, should be certified by an external auditor registered with the Hacienda. Obviously, when the distributing entity ceases to exist, only its results for the year of the split-off are to be certified.

Cancellation of federal taxpayer registration

When the distributing entity ceases to exist, the new entity appointed to the effect in the split-off must file, together with the tax return for the short year of the distributing entity, a notice of cancellation of the tax registration of the distributing entity.

Short year

The tax year of the distributing entities disappearing as a result of a split-off ends on the date of the split-off.

(f) Examples

Use of a split-off may be advisable, among others, in the following situations:

- When an entity simply wants to split-off part of its activities, transferring the corresponding assets to a sister company.
- When only certain assets are to be transferred to another entity, the distributing entity can split-off, allocating the target assets to the new entity, which can then merge into the new owner. Or in a reverse scenario, after the split-off the distributing entity would merge into the new owner, and the new entity resulting from the split-off would hold the assets that were not to be transferred.

- Similarly, when part of a business is to be liquidated, following a split-off the entity with the part to be closed down could be either liquidated or merged into another entity.
- When it is desired to liquidate a given entity, but it has large assets (e.g., real estate) that are not easily saleable, the entity would demerge, leaving only the real property in the distributing entity. The new entity would then be liquidated or merged.
- When merger of a given company with another is desired but for the fact that the first entity has retained earnings that would be taxable in the United States as a result of the merger. Here the assets and liabilities for the contemplated merger would go to the new entity being formed as a result of the split-off, leaving the retained earnings in the distributing company; the new entity would then merge into the desired entity.
- A split-off might be available when a Mexican entity wishes to separate its income-producing activity (say, manufacturing) from its employees, in order to minimize the Mexican 10 percent employee profit sharing. This entity could split-off the manufacturing activities and assets. The new entity would contract for the distributing entity to provide labor services. The largest profit from the operation would be with the new entity, which has no employees and consequently pays no profit sharing. The distributing entity would make a modest profit, which it would share with its employees.

(g) Tax Liability

From a tax liability standpoint, the new entity is jointly liable for the tax liabilities of the distributing entity, in proportion to the net worth of each at the time of the split-off.

13.6 ACQUISITIONS

(a) Stock versus Assets

When considering an acquisition, the first issue from a tax standpoint is whether to acquire the stock or the assets of the target entity. There is no one answer. Several factors must be considered, under individual facts-and-circumstances analyses, in order to achieve the optimal tax result.

(b) Tax Basis for Purchaser

A first consideration is the tax basis the purchaser will acquire in the stock or assets purchased and the tax-recovery period of the investment.

Stock

When purchasing stock, the tax basis for a future sale is the average cost per share. The average cost per share is subtracted from the income per share and

13.6 Acquisitions

multiplied by the number of shares being sold, to arrive at the capital gain or loss. In general terms, the average cost per share is the proportionate cost of acquisition, adjusted for inflation, increased or decreased by the proportionate increase or decrease of the issuing entity's retained earnings during the seller's holding period, also adjusted for inflation. A detailed explanation of the calculation is included in Appendix 13A. This basis is different from the basis for capital redemptions or liquidation of the issuing company, which is, basically, the amount paid by the original stockholders when subscribing issues of stock, minus previous redemptions, adjusted for inflation. The mere capital repatriation is not taxable; however, any distribution resulting from capital redemptions or from liquidations is first considered to be a distribution of retained earnings (i.e., a dividend). The tax benefit of acquiring stock for the purchaser is deferred up to the time of disposition of the stock. No stepped-up basis in the underlying assets of the entity is possible as a result of a stock purchase.

Fixed assets

The price paid for the purchase of fixed assets and intangibles is, in turn, the basis for depreciation or amortization. For these purposes, the statutory percentage of depreciation or amortization (not the historical cost) is indexed for inflation by multiplying it by the inflationary factor resulting from dividing the national consumer price index for the month immediately preceding the month of acquisition by the index preceding the last month of the first half of the period during which the property was used during the tax year. The national consumer price index is published monthly in the Federal Official Gazette. Consequently, to the extent that the price paid is higher than the seller's basis in the assets, the purchaser gets a stepped-up basis. The seller, however, is taxed on the gain because there is no tax-free step-up in basis.

The law sets forth different depreciation and amortization rates that vary depending on the specific type of assets. In general terms, constructions are depreciated in 20 years, office equipment and furniture are depreciated in 10 years, and the deductible portion of automobiles is depreciated in 4 years. Investments in automobiles are depreciable only if the automobile qualifies as class "A" under the Automobile Ownership or Use Tax Law, and then limited to certain statutory amounts. Investments in other classes of automobiles or in excess of the statutory limits are not deductible. Intangibles are amortized between 5 to 20 years. Preoperational expenses, royalties, technical assistance fees, and certain other deferred expenses are entirely deductible in the tax year if it can be shown that the benefit from the investment is limited to the tax year in question.

In the event of a subsequent sale of the assets, the basis is the balance pending depreciation, adjusted for inflation by multiplying it by the factor resulting from dividing the national consumer price index of the month preceding the first half of the year of the sale by the index of the month preceding the date it was purchased by the seller.

Inventory

Mexico allows immediate expensing of inventory. Therefore, when resold, there is no tax basis; thus, the entire proceeds are taxable income for the seller.

Goodwill

Goodwill is not deductible, not even when acquired from a third party. Thus, investments in goodwill represent no tax benefit for the purchaser. When goodwill is involved, reasonable efforts to allocate the value of the goodwill to the other depreciable or amortizable assets may be possible. However, because any excess of the sales price over the market value of all other assets being sold is attributable to goodwill, arbitrary allocation should be avoided. While rarely exercised, the tax administration has the authority to presumptively determine the cost of goods in transactions between unrelated parties, following certain unorthodox methods. Alternatively, when extremely valuable goodwill is involved in the transaction, the purchaser might be well advised to purchase stock instead of assets. That part of the purchase price attributable to the goodwill will be included in the tax basis of the stock for future resale.

Another possibility may be to pay for a covenant not to compete, instead of for the goodwill, provided it has substance. Foreign purchasers, however, may decide to purchase the goodwill directly, if deductible in their home country. Because there is no basis in goodwill, when sold, the entire proceeds are taxable income, both for resident and non-resident taxpayers.

Transfer pricing

The arm's-length principle must be observed in transactions between related parties. The arm's-length method calls for the prices that independent parties would have agreed to in similar transactions under similar conditions. Mexican parties are required to keep contemporaneous documentation to support the arm's-length nature of the consideration in these transactions.

(c) Tax Liability

Of particular concern in determining the type of acquisition is whether the purchaser may be inheriting the seller's or the target's tax liability.

Stock

When the stock of a company is acquired, the purchaser is, in fact, not inheriting but actually taking over all of the tax (and other) history of the target company. The company will be answerable for any such liability with the assets of the purchased entity. From a corporate standpoint, stockholders of a *sociedad anónima* or a *sociedad de responsablidad limitada* (which are the most popular corporate structures, the first similar to a corporation and the second with more partnership-like features) are liable to pay only the value of the shares or quotas they subscribe.

13.6 Acquisitions

From a tax standpoint, stockholders are subsidiarily liable for the tax obligations of the entity during the period they were stockholders and up to their percentage of ownership, but only if one of three conditions are met:

1. The entity fails to register for tax purposes.
2. The entity changes its domicile, without giving notice to the tax authorities, during the course of an audit or after a tax assessment has been served, but not yet paid.
3. The entity fails to carry mandatory books of account.

Proper due diligence, coupled with guaranties from the seller, should greatly minimize this exposure for a buyer of stock.

(d) Assets and Going Concern

Purchase of assets entails no joint tax liability of the purchaser. However, when the full going concern (*negociación*) is purchased, joint tax liability does arise.

A business concern is viewed, in general terms, as the sum of the production factors: capital and labor. A going concern has two main elements, material (assets and liabilities) and human (employees). The assets can represent a variety of forms:

- Fixed and current
- Movable and immovable
- Tangible and intangible (such as intellectual property, client lists, rights under lease agreements, etc.)

When the business concern must be purchased, it might be advisable for several related entities each to acquire one or more of the distinguishable parts of the going concern. For example, one entity could acquire the real property or the lease rights, another the fixed assets including intangibles, a third one could acquire the inventory, another would hire the labor, and a final entity would undertake the actual manufacture or service activity, renting the real property and the fixed assets and hiring labor services from the other entities. Each entity could acquire part of the liabilities. Absent outright simulation, Mexico could not legally disregard the different entities or pierce the corporate veil.

(e) Taxation of Seller

The decision about whether stock or assets should be acquired is often prompted by the seller on the basis of the seller's most favorable tax result.

Tax bases, NOLs

Both the sale of stock and the sale of assets are taxable transactions, but the seller will typically have different bases in each. Other factors, such as net operating losses, may also determine the best structure from the seller's perspective. As indicated earlier, the tax bases for the sale of stock, of fixed assets, and of inventory are different and can, logically, lead to different tax results. The sale of stock or assets is ordinary income—not capital gains—for corporate taxpayers. The sale can be offset with other deductions, including net operating losses of prior years. In the case of nonresidents, the sale of movable property located in Mexico is not subject to taxation unless attributable to a permanent establishment of the nonresident in Mexico.

Alternative structures

It is possible to consider structures other than a straightforward purchase of stock or assets. However, the purchaser should not do the seller's tax planning. If willing to carry on the transaction at the minimal tax cost for the seller, the purchaser must simply state its interest in purchasing the stock or assets from whatever entity may be the rightful owner or under whatever structure the seller may have in place.

Treaty countries

The purchaser might acquire stock from an entity in a country whose tax treaty with Mexico does not provide for taxation by Mexico of capital gains from the disposition of stock issued by a Mexican entity, such as Switzerland. Or the purchaser could purchase the stock from several companies in tax treaty countries where disposition of limited ownership of Mexican stock is not taxed, such as Denmark, the Netherlands, Spain, and others.

Capital increases, redemptions

When the sellers of stock have a high basis for redemption or liquidation purposes, instead of a purchase of stock, the prospective purchaser can make a loan to the target company. The target company would make a capital redemption to the distributing stockholders using such funds, leaving them with an extremely low participation, followed by a capital increase subscribed by the prospective purchaser and paid with the account receivable from the target company. Formerly, these transactions were considered step transactions, which were defined as being tantamount to tax fraud. This characterization has been repealed. Tax fraud would only exist, under distributing rules, if the entire transaction can be considered to be a simulation, which would rarely, if ever, be the case.

Transactions where the capital is first increased and a subsequent reduction takes place within the following two years give rise to a dividend determination on the highest of the following:

- The difference between tax basis for purposes of the redemption and the amount received under the redemption
- The capital gain that would have been realized on the difference between the tax basis for sales purposes and the amount received as a result of the redemption

Such dividends will be taxed to the distributing entity at a 53.85 percent rate and to the recipient, if an individual or a nonresident, at a 5 percent rate. Domestic law provides for a gross up of the dividends paid to individuals or nonresidents by a factor of 1.5385, which increases the 5 percent dividend rate to an effective 7.69 percent rate. The gross up appears to be contrary to treaty provisions. Further, Mexico's courts recently ruled the gross up to be unconstitutional. This provision would not, in the writers' view, apply to the transaction mentioned in the preceding paragraph.

Case-by-case analysis

Needless to say, careful review of the specifics for each transaction should be made before any alternative structure is implemented.

Shams

Participation in outright shams should be avoided. Criminal liability exists for tax fraud (including simulation of transactions). The penalties are imposed not only on the taxpayer but on aiders and abettors as well.

Tax havens

Channeling stock or asset purchases through tax havens is not advisable. Mexico frowns at transactions where tax havens are involved. Transactions with entities residing in tax haven countries are defined by statute as not being at arm's length. Thus, the Mexican tax administration may disregard or adjust the price paid for the stock or assets purchased to a tax haven resident, which could reduce its tax attributes (i.e., the basis to determine the gain in a future sale or the basis for depreciation or amortization).

13.7 WHO SHOULD THE PURCHASER BE?

The selection of purchaser is important for the seller.

(a) Stock

Sale of stock issued by Mexican entities generates Mexican-source income, taxable to nonresidents. Consequently, it might be advisable for the purchaser to be a foreign special-purpose holding company, holding only the Mexican stock to be acquired. This would enable a future sale of the Mexican stock without Mexican tax consequences by selling the stock of the special-purpose holding company.

The same result would be obtained even if the Mexican company owns real estate located in Mexico, representing more than 50 percent of the net worth of the holding company. Domestic law considers the sale of the stock of such a holding company as Mexican-source income, subject to Mexican taxation; most, if not all, tax treaties entered into by Mexico limit taxation by Mexico to sale of the stock of the Mexican entity itself. Alternately, the owner of the stock could be an entity residing in a country with a tax treaty with Mexico, such as Switzerland, preventing Mexico from taxing capital gains from the sale of Mexican stock.

It may also be wise to split ownership of the stock among a few entities. Several Mexican tax treaties exempt taxation of capital gains from the sale of a portfolio interest in Mexican stock, generally of less than 25 percent. Examples of such countries are Denmark, the Netherlands, and Spain.

(b) Assets

When dealing with a purchase of assets, at least a couple of additional major considerations come into play. Mexican taxpayers are subject to assets tax on all of their assets (after deduction of certain liabilities). Nonresidents are also subject to this tax with respect to inventory they keep in Mexico for processing by a third party and to assets kept in Mexico and used by another taxpayer. The U.S.–Mexico tax treaty excludes this inventory from Mexican assets tax.

The assets tax rate is 1.8 percent. This tax is similar to an alternative minimum tax. The taxpayer's income tax is credited against the assets tax liability. Thus, assets tax liability arises only where it exceeds the amount of income tax for the same period. Even here, however, the taxpayer may credit against this liability the excess of income tax over assets tax during the preceding three years. And even where assets tax is paid after the credits, the taxpayer is entitled to a refund of this tax against any excess of income tax over assets tax during the subsequent 10 years.

Based on this analysis, if the target goods are purchased by a Mexican entity, the 1.8 percent assets tax will normally be offset by the entity's income tax. If purchased by a foreign entity and given for a Mexican entity to use, the foreign entity will be subject to a 21 percent income tax withholding, which may be credited against the assets tax. A lower withholding tax, typically of 10 percent, applies under Mexico's tax treaties. Under the U.S.–Mexico tax treaty, U.S. residents may credit, instead of the 10 percent withholding tax, a theoretical 21 percent tax.

Alternately, the lessee may elect to consider the assets as its own for assets tax purposes, crediting, against its assets tax, the taxes withheld on the rental payments. While not free from doubt, it would appear that the lessee may also credit its own income taxes to offset the assets tax on these goods. Under this election, the foreign lessor is dispensed from complying with Mexican formal obligations. A rental structure will require the nonresident lessor to register for VAT purposes in Mexico, issue Mexican invoices in prescribed form, carry Mexican books for tax purposes, and file Mexican VAT returns.

(c) Value-Added Tax (VAT)

Sales of goods located in Mexico at the time of shipment to the purchaser or, absent shipment, physically delivered in Mexico, are subject to VAT, generally at a 15 percent rate (a 10 percent rate applies in border areas). Residents of Mexico who carry on VAT-applicable transactions may recover the VAT paid from VAT collected from their customers or through refunds. Conversely, if the purchaser is a nonresident who does not carry on VAT-applicable activities, the purchaser will not be entitled to recover the VAT paid, which will thus represent a higher cost of the goods purchased.

An exception to this VAT rule is the purchase of intangibles. These sales are subject to VAT only if both the seller and the purchaser are residents of Mexico. Therefore, in certain cases it might be advisable for the U.S. company to purchase certain items, such as goodwill, which a Mexican purchaser could not deduct and the company could not credit any VAT paid, but which is not subject to VAT if purchased by a nonresident.

13.8 CONCLUSION

Acquisitions, mergers, and split-offs are important tax planning tools. None of these options is generally preferable over the other. Individual analyses in each particular case must be made, considering not only the tax implications but also all related legal issues, including corporate, contractual, and labor.

APPENDIX 13A

Average Cost Per Share

CALCULATION

The average cost per share, to determine the gain or loss on the sale of stock, is determined as follows:

1. The acquisition cost of the stock is adjusted for inflation, by multiplying it by the result of dividing the national consumer price index of the month preceding the month of the sale by the index of the month preceding the date of acquisition. The national consumer price index is published in the Federal Official Gazette.
2. The balances of the net after-tax reinvested profits account (CUFINRE) and the net after-tax profits account (CUFIN) of the issuing entity on the date the stock was purchased are adjusted for inflation, by multiplying the said balances by the result of dividing the national consumer price index for the month preceding the month in which they were last adjusted by the issuing entity before the date of acquisition by the index for the month preceding the date of sale.
3. The balances of the CUFINRE and the CUFIN accounts of the issuing entity on the date of sale are adjusted for inflation, by multiplying the said balances by the result of dividing the national consumer price index for the month preceding the month in which they were last adjusted by the issuing entity before the date of sale by the index for the month preceding the date of sale.
4. The sum of the results in 2. is subtracted from the sum of the results in 3.
5. If the difference in 4. is positive, it is divided by the total number of outstanding shares of the issuing entity on the date of the sale and the factor multiplied by the number of shares owned by the seller on the date of the sale. The product is then added to the result in 1.
6. Where the difference in 4. is negative, it is divided by the total number of outstanding shares of the issuing entity on the date of the sale and the factor multiplied by the number of shares owned by the seller on the date of the sale. The product is then subtracted from the result in 1.
7. The result in 5. or 6. is divided by the total number of shares in the entity owned by the seller. This is the average cost per share.

Note, however, that if the result under 6. is negative (if there is an excess of 4. over the adjusted cost of acquisition in 1.) the excess is a deemed profit distribution and thus increases the amount of taxable gain resulting on the sale of the stock.

Further note that the determination of the average cost per share must be made even if only part of the shares owned by the seller are being sold.

Where the number of shares of the issuing entity has changed during the holding period of the seller, the calculations in 2., 3., and 4. may be made for each period, from the date of acquisition through the date of sale, during which the seller has held the same number of shares. The results are then added or subtracted, as the case may be. With this overall result, the calculations in 5., 6., and 7. are continued.

CUFINRE ACCOUNT

The reinvested net after-tax reinvested profits account (CUFINRE) is an account carried by corporate taxpayers who decide to defer part of their corporate tax, from 35 percent to 30 percent, by reinvesting profits. The deferred tax becomes payable whenever the reinvested profits are paid out.

The CUFINRE account is increased with the amount of reinvested net after-tax profits for each tax year and is decreased by the following:

- Profit distributions in cash or in kind (except distributions in stock of the distributing entity and except reinvested distributions), originating from the CUFINRE
- Constructive dividends resulting from capital redemptions, also originating from the CUFINRE

The reinvested profits are the result of adding to the taxable income for the year the following amounts:

- The amount of employee profit sharing taken as a deduction
- Foreign-source losses, claiming deductions on foreign-source income pursuant to article 6 of the Income Tax Law

and subtracting the following:

- The employee profit sharing
- Nondeductible items, with limited exceptions
- Foreign-source gains, claiming deductions on foreign-source income pursuant to article 6 of the Income Tax Law

From the reinvested profits the 30 percent preliminary corporate tax rate paid for the tax year is subtracted, and the result is multiplied by a factor of 0.9286, to arrive at the reinvested net after-tax profits.

CUFIN ACCOUNT

The net-after tax profit account (CUFIN), in turn, is carried to keep track of income already taxed to the corporation, which can be paid out as dividends with-

Cufin Account

out triggering a special 53.85 percent tax, payable by corporations on distribution of previously untaxed income.

This account is increased with the following amounts:

- The net after-tax profit for the year
- The dividends received from corporate entities residing in Mexico
- The income, dividends or profits recognized from investments in low-tax jurisdiction

This amount is reduced by

- The dividends or profit distributions in cash or in kind, except distributions in stock of the distributing entity and except reinvested distributions, originating from the CUFIN
- Constructive dividends resulting from capital redemptions, also originating from the CUFIN

Net after-tax profits are the result of adding to the taxable income for the year the amount of employee profit sharing taken as a deduction and subtracting the following:

- The reinvested profits mentioned in the CUFINRE discussion (i.e., exclusive of the 30 percent tax rate and the 0.9286 factor)
- The employee profit sharing
- Nondeductible items (with limited exceptions)
- The 35 percent income tax paid for the tax year

CHAPTER 14

Taxation of Mergers and Acquisitions in the Netherlands

Olaf Ernst Van Der Donk
George L. Meij
Carl W. A. Van Suchtelen
Ernst & Young, The Netherlands

14.1 Introduction
14.2 Dutch Corporate Income Tax
  (a) Who Is Taxable?
  (b) What Is Taxable?
  (c) Transfer Pricing
  (d) Tax Losses
  (e) Disallowed and Deferred Interest
  (f) Applying the Disallowed and Deferred Interest Provisions
  (g) Interest Deferral Offsets
  (h) CFC Legislation
  (i) Conversion of Debt into Share Capital
  (j) Participation Exemption
  (k) Foreign Finance Companies/CFC Legislation
  (l) EU Subsidiaries
  (m) Foreign Partnerships
  (n) Mergers and Demergers
  (o) Fiscal Unity
  (p) Dutch Finance Regime
  (q) Advance Tax Rulings and Advance Pricing Arrangements
  (r) Dividend Withholding Tax
  (s) Other Withholding Taxes
  (t) Capital Tax
  (u) Real Estate Transfer Tax
14.3 Acquisition Structures
  (a) Asset Transaction–Acquiror's Perspective
  (b) Vendor's Perspective
  (c) Structures
  (d) Allocation and Acquisition Costs
  (e) Value-Added Tax

14.4 Share Transactions
   (a) Acquiror's Perspective
   (b) Seller's Perspective
   (c) Structures
   (d) Value-Added Tax
   (e) Dutch Acquisition Holding
17.5 Other Planning Opportunities
17.6 Dutch Partnerships
17.7 Closing Remarks

14.1 INTRODUCTION

This chapter outlines various methods and techniques available to foreign and Dutch companies to tax effectively acquire either the assets or the shares in a Dutch target company or group of target companies. A Dutch company cannot legally merge with a foreign company under Dutch civil law. As such, we do not discuss cross border mergers in the literal sense. This chapter focuses primarily on inbound investments. Merger and acquisition techniques used by Dutch companies to acquire assets or shares in foreign target companies are discussed at the end of this analysis.

A working knowledge of the Dutch tax system is essential for a clear understanding of the structures and relevant issues described and explained in this chapter. Accordingly, section 14.2 provides a general overview of the Dutch corporate income tax in as far as these tax provisions pertain to mergers and acquisitions, including recent changes that became effective on January 1, 2001. Sections 14.3 through 14.6 address the other types of taxes that may be relevant when planning a merger or acquisition in the Netherlands. Section 14.3 outlines frequently used acquisition structures and their tax consequences.

14.2 DUTCH CORPORATE INCOME TAX

The following description of the Dutch tax system as well as the structures and issues does not purport to be of an exhaustive nature and should not be treated as such.

(a) Who Is Taxable?

Corporate income tax is imposed on the worldwide profits of Dutch tax resident entities. The following types of tax resident entities are subject to corporate income tax:

- NV
- BV
- other companies with a capital that is, wholly or partly, divided into shares
- Dutch "open" limited partnerships

14.2 Dutch Corporate Income Tax

Whether an entity is tax resident is generally determined on the basis of the place where the company is managed and controlled (i.e., effective management). The place of effective management is determined by reference to all relevant facts and circumstances such as the seat of the board, the location of the head office, and where the shareholders meet. Entities incorporated under Dutch law such as the BV and NV are, however, always deemed to be Dutch tax resident entities for the purpose of the corporate income tax, regardless of the place of effective management. A few exceptions apply.

Nonresident entities are subject to corporate income tax on income derived from specific sources within the Netherlands. These entities include all of the following entities:

- Nonresident associations
- Corporate bodies
- "Open" limited partnerships
- Other nonincorporated entities with a capital that is, wholly or partly, divided into shares and
- So-called purpose vehicles (*doelvermogen*) that derive income from specific sources within the Netherlands

The rate of tax is currently 30 percent on the first approximately 22,700€ and 35 percent on the excess, regardless of whether the profits are distributed or not. No distinction is made between capital gains and trading income. Resident taxpayers may be able to claim relief from double taxation of foreign-source profits under the applicable Dutch tax treaties and the unilateral double tax relief rules.

(b) What Is Taxable?

For resident Dutch taxpayers, the taxable amount equals the worldwide profits minus any losses carried over from other years. Profit is defined as the "total income derived from a business, in whatever form and under whatever name" and thus includes capital gains. This profit is then allocated to the appropriate financial years by reference to sound business practice (*goed koopmansgebruik*).

The concept of sound business practice is not statutorily defined and has predominantly developed by case law. It is based on generally accepted accounting principles, but deviates when tax concepts would be violated. Its main principles are the principle of realization, i.e., that income and expense should be allocated to the year in which they belong, and the principle of prudence, i.e., that unrealized losses may be taken into account while unrealized profits may be deferred. Sound business practice allows changes in accounting principles only if that change is compatible with sound business practice. The concept of sound business practice could result in a different taxable profit than commercial profit.

Expenses incurred in connection with the conduct of a business are, in principle, deductible. Assets are generally depreciable. Acquired goodwill and intangibles are also, in principle, depreciable.

Nonresident entities carrying on a business in the Netherlands will be taxed on the income attributable to the branch, including capital gains. The statutory rate for companies also applies to branches. Nonresident entities can also be taxed on income from certain sources, including capital gains on shares in a Dutch company, sale of real estate located in the Netherlands, and interest and dividends received from Dutch resident companies. When a double taxation treaty applies, the Netherlands may have to give up this taxing right in favor of the other jurisdiction.

(c) Transfer Pricing

Currently, the Netherlands has no specific statutory provisions to implement the arm's-length principle (i.e. the principle that safeguards that related parties conduct their transactions as if dealing with third parties). Legislation in this respect has been announced. In the Netherlands, the arm's-length principle originates from the basic concept that the taxable profit comprises all income derived from a business, in whatever form and under whatever name it may arise. As a consequence of this principle, any payment made directly or indirectly to a person in its capacity as a shareholder or made to related persons under conditions that are not at arm's length will be deemed to be distributions of profits to the extent that this payment exceeds the arm's-length amount. Such a distribution is not deductible and dividend withholding tax may become due.

Conversely, if a related company grants a benefit to a Dutch company that originates from its shareholders' relationship rather than from a business relationship, such benefit does not fall within the scope of the corporate income tax. Such benefit is deemed a capital contribution in disguise or an informal capital contribution, which must be excluded from the taxable profit of the company. Such an informal capital contribution may be subject to capital tax.

(d) Tax Losses

Losses may be used to offset taxable profits of the three preceding financial years through carryback and may be carried forward indefinitely. Losses are offset in the order in which they were incurred and the profits made.

The loss compensation rules changed on January 1, 2001. The main features of the new rules are as follows. If the ultimate shareholders of the company changed by more than 30 percent, losses can be offset against future profits only if the following criteria are met:

1. The assets of the company do not consist principally of passive portfolio investments.
2. The activities of the company have not been reduced to less than 30 percent of its original activities.

This continuity rule is aimed at preventing the trade in loss carryovers. This rule should be considered when acquiring the shares of a Dutch company with tax losses.

(e) Disallowed and Deferred Interest

If an instrument qualifies as a loan for Dutch civil law purposes, the instrument will also be treated as a loan for tax purposes. However, there are three exceptions to this rule. For tax purposes, the loan will be treated as equity if the following conditions exist:

1. The parties have always intended the instrument to be equity.
2. The loan has been granted under terms and conditions such that the loan is in fact participating in the equity of the debtor company.
3. At the time the loan was granted is was or should have been obvious to the creditor that the debtor company could never service the loan and/or repay the principle.

If, under these rules, the instrument should, in whole or in part, be considered equity, then interest payments will be requalified as nondeductible dividend payments. If the instrument qualifies as a loan for tax purposes, then it should be determined whether the interest payments are deductible or not.

Under the participation exemption, which is discussed as follows in more detail, interest expenses are not deductible to the extent that these interest expenses relate to loans taken up by a Dutch company to finance investments in shares in foreign entities that qualify for participation exemption. Under the anti-base erosion rules that were introduced into the Dutch corporate income tax act in 1997, interest expenses can further be denied on loans from related companies that are used to finance particular listed transactions. The provisions aim at the introduction of debt in the Netherlands which is, in substance, equity from the group's perspective. Interest deduction is disallowed in two situations:

1. Interest expenses relating to the distribution of profits, capital reimbursements, and capital contributions all left outstanding on intercompany account are not tax deductible for the debtor. The concept of "left outstanding on intercompany account" should be broadly defined. Interest is also disallowed if a so-called circular transaction is performed, for instance if a dividend is distributed to a shareholder and that dividend is immediately lent back to the distributing company. It is even possible that interest is disallowed if a company borrows cash from a third party, for instance a bank, in order to finance the distribution of a dividend to the parent company, while the parent company actually bears the creditor's risk (e.g., by guaranteeing the loan from the bank to its subsidiary company).
2. Interest expenses incurred on loans due to related companies are disallowed in three concrete circumstances:
    a. If this loan is connected with a dividend distribution or a capital refund to a related company or related individual.

b. If this loan is connected with the acquisition of existing or newly issued shares in a related company, except when the ultimate ownership in that company has changed.
c. If this loan is ultimately traceable to equity from a Dutch-resident related company, as a result of which equity actually present in the Netherlands, of which the yield is taxable in the Netherlands, is replaced with debt on which the interest due is deductible against Dutch-taxable income, but of which the proceeds usually are not taxed in the Netherlands.

(f) Applying the Disallowed and Deferred Interest Provisions

Two escape clauses are available for the second set of transactions. The interest deduction will be allowed if it can be demonstrated that the reason for taking up the loan is predominantly business-driven, the motive test. Furthermore, irrespective of the motive test, interest is deductible if the interest is actually taxed in the hands of the recipient, at a tax rate that is considered reasonable from a Dutch perspective. The level of tax is considered reasonable, in general, if both the rate and taxable base are in line with common standards that apply in the Organization for Economic Cooperation and Development (OECD) member states to all tax resident companies.

This reasonableness requirement is obviously not fulfilled if the loan is granted by a related company that is a resident of a tax haven. Neither is this reasonableness requirement fulfilled if the received interest is not actually taxed because the creditor has sufficient losses from previous years with which the received interest can be offset, or because of the fact that the company can otherwise offset its corporate income tax liability on the interest income.

A fiscal unity is often used to simplify an acquisition of a Dutch company. By using a fiscal unity, a Dutch parent company, often the acquisition vehicle, and one or more of its 99 percent-subsidiaries are consolidated for corporate income tax purposes and regarded as one taxpaying entity. The concept of a fiscal unity is discussed in more detail in subsection 14.2(o). A fiscal unity is typically used as a way to push down acquisition debt at the level of the acquiring foreign entity. In such situations, it is often attractive (for the foreign acquiring company) to set up a separate Dutch acquisition company that acquires the target company directly and finances the acquisition by borrowing the funds from a group company. When the acquisition company and the target company both enter into a fiscal unity, interest costs due by the acquisition company on the acquisition loan can be offset against the profits obtained by the target company.

(g) Interest Deferral Offsets

Beginning in 1997, the possibilities to offset interest costs of the parent company against profits obtained by the subsidiary of the fiscal unity are restricted on the basis of the anti-abuse legislation in order to prevent improper use. Interest deductions are deferred if the following conditions apply:

- A fiscal unity exists between a parent company and a subsidiary company.
- One of the companies pays interest on a loan taken out from a related company.
- The loan is related to the acquisition of shares in the subsidiary with which a fiscal unity is formed.
- The acquiring company generates insufficient profit to offset the interest burden.

The interest deduction is deferred during the first eight years after the acquisition of the shares in the subsidiary. Interest deductions can be taken immediately when the parent company has profits of its own. Own profits include profits of group companies already included in a fiscal unity with the parent company on acquisition date. Postponed interest deductions are carried forward to the next year. Any surplus of disallowed interest that remains after eight years is divided in four equal parts and subsequently deducted from income generated by the fiscal unity in the years nine through twelve.

There are two exceptions to these limitations. First, interest due by a company within the fiscal unity can be offset with profits earned by the target company in as far as the group has in turn borrowed from nonrelated parties in order to finance the acquisition. Second, interest expenses due by the group company can be immediately offset with profits of the target companies if the following conditions are fulfilled:

- The ultimate ownership in the subsidiary (the target company) has significantly changed (i.e., a change of at least 30 percent).
- An individual or a group of cooperating individuals own at least 5 percent in the acquisition company, and the other shareholders each hold an interest of less than one-third in the parent company.
- One or more individuals earn income connected with activities performed for the target company, whereas these activities are of substantial volume.

(h) CFC Legislation

The Netherlands has, albeit very limited, controlled foreign corporation (CFC)-type legislation. The rules in question are discussed in Subsection 14.2(j) in relation to the participation exemption.

(i) Conversion of Debt into Share Capital

As of January 1, 2001, a debtor is deemed to have realized a profit equal to the difference between the fair market value of the debt and the nominal value of the debt if two conditions apply:

1. The fair market value of the debt is less than the nominal value.
2. The debt is repaid with shares by being converted into share capital.

This specific rule will also apply if the debt functions as equity without the issuance of shares. According to the Dutch government, such a conversion should be treated in the same way as a forgiveness of debt, which could give rise to taxable profit at the debtor level.

(j) Participation Exemption

One of the pillars of the Dutch corporate income tax system is the participation exemption that seeks to prevent double taxation of business profits at different corporate levels. Under the participation exemption, all capital gains, including currency exchange results, and benefits derived from a qualifying participation in a company are exempt from corporate income tax. Correspondingly, capital losses are not deductible. Under strict conditions, a deduction of losses may be allowed when the subsidiary is liquidated. All corporate taxpayers, resident and non-resident, are eligible for the participation exception, with the exception of qualifying investment institutions.

Costs, including interest and foreign exchange results that are associated with the participation, are nondeductible from corporate income tax. Therefore, interest and foreign exchange losses on borrowings used to finance an investment in shares of a company are not deductible. The foreign exchange gains on these borrowings are not taxable. An exception to this rule applies if the taxpayer can prove that these costs are instrumental in generating taxable profits in the Netherlands. This exemption will generally be the case for costs incurred in relation to resident or non-resident participations that conduct business in the Netherlands. As a result, in general, the interest and costs related to borrowings used to finance the shares in foreign companies are not deductible. To qualify for the participation exemption, a company must meet the following criteria:

- Hold at least 5 percent of the nominal paid-up share capital of a company with a capital divided into shares.
- Not hold the shares as inventory. This test aims at excluding the participation exemption for cash companies that are held by the taxpayer as stock.
- Be subject to a tax on profits levied by a sovereign state where the company is tax resident. A very low rate or tax holiday for a limited period is not an obstacle in satisfying this test.
- Not hold the shares as a portfolio investment. In practice, this test proves to be the most difficult one to satisfy because it is circumstantial. Consequently, companies often request rulings on this issue from the tax authorities.

(k) Foreign Finance Companies/CFC Legislation

The ambiguity in the portfolio investment test has, in the past, created doubt about whether foreign group finance companies were held as a portfolio investment. Under the current rules, foreign finance companies are deemed to be held as a portfolio investment unless the companies are active. Whether a foreign company is conducting active as opposed to passive finance activities is determined by reference to a test in which the substance of the foreign finance company is determined.

14.2 Dutch Corporate Income Tax

For certain 25 percent shareholdings in passive portfolio investments, an annual taxable revaluation is obligatory. As a result of the absence of the participation exemption, any benefits derived from such a shareholding, including the annual revaluation, are taxable in the Netherlands.

(l) EU Subsidiaries

To comply with the Parent-Subsidiary Directive, the Netherlands has introduced rules as a result of which the portfolio investment requirement can be ignored in cases where the taxpayer maintains a holding of at least 25 percent of the nominal paid-up share capital of a company resident in another European Union (EU) Member State. Changes in this regard have been proposed but are now being reconsidered. The proposed change would introduce a credit system with respect to passive finance companies within the EU.

(m) Foreign Partnerships

When a Dutch company owns an interest in a foreign partnership, it is necessary to classify that foreign partnership under the principles of Dutch civil law. Two possibilities exist:

1. The Dutch company derives profits from foreign activities (i.e., the foreign partnership is classified as a transparent entity for Dutch tax purposes).
2. The Dutch company receives income from shares (i.e. the foreign partnership is classified as an entity for Dutch tax purposes).

In the latter case, provided all the conditions are met, the participation exemption may apply.

According to the Secretary of Finance, a foreign partnership qualifies as a non-transparent entity, allowing the partner to obtain the benefits of the participation exemption, if the following additional conditions are met:

- A decision is needed in order for the participants to become entitled to the profits of the partnership.
- The participants are not liable for the debts of the partnership
- The partnership owns the assets that are used to carry on its activities.
- The interest in the partnership can be transferred without the consent of other participants.
- The partnership has a capital divided into shares.
- The partnership itself is subject to a profit tax.

Foreign partnerships that fail to meet these conditions are regarded as hybrid entities. With respect to foreign limited partnerships, the Dutch Ministry of Finance has confirmed that the participation exemption may apply if the limited partnership qualifies as open.

(n) Mergers and Demergers

The tax facilities for the legal merger and the demerger apply to Dutch resident companies as well as, in principle, to EU companies as of January 1, 2001; however, under Dutch civil law the merger between a Dutch resident company and a foreign resident entity is still not possible so that said facilities in practice are restricted to the local Dutch merger.

Business merger

A resident corporate taxpayer transfers all assets and liabilities of its enterprise, or all the assets and liabilities that, together, form an independent part of an enterprise, to another company in exchange for shares. This resident corporate taxpayer may roll over the basis and defer the gain derived on the transfer if certain conditions are satisfied.

Share-for-share merger

Apart from the aforementioned relief for asset mergers, relief for a share-for-share merger is available if a Dutch resident company acquires 50 percent or more of the shares in a Dutch resident company in return for shares. The relief also applies if the EU resident company acquires 50 percent of the voting right in another EU resident company in return for shares. The relief, furthermore, applies if a Dutch resident company acquires 90 percent or more of the shares in any company in return for shares.

Legal merger

A legal merger is a transaction between two or more companies where one company (the absorbing company) receives all assets and liabilities of the other by force of law. Alternatively, a company that is newly incorporated by the merging companies receives all its assets and liabilities by force of law. Because the assets and liabilities are transferred by force of law, the assets do not have to be transferred separately. The companies that transferred all assets and liabilities will cease to exist, without being liquidated as a disappearing company/companies.

A legal merger is available if the disappearing and absorbing companies are Dutch legal entities (e.g., NV, BV, or *stichting*) and the companies involved have matching corporate identities.

Dutch tax rules provide for a recapture rule if a shareholder or a group of collaborating shareholders has certain attributes:

- The shareholder has decisive control over the disappearing company at the time of the legal merger.
- The shareholder retains or obtains decisive control over a company that is party to the legal merger.
- The shareholder loses control within three years of merger because of a transfer of shares.

Corporate income tax will then be due because it is assumed that the legal merger was not predominantly driven by business reasons. This assumption can, however, be rebutted.

Demergers

In 1998, new Dutch company law rules became effective, allowing companies to demerge without liquidating the existing company. Similar to the legal merger, the benefit of a corporate demerger is that the assets and liabilities are transferred to another company by force of law, instead of being transferred separately. In general, two types of corporate demerger can be distinguished: the split-up and the split-off. In a split-up, all assets and liabilities of the transferring company are transferred to at least two existing or newly incorporated acquiring companies. In return, the acquiring companies issue shares to the shareholders of the transferring company. Alternatively, different shareholders of the transferring company become shareholders of a separate acquiring company. The transferring company will cease to exist without being liquidated.

In a split-off, all or part of the assets and liabilities of the transferring company are transferred to at least one existing or newly incorporated acquiring company. The transferring company will continue to exist. The acquiring companies issue shares to the shareholders of the transferring company, to the transferring company, or to both the shareholders of the transferring company and the transferring company itself. If the transferring company is to become the sole shareholder of (one or more of) the acquiring companies, these acquiring companies have to be newly incorporated.

It is also possible to demerge a company and transfer the assets and liabilities of the transferring company to the acquiring company, against the issuance of shares in a parent company of the acquiring company.

(o) Fiscal Unity

Upon request, and subject to certain conditions, Dutch tax resident companies may form a fiscal unity with wholly owned resident subsidiaries and in some cases with nonresident subsidiaries. As a consequence, the companies involved file a consolidated return for corporate income tax purposes. The subsidiary is deemed to be absorbed by the parent company. The main advantages of a fiscal unity are that profits and losses of the subsidiary are deemed to be the profits and losses of the other company. Losses of the subsidiary company can be offset against profits of the parent company and vice versa. Because the subsidiary is deemed to be absorbed, assets can be transferred from one company to another without any taxable income being recognized.

A fiscal unity can only be formed if the following conditions exist:

- The parent company takes the form of an NV, a BV, a cooperative society, or a mutual insurance company.
- The subsidiary company is either an NV or a BV.

- The parent company owns 99 percent of the subsidiary company's shares at the start of and during the entire financial year. New legislation has been proposed to revise the rules for the fiscal unity. Under the proposed legislation, 95 percent ownership is sufficient to form a fiscal unity.
- The parent and subsidiary company have corresponding financial years.
- The parent and subsidiary company are subject to the same tax regime.
- The parent and the subsidiary company file a joint request. If the request is granted, it will be subject to various conditions. The parent and the subsidiary company may object to the denial of their request or to the conditions.

The conditions imposed by the tax authorities are generally identical to standard conditions published by the Dutch Ministry of Finance. These conditions, which are complicated and detailed, serve to preserve the levy and collection of corporate income tax, if there had not been a fiscal unity. These conditions elaborate on many technical aspects such as the consolidation, prefiscal unity losses, antiabuse provisions, and disruption of the fiscal unity.

According to a decision of the Dutch Supreme Court, a fiscal unity can also be formed with a subsidiary that is incorporated under Dutch law, even though the place of its effective management is located outside the Netherlands. Furthermore, in some circumstances, a company that has been incorporated under foreign law, but has its tax residency within the Netherlands, can also be included in a fiscal unity. The foreign company can be either the parent company or the subsidiary company in the fiscal unity. An important condition is that the legal form and the articles of association of the foreign company are comparable to those of a Dutch NV or BV.

(p) Dutch Finance Regime

A Dutch company conducting group financing activities will, provided certain conditions are satisfied, be allowed to establish a provision for the risks connected with those financing activities. The provision is formed solely for tax purposes and can include a provision for risks relating to shareholdings in other companies and foreign branches, held by the group. The company will be able to provide for up to 80 percent of the annual profits from its financing activities. As a result, only the remaining 20 percent of the income related to these financing activities will be immediately subject to tax.

(q) Advance Tax Rulings and Advance Pricing Agreements

The Dutch government announced on November 20, 2000, that it will restructure its ruling practice to be in accord with OECD standards. According to the Dutch Secretary of Finance, the advance tax ruling (ATR) and advance pricing agreement (APA) policy seek to attract international investors to the Netherlands "with real activities which have a certain kind of substance." ATRs and APAs are binding commitments from the Dutch tax authorities on the application of Dutch tax law. Such rulings are obtained before any investment is made. The Dutch government prefers bilateral APAs, but unilateral APAs are also possible.

14.2 Dutch Corporate Income Tax

Generally, an APA is an agreement about the arm's length price to be used between associated enterprises. An ATR is a commitment about the Dutch tax qualification of international structures (e.g., Does the participation exemption apply?). A company cannot obtain an ATR and APA if such an agreement could infringe on the good faith that the Netherlands should observe toward its tax treaty partners.

The consequences of restructuring the ruling practice into a practice that is more OECD-like is that the standard ruling will be replaced with a tailor-made ATR based on economic reality. The standard ruling, such as the holding company ruling, finance ruling, royalty ruling, cost plus ruling, foreign sales corporation ruling, and the informal capital ruling will no longer be applicable. These rulings could offer guidance in developing the APAs and ATRs, particularly because the Dutch government states that the introduction of APAs and ATRs should expand the scope of the rulings.

(r) Dividend Withholding Tax

Dividend withholding tax is levied at a rate of 25 percent on all kinds of profit distributions made by resident companies, including dividends in kind and, in some situations, repayment of paid-in capital. The tax rate may be reduced under double tax conventions. Furthermore, the tax rate drops to zero if the participation in a company falls under the participation exemption (see subsection 14.2(j)). Moreover, dividends paid to EU corporate shareholders that own 25 percent or more of the company for at least one year are exempted from dividend withholding tax. A reduction of the dividend withholding tax payable to the Dutch government can be obtained, provided certain requirements are met.

(s) Other Withholding Taxes

The Netherlands does not levy any withholding tax on interest or royalty payments. Some profit-sharing loans may, however, be subject to dividend withholding tax. Furthermore, no withholding tax is levied on the repatriation of profits from a Dutch permanent establishment to the foreign head office.

(t) Capital Tax

A capital tax is levied at a rate of 0.55 percent on a contribution, in cash or in kind, to the share capital of a resident company. Exemptions apply for certain share-for-share mergers, assets mergers, legal mergers, demergers, and internal reorganizations. It is expected that the capital tax will be further reduced or even abolished in the near future.

(u) Real Estate Transfer Tax

Real estate transfer tax is levied at a rate of 6 percent of the value of any transfer of the legal or economic ownership of real property situated in the Netherlands. The tax is levied from the acquiror of the real estate upon transfer of such property. Shares in companies of which the assets consist of more than 70 percent of Dutch real property are deemed to be real property themselves. Certain transfers are exempted from real estate transfer tax, for instance within the scope of certain reorganizations.

14.3 ACQUISITION STRUCTURES

Whether a transaction takes the form of an asset transaction or a share purchase is often dictated by the vendor. There are numerous business as well as tax reasons why a vendor would choose one over the other. One reason for an asset deal could be that the vendor operates several divisions within a single legal entity and is merely interested in selling off one of these divisions. Another reason could be that the vendor has significant operating losses against which he can offset any capital gains realized on the sale of the assets.

A reason for the seller to opt for a sale of shares is that the capital gain will be exempt at the holding company level as a result of the application of a participation exemption. Where cross-border mergers and acquisitions are concerned, more factors enter into the equation. If it were up to the acquiror, he would probably opt for an asset deal. This way he purchases only those assets and liabilities that he really wants and does not have to deal with other issues such as tax liabilities. In general, one could state that a vendor would prefer a share sale and an acquiror would prefer an asset purchase.

Confronted with an asset deal or a share purchase, the buyer will seek a legal and tax structure that fits its operational objectives as well as its long- and short-term tax strategies. As a result, no specific structure would fit each purchaser. With this in mind, the following paragraphs discuss some commonly used acquisition structures, as well as the affects of the Dutch tax rules on those structures. Unless explicitly stated otherwise, this discussion focuses only on the acquisition of Dutch assets of, or shares in, a company resident in the Netherlands.

(a) Asset Transaction—Acquiror's Perspective

Several advantages can be gained from an asset purchase as opposed to a share purchase. First, the acquiror obtains each asset for its fair market value. The purchaser, therefore, gets to step up the basis of the assets for depreciation purposes, unless the fair market value does not exceed the book value. When assets and liabilities are purchased, which together constitute an independent part of an enterprise and the purchase price includes an amount for goodwill, the acquiror can amortize the goodwill in the Netherlands. Goodwill can generally be written off in a period of five years. The acquiror will probably have to pay the vendor for this depreciation potential.

Furthermore, in principle, no hidden liabilities are transferred to the buyer. The purchaser also has a choice, from a tax perspective at least, regarding how he wishes to finance the acquisition. The anti-base erosion rules that were introduced

14.3 Acquisition Structures

in 1997[1] relate only to certain transactions involving shares. No restrictions, other than general anti-abuse rules, apply to financing the asset acquisition.

The acquiror can choose to have an existing or newly formed Dutch group company purchase the assets and have this Dutch company borrow the acquisition price from a group company. Whether this group company has financed the purchase price with equity or it has itself borrowed from a third party is irrelevant. The interest payments by the Dutch company are deductible in the Netherlands. The acquiror could even choose to have a foreign-formed company act as the acquiring vehicle. Most jurisdictions, including the Netherlands, allow an interest deduction at the branch level to the extent that the head office has borrowed the funds used to finance the asset purchase.

Some disadvantages are attached to an asset acquisition in the Netherlands. The most important issue is more of a civil law issue than a tax issue. Dutch civil law provides that each asset should be transferred according to its own transfer rules. For example, real estate should be transferred by a notarial deed by a Civil Law Notary and receivables should be properly assigned.

These transfers can prove to be an administrative nightmare. Special attention should be paid to licenses and distribution agreements. Some licenses may not be transferred, and a new license should be obtained. A tax and legal due diligence review should help identify these issues.

As mentioned previously, an advantage of acquiring the assets and liabilities is that no hidden liabilities are transferred. Some caution is due here. Under Dutch law, most tax and other liabilities remain with the selling legal entity. This entity will remain liable for taxes that are due up to the date of sale. In some instances, prospective liabilities can transfer to the acquiror. For example, under Dutch civil law when the assets and liabilities of a business are purchased as a going concern, the employees are also transferred by force of law to the acquiror. The acquiror is in principle bound by the employment agreement that was entered into by the employee and the seller. If this contract provides for excessive expense reimbursements, this may lead to a wage tax liability for the acquiror.

(b) Vendor's Perspective

In the Netherlands, no distinction is made between operating income and capital gains; both amounts are considered the income of the company taxable at the statutory rate of 35 percent (or 30 percent). The same applies for losses. Operating losses and capital losses can equally be used to offset income of the company. As such, a vendor may choose to have the capital gains realized on the sale of the assets offset by operating losses carried forward from previous years. If no losses are to be carried forward, the gain is in principle taxable.

Another advantage that may be available to the vendor is to postpone taxation on the gain by forming a reinvestment reserve. The reinvestment reserve was introduced as of January 1, 2001, and replaces the replacement reserve.

---

[1] These rules are discussed in subsection 14.2(j).

It is now possible to form a reinvestment reserve for a reinvestment in other assets as long as they are purchased in the same year or in the following three years as the disinvestments are made and the intention to reinvest exists. The reserve is rolled over to the purchase price of the new assets. The joint new book value of the new asset(s) may not be less than the book value of the asset(s) sold. Ultimately, the gain on the sale of these assets will be taxed, so that the advantage is time value of money.

An exit tax is levied to the extent that the vendor ceases to generate taxable profits in the Netherlands. All gains realized upon leaving the Netherlands will be taxed at that time unless a specific exemption is applicable. Gains realized on shares could fall under the participation exemption.

Disadvantages to the vendor could be the effect of loss restriction rules. These rules can disallow the use of losses in the event that the activities of the vendor have substantially decreased, and a change in ultimate ownership takes place. These rules are complex and should be considered carefully. The vendor will want to be compensated for the additional tax burden that exists as a result.

(c) Structures

The acquisition can be structured as follows: The foreign company sets up a new Dutch company to act as the acquisition vehicle. The company should be financed with at least the minimum equity required under Dutch law (approximately 20,000€). The remainder of the acquisition price could be furnished through a loan to the acquisition vehicle. Although there are no thin capitalization rules in the Netherlands, it is advisable not to fully leverage the BV. The acquisition vehicle then purchases the target assets.

The interest expenses due by the acquisition vehicle are fully deductible against the operating profits of the acquired assets. Relief for interest expenses is given on an accruals basis. It is not required to make actual payments in order to obtain the benefit. The interest deduction disallowance rules do not apply when assets are acquired. There is no withholding tax in the Netherlands on interest. Without further planning, the interest payments are probably fully taxable in the hands of the recipient. Further tax planning, depending on the jurisdiction concerned, could either postpone or reduce taxation of the interest received or accrued.

If the foreign company chooses to purchase the assets itself, so that the assets constitute a branch or permanent establishment in the Netherlands, this asset acquisition has the advantage that losses incurred at the branch level may be offset against the operating income of the head office company. An additional advantage is that the Netherlands does not levy branch remittance taxes. When the acquisition of assets is funded through a loan, care should be taken that the Dutch tax authorities cannot dispute that this loan and the corresponding interest deduction should be allocated to the Dutch branch.

(d) Allocation and Acquisition Costs

When an overall purchase price is agreed upon for all assets, the purchase price should be allocated to the separate assets for depreciation purposes. This alloca-

14.4 Share Transactions

tion should be accomplished on an arm's-length basis. The tax authorities could challenge the allocation if it does not equate with an arm's-length allocation. The tax authorities could even challenge an allocation of the purchase price that has been agreed upon between the seller and buyer, although this does not occur often.

Costs relating to the acquisition of the assets need to be capitalized on the balance sheet and can be depreciated if, and to the same extent as, the assets themselves. When acquisition costs cannot be directly linked to an asset, they are deductible in the year in which they occur, subject to the general rules.

(e) Value-Added Tax

A cashflow disadvantage could occur when the transfer of the assets is subject to Dutch value-added tax (VAT) at a rate of 19 percent. The seller is obliged to charge VAT. The buyer, if it qualifies as a VAT entrepreneur, can recover the VAT from the tax authorities; however, a VAT exemption could be applicable if the assets form an enterprise or an independent part of an enterprise.

14.4 SHARE TRANSACTIONS

(a) Acquiror's Perspective

There are both advantages and disadvantages when the purchaser acquires the legal entity in which the desired business is carried out. An advantage could be that losses can survive the change of ownership and be available to the purchaser. Any tax attributes, such as reinvestment reserves, could also survive the transfer of ownership. However, the downside is that the purchaser also acquires the company's tax history and any other claims that may arise from the company's business, such as environmental claims. Where the target company was part of a fiscal unity, either for VAT or corporate income tax purposes, the target company remains severally liable for the taxes due by the fiscal unity during the period in which the target was part of the fiscal unity. The share purchase agreement (SPA) should contain appropriate warranties and indemnities to safeguard the purchaser against such claims.

Careful planning is required to push down acquisition debt to the target company. A potential pitfall is that a purchaser that is interested in purchasing an entire group and would wish to purchase shares in several companies separately is often faced with the fact that it is forced to buy the shares in the holding company of the group.

From a tax perspective, it may be preferable to acquire certain shares out from underneath the holding company before the acquisition of the holding company. This would help sustain the fact that the shares in these companies were acquired directly from a third party. Now the purchaser may be forced to reorganize the target group after the acquisition of the holding company. From a Dutch perspective, this approach increases the risk that the interest deductions on the acquisition debt that is pushed down to the Netherlands is not deductible because these companies are acquired from a related party.

In a share transaction, no goodwill included in the purchase price can be amortized. Such costs are allocated to the basis of the acquired shares.

(b) Seller's Perspective

The sale of shares by the vendor usually results in application of the participation exemption, assuming that the shares are held by a Dutch holding company. The situation in which individuals resident in the Netherlands are the vendors is more complicated. Where an individual owns more than 5 percent of the share capital of a Dutch company, he is considered to own a substantial interest. If shares in a substantial interest are sold, the capital gain is taxed at the individual level with personal income tax. Special taxation rules apply to these situations. Careful tax planning is required in these types of situations.

(c) Structures

The most important tax objective of designing an acquisition structure is usually to push down as much of the acquisition debt as possible to the target jurisdiction. As mentioned previously, this has become increasingly difficult where share transactions are concerned because of recent law changes. The second most important objective is to try to avoid or mitigate taxation on the interest income at the recipient level. How this can be done falls outside the scope of this chapter. The following structures are often contemplated and implemented.

A Dutch holding company is incorporated before the acquisition. This company will be highly leveraged. This holding company will subsequently acquire the shares directly from the seller, which is not a related company. The holding company and the target form a fiscal unity.

To the extent the buyer can prove that the debt in the holding company corresponds to third-party debt (e.g., bank debt), the interest on the debt is deductible from the profits of the operating company. To the extent, for example, the parent company of a multinational group has borrowed funds from a third-party bank *and* raised equity through a public share offering to finance the acquisition of the Dutch target, and has loaned the entire acquisition price to the acquisition holding. In principle, only the interest expenses related to the loan taken up by the parent company from the bank are deductible against the profits of the target company. The interest due on the remainder of the loan will not be disallowed, but will be deferred over a period of eight years. This deferral is obviously a major drawback of such a structure.

It is also possible that only part of the funds obtained by the parent through the bank and the public offering is loaned to the acquisition vehicle. Assume that the entire amount of funds raised through the bank is 100 million; 25 million is equity. Assume also that the acquisition price is 75 million. The parent companies grant the Dutch acquisition company a loan of 75 million. In that case, the acquiror will argue that the amount of the loan to the Dutch company stems entirely from the bank loan. The tax authorities would preferably argue that 25є million of the loan stems entirely from the equity part, so as to minimize any interest deduction in the Netherlands. Unless the acquiror can actually demonstrate that the loan can indeed be traced back to the bank loan, it is arguable that a pro rata part of the interest deductions in the Netherlands will be deferred.

Interest deduction could be denied altogether if the acquisition debt is borrowed from a related company and the shares are also acquired from a related company (e.g., sale of the shares against indebtedness). This denial of the interest deduction could also occur if the third-party debt is guaranteed by its shareholder or group company.

It is possible to create acquisition structures whereby beneficial tax results can be obtained in the jurisdiction of the interest recipient. These results vary from temporary deferral of taxation in that jurisdiction to permanent deferral or double dip of expenses. The benefits and the complexity of these structures depend largely on the tax jurisdiction of the income recipient. Most jurisdictions do, however, provide for some variation of the aforementioned planning techniques.

Dividends distributed to the shareholders are subject to a 25 percent dividend withholding tax. Under most double tax conventions, the rate is decreased and can be as low as zero percent. If the EU Parent-Subsidiary Directive applies, the dividend withholding tax is reduced to nothing. If the creditor is resident in a country to which dividend distributions are subject to withholding taxes, an additional benefit of introducing leverage is that income can be remitted to that jurisdiction free of withholding taxes in the form of interest payments and repayment of principal.

(d) Value-Added Tax

Attention should be paid to the VAT position of the holding company during the structuring of the transaction. The holding company will acquire all shares. Often, all fees of external advisors, such as lawyers, tax advisors, accountants, and investment banks, will be invoiced to the holding company. These advisors should charge VAT in most cases. The holding company can recover such VAT only if it qualifies as an entrepreneur for VAT purposes. The VAT cannot be recovered if the holding company holds the shares only in the subsidiaries and does not perform any other services to the subsidiaries. A holding company may be entitled to VAT if the holding company is active in managing the subsidiaries and receives a compensation for those services.

(e) Dutch Acquisition Holding

Traditionally, the Netherlands has been an ideal location to set up a holding company for foreign participations. The participation exemption, the favorable treaty network, the absence of withholding taxes on interest, and the ability to obtain rulings from the Dutch tax authorities before actually making an investment makes the Netherlands an attractive location to set up such holding activities. As such, a Dutch company is often used as an acquisition vehicle for acquisitions of foreign entities by foreign multinationals. Therefore, the following paragraph addresses some of the issues a foreign multinational using the Netherlands faces.

Interest paid by the Dutch holding company on debts assumed to acquire the shares in resident and nonresident companies is deductible only to the extent that these costs relate to profits that are taxable in the Netherlands. In general, this exclusion leads to the denial of interest deduction for interest paid on debt assumed to acquire shares in foreign, non-Dutch, companies. This exclusion rule provides the refutable assumption that debts agreed upon six months before the acquisition are deemed to be entered into to acquire the shares in the subsidiary. The burden of proof is therefore shifted to the taxpayer.

One possibility to solve this interest deduction issue is to incorporate local holding companies in all relevant countries. The acquisition debt assumed by the Dutch acquisition company is pushed down to the local holding companies. The Dutch company acts as a conduit financing company.

The interest paid on the acquisition debt should be deductible to the extent that it relates to the financing of the debt to the local holding companies. The Dutch company will be required to report a spread in the Netherlands. The local holding companies use the funds to acquire the target companies. Where this is not possible, this debt pushdown can be implemented after the acquisition, although given the anti-base erosion rules, this can prove more difficult.

Many acquisitions structured through the Netherlands combine the use of a Dutch holding company with a tax-effective financing structure. Many non-European multinationals structure and have structured their acquisitions through the Netherlands.

14.5 OTHER PLANNING OPPORTUNITIES

Every civil law and tax law system creates its own possibilities. Where two different systems meet, planning opportunities often arise because of mismatches between the civil law systems, the tax systems, or between the civil law and the tax law of the jurisdictions. Consider the following examples:

- Differences in entity classification, resulting in the same entity being treated as a company by one jurisdiction and as a partnership by the other jurisdiction
- Differences in income qualification, resulting in a payment being treated as an interest payment in one country and as a dividend payment in the other country

Some of these differences may be resolved by tax treaties, but this is only rarely the case. An example of a difference in entity classification can be demonstrated in the following example involving a U.S. company acquiring a Dutch target company.

This U.S. company (USCO) incorporates a Dutch BV (BV). BV will acquire the target company. BV will have to be funded to provide it with the means to acquire the target company. Therefore, USCO grants a loan to BV, which itself had obtained from a nonrelated bank. BV and target form a fiscal unity. As such, the BV may offset the interest charges against the profits of the target company.

USCO elects to "check the box" on the BV such that the BV will be treated as a branch for U.S. corporate income tax purposes. The "check-the-box" rules allow U.S. shareholders for entity classification purposes to treat certain foreign companies either as a branch, legal entity, or partnership, provided that some requirements are met. The election has no impact on the Dutch tax treatment of BV.

As a result, the loan between USCO and BV will be ignored from a U.S. perspective because a loan between the branch office and the head office cannot exist under U.S. tax rules. The interest is, therefore, not taxable at the level of USCO, while the interest is deductible at the level of BV. Moreover, USCO will pay interest on the third-party debt, which should also be deductible. The example illustrates the results of differences in entity classification rules in the various jurisdictions. Of course many other variations are possible.

14.6 DUTCH PARTNERSHIPS

A vehicle that often gives rise to classification issues is a partnership. Inserting a partnership in the right jurisdiction can result in interest being deducted in one country without being picked up in the other country.

The two most used partnerships in the Netherlands are the general partnership and the limited partnership. According to Dutch civil law, partnerships are not separate legal entities but a contractual arrangement between the partners. The partnership is regarded as a fully transparent entity. From a corporate tax law point of view, the partnership is also regarded as fully transparent, unless the partnership has a capital divided into shares.

For Dutch corporate income tax purpose, the so-called open partnership is a taxable entity to the extent of the limited partner's share in the profits. The so-called closed partnership is a fully transparent entity for tax purposes. Whether a limited partnership is open or closed depends on the corporate characteristics of the partnership agreement. Full transparency means that the partners in a general partnership and the general partner in a limited partnership are in fact the owner of the business or trade. The taxable profit is calculated at the level of the partner. Therefore, each partner can choose its own profit calculating system in so far as this does not contradict the principle of sound business practice and is not bound by the system of its partner. Each of the partners is liable for the corporate income tax due on the part of the profits to which it is entitled under the partnership agreement.

14.7 CLOSING REMARKS

This chapter is a description of some of the more important issues facing Dutch and foreign companies when trying to structure an acquisition in the Netherlands. This discussion shows that there is not a "one size fits all" structure available in the Netherlands. Each deal, whether an asset deal or a share purchase, should be judged on its own merits in order to determine the most suitable structure.

Having said that, the Netherlands provides several opportunities to create a tax effective acquisition structure that allows, within the parameters described, for a maximum deduction of interest. More elaborate tax planning can also create a structure that maximizes the benefit in the jurisdiction of the acquiring company.

CHAPTER 15

Taxation of Mergers and Acquisitions in Norway

Espen Ommedal
International Tax Services, Ernst & Young, Norway

15.1 Introduction
15.2 Taxation Structure
    (a) Corporate Income Tax
    (b) Value-Added Tax
    (c) Other Taxes
15.3 Asset Acquisitions
    (a) Seller
    (b) Buyer
15.4 Stock Acquisitions
    (a) "RISK" Adjustments
    (b) Seller
    (c) Buyer
15.5 Mergers and Demergers
    (a) Mergers and the Merger Directive
    (b) Mergers Applications
    (c) Demergers
15.6 Cross-Border Transactions
15.7 Anti-Avoidance

15.1 INTRODUCTION

The Norwegian tax treatment of mergers was historically based on case laws and tax practice by tax authorities; however, in 1997 legislation was introduced that is now embedded in the General Tax Act of 1999 (GTA), Chapter 11. The rules introduced largely enacted the historic practice that had developed for corporations. In addition, as part of the law, similar rules were introduced for partnerships.

Since 1961, Norway has had specific rules for intergroup tax-free reorganizations. These rules have also given the tax authorities a discretionary right to grant tax deferral on various acquisitions. This discretionary right has especially and increasingly been used in relation to cross-border acquisitions and mergers. These rules are also embedded in the GTA, Chapter 11.

This chapter analyzes the tax effects of mergers and acquisitions in Norway. In addition to the tax effects, deciding the final structure of such transactions should include evaluating a range of other factors as well, including operational optimalization, legal constraints, public concessions, and customs duties. These issues are not dealt with in this chapter.

15.2 TAXATION STRUCTURE

The Norwegian budget for 2001 was passed late in 2000, and the general taxation structure in Norway is summarized as follows. The Norwegian government has stated that tax reform is scheduled for 2002. The content of this reform is not yet known, but the reform will certainly introduce rules that will affect transactions as mergers and acquisitions.

(a) Corporate Income Tax

Resident corporations are subject to taxes on worldwide income. Nonresident corporations are subject to the same taxes, but are restricted to income attributable to Norwegian business operations. A corporation is resident in Norway if it is incorporated (i.e., registered) in Norway or if its central management and control are effectively exercised in Norway. For 2001, the corporate tax rate was 28 percent.

Capital gains derived from the disposal of business assets and shares of stock are subject to normal corporate taxes; however, capital gains derived by a foreigner from the sale of stocks in a Norwegian corporation are generally not subject to tax.

Taxable income is based on book income shown in the annual financial statements, which must be prepared in accordance with generally accepted accounting principles. An item must be included in the statutory accounts to be deductible for tax purposes. In general, all expenses, except gifts and entertainment expenses, are deductible.

Inventory is valued at cost, which must be determined on a first-in, first-out (FIFO) basis. Depreciation on fixed assets must be calculated using the declining balance method at any rate up to a given maximum. Fixed assets are allocated to one of the following eight different groups:

1. Office equipment and similar items — 25%
2. Acquired goodwill — 20%
3. Trailers, trucks, buses, taxis and vehicles for transportation of disabled persons — 20%
4. Cars, tractors, other movable machines, other machines, equipment, instruments, furniture, fixtures, and similar items — 15%
5. Ships, vessels, drilling rigs, and similar items — 14%
6. Aircraft and helicopters — 12%

15.2 Taxation Structure

7. Industrial buildings, hotels, rooming houses, restaurants and similar buildings, and electronic equipment in power stations, but with higher rate if less than 20 years economic life   6%

8. Office buildings, but a higher rate if less than 20 years economic life   1%

Assets in groups 1 through 4 are depreciated on an aggregate basis, whereas assets in groups 5 through 8 are depreciated individually.

(b) Value-Added Tax

The value-added tax (VAT) is a general tax on supply of goods and some specific services rendered in Norway. The VAT is levied on the delivery of goods and/or the provisions of specific services by any individual or legal entity conducting an economic activity, and on the importation of goods, and on the importation of certain services to be used or exploited in Norway.

Under the VAT system, the tax is levied at each stage of the manufacturing and distribution process on a noncumulated basis. The accumulation of tax is avoided through the deduction of VAT invoiced to the entity. The entity collects VAT on the total amount invoiced in each tax period, but the entity is entitled to recover the input VAT, which was invoiced to the entity during the same period. If, in any tax period, the credit for input VAT is higher than the amount of VAT due on output, the entity is entitled to a refund.

A VAT reform is to be introduced, probably as of July 1, 2001. By this VAT reform, the VAT obligation on rendering of services will be increased because all services, unless explicitly exempted, will be liable for VAT. The general VAT rate has been 23 percent for a long time, but was increased to 24 percent as of January 1, 2001.

In general, VAT is not a problem in mergers and acquisition. VAT is not levied on sale of stocks, and acquisitions of whole or part of the business through assets deals are normally exempted according to the Value Added Tax Act of 1969, § 16 (6), provided specific conditions are satisfied.

(c) Other Taxes

No additional turnover tax is levied in Norway. Stamp duty in Norway is levied only on transfer of legal ownership of real estate. The stamp duty rate is 2.5 percent, calculated on the fair market value of the real estate. An investment tax is a specific tax on purchased goods not intended for resale or for the production of goods for sale. Manufacturing equipment is exempted. The tax rate is 7 percent. The authorities indicate that this tax will be abolished on April 1, 2002. Various other duties may be incurred in Norway, such as re-registering legal ownership of cars, re-registering legal ownership for other assets than real estate, and so forth. However, such duties are normally negligible.

15.3 ASSET ACQUISITIONS

This section deals with the tax aspects of a taxable purchase and sale of a business that takes the form of a sale of corporate assets.

(a) Seller

Income tax

The seller will have to recognize capital gains or losses from a bulk sale. Capital gains are considered as ordinary income, and losses from such sales are deductible from ordinary income. Gains or losses can be recognized in the year of transaction if the company is liquidated as part of the process. Otherwise the sales proceeds are related to the fixed assets group as follows:

If the taxpayer sells fixed assets in groups 1 through 4, as discussed in section 15.2 (a), the proceeds reduce the balance of the group of assets and consequently the basis for depreciation. If a negative balance results within groups 1, 3, or 4, part of the negative balance must be included in income. In general, the minimum amount to be included as income is determined by multiplying the negative balance by the depreciation rate for the group. If the negative balance is less than 15,000 Norwegian kroner (NOK), however, the entire negative balance must be included in taxable income (1 USD = approx NOK 9). A negative balance in one of the other groups (2 and 5 through 8), as discussed in section 15.2 (a), must be included in a gains and losses account. Twenty percent of a positive balance in this account must be included in taxable income.

VAT

The sale of goods subject to VAT taxation (e.g., inventories and fixed business assets) will not incur VAT if the transaction is part of a transferral of the total business or a separate part of the business. In case law and practice, certain specific conditions are set up which must be satisfied, which they normally will be. One of these conditions includes that the business or the separate part in question is essentially continued by the acquiror.

(b) Buyer

Income tax

The allocation of the purchase consideration is relevant to the buyer because it establishes the tax basis for each of the newly acquired assets. This allocation by the buyer must be similar to the one done by the seller.

The acquired assets are depreciable under the ordinary rules described in section 15.2 (a) (i.e., depreciation under the declining balance method). This acquisition applies to acquired goodwill, which is depreciable on the declining balance method at a rate of 20 percent. The overall procedure to establish the value of goodwill is the "residual method," by which the difference between the purchase consideration and fair market value of fixed assets and identifiable intangibles is goodwill.

As a result of the favorable treatment of depreciation of goodwill, the tax authorities have focused on the definition of goodwill. Intangible assets, such as company names, brand names, patents, and so on have to be treated separately. Such assets might be depreciable provided a declining economic value can be argued, and then the values are amortizable over the asset's economic life. We recommend that the taxpayer establish a careful documentation package in order to avoid potential challenges from the tax authorities.

VAT

The buyer will normally not have paid any input VAT in an asset transaction; however, ordinary output VAT will have to be charged when goods subject to VAT taxation are sold. The ordinary exemptions on exports will be applicable if the buyer is a non-Norwegian tax resident. No investment tax will be levied given that the transaction is exempted from VAT.

15.4 STOCK ACQUISITIONS

This section deals with the tax aspects of a taxable purchase and sale of a corporate business that takes the form of a sale of the stocks (shares) of the corporation.

(a) "RISK" Adjustments

Norway has introduced the RISK method to avoid double taxation of the gain on transfers of stocks of Norwegian corporations. RISK is an acronym for the Norwegian phrase meaning "adjustment of cost price for taxed capital." Changes in the corporation's taxed capital during the shareholder's period of ownership are taken into account in computing the gain on transfers of stocks of Norwegian corporations. Taxed capital is undistributed income that has been previously subject to tax at the corporation level. The original cost of the stocks is increased by the net increase or decreased by the net decrease in the corporation's taxed capital during the shareholder's period of ownership. Corporations calculate changes in taxed capital each year at year end.

(b) Seller

Income tax

Sale of stock is a taxable event for a Norwegian tax resident irrespective of the number/percentage of stocks sold and irrespective of whether the stocks have been held for trading or investment purposes. Gains are taxable as ordinary income and taxed at a rate of 28 percent, and correspondingly losses are deductible against other ordinary taxable income. Gain or loss will be calculated as the difference between the purchase consideration and the tax base, including adjustments after the RISK method.

As a result of special transitional rules introduced as part of the Norwegian tax reform of 1992, several sellers got a step-up of their tax basis in the stock as of January 1, 1992. The rules for this step up were rather liberal, resulting in rather high upward regulations for several stockholders. Thus, through a sale of the stocks, several sellers will get a relatively low taxable gain. A special rule introduced in 1992 preventing tax-deductible losses due to any excess upward regulations will be abolished in 2002. A non-Norwegian tax resident seller will normally not be taxable for any gain in Norway, and correspondingly not get any deductions. The sale of stocks is exempt from VAT.

(c) Buyer

The purchase consideration for the stock will be the tax basis for the buyer. This purchase amount is not depreciable, but the taxpayer must capitalize this amount. The purchase consideration will be deductible only on later alienation of the acquired stocks (e.g., in an onward sale or liquidation of the corporation). The assets will retain the tax basis when the ownership of the corporation changes hands. If the assets have a tax basis lower than their marked value, and hence lower than the price paid for the business, this situation may be unsatisfactory to the purchaser, especially with respect to inventory or depreciable property.

A stock purchase also involves taking over other tax attributes such as the tax basis, tax credits, net operating losses carryforwards, and so on. These tax attributes will not be abolished unless tax avoidance rules apply. In addition, the corporation may have liabilities which the purchaser does not wish to assume indirectly.

Therefore, the buyer often desires to buy the assets rather than the stocks, unless a discount is achieved. Through the RISK method, however, the buyer may get to a situation equivalent to an assets deal in terms of depreciation, even though the stocks are acquired. This involves the following:

1. Setting up a Norwegian acquiring corporation
2. Purchasing shares
3. Transferring of the asset to the acquiring corporation, given a taxable situation in the acquired corporation, but with a corresponding RISK adjustment
4. Liquidating of the acquired corporation, which will give an off-settable liquidation loss equivalent to taxable gain in the acquired corporation due to the RISK adjustment.

If the buyer is a non-Norwegian tax resident, the acquisition will not generate any tax effects in Norway for the buyer as such. The future sale of the stocks in the acquired Norwegian corporation will normally not be taxable in Norway by the foreign seller.

Dividends paid to nonresident stockholders are subject to a 25 percent withholding tax. The withholding tax rate may be reduced by tax treaties. If the buyer is a corporation owning at least 25 percent of the Norwegian corporation and established in a tax treaty country, under several tax treaties the withholding tax rate is reduced to zero. Norway does not levy withholding tax on interest payments or royalty payments.

The change of ownership of the shares of the acquired company does not release the corporation from any tax and social security liabilities that are not abolished by the applicable statute of limitations that may exist. In other words, upon purchasing the stocks of a corporation, the new investors acquire all the tax and social security contingencies of such corporation. In this regard, and according to legislation, the actions and powers of the tax authorities to determine and demand the payment of taxes are in practical life abolished by the statute of limitations after 10 years.

15.5 MERGERS AND DEMERGERS

This section deals with transactions involving combining business activities through mergers or division of business activities through demergers, as defined as follows. The rules to be described apply only to mergers and demergers involving Norwegian tax resident corporations (i.e., corporations registered in Norway and foreign-registered corporations that are tax residents to Norway through effective management in Norway).

(a) Mergers and the Merger Directive

Norway is not part of the Merger Directive enforced within the European Union (EU). The rules in the Merger Directive on mergers, demergers, and the transfer of assets and exchange of shares concerning corporations of the EU Member states are therefore not applicable to cross-border transactions involving Norwegian companies. However, upon application to the Ministry of Finance, tax deferrals may be achieved on cross-border transactions, resulting in a deferred taxation similar to the ones achievable under the Merger Directive. See section 15.6.

The tax deferral achievable under the Norwegian merger and demerger rules are exemptions to the main rule that transfer of stocks/assets are to be taxed as ordinary income. Ordinary taxation will result if the conditions for tax deferral are not fulfilled.

One of the basic conditions is that the merger or demerger complies with the rules of the Norwegian corporation laws—the Act on Limited Liability Corporations (AS) of 1997 and the Act on Public Limited Liability Corporations (ASA) of 1997. The basic rules on mergers are the same in both of these laws, with more thorough documentation and procedure requirement in the ASA law. If one of the corporations involved is an ASA, the ASA law applies.

(b) Mergers Applications

Type of mergers

According to the corporation laws in Norway, a merger may be characterized as a transaction whereby one corporation, the transferee corporation, is taking over the other corporation's, the transferor corporation, assets and liabilities as a whole. The stockholders in the transferor acquire stocks in the transferee as consideration. The consideration may also be given in the form of cash for up to 20 percent of the consideration value. Similarly, a merger may involve the foundation of a newly established corporation absorbing two or more existing corporations.

If the transferee corporation belongs to a group, the consideration may instead consist of stocks in the parent corporation. Group arrangements are often expedient when the transferee corporation is the subsidiary of a parent corporation in which the liquidity of the stocks is high (e.g., a listed corporation). The prerequisite for implementing a group merger is that the transferee corporation be more than 90 percent owned by the parent corporation or other group corporations.

In addition to fulfilling the requirements with regard to the legal form of the transfer, various formalities must be complied with, including the following:

1. Providing a merger plan
2. Approvals by the Board and the General Assembly
3. Reports of the auditor's notification to the Norwegian Register of Business Entities, the Registrar, and so on.

The taxpayer's accounting must show the financial realities of the merger, which normally implies that this transaction has to be booked at the fair market value, the so-called purchase method. This structure implies that goodwill often has to be accounted for. In some instances, accounting may be done on a continued value basis, the so-called continuity method. This may be the case when the merger represents pooling of interest.

Tax consequences

A tax-exempt merger implies that the merger will not result in any taxation of the corporation involved or the stockholders. Thus, the surviving (transferee) corporation will continue the tax basis in the assets transferred. The surviving corporation will also continue the tax positions such as losses carried forward and deferred taxation. The stockholders will carry over their tax basis in their stocks in the transferor corporation to the stocks they receive in the surviving (transferee) corporation.

A nontax resident stockholder needs to focus on the fact that a merger in Norway requires that the transferor company be liquidated. In the country of residence, the stockholder may be taxed as a result of this action because this tech-

15.5 Mergers and Demergers

nically can be seen as a liquidation gain combined with a capital subscription in the (transferee) surviving corporation. The merger is considered to take effect in the tax year wherein all formalities have been finalized, especially the notification of the final decision of the merger to the Registrar.

(c) Demergers

Type of demergers

According to the corporation law, a demerger may be described as a transaction in which the corporation's assets and liabilities are to be distributed between the corporation itself (the transferor corporation) and one or more transferee corporations whereby all or some of the stockholders in the transferor corporation become stockholders in the transferee corporation(s). In addition to consideration in stocks, the stockholders may receive consideration cash, which must not exceed 20 percent of the total consideration. The consideration in stocks may consist of stocks in a group corporation (owned more than 90 percent) of which the transferee corporation forms part.

As described in relation to mergers, several similar requirements set in the corporate laws have to be fulfilled. Correspondingly, the accounting requirements must be met. In addition, the GTA prescribes that the share capital is to be divided in the same proportions as the underlying values.

Tax consequences

The following type of demergers are exempt from tax:

- The transferor corporation, which is to be split up, forming a new transferee corporation and transferring the operating unit, which is to be distributed to the new corporation
- The transferor corporation, which is to be split up, forming two or more new transferee corporations, transferring assets, rights, and liabilities to these entities and is thereafter "deregistered"
- The operating unit, which is to be distributed, being transferred to an already existing corporation with shares in the transferee corporation as consideration

Tax exemption implies that the tax basis for the stockholders and the corporations is carried over; i.e., no gains or losses are realized. Specified rules apply to the division of tax positions, tax basis in the shares, and so on. The two critical indicators here are the division of the business activities, which may influence the division of the losses carried forward, and the division of the share capital, which will have to be divided in the same way as the net real values are divided, This division may influence the tax basis for the stockholders and, in some instances, the division of losses carried forward.

The demerger will take effect when the capital decrease in the transferee corporation and the new corporation have been formally registered, which necessitates that the creditor's notice period has elapsed, or if the transfer is to an existing corporation, when the capital increase in the company has been registered.

15.6 CROSS-BORDER TRANSACTIONS

Under the GTA, § 11-22, the Ministry of Finance is given a special authority to grant tax deferrals. This rule is used rather extensively in relation to transactions involving cross-border issues. Under this rule, the tax authorities may grant tax deferrals on the transfer of stocks and business assets from Norwegian tax residents in cross-border mergers or cross-border acquisitions. The Norwegian stockholders must receive stocks in the surviving company/acquiring company, and not cash.

The granting of tax deferral is discretionary, and the following elements are critical to the decision by the Ministry of Finance:

- Most of the stocks/business assets must be transferred.
- The transaction must enhance the Norwegian corporation's efficiency (i.e., this entity's future growth and profit potential). Efficiencies in terms of administrative and/or financial issues are not relevant, and neither are the efficiencies of pure consolidation of management.
- The Norwegian tax basis (i.e., the taxable activity done in Norway) must not be weakened by the transaction.
- Obtaining a tax deferral is to be critical to the transaction (i.e., an application must be filed before the transaction is done), and the tax deferral must be a condition for carrying through the transaction.

The Norwegian government publishes an annual overview of the administrative practice by the Ministry of Finance in relation to this rule in connection with the presentation of the budget proposal.

15.7 ANTI-AVOIDANCE

Legislation permits the tax authorities to disregard a transaction or to tax the transaction hereunder to disallow transferrals of losses carried forward and other tax positions, if the transactions are not considered consistent with the "spirit of" the Norwegian tax legislation. Special anti-avoidance rules apply in relation to mergers and demergers, which are especially aimed at abolishing favorable tax positions if the transactions are not backed by satisfactory business reasons.

CHAPTER 16

Taxation of Mergers and Acquisitions in Russia

Joel M. McDonald
Oleg Y. Konnov
Andrei Shishkov
Salams, Hertzfeld & Heilbronn, Moscow

16.1 Introduction
16.2 Overview of the Tax and Legal System in Russia
    (a) Corporate Taxes
    (b) Major types of Taxes
    (c) Federalism and Taxes
    (d) Transfer Pricing
16.3 Commercial and Corporate Law
16.4 Currency Control
16.5 Anti-Monopoly Regulation
16.6 Restrictions on Foreign Ownership of Domestic Business
16.7 Analysis of Types of Mergers and Acquisitions
16.8 Share Purchases
    (a) Acquisition Vehicles
    (b) Legal Documentation and Filings
    (c) Tax Consequences
    (d) Advantages and Disadvantages of Share Purchases
16.9 Asset Purchases
    (a) Acquisition Vehicles
    (b) Legal Documentation and Filings
    (c) Corporate Profits Tax
16.10 Value-Added Tax
16.11 Turnover Tax
    (a) Taxation of a Buyer of Assets
    (b) Corporate Profits Tax
16.12 VAT Applications
16.13 Property Tax
16.14 Advantages and Disadvantages of Asset Purchase
16.15 Reorganizations
16.16 Legal Documentation and Filings

16.17 Tax Consequences
    (a)   Taxation of Reorganized Companies and their Shareholders
    (b)   Carryover of Tax Attributes
    (c)   Tax Liabilities, Penalties, and Interest
    (d)   Tax Credits
    (e)   Cost Basis of Assets and Shares
    (f)   Net Operating Losses

16.18 Advantages and Disadvantages of Reorganizations

16.19 Financing
    (a)   Equity
    (b)   Debt
    (c)   Shareholder/Related-Party Loan
    (d)   Back-to-Back Loan Through a Russian Bank

16.20 Repatriation of Capital and Profits
    (a)   Management Fees
    (b)   Royalties
    (c)   Interest
    (d)   Leasing
    (e)   Dividends
    (f)   Repayment of Debt
    (g)   Redemption of Shares
    (h)   Sale of Shares

16.21 Conclusion

16.1   INTRODUCTION

Since the breakup of the Soviet Union in December 1991, Russia has experienced a remarkably speedy, though often turbulent, transition from a command economy to a market economy. The 1990s witnessed positive steps in Russia, such as the liberalization of prices, mass privatization, and enactment of a new Civil Code and other commercial legislation. Russia had faced calamities such as the financial crisis that began in August 1998 when the ruble was devalued and the Russian government defaulted on its debts. The new millennium has brought renewed optimism about Russia's economic prospects, and investors are once again recognizing the attraction of Russia's vast mineral resources and highly educated and resilient population of 150 million people.

   As backdrop to a discussion of the taxation of mergers and acquisitions in Russia, it is important to briefly touch on the current Russian legal and tax environment and its effect on investment in general. Mergers and acquisitions proliferate in industrialized countries because, aside from the underlying business strengths, those countries have well-developed bodies of corporate and tax law, a competent and fair judiciary, functioning banking systems, and capital markets. Although Russia has enormous economic potential, it is still continuing to build the legal and financial infrastructure that is critical to a robust market economy. The result is that while investments are being made in Russia, the relative sim-

16.2 Overview of the Tax and Legal System in Russia

plicity of the investment structures that are used are a reflection of the legal and tax uncertainties associated with more complex transactions.

This chapter discusses the following:

- An overview of the tax and legal system in Russia, including areas such as corporate taxes, corporate and commercial law, currency control, and anti-monopoly regulations.
- The types of mergers and acquisitions used in Russia at present, namely share purchases, asset purchases, and reorganizations.
- Financing structures that are used in connection with mergers and acquisitions.
- The capital and profit repatriation methods that are used by foreign investors in Russia.

16.2 OVERVIEW OF THE TAX AND LEGAL SYSTEM IN RUSSIA

In order to provide context for an analysis of the taxation of mergers and acquisitions in Russia, this section sets forth an overview of the tax and legal system in Russia. In particular, the section briefly discusses five attributes:

1. Corporate taxes
2. Commercial and corporate law
3. Currency control
4. Anti-monopoly regulation
5. Restrictions on foreign ownership of domestic businesses

(a) Corporate Taxes

Since its inception in late 1991, the Russian tax system has been widely criticized as one of the main deterrents to investment in Russia. An excessive cumulative tax burden and arbitrary enforcement by the tax authorities have been among the major complaints. However, the introduction of Part I of the Tax Code in early 1999 strengthened taxpayers' rights considerably. The entry into force of a portion of Part II of the Tax Code at the beginning of 2001 lowered the tax burden. Although more changes are needed to establish a tax system that is suitable for a market economy, significant improvements to the tax rules are at last being made.

(b) Major Types of Taxes

At present, approximately 50 federal, regional, and local taxes may apply in Russia. However, the bulk of the total tax liability of a typical corporate business is generally attributable to six categories of taxes:

1. Profits tax
2. Value-added tax (VAT)
3. Customs duties
4. Labor taxes
5. Property taxes
6. Turnover taxes

Certain types of corporate businesses, such as those involved in natural resources or production and the sale of alcohol and tobacco, are subject to additional taxes, such as excise taxes and royalties.

The major types of taxes that apply to corporations in Russia are superficially similar to the major taxes that apply to corporations in industrialized countries. However, the distinguishing feature of the Russian versions of these taxes is that these taxes often do not apply mechanically or economically in a manner similar to their counterpart versions in industrialized countries. For example, many important business expenses, such as interest, advertising, training, and insurance, are subject to strict restrictions on deductibility for profits tax purposes. In addition, limitations on the creditability of VAT means that businesses often bear a VAT cost that they would not otherwise bear under a traditional VAT system. The result is that the total tax burden of a Russian business is usually higher than would apply in an industrialized country with similar statutory rates.

Exhibit 16.1 summarizes the major Russian taxes, the tax bases for the taxes, and the generally applicable tax rates.

Exhibit 16.1

MAJOR TAX SUMMARY

Type of tax	Tax base	Tax rate
Profits tax	Net income of Russian companies and permanent establishments of foreign companies	35% maximum rate for most companies; 43% maximum rate for banks, brokers, insurance companies, and intermediaries
Value-added tax	Turnover from domestic sales of goods and services and the value of imported goods	20% for most goods and services; 10% for certain food and children's goods; 0% for exports (including, from July 1, 2001, to CIS countries)
Customs duties	Value and/or unit of imported goods and limited number of exported goods	*Ad valorem* rate categories are 5%, 10%, 15% and 20%; Various per unit rates; some combined *ad valorem* and per unit rates

16.2 Overview of the Tax and Legal System in Russia

Exhibit 16.1   Major Tax Summary (*cont'd*)

Type of tax	Tax base	Tax rate
Personal income tax	Worldwide income of Russian residents and Russian source income of Russian non-residents	Flat 13% rate applies to most types of income earned by residents; 30% rate applies to non-residents; 35% rate applies to certain insurance proceeds, gambling winnings, and bank deposit interest
Unified social tax	Wages paid by Russian companies and foreign companies doing business in Russia	Regressive rate scale from 35.6% to 2% (5% in 2000)
Property tax	Book value of assets	2%
Road users tax	Gross receipts	1% (abolished from January 1, 2003)
Excise taxes	Turnover from or units of domestic sales of excisable goods by producers and value or unit of imported excisable goods	Various per unit and *ad valorem* rates on alcohol, alcohol products, wine, beer, tobacco, gasoline, diesel fuel, motor oil, jewelry, automobiles, crude oil, and natural gas
Advertising tax	Cost of advertising services	5%
Sales tax	Cash and credit card sales	5%

(c) Federalism and Taxes

Note the effect of Russia's federal governmental system on taxation: Russia has a federal form of government consisting of three levels: the federal government, 89 regional governments (or "subjects" of the Russian Federation), and local governments. Under the Russian Constitution, each level of government may impose its own taxes, so there could be federal, regional, and local taxes in Russia.

Federal legislation defines a closed list of federal, regional, and local taxes. Most of these major taxes payable by most Russian businesses are federal taxes, and the applicable rates and tax base are fixed by federal law. Although the tax base for the profits tax is defined by federal legislation, the revenues from the tax are shared among the federal, regional, and local governments, depending on the applicable rate set by each level of government.

The federal profits tax rate is fixed at 11 percent, each region is allowed to choose a rate between 0 percent and 19 percent (27 percent for banks, brokers, insurance companies, and intermediaries), and each locality is allowed to choose a rate between 0 percent and 5 percent. Although the typical combined profits tax rate that applies in Russia is 35 percent, actual rates can vary because of regional and local government rate discretion. Finally, the property tax, advertising tax, and sales tax are regional or local taxes. The rates, and even the imposition, of these taxes can vary from region to region and from locality to locality.

(d) Transfer Pricing

"Transfer pricing" rules have applied in Russia since 1999. The Russian transfer pricing rules are similar to the rules used in OECD countries, although there are some differences. Generally speaking, the Russian tax authorities may substitute the market price for the price used by the parties to certain types of transactions if the price used by the parties deviates from the market price by more than 20 percent in either direction. The types of transactions to which the transfer pricing rules may be applied include transactions between related persons, cross-border transactions, and barter transactions. The transfer pricing rules do not currently apply to sales of securities.

16.3 COMMERCIAL AND CORPORATE LAW

Russia has a reasonably well-developed body of commercial and corporate law. For example, a Civil Code has been in effect since the mid-1990s and provides a legal framework for major types of business transactions. Separate laws govern the two main types of legal entities in Russia—joint stock companies and limited liability companies (LLCs). Most mergers and acquisitions involve either or both of these types of legal entities.

A joint stock company is a legal entity that is similar to a corporation in Western countries. A shareholder of a joint stock company is generally liable for the debts of the company only up to the amount of the shareholder's investment. A joint stock company may be a "closed" joint stock company, which means that it cannot have more than 50 shareholders and its shareholders have a preemptive right to acquire shares sold by other shareholders. Alternatively, a joint stock company can be an "open" joint stock company, which means that the company can have an unlimited number of shareholders and its shares may be freely traded. A 0.8 percent securities issuance tax is imposed on the issuance of shares in joint stock companies, with some exceptions. In addition, joint stock companies are regulated by the Russian Federal Securities Commission and are subject to voluminous reporting and record-keeping requirements.

An LLC is a legal entity established by one or more "participants," each of whom is generally liable for the debts of the company to the extent of such participant's investment in the company. Unlike a joint stock company, an LLC does not issue shares of stock. Instead, an LLC issues "participatory interests" to its participants. A participant in an LLC has the unilateral right to withdraw from the company at any time and demand redemption of the participant's participatory interest in exchange for the net asset value of the interest. No tax applies to the issuance of participatory interests in an LLC. In addition, LLCs are not regulated by the Russian Federal Securities Commission and are subject to a reasonable amount of reporting and record-keeping requirements.

16.5 Anti-Monopoly Regulation

LLCs have become the preferred investment vehicle for investors that operate through a wholly owned Russian subsidiary. However, because of a participant's unilateral right to withdraw from an LLC at any time, entities that have more than one shareholder are usually formed as joint stock companies.

A couple of important deficiencies in Russian commercial and corporate law should also be mentioned:

- Creditors' rights are relatively weak. Collection of debts is hindered not only by inadequate laws, but also by uneven judicial enforcement, which is often influenced by corruption. Although a bankruptcy law does exist, it has been criticized for facilitating various abuses of both shareholders and creditors.
- The rights of minority shareholders in Russian companies are often not sufficiently protected. Current legislation arguably provides minority shareholders with adequate legal safeguards. Nevertheless, judicial and administrative enforcement of sanctions against majority shareholders and management for abuses such as asset-stripping and share dilution (among other things) have been rare. One consequence of this treatment of minority shareholders is that a seller of a Russian company usually prefers to receive the sales price in cash rather than as a minority share interest in the acquiror.

16.4 CURRENCY CONTROL

The Russian ruble is not a fully convertible currency. The use of both rubles and foreign currency in Russia is strictly regulated by Russian currency control legislation. Mergers and acquisitions in Russia, particularly those involving foreign parties, must be structured to consider the currency control rules.

In particular, Russian companies are restricted regarding their ownership of foreign currency, foreign currency–denominated securities, and foreign bank accounts. A limited number of transactions may be carried out in foreign currency by a Russian company without Russian Central Bank approval. All other transactions may be carried out only with Russian Central Bank approval. In addition, foreign companies that transact in rubles in Russia are required to open special types of ruble accounts with Russian banks.

16.5 ANTI-MONOPOLY REGULATION

Russia has rather broad anti-monopoly legislation that has a direct impact on a wide range of commercial transactions. Parties who are involved in mergers and acquisitions in Russia should take careful note of the rules.

A business with a "dominant" market position is subject to several restrictions and controls, including on mergers and acquisitions. In addition, transfers of shares or assets, and various forms of reorganizations, may require notification or prior approval of the Russian anti-monopoly authorities. Failure to obtain prior approval from the anti-monopoly authorities, which requires the submission of a lengthy and complex application, can result in the imposition of penalties and, in some cases, invalidation of the relevant transaction.

16.6 RESTRICTIONS ON FOREIGN OWNERSHIP OF DOMESTIC BUSINESSES

As in most countries, Russia restricts the foreign ownership of certain types of domestic businesses. Any foreign company considering acquiring a Russian business should determine whether any foreign ownership restrictions apply to the industry or company involved.

For instance, there is a 15 percent quota on foreign ownership of the total capital of all licensed Russian insurance companies, as well as other operational restrictions that apply to certain foreign-owned Russian insurance companies. There is a similar 12 percent quota on foreign ownership of the total capital of all licensed Russian banks. Foreign ownership of the Russian natural gas monopoly, Gazprom, is limited to 14 percent of its capital, and foreign ownership of the national electric utility, Unified Energy Systems, is limited to 25 percent of its capital, although Unified Energy System's foreign ownership threshold has been breached in practice.

16.7 ANALYSIS OF TYPES OF MERGERS AND ACQUISITIONS

Under Russian civil and tax legislation, three basic categories of transactions fall under the rubric of mergers and acquisitions:

1. Share purchases
2. Asset purchases
3. Reorganizations

Each of these three categories of transactions is discussed in more detail as follows; however, the following general points should be noted at the outset:

- In industrialized countries that have a well-developed body of corporate law, a fully convertible currency, relatively stable tax rules, and a competent judiciary, a company that wishes to acquire another company may choose among a broad range of both simple and complex acquisition structures. Russia currently lacks, to varying degrees, all of these characteristics of industrialized countries. As such, the choices for structuring acquisitions of businesses in Russia are far fewer than in industrialized countries. Given the relatively undeveloped and unclear aspects of Russian commercial and tax legislation, most acquirors of businesses in Russia therefore choose to structure their acquisitions in the simplest way possible.

16.8 Share Purchases

- At present, most acquisitions of Russian businesses are effected either through straightforward share or asset purchases for cash. Between these two forms, share purchases for cash are more common. Generally speaking, the costs of the assumption of both known and unknown liabilities of an acquired company are outweighed by the VAT costs of an asset purchase and the fact that a tax-free step-up in the book value of a company's fixed assets to fair market value may arguably be achieved without an actual sale of the assets.
- Russian law provides a basic legal framework for reorganizations that is generally consistent with mergers, divisions, and the like as applied in industrialized countries. Furthermore, reorganizations are arguably tax-exempt. However, because of significant uncertainties regarding the legal mechanics of reorganizations and the interpretation of relevant legislation by government agencies and the courts, reorganizations are, at this time, rarely used in the acquisition and restructuring of Russian businesses.

16.8 SHARE PURCHASES

Following is a discussion of four facets of share purchases:

1. The acquisition vehicles used for share purchases
2. The required legal documentation and filings
3. The tax consequences to the seller and the buyer
4. The advantages and disadvantages of share purchases

Equity interests in LLCs are technically referred to as participatory interests. Nevertheless, references to shares in the following text, for the sake of convenience, encompass both equity interests in joint stock companies and LLCs.

(a) Acquisition Vehicles

Generally speaking, a foreign acquiror will use a foreign company, rather than a Russian company, to purchase and hold the shares of a Russian target company. This choice is made principally because a Russian holding company structure is tax-inefficient. Specifically, no tax consolidation is available to commonly owned groups of Russian companies. Dividends paid by a Russian company to another Russian company, even a 100 percent parent, are subject to a scheduled 15 percent withholding tax.

The jurisdiction of the foreign holding company is often a country with which Russia has entered into a tax treaty. Because of its favorable tax treaty with Russia and low local tax (4.25 percent), Cyprus is currently the jurisdiction of choice for most foreign owners of shares of Russian companies. Sometimes a company incorporated in a pure tax haven with no tax treaty with Russia is used to hold Russian shares if the return from the investment is expected to be from capital gains rather than dividends.

A Russian acquiror of a target Russian company will often use a Russian holding company in the acquiror's corporate group. Because of the tax inefficiencies noted previously, most Russian corporate groups do not extend beyond a single tier below the Russian holding company. Although Russian residents are required to obtain a license from the Russian Central Bank in order to establish or acquire a foreign company, some Russians avoid this requirement through various means and use foreign companies to acquire shares of Russian companies.

See the following section for a discussion of the types of financing used by acquisition vehicles for share purchases.

(b) Legal Documentation and Filings

The primary legal documentation for a share purchase is normally a basic sales contract. No special contractual provisions are required under Russian civil law. Several filings with Russian governmental agencies are required in connection with a share purchase. For example, an acquiror must obtain advance permission from the Russian anti-monopoly authorities for any acquisition of more than 20 percent of the voting shares of a Russian company if the aggregate book value of the assets of the acquiror's group and the target company exceeds approximately $350,000. Some foreign purchasers prefer to avoid this filing by acquiring a foreign holding company of the target Russian company. In addition, if shares in a Russian joint stock company are acquired, a filing must be made with the Russian Federal Securities Commission after the acquisition is complete.

Various Russian corporate-level approvals are also normally required for a share purchase. For example, if the value of the shares is 25 percent or more of the book value of the seller's assets (a so-called major transaction), then either the seller's Board of Directors (if the value of the shares is between 25 percent and 50 percent of the book value of the assets) or the seller's shareholders (if the value of the shares is more than 50 percent of the book value of the assets) must approve the sale. In addition, the approval of either the disinterested shareholders or Board members (depending on the market value of the shares) of both the seller and buyer is required if the sale is made to a related party (a so-called interested transaction).

The Russian currency control rules must also be observed in payment of the purchase price. If both the acquiror and seller of the Russian shares are foreign, then the payment may be made in foreign currency; however, if either the acquiror or the seller is Russian, then the payment must be made in Russian rubles, unless the Russian party (or parties) has obtained a license from the Russian Central Bank. A foreign acquiror or seller must also establish a special ruble bank account with a Russian bank in order to effect the ruble payment.

(c) Tax Consequences

Following is a discussion of the tax consequences of a share purchase to the seller and the buyer.

16.8 Share Purchases

Taxation of a seller of shares

A Russian seller of shares of a Russian company, either a joint stock company or an LLC, is subject to Russian corporate profits tax or personal income tax, if the seller is an individual. Gain is taxed on the excess of the selling price over the acquisition price of the shares, including expenses connected with both purchase and sale. Subject to certain limitations, losses on sales of securities (e.g., shares in a joint stock company) realized by Russian companies may be offset against gains from sales of securities of the same type.

A foreign company that sells shares of a Russian company other than through a permanent establishment of the foreign company in Russia is subject to a 20 percent withholding tax on any gain on the sale. This 20 percent tax may be reduced or eliminated under an applicable tax treaty. If an advance treaty exemption from the 20 percent tax is not obtained, then a Russian buyer of the shares will withhold Russian tax equal to 20 percent of the gain from the sale proceeds, or 20 percent of the gross sale proceeds if the seller cannot establish its cost basis in the shares. If the buyer is another foreign company with no permanent establishment in Russia, then in practice there is normally no withholding, even in the absence of a tax treaty, because there is no mechanism for the foreign seller to pay the withheld tax. A seller of Russian shares is not liable for any other taxes on the sale, such as VAT or stamp duty.

Taxation of a buyer of shares

The only tax that a buyer of Russian shares may be liable for is the 20 percent withholding tax that may apply, as discussed previously, if there is a foreign seller.

An ownership change as a result of a share purchase does not restrict the acquired company's future use of its tax attributes, such as net operating losses and excess VAT credits; however, because of various limitations on their use that apply even in the absence of an ownership change, the value of such attributes is generally not high in many cases.

(d) Advantages and Disadvantages of Share Purchases

The documentation for a share purchase is a simple sales contract. The transaction is well understood by buyers and sellers, governmental agencies, and the courts. Although governmental filings that take time and effort are required, the filings are generally manageable.

Through voluntary asset revaluation procedures under the Russian accounting rules, it is possible for a Russian company to step up the book value of its fixed assets to fair market value without any profits tax liability (see further discussion). Thus, a buyer of shares of a Russian company can obtain a tax-free step-up in the book value of the target company's fixed assets. Although the same result could be achieved through an asset purchase, there may be a significant VAT cost to a buyer of assets (see section 16.9).

The main disadvantage of a share purchase is that a buyer of shares acquires, in addition to the assets of the target company, both the known and unknown liabilities of the target. A careful due diligence should identify most or all of the liabilities of a target company. A buyer should be especially cautious in acquiring shares of a company that has undergone privatization because many privatizations of Russian companies carried out during the 1990s did not fully comply with applicable legislation. As a result, there is a risk that such privatizations may be challenged in court and possibly unwound.

16.9 ASSET PURCHASES

An asset purchase may qualify either as the acquisition of individual assets or as the acquisition of "a whole business." An acquisition of a whole business is subject to special rules under Russian civil legislation, including assumption by the buyer of all liabilities connected with the business. In practice, almost no asset purchases are structured as acquisitions of a whole business, largely because of various legal and tax uncertainties.

(a) Acquisition Vehicles

Asset purchases are almost always made by Russian companies. Although it is theoretically possible for a foreign company to purchase assets in Russia and directly operate a business, the various legal and tax consequences of operating a branch of a foreign company are unclear. Thus, nearly all foreign acquirors of Russian assets establish a wholly owned Russian subsidiary to purchase and use the assets.

(b) Legal Documentation and Filings

An asset purchase that does not qualify as the acquisition of a whole business is documented with one or more simple sales contracts. Special contractual provisions may be required depending on the type of assets sold, in particular real estate.

Under Russian civil legislation, a special contract (called a "contract for the sale of an enterprise") is required for an asset purchase that qualifies as the acquisition of a whole business. The contract is also subject to State registration.

A buyer of assets is required to obtain preliminary approval from the antimonopoly authorities if the purchase price of the assets exceeds 10 percent of book value of the seller's assets and the combined book value of the assets of the buyer's group and the seller exceeds approximately $350,000. The purchase is also subject to the corporate-level approvals discussed previously (i.e., if the purchase is a "major transaction" or an "interested transaction").

As in the case of a share purchase, the Russian currency control rules must also be observed in payment of the purchase price. The same basic rules discussed previously apply to asset purchases.

(c) Corporate Profits Tax

As a general rule, a seller of assets is subject to profits tax on the excess, if any, of the selling price of the assets over the seller's cost basis in the assets.

A Russian company can step up the cost basis of its fixed assets, but not, for example, for inventory and securities on a tax-free basis. This step-up can be done either on a quarterly basis using inflation indices published by the Russian State Statistics Committee or as of January 1 of each year using the fair market value of the assets on such date. Under the prevailing view, no income or gain is recognized as a result of the write-up to fair market value. Many Russian companies exploit the January 1 fair market value revaluation rule by completing major asset sales at the beginning of the year in order to minimize the recognition of taxable gain.

In general, a Russian company can offset losses from sales of its assets against gains from sales of its assets; however, there are limits on the deductibility of losses from sales of securities. In addition, the Russian tax authorities take the position that losses from sales of fixed assets are not deductible, although the legal basis for this position is questionable.

A Russian company can take a current deduction for the cost of certain "capital investments," in particular the acquisition of fixed assets. However, if a Russian company uses this tax privilege in connection with the acquisition of a fixed asset, and then disposes of the fixed asset within two years, the Russian company is required to recapture as income the cost of the fixed asset that was originally deducted.

A significant uncertainty associated with asset purchases is the allocation of the total sales price among the individual assets that are sold. Unfortunately, the Russian tax authorities have not issued any clear guidance in this area.

Regarding an asset purchase that is not the acquisition of a whole business, it would be reasonable for the parties to specify sales price allocations to particular assets in the sales contract, subject to application of the transfer pricing rules.

Regarding an asset purchase that qualifies as the acquisition of a whole business, the prevailing view is that the total sales price should be apportioned among the assets using the ratio of the total sales price to the aggregate book value of the assets, with the book value of securities and receivables not taken into account. Although the acquisition of a whole business involves assumption of the liabilities of the acquired business, it is not clear how the assumed liabilities are reflected in the sales price allocation.

16.10 VALUE-ADDED TAX

Sellers of assets in Russia are generally subject to a 20 percent VAT on the selling price of the assets. A 10 percent VAT rate applies for food and children's goods. Certain assets, such as pharmaceuticals and securities, are exempt from VAT. Unlike in other countries, no VAT exemption is given in Russia for bulk sales of assets, including sales of whole businesses.

Thus, in a typical asset purchase, the seller would charge VAT to the buyer based on the types of assets sold and their allocated selling prices. As a general rule, the seller is able to credit VAT (known as "input VAT") that the seller paid for goods and services used in its business during the period of the sale of the assets. In addition, the seller may credit VAT that it had previously paid in connection with the acquisition of any of the sold assets that the seller could not credit at the time of the acquisition because the assets were used in VAT-exempt activities.

For example, if the seller of assets is engaged in banking activities (which are VAT-exempt), the seller could not credit VAT paid on the acquisition of assets used in carrying out the banking activities. Instead, such VAT is added to the cost basis of the assets and depreciated for profits tax purposes; however, when the assets are sold, the seller may credit the undepreciated portion of the VAT against its VAT liability on the sale.

Like the profits tax, a major uncertainty in the application of VAT to asset purchases is the allocation of the total selling prices among the assets. In particular, it is not clear whether goodwill is subject to VAT, but there is somewhat more clarity for VAT purposes because the VAT chapter in the new Russian Tax Code that went into effect on January 1, 2001, includes specific rules for calculating the VAT liability of the seller of a whole business. These rules are basically consistent with the prevailing view on the application of profits tax to sales of whole businesses.

16.11 TURNOVER TAX

Until January 1, 2003, a seller of assets is subject to a 1 percent road users tax on sales of inventory, not on sales of fixed assets. The tax base for this so-called turnover tax is the excess of the selling price of the inventory over its acquisition price in the case of inventory acquired for resale or the selling price of the inventory in the case of self-produced inventory.

(a) Taxation of a Buyer of Assets

Three principal taxes are relevant to a buyer of assets:

1. Corporate profits tax
2. VAT
3. Property tax

(b) Corporate Profits Tax

Generally speaking, a buyer of assets will account for each acquired asset at its acquisition cost, which may include various expenses connected with the acquisition.

A buyer of assets faces the same significant uncertainty that the seller faces—the proper allocation of the total selling price among the purchased assets. The previous analysis regarding sellers of assets is relevant here as well.

Since 1999, the Russian accounting rules have provided for the recognition of goodwill and "badwill" on acquisitions of whole businesses. To determine goodwill or badwill, the buyer must compare the total selling price of the assets with the aggregate book value of the assets and liabilities. A positive difference is accounted for as goodwill, and a negative difference is accounted for as badwill. Although goodwill is deductible for accounting purposes, it apparently is not deductible for profits tax purposes.

Depreciation periods for fixed assets in Russia generally far exceed the economic lives of the assets. For example, computers are depreciated on a straight-line basis over 10 years, automobiles are depreciated over 6 to 9 years, and buildings are depreciated over 8 to 250 years.

As indicated earlier, a Russian company can take a current deduction for the cost of certain capital investments, in particular the acquisition of fixed assets. Thus, a buyer of qualifying fixed assets can deduct the cost of the assets in the year of acquisition; however, the benefit of the deduction is generally limited to 50 percent of the taxable profits of the buyer in the year the assets are purchased. If the purchase is financed by a loan from a Russian bank, then the deduction is taken with respect to each repayment of the loan. This can mitigate the effect of the 50 percent rule by spreading the deduction over two or more years, depending on the loan repayment period.

16.12 VAT APPLICATIONS

A seller of assets will charge VAT (generally at a rate of 20 percent) to the buyer. The buyer will be able to credit such VAT to the extent the assets purchased are used to carry out activities that are subject to VAT. If the assets are not used in a taxable VAT activity (such as banking), then the VAT is capitalized in the cost of the assets and depreciated for property tax purposes. It is not clear whether any goodwill component of the overall purchase price is subject to VAT or whether such VAT would be creditable by the buyer.

The main tax cost of an asset purchase to a buyer is VAT. Assuming that the buyer is engaged in a taxable VAT activity and thus is entitled to credit VAT paid on purchases, the problem is that, in most cases, the amount of VAT paid on the acquisition of assets constituting most or all of a business will exceed the buyer's VAT liability on its sales for the tax period during which the purchase occurs. This results in the creation of an "excess VAT credit."

Before January 1, 2001, a taxpayer could carry forward an excess VAT credit and apply the credit against the taxpayer's VAT liability in future periods; however, because the amount of the credit did not accrue interest and was not inflation-adjusted, the taxpayer would not fully recover the VAT paid and thus would bear a VAT cost. From January 1, 2001, a taxpayer with an excess VAT credit may apply for a refund if the credit has not been used up within three months. If the refund is not paid within approximately one month, then the refund will accrue interest until it is paid. Although the new refund and interest mechanism is preferable to prior law, it is still not clear to what extent taxpayers with excess VAT credits will bear a VAT cost.

16.3 PROPERTY TAX

For property tax purposes, a buyer of assets will account for each acquired asset at its acquisition cost, which may include various expenses connected with the acquisition. The buyer will be liable for property tax on the book value of each asset with some exceptions, such as securities. The generally applicable property tax rate is 2 percent.

16.14 ADVANTAGES AND DISADVANTAGES OF ASSET PURCHASES

The main advantage of an asset purchase is that, if properly structured, the buyer does not assume any of the liabilities of the business from which the assets are purchased. The main disadvantages of an asset purchase are as follows:

- Normally, the buyer will pay a large amount of VAT on the purchase of the assets. Because it may take several months for the buyer to recover fully this VAT, asset purchases may result in a significant VAT cost.
- If the asset purchase constitutes the acquisition of a whole business, then the buyer will be liable for all the liabilities of the business from which the assets are purchased.
- The allocation of the total selling price among the purchased assets is unclear, including the calculation and taxation of goodwill and badwill.
- Several nontax-related costs are imposed, such as re-registration of assets, reissuance of licenses, and transfer of employees.

16.15 REORGANIZATIONS

Under Russian civil legislation, two basic categories of reorganizations are relevant in the context of mergers and acquisitions:

1. *Mergers* involve either the establishment of a new company into which the assets and liabilities of two or more companies are transferred and the termination of the transferor companies, or the transfer of the assets and liabilities of one or more companies into an existing company and the termination of the transferor companies.

2. *Divisions* involve the transfer by an existing company of its assets and liabilities to two or more newly established companies and the termination of the transferor company (a "split-up"). Alternately, a division involves the transfer by an existing company of part of its assets and liabilities to one or more newly established companies without the termination of the transferor company (a "spin-off").

16.17 Tax Consequences

The legal framework exists in Russia for mergers and divisions as are understood in industrialized countries. Nevertheless, there continues to be a significant amount of legal and tax uncertainty regarding the application of reorganization rules in Russia. This uncertainty exists not only among lawyers, but also, more importantly, among the courts and relevant governmental agencies. Thus, at the present time, mergers and divisions are infrequently used in Russia.

16.16 LEGAL DOCUMENTATION AND FILINGS

Companies participating in a merger are required to conclude a merger contract providing for terms of the merger and the procedure for converting the shares of the transferor company(ies) into the transferee company. All rights and obligations of the transferring company(ies) pass to the transferee company in accordance with a transfer act.

In a division, the shareholders of the company that is to be split up, or from which one or more companies will be spun off, decide on the terms of the division and the procedures for converting the shares of the dividing company into the split-up or spun-off companies.

Mergers of Russian companies require preliminary approval of the anti-monopoly authorities if the aggregate book value of the assets of the merged companies exceeds approximately $350,000. Mergers are also subject to approval by the shareholders of each of the merged companies. Finally, share issuances in connection with a merger must be registered with the Russian Federal Securities Commission.

16.17 TAX CONSEQUENCES

In reorganizations, there are transfers of assets and liabilities between companies and exchanges of shares. As a result of these transactions, the two principal tax issues that arise from reorganizations are the taxation of the reorganized companies and their shareholders, and the carryover of tax liabilities and tax attributes.

(a) Taxation of Reorganized Companies and Their Shareholders

Russian tax legislation specifically exempts a company that is being reorganized from taxation on transfers of assets to its legal successor. Thus, the transferring company in a merger that is terminated in connection with the merger and the transferring company in a division that is either terminated (in the case of a split-up) or not (in the case of a spin-off), are not subject to tax on the asset transfers that they make.

As a general rule, share issuances by Russian companies are subject to a 0.8 percent securities issuance tax that is assessed on the nominal value of shares issued. However, shares issued in connection with mergers and divisions are exempt from this tax.

Although there is no clear statutory exemption, the prevailing view is that shareholders involved in mergers and divisions who receive new shares in exchange for their shares in a reorganized company are not subject to tax on the exchange.

(b) Carryover of Tax Attributes

A company can transfer all assets and liabilities in the case of a merger or split-up, or some assets and liabilities in the case of a spin-off, to one or more other companies in connection with a reorganization. An important issue then arises regarding the extent to which the tax attributes of the transferring company carry over to the transferee company.

(c) Tax Liabilities, Penalties, and Interest

Russian tax legislation provides specific rules for the carryover of the transferring company's liabilities for taxes, penalties, and interest to the transferee company.

In the case of a merger, the transferee company is liable for all unpaid tax obligations and interest owed by the transferring company, even if the liabilities were unknown at the time of the reorganization. The transferee company is only liable for the tax penalties of the transferring company that were imposed before the end of the merger.

In the case of a split-up, all unpaid tax obligations, penalties, and interest owed by the transferring company are allocated between the newly established transferee companies based on the relative amounts of the transferring company's net assets received by the transferee companies. Under certain circumstances, the transferee companies may be jointly and severally liable for the transferor company's tax-related obligations.

In the case of a spin-off, the general rule is that the unpaid tax obligations, penalties, and interest owed by the transferring company are not assumed by the newly established company(ies) that received certain of the transferring company's assets and liabilities; however, if the transferring company cannot pay its tax-related obligations as a result of the spin-off, then a court may rule that the spun-off companies are jointly and severally liable for the transferring company's tax-related obligations.

(d) Tax Credits

A transferring company may have overpaid certain taxes. The general rule is that a transferee company is entitled to credit such overpaid amounts against the transferring company's tax-related obligation assumed by the transferee company. If a credit remains, the transferee company is entitled to a refund. The application of this general rule to excess VAT credits is unclear.

(e) Cost Basis of Assets and Shares

The assets received by a transferee company from a transferor company are accounted for in the records of the transferee company at the book value of the assets, as reflected in the transfer company's balance sheet at the time of the reorganization.

Shareholders involved in mergers and divisions who receive new shares in exchange for their shares in a reorganized company have a cost basis in the new shares equal to their cost basis in the shares they exchanged.

(f) Net Operating Losses

A Russian company with a net operating loss in a particular tax year can carry forward the loss for five years. It is unclear whether a transferee company is entitled to any unused net operating losses of a transferor company.

16.18 ADVANTAGES AND DISADVANTAGES OF REORGANIZATIONS

The main advantages of reorganizations are the following:

- Subject to some uncertainty, reorganizations can be accomplished tax-free.
- No cash is required because the consideration paid is the acquiring company's shares.

The main disadvantages of reorganizations are the following:

- Significant uncertainty exists among lawyers, judges, and government officials regarding the legal requirements of reorganizations.
- The tax authorities almost always conduct a thorough audit of a reorganized company that will be terminated. Companies with questionable past tax reporting practices, which even the most compliant taxpayers often have, may therefore prefer to avoid reorganizations.
- Because capital markets in Russia are not particularly liquid, shareholders of companies that are acquired pursuant to reorganizations may prefer to receive cash rather than shares in another company. The weak legal protection that is provided to minority shareholders is another reason why a seller might prefer cash rather than a minority share interest in the buyer.

16.19 FINANCING

In the case of a share purchase or asset purchase, the buyer will normally pay cash to the selling shareholders or selling company, respectively. In a merger, most if not all of the consideration is shares of the acquiring company.

An important issue is how the acquiring company will fund the payment of the purchase price. The two basic choices are equity and debt.

(a) Equity

If a Russian company is the acquiring company, then the shareholders of the Russian company make cash equity investments by contributing cash to the charter capital of a Russian company in exchange for shares.

The complexity of the corporate procedures required to make a cash equity contribution depends on the type of Russian company involved. The procedure is far more complicated and time-consuming for joint stock companies than for LLCs.

Russian shareholders of Russian companies are required to make their capital contributions in rubles, whereas foreign shareholders may make their contributions in either foreign currency or rubles. Under certain circumstances, foreign shareholders may also make "gratuitous transfers" (i.e., gifts) of foreign currency to their Russian subsidiaries.

If a foreign company is the acquiring company, then the relevant corporate legislation of the jurisdiction in which the foreign company is established should be considered.

(b) Debt

If a Russian company is the acquiring company, then there are two ways to provide debt financing:

1. Shareholder/related-party loans
2. Back-to-back financing through a Russian bank

(c) Shareholder/Related-Party Loan

During the Soviet era, one state-owned enterprise could not lend money to another state-owned enterprise on a commercial basis. Nonbank loans are not prohibited under current Russian legislation unless these loans represent a licensable banking activity, but certain unfavorable tax and currency control rules apply to these loans. Despite these disadvantages, intercompany loans are often used in Russia.

For tax purposes, interest on a loan paid by a Russian company to another company other than a Russian bank is generally not deductible; however, Russia is a party to several tax treaties that permit Russian companies that are partially or wholly owned by shareholders resident in those treaty countries to deduct interest regardless of whether the lender is a Russian bank. These treaties include the following:

- U.S.–Russia Treaty
- UK–Russia Treaty
- Netherlands–Russia Treaty
- Germany–Russia Treaty
- Canada–Russia Treaty
- France–Russia Treaty

16.19 Financing

Interest paid by a Russian company to a foreign lender that is not attributable to a permanent establishment of the foreign lender in Russia is subject to a 15 percent Russian withholding tax, but the tax is reduced or eliminated under most Russian tax treaties. It is usually possible to obtain an advance treaty exemption from the withholding tax.

In order to avoid the tax problems associated with interest payments, some foreign shareholders have made 0 percent interest loans to their Russian subsidiaries. Before the Russian transfer pricing rules came into effect on January 1, 1999, there was generally considered to be no risk of adverse Russian taxation under such an arrangement. However, it is unclear whether the Russian tax authorities will use the new transfer pricing rules to attack 0 percent interest loans.

The currency control aspects of a foreign shareholder loan must also be considered. As a general rule, a foreign company may provide a loan to a Russian company only in foreign currency. Furthermore, if the term of the loan exceeds 180 days, certain currency control restrictions and formalities apply.

(d) Back-to-Back Loan Through a Russian Bank

Because of the tax and currency control disadvantages of shareholder loans, many foreign investors debt-finance their Russian subsidiaries via back-to-back loans through a Russian affiliate of a Western bank. The loan is secured either with an offshore deposit of a member of the foreign investor's group or with a guarantee.

For tax purposes, interest paid by a Russian company to a Russian bank is generally deductible, but subject to certain limitations. In order to permit full deductibility of arm's-length interest paid to a Russian bank, foreign investors sometimes try to arrange for their Russian company to be owned by a shareholder resident in a country that is party to one of the tax treaties listed previously. The Russian tax authorities normally do not attempt to recharacterize such a back-to-back loan as a loan directly from the offshore guarantor or security provider to the Russian company.

An important advantage of a back-to-back loan through a Russian bank, as compared with a shareholder or related-party loan, is that the benefit of the capital investment deduction may be enhanced because the deduction is generally limited to 50 percent of taxable profit, but the deduction is taken for each loan repayment if the investment is financed with a loan from a Russian bank. This loan arrangement can permit the taxpayer to spread the deduction over two or more years, depending on the loan repayment term.

For currency control purposes, licensed Russian banks are free to provide loans to Russian companies in either rubles or foreign currency without special authorization from the Central Bank. The main disadvantage of a back-to-back loan is the financing cost charged by the Western bank and its Russian subsidiary. The cost is usually spread between the interest on the offshore deposit and the interest charged to the Russian company.

16.20 REPATRIATION OF CAPITAL AND PROFITS

A foreign investor who acquires a Russian business will need to consider mechanisms for repatriating capital and profits from Russia. The taxation aspects of the most commonly used repatriation mechanisms are discussed as follows. Before analyzing the taxation of repatriation, it is important to mention the potential currency control implications. The ruble is currently not a fully convertible currency, and foreign investors must either receive foreign currency directly from their Russian subsidiaries or convert rubles paid by the Russian subsidiaries into foreign currency before repatriation. Because of the capital flight problem in Russia, the Russian Central Bank continues to impose restrictions on the outflow of foreign currency. Although these restrictions are intended to stem illegal outflows, legitimate repatriation by foreign investors can sometimes be problematic.

(a) Management Fees

It is common practice for foreign investors or their foreign affiliates to provide certain management services to their Russian subsidiaries. Generally, these services are structured so that they are performed offshore to avoid taxation in Russia. The Russian tax authorities generally take the position that such services performed in Russia give rise to a taxable permanent establishment.

Management fees are generally deductible by the Russian subsidiary. However, the Russian tax authorities often deny a Russian company a deduction for management fees paid to a third party if responsibility for the management services for which the fees are paid is given to the company's employees in the company's job chart or description of responsibilities. If the services are performed outside Russia, there are good arguments that no Russian withholding tax applies. VAT usually applies to the fees via withholding. The Russian version of reverse charge VAT is applied in the European Union, but should be creditable by the Russian subsidiary.

(b) Royalties

Foreign investors often license certain rights or technology to their Russian subsidiaries. The royalty payments under a license are normally deductible by the Russian subsidiary. The royalty payments are also subject to a 20 percent Russian withholding tax; however, the withholding tax is reduced or eliminated under most Russian tax treaties. It is usually possible to obtain an advance exemption from the withholding tax.

Under the current interpretation of the Russian VAT rules, the license of intangibles is treated as a service, the place of supply of which is the place of economic activity of the licensor. So long as the foreign licensor does not conduct business activities in Russia, the royalties should not be subject to Russian VAT. In any case, most foreign investors choose to license, rather than assign, intangibles to their Russian subsidiaries because they want to retain ownership of the intangibles.

(c) Interest

Some foreign investors use back-to-back loans through Russian affiliates of Western banks in order to repatriate profits through tax-deductible interest payments because of certain unfavorable tax and currency control consequences of shareholder loans.

(d) Leasing

Cross-border leasing is currently not widely used in Russia because of the absence of clearly defined legal and tax rules.

(e) Dividends

Dividends paid by a Russian company to a foreign legal entity shareholder are subject to a 15 percent withholding tax. Dividends paid to a nonresident individual shareholder are subject to a 30 percent withholding tax. Dividends are not deductible by the Russian company. Most Russian tax treaties provide for reduction or elimination of the withholding tax on dividends. It is usually possible to obtain an advance exemption from the withholding tax.

(f) Repayment of Debt

Repayment of debt principal by a Russian company to a foreign shareholder or affiliate is not subject to Russian tax. Similarly, repayment of debt by a Russian company to a Russian bank subsidiary of a Western bank, along with release of an offshore deposit or guarantee, are not subject to Russian tax.

Some multinational foreign investors in Russia have preferred to fund their Russian subsidiaries primarily with debt because repatriation of a debt investment is easier than repatriation of an equity investment (see next section); however, some issues may discourage the use of debt. First, a significant amount of foreign-currency denominated debt may cause the Russian company's net asset value to fall below its charter capital or minimum charter capital and result in a risk of forced liquidation under Russian corporate law. Second, if the Russian company is expected to generate taxable losses before deductions for interest expense, it may be more tax-efficient for the foreign investor's worldwide group to place the borrowing for the investment in the Russian subsidiary in a jurisdiction in which a deduction for interest expense may be utilized currently.

(g) Redemption of Shares

The redemption of a foreign shareholder's shares in a Russian company is normally treated as giving rise to Russian-source income. The foreign shareholder's gain on the redemption of shares (or the entire redemption proceeds if the amount of gain cannot be established) is subject to a 20 percent withholding tax, unless reduced or eliminated under a tax treaty.

(h) Sale of Shares

Like a redemption, the sale of shares of a Russian company by a foreign shareholder is normally treated as giving rise to Russian-source income, regardless of whether the sale is attributable to a permanent establishment in Russia of the seller. The foreign shareholder's gain on the sale of the shares (or the entire sale proceeds if the amount of gain cannot be established) is subject to a 20 percent withholding tax, unless reduced or eliminated under a tax treaty. If a foreign legal entity sells the shares to another foreign legal entity and neither has a taxable presence in Russia, there is currently no mechanism for enforcement or even payment of the tax.

16.21 CONCLUSION

After following a sometimes tortuous path from a command economy to a market economy during the 1990s, Russia is entering the new millenium with renewed hope that its economy has stabilized and that it will be able to attract the substantial investment needed to replace the crumbling infrastructure inherited from the Soviet era. As Russia's legal and tax rules evolve further and the "rule of law" strengthens, investors should begin to focus on opportunities in areas such as oil and gas, electricity, telecommunications, high technology, and manufacturing. Although mergers and acquisitions in Russia at present are mostly in the form of simple share and asset purchases for cash, it is expected that more complex structures will be used as the investment climate improves.

This chapter has outlined the basic legal and tax rules that currently apply to mergers and acquisitions in Russia. It is important to emphasize that the rules will likely be fluid for several years to come, and any investor contemplating a merger or acquisition in Russia should consult a qualified lawyer in order to ensure compliance with applicable law.

CHAPTER 17

Taxation of Mergers and Acquisitions in Spain

Rocío Reyero
Laura Ezquerra
Adriana Ojeda
Ernst & Young, Abogados

17.1 Introduction
 (a) Merger
 (b) Spin-Off
 (c) In-Kind Contribution of Branch Activity
 (d) Exchange of Shares Transaction
17.2 Taxation of Operations Under the Rollover Regime
 (a) Capital Tax
 (b) Value-Added Tax
 (c) Urban Land Appreciation Tax
17.3 Corporate Income Tax/Personal Income Tax
 (a) Entity Making the Transfer
 (b) Entity Acquiring the Assets
 (c) Waiver of the Regime for Corporate Income Tax Purposes
17.4 Shareholders or Partners
 (a) Merger and Spin-Off
 (b) Share-for-Share Exchange
17.5 Merger Goodwill
17.6 Transfer of Tax Benefits and Obligations
17.7 In-Kind Contributions
17.8 Rules to Avoid Double Taxation
17.9 Allocation of Income Obtained by the Disappearing Company
17.10 Application of the Rollover Regime

17.1 INTRODUCTION

Spain has implemented Directive 90/434/CEE into its domestic legislation. The directive provides a special rollover regime for reorganizations, the main feature of which is that it aims to provide a tax deferral frame to facilitate business reorganizations.

The application of the rollover regime does not require the tax authorities' authorization. A simple notification to the competent tax authority suffices if the entities taking part in the reorganization opt to benefit from the rollover. This notification does not preclude the possibility that the tax authorities thereafter can analyze whether the regime has been unduly applied.

Spanish tax law provides a closed list of the operations that may benefit from this special regime and defines these operations. Only operations that fit the definitions contained in the Corporate Income Tax Law may benefit from this special regime, notwithstanding the additional requirements that must be met for the regime to be applicable. The following are the definitions of the terms *merger, spin-off, contribution of branch of activity,* and *exchange of shares* transaction, as currently provided under the Spanish Corporate Tax Law.

(a) Merger

The following transactions qualify as a merger for the application of the rollover regime.

One or more entities transfer all of their assets and liabilities to another already existing entity. This transfer takes place at the moment of the dissolution without liquidation of the former entities. The shareholders or partners of the disappearing entities are given shares or securities that represent the capital stock of the company receiving the assets and liabilities, and, if applicable, a monetary consideration. This monetary consideration cannot exceed 10 percent of par value of the shares or securities received or, in the absence of such par value, of the value equivalent to the par value of said securities as may be deduced from accountancy.

For example, Company A absorbs Company B. As a result of the merger, for each of the shares of Company B, the shareholders of this company receive two shares of Company A and a monetary consideration amounting to €10. The par value of the shares of Company A is €500, so the monetary consideration received does not exceed 10 percent of the par value of the shares received.

Two or more entities transfer all of their assets and liabilities to another newly incorporated entity. This transaction takes place at the moment of the dissolution without liquidation of the former entities. The disappearing entities' shareholders or partners are attributed shares or securities that represent the capital stock of the company receiving the assets and liabilities, and, as the case may be, a monetary consideration. This monetary consideration cannot exceed 10 percent of par value or, in the absence of such par value, of the value equivalent to the par value of said securities as may be deduced from accountancy.

An entity transfers, as a consequence of its dissolution without liquidation and at the moment thereof, all of its corporate assets and liabilities to the entity that is its sole shareholder or partner. Dissolution implies that a company ceases to exist but does not necessarily imply that its assets are sold out. Liquidation is the procedure by which the company's assets are sold out and its shareholders are paid with the proceeds.

17.1 Introduction

(b) Spin-Off

Complete spin off: As a consequence of its dissolution without liquidation, an entity divides its net equity into two or more parts and transfers the same to two or more already existing or newly incorporated entities. The disappearing entity's shareholders or partners are attributed shares or securities representing the capital stock of the entities acquiring the contribution and, if applicable, a monetary consideration. This monetary consideration cannot exceed 10 percent of par value or, in the absence of such par value, of the value equivalent to the par value of said securities as may be deduced from the accounting.

Partial spin off: An entity segregates one or several parts of its net equity that must form branches of activity and transfers them to one or several newly incorporated or already existing entities. The entity reduces its share capital and reserves in the relevant amount, and the securities that represent the share capital of the company/ies receiving the branches of activity are proportionally given to the shareholders or partners of the transferring entity. Additionally, if applicable, shareholders or partners may receive a monetary consideration under the conditions set out in the preceding paragraph.

The principal difference between a partial and a complete spin-off is that in the case of a partial spin-off, it is mandatory that the segregated assets and liabilities form a branch of activity. In contrast, in the case of a complete spin-off, the company's equity may be freely divided; that is, the divisions must not necessarily constitute branches of activity. (The definition of branch of activity for tax purposes is detailed in a following section).

Financial spin-off: An entity segregates a part of its net equity, which must be made up of shares or participations in other entities that represent the majority of the share capital of the latter entities (more than 50 percent), and reduces its share capital and/or reserves.

Reserves are retained earnings corresponding to prior years. When a company segregates some of its assets, it must proportionally reduce its share capital and reserves. Exhibit 17.1 illustrates the balance sheet of a company before and after the spin-off.

Exhibit 17.1

SPIN-OFF EXAMPLE

Prior to the Spin-off		
10.000 Shares of Company C	Capital	5,000
10.000 Other assets	Reserves	15,000

After the Spin-off		
10.000 Other assets	Capital	2,500
	Reserves	7,500

The participations or shares are transferred to an already existing or newly incorporated entity, and the securities of the latter entity are proportionally attributed to the shareholders or partners of the entity spinning off its portfolio. Additionally, if applicable, the shareholders or partners may receive a monetary consideration. This monetary consideration cannot exceed 10 percent of par value of the same or, in the absence of such par value, of the value equivalent to the par value of said securities as may be deduced from the accounting.

In the case that two or more entities acquire the split assets, the distribution of a shareholding in each of the acquiring entities to the transferring entity's shareholders or partners in an unequal proportion will only be possible to the extent that the segregated assets form a branch of activity.

For example, a company has two shareholders that hold individually a 50 percent participation. The company's net assets amount to 10,000 (5,000 correspond to the branch of activity A and 5,000 correspond to the branch of activity B). The company is completely spun-off in order to form two newly incorporated companies (Company A and Company B), and each of the branches of activity is attributed to one of the newly created companies. It is possible that one of the shareholders receives 100 percent of the shares of Company A and the other shareholder receives 100 percent of the shares of Company B. On the contrary, if the segregated assets did not constitute branches of activity, each of the shareholders should receive 50 percent of each of the new companies.

(c) In-Kind Contribution of Branch Activity

This transaction is defined as the contribution of one or more branches of activity to an already existing or newly incorporated entity in exchange for shares or participations in the latter entity. The entity making the contribution is not dissolved as a consequence of the same.

Spanish law provides a definition of branch of activity for these purposes (and for purposes of a spin-off). A branch of activity is deemed to be a group of assets and liabilities that constitutes an autonomous economic unit defining an economic activity; that is, an overall unit capable of functioning by its own means. The relevant characteristic of the definition of branch of activity is that the assets and liabilities integrating it should constitute an economic unit in the entity acquiring it, and not necessarily in the transferring entity.

(d) Exchange of Shares Transaction

An exchange of shares transaction is defined as the operation whereby a shareholder or partner (who may be an individual or a corporation) contributes the shares it holds in another entity to an already existing or newly incorporated company. The company receiving the shares must obtain the majority of the voting rights in this company and issue shares or participations to the shareholder or partner making the contribution.

17.2 TAXATION OF OPERATIONS UNDER THE ROLLOVER REGIME

(a) Capital Tax

The transactions that may benefit from the rollover regime may entail the incorporation of new entities or a share capital increase in already existing companies. Both events are generally subject to capital tax at a 1 percent rate on the amount of the share capital, but Spanish law grants an exemption from this tax to transactions carried out under the rollover regime.

(b) Value-Added Tax

The transfer of all the assets and liabilities of a company or of the assets and liabilities of one or several branches of activities does not create value-added tax (VAT) if the transfer is carried out under the rollover regime. The rollover includes a transfer that takes place as a consequence of a merger, a spin-off, or an in-kind contribution, which benefit from the special rollover regime. The transfer of the shares of an entity is generally exempt from VAT. Therefore, an exchange of shares transaction entails no indirect tax cost from this point of view.

(c) Urban Land Appreciation Tax.

Urban land appreciation tax accrues when urban land within the Spanish territory is transferred. One of the benefits of the rollover regime is that this accrual is avoided when urban land is transferred as a consequence of a transaction that is carried out under the rollover regime.

17.3 CORPORATE INCOME TAX/PERSONAL INCOME TAX

(a) Entity Making the Transfer

The transfer of assets and liabilities by means of a merger, an in-kind contribution, a spin-off, or an exchange of shares, which does not benefit from the rollover, gives rise to capital gain or loss in the company making the transfer. The amount of this loss or gain is generally equal to the difference between the net book value of the assets transferred and the fair market value of the assets. The gain must be included in the transferring entity's taxable base for corporate tax purposes. However, the company transferring the assets may opt to exclude the aforementioned taxable gain from its taxable base for corporate income tax purposes if any of the transactions are carried out under the rollover regime.

Certain requirements must be met to allow the exclusion of the gain from the transferring company's taxable base. Basically, the operation must fit one of the descriptions provided by the Corporate Tax Law for mergers, in-kind contributions, spin-offs, or exchange of shares. Capital gains derived from the following operations can be excluded from the transferring entity's taxable base:

- Capital gains derived from the transfer of assets located in the Spanish territory: If the entity acquiring the assets is not a Spanish resident, the capital gain can only be excluded from the transferring entity's taxable base when the assets remain linked to a permanent establishment of the acquiring entity in Spain.
- Capital gains derived from the transfer of Spanish permanent establishments by non-Spanish resident entities: As in the prior case, if the acquiring entity is also a nonresident, the rollover regime may only be applied to the capital gains derived from assets that remain linked to a Spanish permanent establishment of the acquirer.
- Capital gains derived from transfers made by Spanish resident entities of permanent establishments in a European Union (EU) Member State, provided the company acquiring the assets is an EU resident entity incorporated under any one of the forms listed in the Annex to Directive 90/434/CEE, which is subject (and not exempt) to tax as provided under Article 3 of the directive
- Capital gains derived from the transfer by Spanish resident entities to Spanish resident entities of permanent establishments in a non-EU Member State

(b) Entity Acquiring the Assets

From the perspective of the acquiring entity/ies, the application of the rollover regime entails that these companies must register or value these assets, for tax purposes, at the same value they had in the transferring entity. Therefore, no step-up of the value of the assets is achieved for depreciation or amortization purposes or for future transfers of the assets. Additionally, it is deemed that the assets have been held by the acquiring entity since the date they were originally acquired by the transferring entity.

(c) Waiver of the Regime for Corporate Income Tax Purposes

Spanish law provides that a taxpayer can opt for the application of the rollover regime for indirect tax purposes (i.e., VAT, capital tax, urban land appreciation tax), but simultaneously waive the application of the rollover regime for corporate income tax purposes. In these cases, a capital gain or loss, as the case may be, arises in the company transferring the assets. This capital gain or loss must be included in the company's corporate tax base. The result from the acquiring entity's standpoint is that the value of the assets is stepped up for tax purposes (i.e.. for future transfers).

This alternative can be tax efficient if, for instance, the transferring entity has tax losses. In that event, the taxpayer could waive the application of the rollover regime for corporate tax purposes and use the losses to avoid effective taxation of this capital gain, so that the step-up of the value of the assets for tax purposes would be achieved. The application of the regime for indirect tax purposes would, nevertheless, sensibly reduce the overall tax cost of the reorganization.

It is also possible to waive the application of the rollover regime only for the capital gain derived from the transfer of part (in lieu of all) of the assets involved in the reorganization. In this case, the entity transferring the assets would include in its taxable base only the capital gain derived from the transfer of the selected assets. Of course, only the value of these assets would be stepped up for tax purposes. The remaining assets would have to be registered for tax purposes by the acquiring entity at the same tax value they had in the transferring company. As addressed previously, this partial waiver of the rollover regime does not preclude the right to apply the same for indirect tax purposes.

Under Spanish law, it is not mandatory to notify the tax authorities of the waiver of the regime for corporate tax purposes. The waiver is effective as of the moment the entity making the transfer includes the capital gain in its taxable base in the relevant corporate income tax return.

17.4 SHAREHOLDERS OR PARTNERS

(a) Merger and Spin-Off

A merger or spin-off might not benefit from the rollover regime. In that event, the partners or shareholders of the entities register a taxable gain or loss. This taxable gain or loss is equal to the difference between the acquisition value of the shares or securities they initially held and the fair market value of the shares or securities they receive of the merged company or in the entity/ies receiving the assets. This is the situation, irrespective of whether the partners are individuals, and therefore subject to individual income tax, or corporations subject to corporate income tax.

This capital gain will not be taxable at the partners' or shareholders' level if the merger or spin-off benefits from the roll-over regime; however, for this nontaxable result to be the case, the following requirements must be met:

- The partners or shareholders must be Spanish or EU residents.
- If this is not the case, the rollover regime may apply only if the shares or securities received by the partners or shareholders correspond to a Spanish resident entity.

Under the rollover regime, the shares or securities representing the share capital of the acquiring entity will be valued, for tax purposes, at the same value the old shares had before the reorganization. That is, the value for tax purposes of the shares received will be equal to the value of the shares for which these new shares have been exchanged.

Further, the period during which the original shares or securities was held will roll into the shares received in exchange for the old shares. The holding period is relevant in order to compute the Spanish individual income tax payable in case of transferring the shares.

Subsequent disposals of the shares will trigger tax on the capital gain produced in the transaction. In addition, personal or corporate income tax will be triggered if the partner ceases to be a Spanish tax resident unless the partner guarantees the tax due to the Spanish Public Treasury.

(b) Share-for-Share Exchange

The partners exchanging the shares will normally register a gain or loss in a share-for-share exchange transaction. This gain or loss is equal to the difference between the acquisition value of the shares contributed and the fair market value of the shares received in exchange for the old shares. This is the situation, as in the case of mergers or spin-offs, irrespective of whether the partners are individuals, and therefore subject to individual income tax, or are corporations subject to corporate income tax.

This capital gain will not be taxable if the share-for-share exchange benefits from the rollover regime. If the roll-over regime is applicable, the shares received by the entity making the exchange of shares from the former shareholders or partners will be valued, for tax purposes, at the same value as the original shares. An exception applies where the market value is lower. In that event, the lower value prevails.

Under a recent modification, it is now provided that the value for tax purposes of the shares received would be the value agreed upon among the parties. This agreement applies if the capital gain derived from the exchange is not taxable in Spain, i.e., the partner or shareholder is not a Spanish resident covered by a tax treaty. This value may not exceed the market value of the shares.

Under the special regime, the shareholders will get rollover basis in the shares they receive in a share-for-share exchange transaction if the following requirements are met:

- The partners carrying out the share-for-share exchange must be resident in Spain or in an EU Member State. If this is not the case, the partners must receive the shares or securities of a Spanish resident company as a consequence of the exchange.
- The recipient company must be a Spanish company or a company included within the scope of Directive 90/434/EU, and not subject to a special tax regime. Before a recent amendment, it was further mandated that these requirements had to be met by the companies the shares of which were contributed.

Similarly to mergers and spin-offs, in share-for-share exchanges the period during which the original shares were held will roll into the shares received in exchange for the same, and subsequent disposals of the shares will trigger tax on the capital gain produced in the transaction. Personal or corporate income tax will also be triggered if the partner or shareholder ceases to be a Spanish tax resident, unless the tax due before the Spanish Public Treasury is guaranteed.

17.5 MERGER GOODWILL

A special tax treatment is provided for those mergers in which the surviving entity holds a participation exceeding 5 percent in the share capital of the disappearing entity before the merger. In essence, it is provided that, under certain circumstances, the cancellation of this stake in the absorbed entity may create a merger goodwill that may be amortized for tax purposes by the surviving entity.

17.5 Merger Goodwill

The treatment of this merger goodwill is provided under Article 103.3 of the Spanish Corporate Tax Law, which reads as follows:

The assets acquired through a merger will be valued, for tax purposes, according to the rules of article 99 (That is, the assets will be registered by the surviving company at the same value they had in the disappearing company).

If the surviving entity owns at least 5 percent of the disappearing entity, the difference between the acquisition price of the shares of the disappearing entity and its net equity value will be allocated to the assets and rights which are acquired, following the accounting rules of valuation. The portion of this difference that cannot be allocated to any specific asset will be tax deductible with an annual 10 percent limit if the following requirements are met:

a) The shareholding in the disappearing company has not been purchased from:

- Nonresident entities or individuals, or
- Individuals who are resident in Spain if they are related to the absorbing entity, or
- A related company if the latter, in turn, purchased the shares from any of the above-referred individuals or entities.

This requirement will be deemed to have been met under certain circumstances:

a) In the case of shares acquired from nonresident entities or individuals or from a related party which, in turn, acquired the shares from the aforementioned entities or individuals, the requirement will be deemed to have been met when the amount of the difference mentioned in the preceding paragraph has been taxed in Spain in any prior transfer of the shares.

The requirement will also be deemed to have been met when it is proven that an amount equal to this difference has effectively been taxed in another EU State in a manner equal to that which would have resulted if the Spanish Corporate or Individual Income Tax had been applicable to prior transfers by nonresident individuals or entities. This provision does not apply to tax haven residents.

b) In the case of shares purchased from Spanish resident individuals related to the surviving company or from a related entity which, in turn, acquired the interest from the mentioned individuals, the requirement will be deemed to have been met when it can be proved that more than 50 percent of the capital gain obtained by such individuals has been included as taxable income for individual income tax purposes.

b) The entity acquiring the interest is related to the entity that transferred the shares because these entities form a consolidated group as described under Article 42 of the Commercial Code. For the purposes of this provision, it will be understood that the circumstances provided for in Article 42 of the Commercial Code are those included in Section 1 of Chapter One of the rules for formulation of consolidated annual accounts, approved by Royal Decree 1815/1991, December 20, 1991. This requirement is not applicable to the acquisition price of the shares paid by the transferring individual or entity when the latter individual or entity, in turn, acquired the shares from unrelated individuals or entities resident in the Spanish territory.

When the requirement listed in letter b) above are not met, the depreciation of the difference between the price of acquisition of the shares and their net asset value will be deductible if it the taxpayer can prove this amount corresponds to an irreversible decline in value.

These requirements are summarized in Exhibit 17.2.

Exhibit 17.2

GOODWILL PARTICIPATION SUMMARY

Merger goodwill *cannot* be depreciated	Exceptions: Merger goodwill *may be* depreciated
If the absorbing entity has acquired its participation in the absorbed entity from a...	
a) 1. Non-resident entity or individual	1'. If the difference between the acquisition price of the shares of the absorbed entity and its net equity value has been taxed in Spain in any prior transfer of the shares. Also when it is proven that an amount equal to this difference has effectively been taxed in another EU State in a manner equal to that which would have resulted if the Spanish Corporate or Individual Income Tax had been applicable to prior transfers by non-resident individuals or entities. This provision does not apply to tax haven residents.
2. Resident individual related to the absorbing entity	2'. If more than 50% of the capital gain obtained by the individual has been included in his taxable base for Personal Income Tax purposes.
3. An entity related to the absorbing entity that, in turn, purchased the shares from 1) or 2) above	3'. If the requirement described under 1') or 2') above is fulfilled respectively.
b) An entity related to the absorbing entity because they belong to a group as defined in article 42 of the Spanish Commercial Code.	Merger goodwill may be depreciated in respect of the acquisition price paid by the entity that transferred the shares to the absorbing entity, if the former, in turn, acquired the participation from unrelated persons or entities that are resident in Spain.

17.6 Transfer of Tax Benefits and Obligations

Consequently, if the requirements of Article 103.3 of the Spanish Corporate Tax Law are met, a merger under the rollover regime may give rise to a merger goodwill that can be amortized for tax purposes. That is, the difference between the acquisition price of the shares and the net equity of the absorbed entity must be allocated to the assets of the latter until the assets reach their market value. The excess, if any, qualifies as merger goodwill and can be amortized, for tax purposes, over a 10-year period.

Certain authors maintain that, additionally, the part of the difference between the acquisition cost of the shares and the equity of the disappearing entity that must be allocated to the disappearing entity's assets until they reach their market value steps up the value of these assets for tax purposes. However, the tax authorities have repeatedly ruled that this allocation has no tax effect.

17.6 TRANSFER OF TAX BENEFITS AND OBLIGATIONS

Tax benefits and obligations are generally transferred to the entity acquiring the assets and liabilities. The entity receiving the assets may benefit only from the tax rights, such as tax credits, that are directly linked to the assets acquired by means of the operation carried under the tax-free regime. This treatment applies to the case of partial spin-offs, exchange of shares transactions, and in-kind contributions of branches of activities. The entity/ies acquiring the assets and liabilities acquire all the tax benefits and obligations of the disappearing entity in those cases when the transferring entity is dissolved as a consequence of the transaction, which is the situation in the case of mergers and complete spin-offs.

Special rules are provided regarding the tax losses: Losses are only transferred in the case of complete spin-offs and mergers (i.e., in those cases when the entity that generated the losses is dissolved and can no longer make use of these losses). Nevertheless, even in these cases, certain restrictions are provided to the transfer of tax losses, in order to avoid double dips. The double deduction of tax losses takes place when the surviving entity receiving the tax losses has registered a provision for the decline in value of the shares in the disappearing entity and this provision has been duly deducted for tax purposes.

These restrictions are provided under Article 104.3 of the Corporate Tax Law, which reads as follows:

> The disappearing company's tax losses carryforwards are transferred to the surviving company.
>
> When the absorbing company holds an interest in the absorbed company, or if both companies belong to the same group of companies as described under Section 42 of the Spanish Commercial Code, the carryforward tax losses of the absorbed entity must be reduced. The reduction is equal to the positive difference between the contributions of the shareholders corresponding to that interest and its book value, or equal to the positive difference between the contributions of the shareholders corresponding to the interest the companies of the group have in the absorbed entity and the book value of such interest.

The disappearing company's tax losses carryforwards may not be transferred to the surviving company if these losses have caused the surviving entity to reflect the expense derived from the decline in value of the shares in the disappearing company. The disappearing company's tax losses carryforwards may not be transferred to the surviving company either, if those losses have caused another company of the same group of companies to reflect the expense derived from the decline in value of the shares in the disappearing company.

As regards the interpretation of the wording of Section 104 of the Corporate Tax Law, it must be noted that the same literally refers to "groups of companies as defined under Section 42 of the Commercial Code." Section 42 provides the rules to determine in which cases a group of companies must file consolidated annual accounts with the Commercial Registry.

According to Section 42 of the Spanish Commercial Code, a consolidated group exists if the dominant company holds the majority of the voting rights of another company or if a company has the capacity to appoint or terminate most of the members of the administrative body of the other company. Section 42 further provides that the voting rights of the companies that are held by the dominant company must also be taken into account for the purposes of determining which companies form part of a consolidated group. That is, these voting rights are considered to be part of the dominant company's voting rights. Following this definition, nonresident entities will also be considered as group companies.

The following example illustrates the mechanism provided by Article 104.3:

The net book value of the shares of the disappearing entity held by the parent company at the date of the merger is as follows:

Acquisition cost of the shares (equal to the disappearing company's share capital):	1,000,000
Allocation to the provision for the decline in value:	(900,000)
Net book value	100,000

Shareholder's contributions to the disappearing company:

Share capital:	1,000,000
Shareholder's contributions	1,000,000
Net book value of the shares	100,000
Difference	900,000

Therefore, if the disappearing company had, for instance, 900,000 tax losses, none could be transferred (900,000–900,000 = 0) to the surviving entity in order to preclude that the tax losses are used twice. If no restriction were applied, losses would occur in two occasions: once when the parent company registered a tax-deductible expense for the decline in value of the shares it held in the disappearing company, and again when the tax losses are transferred to the parent company as a result of the merger.

17.7 IN-KIND CONTRIBUTIONS

Spanish law has extended the application of the rollover regime to certain operations that are not included in Directive 90/434/CEE. In this sense, in-kind contributions of assets may benefit from this regime, but with certain peculiarities.

The assets contributed need not qualify as a branch of activity and, therefore, any independent asset may be so contributed. However, for the rollover regime to apply, it is required that the entity receiving the contribution must be a Spanish resident or must have a permanent establishment in Spain to which the assets so contributed must be allocated. Additionally, the entity or individual making the contribution must reach a participation of at least 5 percent in the entity receiving the contribution. However, the tax authorities have admitted that once the 5 percent participation is reached, additional in-kind contributions may also benefit from the rollover regime.

If the contribution is made by an individual, it is further required that the assets contributed must be used for the purposes of the individual's business activity. The individual must be obliged to keep official accounting books and records in the performance of this business activity.

From a direct tax perspective, this operation offers no difference from that of an in-kind contribution of a branch of activity, and the indirect tax benefits analyzed previously are also fully applicable, but with two exceptions:

- In-kind contributions of this kind are subject to VAT, and not exempt from VAT, provided the transfer of the asset so contributed is subject to this tax. That is, a contribution of shares, which is exempt from VAT (with certain exceptions) under the generally applicable Spanish legislation, will not give rise to this tax.
- In-kind contributions of this kind will trigger urban land appreciation tax.

17.8 RULES TO AVOID DOUBLE TAXATION

Share-for-share exchange transactions and in-kind contributions benefiting from the roll-over tax regime may give rise to a double taxation issue as a result of the application of the aforementioned valuation rules for the following reasons:

- The entity acquiring the assets must value, for tax purposes, the assets received at the same value they had in the transferring entity.
- The shares received by the shareholders participating in a share-for-share exchange or the entity that contributed the assets must also be valued, for tax purposes, at the same value of the shares or assets contributed.

Thus, the same capital gain may be taxed twice (once in the hands of the entity that received the shares or assets, and again in the hands of the shareholders). In order to avoid a double taxation of the same capital gain, Article 109 of the Corporate Tax Law provides the following two rules:

1. If the entity that received the assets or shares did not step up for accounting purposes the value of the assets or shares received, double taxation will be avoided because profits distributed against the income derived from the assets or shares contributed gives the right to a tax credit/tax exemption to avoid domestic/international double taxation, regardless of the interest held in such entity and regardless of the period during which this interest was held. A tax credit/tax exemption is available if the interest held in the entity that received the assets or shares is transferred.
2. If the entity that received the assets or shares stepped up for accounting purposes the value of those assets or shares, no accounting profits arise when said entity transfers the assets or shares received. Thus, double taxation may not be avoided by applying the rules described. In such cases, the entity that received the assets or shares may carry out a negative tax adjustment in the moment of its extinction. This negative tax adjustment is equal to the positive tax adjustments previously carried out as a result of not having stepped up for tax purposes the value of the assets received.

Under a recent modification, it is now provided that said negative tax adjustment may be carried out by the entity that received the assets or shares before its extinction. This provision applies if it is proven that the shareholders have transferred their shares in such entity and the shareholders have been taxed for the capital gain derived from this transfer. In this case, the negative tax adjustment may not exceed the taxable capital gain obtained by the shareholders.

The following example illustrates the rules provided by article 109 to avoid double taxation:

A Spanish resident entity (A) contributes certain assets to another resident entity (B). The value of the assets contributed is the following, and B has no other assets or liabilities:

- Net book value: 100
- Fair market value: 500

B sells the assets received for 500 and A sells the shares in B in two situations:

1. After B has distributed the profit derived from the sale of the assets
2. Before the profit distribution

The example will analyze the application of Article 109 under two alternatives:

1. B *has not* stepped up for accounting purposes the assets received.
2. B *has* stepped up for accounting purposes the assets received.

B has not stepped up for accounting purposes the assets received. Thus, B has registered the assets for accounting and tax purposes at 100.

17.8 Rules to Avoid Double Taxation

A transfers the shares in B after B makes its profit distribution. The sale price of the share amounts is 100. This amount is equal to the market value of the cash received by B from the sale of the assets (500), less the tax due for the capital gain in B (35% × 400 = 140), and less the cash distributed as dividends.

	A	B	TOTAL
Profit derived from the sale of assets received:		400	400
Dividends received from B (400–140):	260		260
Tax credit to avoid double taxation:	(260)		(260)
Profit derived from the transfer of shares in B (100–100):	0		
TOTAL	0	400	400

A transfers the shares in B before a profit distribution by B. The sale price of the shares amounts to 360, which is equal to the market value of the cash received by B from the sale of the assets (500), less the tax due for the capital gain in B (35% × 400 = 140):

	A	B	TOTAL
Profit derived from the sale of assets received:		400	400
Profit derived from the transfer of shares in B (360–100):	260		260
Tax credit to avoid double taxation:	(260)		(260)
TOTAL	0	400	400

B has stepped up the assets received for accounting purposes. Thus, B has registered the assets for accounting and tax purposes at 500.

B sells the assets received and registers no accounting profit. A transfers the shares in B. The sale price of the shares amounts to 360, which is equal to the market value of the cash received by B from the sale of the assets (500), less the tax due for the capital gain in B (35% × 400 = 140):

	A	B	TOTAL
Tax profit derived from the sale of assets received:		400	400
Tax profit derived from the transfer of shares in B (360–100):	260		260
Dividends received from B:	0		
Tax credit to avoid double taxation:	(0)		
TOTAL	260	400	660

In order to avoid double taxation, B may carry out a negative tax adjustment amounting (260) once A has transferred its shares in B. The overall taxable capital gain amounts to 400 (260 in A and 140 in B).

17.9 ALLOCATION OF INCOME OBTAINED BY THE DISAPPEARING COMPANY

The Corporate Tax Law provides that the income derived from the activities performed by the entities disappearing as a result of the operations that benefit from the rollover regime will be allocated pursuant to the provisions of the mercantile rules. According to these rules, the merger or spin-off project that must be prepared by the entities should include the date from which the income obtained by the disappearing entities is deemed to be obtained by the surviving entities. This date must be considered for both accounting and tax purposes. According to the Corporations Law, this date can be fixed retroactively. This rule regarding the allocation of income is only applicable to mergers and complete spin-offs, but not to any other operations where there is not a disappearing company.

17.10 APPLICATION OF THE ROLLOVER REGIME

The rollover regime seeks to provide tax deferral to facilitate and make attractive business reorganizations that seek a sound business aim, such as creating a more efficient organization, reducing global costs, or complementing the business of any of the companies involved in the transactions. The Spanish law provides that this regime is not applicable to operations, the main aim of which is tax fraud or tax evasion. Spanish law further provides that the rollover does not apply if the reorganization is not carried out for valid business reasons (such as the restructuring or rationalization of the activities of the entities taking part in the reorganization), but only seeks to obtain a tax advantage. The wording of this anti-abuse rule has been recently amended and mirrors a decision from the EU Court of Justice dated July 17, 1997.

There is no need to apply for the rollover regime. Communication to the tax authorities before the granting of the relevant public deed suffices. A recent amendment to the Law has introduced a detailed regulation of the rules to communicate the option for this rollover regime. This communication should be included in the shareholders' resolution or/and in the public deed executing the operation.

CHAPTER 18

Taxation of Mergers and Acquisitions in Ukraine

Oleg V. Batyuk
Vladimir N. Zakhvataev
Salans, Hertzfeld & Heilbronn, Ukraine

18.1 **Introduction**
    (a) Developments
    (b) Forms of Reorganization
    (c) Objectives
18.2 **Overview of Tax and Legal System in Ukraine**
    (a) Corporate Taxes
    (b) Currency Control
    (c) Corporate Law
    (d) Securities Law
    (e) Limited Liability Companies
    (f) Reorganizations
    (g) Specified Corporate Procedures
    (h) Anti-trust
    (i) Obtaining Permission from the Anti-Monopoly Committee
    (j) Failure to Obtain Permission from the Anti-Monopoly Committee
    (k) Restrictions of Foreign Ownership of Domestic Businesses
18.3 **Analysis of Types of Mergers and Acquisitions**
18.4 **Aquisitions of Assets**
    (a) Legal Form
    (b) Foreign Purchasers
    (c) Tax Consequences to Seller
    (d) VAT Consequences to Seller
    (e) Notarization
    (f) Tax Consequences to Buyer
18.5 **Acquisition of Shares**
    (a) Legal Form
    (b) Types of Stock Acquisition
    (c) Formerly State-Owneed Shares
    (d) Cash Payments
    (e) Subscription to a Joint Stock Company
    (f) Tax Consequences to Seller
    (g) Tax Consequences to Buyer

18.6 Mergers
- (a) Legal Forms
- (b) Timing Issues
- (c) Basic Types of Reorganization
- (d) Tax Consequences to Target and Shareholders
- (e) Tax Consequences to Acquiror

18.7 Divisions
- (a) Legal Forms
- (b) Splitting-Up Process
- (c) Splitting-Up Procedure Process
- (d) Spinning-Off Procedure
- (e) Tax Consequences to a Distributing Company

18.8 Tax Consequences to Recipient Shareholders
- (a) Tax Liability
- (b) VAT Issues
- (c) Debt Issues

18.9 Carryover of Tax Attributes
18.10 Consolidation
18.11 Financing
18.12 Repatriation of Capital and Profits
- (a) Source of Income
- (b) Exceptions

18.13 Conclusion

18.1 INTRODUCTION

Ukraine embarked on the road to the world market economy beginning with the Ukrainian parliament's adoption of "On Proclamation of Independence of Ukraine" on August 24, 1991. From the first days of independence, Ukraine had faced fundamental tasks of replacing the legal substratum of the moribund Soviet economy, state property, and the overwhelming system of state-owned enterprises. Ukraine initiated a modern market economy law, private ownership, and private companies—or more accurately, non–state-owned companies—as precursors of the emerging economic order.

(a) Developments

Ukraine gradually adopted new laws and regulations governing new corporate and tax processes in Ukraine, including the following:

- The establishment of private ownership
- Privatization of state-owned enterprises
- The inflow of foreign investments from developed countries
- The spawning of thousands of new companies
- The reorganization and amalgamation of such companies
- The development of international business

(b) Forms of Reorganization

Under Soviet law, only three forms of reorganization existed:

- Amalgamation
- Joining
- Splitting up

All of these reorganizations pertained to state-owned companies. The currently existing *spinning off* and *transformation* of privatized companies were alien to the old Soviet law system; however, the reorganizations of non–state-owned companies are not quite frequent in Ukraine despite certain new developments in legislation in this area and despite thousands of reorganizations of state-owned companies. There is no express law in Ukraine governing the complex issues of mergers, divisions, and transformations of such companies.

(c) Objectives

This chapter develops a concise, practical guide for foreign investors interested in potential investments and corporate business in Ukraine. In light of this practical objective, this chapter is designed to cover the main Ukrainian law issues relating to mergers and acquisitions, with a particular emphasis on taxation of such operations. Specifically, the chapter deals with the tax issues resulting from acquisition of companies' assets, shares, from mergers, divisions, as well as with the carrying over of tax attributes, consolidation, financing, and repatriation of profits.

18.2 OVERVIEW OF TAX AND LEGAL SYSTEM IN UKRAINE

The tax issues are the main focus of this chapter. Nevertheless, we find it advisable to familiarize the reader, albeit by way of introduction, with the most general features of the Ukrainian tax system. This introduction includes the following:

- Corporate taxes
- Major types of companies existing in Ukraine
- Currency control rules
- Securities law
- Antitrust legislation
- Foreign ownership

It is anticipated that this brief background of the current Ukrainian law will serve as an instrument for perceiving the specifics of Ukrainian tax law in the area of mergers and acquisitions.

(a) Corporate Taxes

As elsewhere in the world, Ukrainian taxes and other mandatory payments are classified based on the object of the taxation. As regards corporations, to date, there are about 30 taxable objects in Ukraine, which correspond to 30 types of taxes. Of this general number, about 20 types of taxes are payable to the State Treasury and include various types of central funds, such as the Social Security Fund, Pension Fund, Chernobyl Disaster Fund, Innovation Fund, and so forth. The remaining taxes, such as advertisement tax, communal tax, and mandatory payments, are payable to the local Treasury. Major Ukrainian taxes that apply to corporations are summarized in Exhibit 18.1.

Exhibit 18.1

UKRAINIAN TAXES THAT APPLY TO CORPORATIONS

Type of tax	Tax base	Tax rate
Profits tax	Net profits (determined as the difference between the gross income of the corporation and its gross expenses, including amortization payment)	30 percent of the tax base
Value-added tax (VAT)	Contractual price (which also includes applicable taxes and duties) both for domestic sales of goods and services (including leasing) and import (including leasing) and export of goods and services	20 percent (added to the price) for most goods and services; 0 percent for goods that were exported and for labor/services to be used outside of Ukraine; Note: sales of goods for the disabled, sale of books produced in Ukraine, and some other sales are exempt from VAT
Customs duties	Value and/or unit of imported goods and limited number of exported goods	*Ad valorem* rate categories are 5 percent, 10 percent, 15 percent and 20 percent; various per unit rates; some rates combine *ad valorem* and per unit rates. Property that is imported by foreign investors as their contribution to the Charter Fund of a company, whether a wholly-owned subsidiary or a joint venture, is exempt from customs duties. However, where this property is sold or alienated otherwise prior to expiration of 3 years, the company is obliged to pay the relevant customs duties.

18.2 Overview of Tax and Legal System in Ukraine

Exhibit 18.1 Ukrainian Taxes that Apply to Corporations (*cont'd*)

Type of tax	Tax base	Tax rate
Personal income tax	*Ukrainian residents:* taxed on worldwide income for a calendar year	*Rate for residents at the principal place of work:* Progressive rates apply, depending on the amount of wages/salary: tax rates essentially range from 10 percent to 50 percent
	Ukrainian non-residents (i.e. foreigners who live in Ukraine less than 183 days in a calendar year)—Taxed on Ukrainian source income	*Rate for non-residents and for residents for income obtained outside of main place of work*—20 percent
		Rate for dividends and for other similar corporate right incomes—15 percent
Chernobyl Disaster Fund	Amount of wages/salaries paid to the employees	Rate is 10 percent of the total amount of wages/salaries. Payments to the Chernobyl Fund are attributable to the gross expenses of the payers
Tax on Immovable Property	Note: the tax is envisaged by the law on the System of Taxation, however to date this tax is not levied, as no Immovable Property Tax Law was adopted	To date no tax is levied
Excise taxes	a) Turnover from sales of excisable goods of Ukrainian origin b) Turnover from sales, transfer of excisable goods or products for company's own use or for industrial production c) Customs value of excisable goods or products imported in Ukraine	Tax rates vary, depending on types of excisable goods. In most cases *ad valorem* percentage rates apply; however, on certain occasions per unit rates are applicable. For the most part, excise tax applies to acquisitions of vehicles, alcohol beverages, beer, various types of gasoline, jewelry, tobacco and to some other limited types of goods.
Advertising tax	Value of advertising services	Tax is established by municipal authorities. Tax rate must not exceed 0.1 percent for single time advertising and 0.5 percent for advertising that has duration in time

Exhibit 18.1   Ukrainian Taxes that Apply to Corporations (*cont'd*)

Type of tax	Tax base	Tax rate
Payments to certain mandatory social insurance funds:		
(a) fund designated to compensation for temporary disability of employees	Amount of wages/salaries paid to the employees	a) for employers: 2.5 percent
(b) unemployment insurance fund		b) for employers: currently 2 percent; as of July 1, 2001, 2.5 percent

Repatriation tax is classified as a type of profit tax and is levied at a rate 15 percent of the profit, unless an applicable international treaty provides otherwise.

(b) Currency Control

All currency operations in Ukraine are subject to currency control. The control is exercised by the National Bank of Ukraine (NBU), the authorized Ukrainian banks, the State Tax Administration, and the Customs Service authorities, each acting within the scope of its respective competence envisaged by Ukrainian law. These currency control officials exercise rigid control over the currency transactions with participation of Ukrainian residents and nonresidents. Pursuant to the currency regulations, any payments between national corporations are to be made in Ukrainian currency—*Hryvnias* (UAH). All payments between residents and nonresidents are effected in hard currency via the authorized Ukrainian banks (i.e., through those banks that have a relevant license issued by the NBU).

Ukrainian resident companies use their hard currency funds or purchase hard currency through authorized Ukrainian banks at the inter-bank currency market to make payments in hard currency. The NBU is generally authorized to establish the specific margin limits on the inter-bank currency transactions. Payments between residents and nonresidents in Ukrainian currency are permitted only in the event that one of the parties to the transaction has obtained an NBU hard currency license. Ukrainian companies' hard currency located or deposited abroad is subject to mandatory declaration with the NBU in accordance with the established procedure.

Authorized Ukrainian bodies are entitled to obtain from Ukrainian residents and nonresidents the full scope of information as to the relevant currency operations and the status of their foreign currency bank account. Relevant provisions of Ukrainian laws limit such controlling powers. Any unauthorized currency operations, by Ukrainian residents or nonresidents, involving purchase, sale, exchange, or other unlawful use of currency as a means of payment, results in administrative liability in the form of various financial sanctions. The amount of a particular sanction depends on the seriousness of the violation and may be as high as the amount involved in the unlawful currency transaction.

18.2 Overview of Tax and Legal System in Ukraine

In sum, unless one of the parties has a relevant NBU currency license permitting payments in Ukrainian currency, all mergers and acquisition transactions between Ukrainian resident corporations and nonresident corporations must be effectuated in hard currency and in full compliance with the applicable currency law provisions.

(c) Corporate Law

Ukrainian law determines the form of all entrepreneurial activities in Ukraine. The principle of freedom of entrepreneurial activities permits the entrepreneur to choose a particular form for its activities. The most common corporate entities in Ukraine are joint stock companies and limited liability companies (LLCs). The joint stock company may be in the "open" or "closed" form, depending on whether the company's shares may be offered to the public. The LLC does not issue shares because its shares refer only to "participation interests" in the LLC.

Ukrainian law provides for three additional corporate forms. These forms are not frequently used in Ukraine. Such forms are as follows:

1. A quasi-LLC, which is similar to an LLC, except that the owners of the company agreed to be liable in a specified amount beyond the authorized fund of the quasi-LLC
2. A general partnership, where the partners are jointly and severally liable vis-à-vis a third party
3. A limited partnership, where the general partners are subject to limited liability on a joint and several basis, while the limited partners are only liable to the extent of their capital contributions. Partnerships are deemed to be legal entities under Ukrainian law and are taxable at the partnership level for tax purposes.

Enterprises can be formed under the law "On Enterprises in Ukraine." These enterprises are similar to sole proprietorships or may be viewed as wholly owned by a single founder. This structure for private entrepreneurs is less common in Ukraine; however, most of the companies created by Ukraine have the status of enterprises.

(d) Securities Law

Ukraine permits various types of business structures, but only open and closed joint stock companies are entitled to issue shares. The principal difference between shares of an open joint stock company and a closed joint stock company are the following:

- Shares of an open joint stock company are offered for an opened subscription and may be traded in the stock markets.
- Shares of the closed joint stock company are distributed only among the founders and may not be traded at the stock exchange.

Shares of an open joint stock company may be purchased on the basis of an agreement with the owner or the holder of such shares, at the price determined by the parties or at the price that has been formed at the stock exchange. An open joint stock company is entitled to issue all types of shares, such as registered shares, privilege shares, bearer's shares, and ordinary shares, whereas a closed joint stock company may issue only registered shares. All types of shares are denominated in Ukrainian currency.

Unlike in an open joint stock company, all shareholders in a closed joint stock company are considered to be its founders. As such, all shareholders must be signatories to the founders' agreement. All existing shareholders are contracting parties to the founders' agreements. Any share transfer would require a modification of the founders' agreement, such as the inclusion of a new founder or exclusion of existing shareholders through the transfer. The contracting parties to the founders' agreement must assent to the modification.

The primary distinguishing points between a closed joint stock company and an LLC are the following:

- The shareholders in a closed joint stock company receive shares in the company in exchange for their charter founding contribution
- The participants in an LLC hold "share interests" only, participatory percentage, or stakes in the charter of the company. Such share interest is not considered as securities under Ukrainian law.

Certificates issued by the LLC evidence the holdings of share interests in an LLC by the participants, which are made the contributors in full. A closed joint stock company must register the issuance of its shares with the State Commissions for Securities and the Stock Market of Ukraine. The company must also maintain an official register of shareholders, either on its own or, when the company has more than 500 shareholders, through an independent share register who holds a relevant license.

(e) Limited Liability Companies

Shares of the closed joint stock company are not freely tradable by shareholders. A participant in an LLC may transfer its share interest to one or more participants of such a company, but only upon consent of the remaining participants. Subject to such a unanimous consent, as well as to any specific provision of the LLC foundation documents, such a participant may also transfer its shares to third parties.

A participant of an LLC has an absolute right to a unilateral withdrawal from LLC, whether or not the other parties wish to acquire the share interest of the participant and without the consent of the other parties. In such a case, the LLC must compensate the participant with the share of the company's assets and profits proportional to the participant's share interest in the LLC at the time of withdrawal. The amount of such compensation may differ, and in most cases will differ from the amount of the original contribution of the relevant participant.

18.2 Overview of Tax and Legal System in Ukraine

Voting and quorum requirements differ in the case of a shareholders' meeting of a closed joint stock company and participants' meetings of an LLC, with an LLC providing greater opportunity for a minority participant to block decisions on significant issues affecting the company.

(f) Reorganizations

The following basic legal rules must be observed in the event of reorganization of companies as to merger, division, or transformation:

- To protect the minority shareholders' interests, where a joint stock company issued a decision for a reorganization (merger, division, transformation), such company must value and buy out the shares of those shareholders who so require, provided that such shareholders did not vote for the reorganization. The buy-out price is determined by agreement of the parties but may not be lower than the par value of the shares.
- Shares are not sold when new shares have been issued as a result of reorganization (merger, division, or transformation). Under such circumstances, the shares (share interests in the charter fund) of the demised companies are exchanged for the shares (or share interests in the charter fund) of the company. The reorganization effects the shares of the joint stock company whose charter fund is being increased as a result of the joining of this company by another one.
- Under reorganization (merger, division, joining), the total amount of the charter funds of all participants of reorganization (as of the date of reorganization) must be equal to the total amounts of the charter funds of all of the companies resulting from the reorganization (as of the date of registration of shares). The registration of the issue of shares of the open joint stock companies is effected simultaneously.
- The par value of shares of the companies participating in reorganizations might not permit them to exchange such shares for the shares or share interests in the charter fund in accordance with applicable legal requirements. In that event, companies must undertake a prior denomination of their shares.

(g) Specified Corporate Procedures

Ukrainian law prescribes a set of specific steps for each of the existing types of reorganization of companies, which are to be undertaken in accordance with the sequence expressly contemplated by law. The steps in a merger include the following:

1. Adopting a merger decision by the chief corporate body of each of the merging companies
2. Confirming a relevant draft of an amalgamation/joining agreement that reflects the specific conditions of the merger
3. Signing the agreement

4. Confirming the merger balance sheet
5. Valuing and buying out by the reorganized company of the share stock from the shareholders
6. Establishing a procedure for the exchange of shares (or share interests) in the charter fund of the target companies for written obligations of the newly created company to grant to the shareholders a relevant number of shares/share interests
7. Obtaining consent of the Anti-Monopoly Committee of Ukraine (where applicable)
8. Confirming the charter of the newly created company

(h) Anti-trust

Ukraine established anti-trust rules to protect businesses from unlawful restrains and monopolies. Such rules are envisaged by the Ukrainian anti-trust legislation. Under Ukrainian anti-trust law, the following transactions are viewed as economic concentration:

- The creation, reorganization (merger, joining) of companies (associations, concerns, corporations, consortiums)
- The joining of one or two companies and association of companies
- The direct or indirect acquisition or the obtaining for management (use) of shares (share interests, portions), as well as the acquisition of assets in the form of entire integral property complexes of companies or structural units of such companies
- The liquidation of companies, the creation of industrial and financial groups, and the acquisition by any other means of control of one company over another

(i) Obtaining Permission from the Anti-Monopoly Committee

In instances envisaged by law, any operation that leads or may lead to economic concentration requires the obtaining of a prior permission from relevant bodies of the Anti-Monopoly Committee of Ukraine. Under Ukrainian anti-monopoly regulations, unless the law expressly envisages otherwise, the following operations, *inter alia,* require permission from the Anti-Monopoly Committee:

- The creation by a company of one or several companies may require permission from the Anti-Monopoly Committee. The permission is required in the event where the joint value of assets or the joint volume of sales of companies involved for the preceding financial year surpassed the specified amount denominated in Ukrainian currency. This specified amount is equivalent to US$12 million at the official exchange rate operative at the end of the last financial year. This rule, however, is triggered only in the event where each

18.2 Overview of Tax and Legal System in Ukraine

of at least two founding companies, not controlling each other, has the value of assets or the volume of sales of goods that surpasses the amount equivalent to US$1 million

- The creation of a company by two or more companies, where the joint portion of the founding companies at a particular market exceeds 35 percent or if at least one of these companies has a monopoly status in the market
- The creation of a company, the portion of which clearly exceeds 35 percent of a particular market
- The accession of one or several companies to an association, where the joint value of assets or the joint volume of sales of the acceded companies and the association, together with its founder participants, surpasses the amount equivalent to US$12 million. Alternately, this applies to where at least one of the companies or the association has the status of a monopoly unit at a particular market. This also applies where the entire portion of the founders (participants) of the association after the accession of the new companies exceeds 35 percent in a particular market.
- The merger of companies or the joining of one company by another, where at least one of such companies has a monopoly status in a particular market
- The merger of companies or the joining of one company by another, where such companies operate in a particular market and their joint portion in this market surpasses 35 percent
- The merger of companies or the joining of one company by another, where none of such companies has a monopoly status; however, this status applies where the joint value of assets or the joint volume of sales of such companies for the preceding financial year surpasses the amount equivalent to US$12 million. This rule is triggered in the event where the value of assets or the volume of sales of each of at least two companies surpasses the amount equivalent to US$1 million.
- The direct or indirect acquisition or obtaining in management (by one act or by several acts) of shares that reach or exceed 25 percent, 50 percent of the voting rights in the chief corporate body of the company. This rule is triggered in the event that both of the following two conditions are met:

    1. The total value of assets or the total of sales of this company and the acquiring company for the last financial year exceeds the amount equivalent to US$12 million
    2. The value of assets or the volume of sales each of the two companies exceeds the amount equivalent of US$1 million

(j) Failure to Obtain Permission from the Anti-Monopoly Committee

The failure to obtain permission from the Anti-Monopoly Committee is deemed to have occurred, depending on concrete transaction, from the date of registration of the company or the acquiring title to the shares (share interest) or the obtaining of shares (share interest) in management. Such a failure may result in various sanctions, including the imposition of a fine, cancellation of unlawful concentration decisions, and so on.

Concentration may lead to a substantial enhancement of the monopoly status of the company or substantially limit competition in the entire market or in a significant part thereof. In that event, the Anti-Monopoly Committee is entitled to file with a court a claim seeking the invalidation of relevant agreements, decisions, and cancellation of registration of the relevant company.

(k) Restrictions of Foreign Ownership of Domestic Businesses

Ukrainian law is based on the principle of freedom of entrepreneurial activities; as such, there are few limitations regarding the ownership of businesses. Those limitations that do exist apply, for the most part, both to foreign and Ukrainian domestic owners equally. Restrictions apply to ownership of companies involved in the production of controlled substances, weapons, ammunition, rockets, and so on.

The creation in Ukraine of teleradio organizations by foreign legal entities and by physical persons without Ukraine citizenship is prohibited. Ukraine prohibits the creation and activities of teleradio organizations with foreign investments if such investments take more than 30 percent of the charter fund of the relevant Ukrainian teleradio company.

18.3 ANALYSIS OF TYPES OF MERGERS AND ACQUISITIONS

The most frequently occurring form of reorganization of companies is reorganization by way of privatization of state-owned companies, i.e., by way of transformation (acquisition) of the existing state-owned companies. The reorganization of non–state-owned companies does not appear to be frequent as of now. Ukraine does not have an express law governing the complex issues connected with the merger and acquisition of companies.

Legal issues pertaining to mergers and acquisitions are becoming important in Ukraine because of foreign capital for corporate business, development, and the growth potential of Ukrainian companies with foreign participation. This process should proceed more rapidly once the privatization process in Ukraine has been completed and the Ukrainian economy is stabilized. Therefore, it is important to know the various merger and acquisition rules that are scattered in several current Ukrainian laws.

18.4 ACQUISITIONS OF ASSETS

(a) Legal Form

Ukraine is still in a state of transition and is undergoing the process of privatization of state-owned property. Therefore, the main types of acquisitions of assets by foreign companies are effected pursuant to the laws and regulations governing privatization of state-owned enterprises in Ukraine.

18.4 Acquisitions of Assets

Under Ukrainian law, the acquisition of assets of state-owned enterprises takes place only on a competitive basis via a stock market, a tender, or through an auction. The procedure for such an acquisition in each case is established by the State Property Fund (SPF) of Ukraine. The principal acquisition instrument is a sale purchase agreement, ordinarily prepared on the basis of a specific model developed by the SPF.

The execution of such a sale purchase agreement requires notarization. Importantly, failure to notarize the agreement results in the invalidity of the agreement. The ownership rights to the acquired assets pass to the foreign buyer in accordance with terms and conditions set forth in a sale purchase agreement. The transfer of assets is effected on the basis of the Delivery-Acceptance Act duly executed by the parties. The list of the transferred assets must be in full compliance with the Inventarization Act compiled by the privatization commission and attached to the sale purchase agreement.

The acquired assets may be immovable property in the form of buildings. In addition to notarization of the sale purchase agreement, the new owner must register the property with the local Bureau of Technical Inventorization responsible for maintenance of the ownership records and technical parameters of the buildings. In addition, where the acquisition was made pursuant to a privatization scheme, the sale purchase agreement must be registered with the relevant municipal authorities within a one-month period.

(b) Foreign Purchasers

Foreign legal entities or physical persons may acquire fixed assets. Such entities, while acquiring ownership rights to the assets, do not acquire the title to the attached land. Under such circumstances, relevant land is granted to the foreign buyer only for use pursuant to a specific land use act issued by the relevant municipal authorities.

The acquired assets may not constitute the "entire property complex," an autonomous integral business unit that effects independent entrepreneurial activities on a constant and regular basis. In that event, the state-owned enterprise acts in the capacity of the seller; however, in other instances, the assets do constitute an entire property complex. In that event, the seller is a relevant body of the SPF. In each instance involving the acquisition based on a privatization scheme, the purchase price is determined by the results of the tender/auction, confirmed by a privatization commission, or by the applicable stock market procedures. In either case, goodwill is typically not reflected in the assets acquisition agreement.

Foreign companies acquiring Ukrainian assets are not required to establish a particular acquisition vehicle in Ukraine. Consequently, foreign companies may make the acquisitions directly; however, the operation of the acquired assets by foreign companies connected with obtaining profits from such assets requires registration of a permanent establishment in Ukraine in accordance with the specific procedure set forth by Ukrainian law. Once registered, the permanent establishment must submit tax and other reports to relevant Ukrainian authorities.

In most instances, however, the specific purpose for the acquisition of Ukrainian assets by foreign companies is not a direct operation of such assets but rather is the creation of a legal entity in Ukraine, be it a jointly owned company or a 100 percent foreign-owned subsidiary. Under this scheme, the acquired assets are contributed into the charter fund of the newly created company. When a foreign entity already has its subsidiary in Ukraine or when it is a co-owner of a joint venture, acquisitions of assets are typically made to make additional contribution into the charter fund of the subsidiary/joint venture for the purposes of enhancing its business potential.

(c) Tax Consequences to Seller

Privatization sales of Ukrainian assets are for cash and/or privatization certificates. The payment for the acquired assets can be made in shares when the acquisition does not involve state-owned assets; however, when the payment shares are of a foreign origin, the Ukrainian asset seller must obtain a license from the National Bank of Ukraine before receiving such shares because the acquisition of a foreign company's shares is viewed as a Ukrainian investment abroad. Under Ukraine investment law, this transaction requires obtaining a relevant license.

(d) VAT Consequences to the Seller

Pursuant to Ukrainian profit tax law, profits obtained by the seller from the sales of assets (whether for cash or for shares) are included into the seller's gross income. These operations are taxable in Ukraine. The applicable profit tax rate is 30 percent of the net profits of the seller. Pursuant to the general rule, the seller is responsible for obtaining from the buyer and paying to the State Treasury value-added tax (VAT) at the rate of 20 percent of the contractual price of the assets sold.

A sale does not constitute a VAT-taxable object pursuant to Ukrainian law when the object of sale is "the agglomeration of gross assets of the taxpayer (including goodwill) which is being transferred to another taxpayer." The sale of an agglomeration of gross assets is understood as a sale of an enterprise as a separate object of entrepreneurship or the inclusion of gross assets of the enterprise. The assets become part of the buyer's company, provided that the buyer's company becomes the legal successor of the enterprise that sells such assets. This position is confirmed by Letter No. 1419/5/16-12-14 of the Ukrainian State Tax Administration dated February 26, 1999.

(e) Notarization

A buyer that acquires assets of an entire property complex obtains the ownership rights to such assets from the date of notarization of the transaction. In turn, the notarization requires payment of state duties at the rate of 1 percent from the value of such a property complex. When the object of sale is a vehicle, this transaction is also subject to notarization, and the state duties are levied at the rate of 5 percent of the value of the vehicle.

18.5 Acquisition of Shares

Technically, the state duties may be paid either by the seller or the buyer; however, the state duties are payable by the buyer in the event of acquisition of assets under a privatization scheme.

(f) Tax Consequences to Buyer

The fair market value of the assets is ensured by a particular competitive procedure in which the acquisition of assets takes place under a privatization scheme. Such a procedure requires that the information on privatization be published no later than 30 days before the date of the tender/auction. The publication must be made in the official privatization bulletins, as well as in the Ukrainian central and local mass media.

The published competitive sales information must provide, *inter alia,* the following information:

- The full characteristics of the assets
- The starting price of the sale
- The means of payment (cash, privatization certificates, etc.)
- The size of the land plot on which the assets are located
- The amount of the deposit to be made by the participants of the sales
- Terms for the determination of the winner
- Conditions for utilization of the assets by the new owner, if any

The acquisition of assets by foreign entities may be made outside of the privatization procedure, i.e., where no state-owned assets are involved. The fair market value is ensured by relevant provisions of Ukrainian law, pursuant to which the contractual price must be determined by agreements of the parties in accordance with conditions and prices existing in the world market.

Ukrainian law requires the buyer to pay to the seller the 20 percent VAT, regardless of the means used as a payment for the assets. This sum is added to the contractual price unless the object of sale constitutes an agglomeration of gross assets of the tax payer, including goodwill.

Under Ukrainian law, goodwill is defined as a nonmaterial asset. This value is determined as the difference between the balance sheet value of assets of an enterprise and the usual price of the enterprise as an entire property complex, which arises as a result of best management, domination in a market, the use of new technologies, and so on. The value of goodwill is not subject to amortization and is not counted when determining the value of gross expenses of the taxpayer.

18.5 ACQUISITION OF SHARES

(a) Legal Form

Among the existing forms of companies contemplated by Ukrainian law, only joint stock companies are entitled to have shares. Shares of closed joint stock companies are distributed among the founders and are not traded publicly.

Foreign entities acquire shares from Ukrainian open joint stock companies in most cases. Shares may be sold at the par value or at the market price, which can be higher or lower than the par value. The acquisition of shares of joint stock companies as well as the acquisition of share interest in other companies must be effectuated in compliance with the anti-monopoly requirements discussed previously.

The transfer and effectuation of the ownership rights to shares are subject to Ukrainian law, regardless of by which law a relevant agreement is expressed to be governed. Upon creation of an open joint stock company, its shares are purchased by shareholders on the basis of an agreement with the founders; however, in the event of the sale of newly issued shares resulting from the increase of the charter fund, such shares are purchased from the company itself. Generally, shares may be purchased on the basis of an agreement with their owner or holder at the price determined by the parties or at the one that has been formed at the stock market.

(b) Types of Stock Acquisition

Ukraine permits three basic types of acquisition of shares for open joint stock companies. Apart from the initial subscription for shares issued on forming of the company, one can distinguish the acquisitions of shares using the following criteria:

- On a competitive basis from Ukraine, as a result of privatization of a state-owned company that has been transformed into an open joint stock company
- Shares newly issued by open joint stock companies (e.g., as a result of the increase of their charter fund)
- Circulating shares in the secondary market through a stock market or via individual shareholders who wish to sell their shares directly

(c) Formerly State-Owned Shares

There are three basic types of acquisitions of formerly state-owned shares apart from the acquisition of such shares at the stock exchange market:

1. On the basis of a commercial tender, where the winner becomes the one who offered the highest bid and undertook to fulfill all obligations set forth by the conditions of the tender
2. On the basis of a noncommercial tender, where the winner becomes the one who offered a maximum investment in accordance with the business plan and pays a fixed price for the block of shares
3. On the basis of an open auction, where the winner is deemed to be the one who offered the highest bid for the shares

18.5 Acquisition of Shares

(d) Cash Payments

Where the sale of state-owned shares is effectuated for cash, the acquisition price for each of such a share may not be lower than the following:

- By 30 percent of the initial price and not lower then the par value of the share, with respect to companies of strategic importance
- By 75 percent of the initial price, for most other privatized companies

(e) Subscription to a Joint Stock Company

The charter fund of a joint stock company can be increased either by the issue of new shares, by the exchange of debentures for shares, or by the increase of the nominal value of the shares. In the event of an issue of new shares, the existing shareholders have priority for the acquisition of the additionally issued shares in the number that is proportionate to their respective stock ownership. As a result of the existing priority, the subscription to the additionally issued shares is effected at two stages:

1. The shares are offered to the existing shareholders in proportion to their portion of shares.
2. The shares are offered both to new investors and to the existing shareholders who wish to acquire shares in excess of their proportionate right.

Share acquisition applications of the new investors are considered only at the second stage of subscription. At the second stage, the existing shareholders have priority over the new investors. Whether the additionally issued shares are sold to the existing shareholders or to new investors, the purchase price for the newly issued shares pursuant to the increase of the charter fund may not be lower than the par value of such shares. Ukrainian law expressly prohibits open joint stock companies from establishing any privileges for investors, whether the existing investors or the new investors as to the acquisition of newly issued shares, except for the existing shareholders' priority right mentioned earlier.

(f) Tax Consequences to Seller

Ukrainian VAT law does not view operations involving the issue of or subscription to shares, as well as the sale of shares for cash or the exchange of such shares for other shares or other securities, as a VAT-taxable object. The seller is not obliged to add VAT to the contractual price and remit the VAT to the State Treasury, as would be the case for most other objects of sale where the shares are traded for cash or other shares/securities.

Regarding the profit tax, the revenues from the sales of shares are generally included into the gross income of the seller. Net profit obtained from such sales is generally taxable at the normal rate of 30 percent as contemplated by Ukrainian law. The applicable rules in this area are as follows.

The seller of shares and any other securities is required to maintain separate accounting records for taxation. Expenses incurred by the taxpayer for the acquisition of shares (and other securities) might exceed the revenues obtained from the sales of shares (and other securities) during the same period, i.e., in the event of a negative sale balance. In that event, the balance losses incurred by such a taxpayer are carried over to the next reporting periods (up to 12 such periods) and are used to decrease the revenues obtained from share/securities sales. If such a balance is positive, this balance must be included in the gross income of the taxpayer for the relevant reporting period and taxed in accordance with the general rule.

The operations involving the issue and sale of the newly issued shares (initial subscription) are not subject to profit tax. The same exception applies to operations involving the initial sale of shares resulting from the increase of the charter capital of the company because this operation is viewed as the initial subscription, which is not deemed as a taxable operation.

(g) Tax Consequences to Buyer

The issue and subscription of shares and the sale of these shares for cash as well as the exchange of shares for other shares/securities do not constitute an object of VAT taxation. As such, the acquisition of shares by subscription, by purchase for cash, or by way of exchange for other shares/securities do not have VAT consequences for the buyer. Ukrainian law does not envisage separate rules for such a buyer regarding the profit tax obligations of the buyer of shares. The profit tax rules that are applicable to the seller should also apply to the buyer.

18.6 MERGERS

(a) Legal Forms

Reorganization of companies, including mergers, generally falls within the competence of the owners of such companies, with the exception of a forced reorganization envisaged by the anti-monopoly law. The reorganization of state-owned enterprises is effectuated by decision of relevant state bodies. The reorganization of non–state-owned companies is made pursuant to decisions made by the highest corporate body of such companies, i.e., general meetings of shareholders of a joint stock company, meetings of participants of an LLC, and so forth.

A reorganization is to be structured in accordance with the specific model restructuring methods developed by the Ministry of Economics of Ukraine in the event of reorganization of state-owned companies. This reorganization involves an economic analysis of the company and the choice of a particular reorganization method. Such methods envisage merger models, splitting-up, and spinning-off and are effected on the basis of appropriate orders issued by the relevant state agency.

(b) Timing Issues

An enterprise is deemed to be reorganized from the date of its deletion from the State Registry of Companies of Ukraine. Joint stock companies and other companies falling under the law of Ukraine entitled "On Business Companies" are deemed to be reorganized from the date when a relevant entry is made in the State Registry of Companies.

The date when assets, rights, and obligations of the target companies pass to the newly created companies in the event of a merger or splitting up of companies is deemed to be the date of the signature of the transfer or the division balance sheet. Newly created enterprises that succeed to the property obligations of the target companies are responsible for such obligations in the event that the assets accepted by them do not cover creditors' claims. Limits are established by the company's constituent documents governing the reorganization of the target company pursuant to Explanation No. 02-5/334 of the Supreme Arbitration Court dated September 12, 1996, as amended.

(c) Basic Types of Reorganization

Three basic types of reorganizations of companies exist under Ukrainian law:

1. Mergers
2. Divisions
3. Transformation

There are two distinct types of mergers:

1. Amalgamation
2. Joining

Amalgamation is defined as a merger of two or more original companies, all of which, as legal entities, cease to exist and which gives rise to the emergence of, in their stead, a new company. Pursuant to the amalgamation scheme, all rights and obligations of the demised companies are devolved on the newly created company. In other words, as a result of amalgamation, the newly created company becomes the sole legal successor of all of the companies that have participated in the amalgamation.

Joining is defined as a merger in which one or more target companies join some other company. Under the joining scheme, all of the joining target companies, as legal entities, end. The company that is being joined remains in existence and maintains its status of a legal entity. As the result of joining, all rights and obligations of the demised companies devolve on the company that is being joined. Under the joining scheme, the surviving company, while retaining its own rights and obligations that existed before the merger, assumes all of the rights and obligations of the demised companies.

Transformation does not fall within either the merger or the division scheme, but by its nature it is closer to merger than to division. Under the transformation scheme, an original company changes its legal status. As a result of the transformation, all rights and obligations of the original company, which is deemed to be terminated, pass on to the newly created company, which is viewed as the legal successor of the original company. A typical example of transformation of the company would be the conversion of a state-owned enterprise into an open joint stock company as a result of the corporatization/privatization process.

Companies that owe debts to their creditors under Ukrainian law must comply with the express rules that govern the transfer of debts as envisaged by the Civil Code of Ukraine. All transactions involving any types of reorganizations must be carefully structured from the legal point of view because any failure to comply with the applicable Ukrainian law provisions and formalities may result in invalidity of such transactions.

(d) Tax Consequences to Target and Shareholders

Ukrainian law provides that the inspection of its tax records and reports by tax authorities is mandatory in case of reorganization of a company. Ukrainian law does not provide any specific rules regarding the companies participating in the reorganization. The general succession rule discussed previously should apply to the tax obligations resulting from reorganization. Specifically, the tax consequences should be as follows in the event of a merger.

As a result of amalgamation, all of the tax rights and obligations of each of the companies participating are passed on to the newly emerged company. In other words, the tax rights and obligations of the target company(ies) pass to the newly created company by way of succession.

In the event of joining, all of the tax rights and obligations of the joining target company pass on to the surviving company. This company must retain its own tax rights and obligations preceding the joining procedure. In this type of reorganization, the company that is being joined should be viewed as the legal successor because all rights and obligations of the target company as a legal entity have ended.

Tax consequences are determined on the basis of a relevant amalgamation/joining, which reflects, *inter alia,* settlements with the Treasury involving all relevant types of tax debts. The basis for the transfer of such debts to the balance sheet of the newly created company is the data of the so-called analytical accounting of the merging companies. In the event of amalgamation, if the target companies have any funds on their accounts, such funds must be used to repay the taxes, including payments to the Pension Fund, Social Insurance Fund, and so on before the amalgamation.

The amalgamation/joining balance should reflect any tax credits and other debts of the budget vis-à-vis the participants of amalgamation/joining. Such credits are transferred to the newly created company in accordance with the provisions of the relevant balance. Ukrainian law does not expressly envisage any tax consequences for individual shareholders resulting from the merger.

18.7 Divisions

In case of transformation, all tax rights and obligations of the target company pass on to the company that is created in its stead. The newly created company becomes the legal successor of the target company at its termination.

(e) Tax Consequences to Acquiror

In the event of amalgamation, the newly created company succeeds all tax rights and obligations of the companies that participated in the amalgamation. These companies then terminate. Under the joining scheme, the surviving company (the acquiror) is deemed to succeed all tax rights and obligations of the target company(ies).

18.7 DIVISIONS

(a) Legal Forms

Under Ukrainian law, two types of company divisions exist:

- Splitting-up
- Spinning-off

(b) Splitting-Up Process

Under the splitting-up procedure, the target company ceases to exist. All of its rights and obligations pass on to the newly created companies pursuant to the split-up balance. The highest corporate body of the target company confirms these transfers. Ukrainian law does not envisage an express requirement for deleting the target company from the tax registry in the event of the splitting-up; however, because the target company ceases to exist, we believe that the company should submit to the tax authorities, within a three-day period, an application and other relevant documents required in the event of liquidation of the company, seeking its deletion from the tax registry. The newly emerged companies must be registered with the tax authorities in accordance with the procedure established by Ukrainian law.

The Ministry of Economy of Ukraine, the Ministry of Statistics of Ukraine, and the Anti-Monopoly Committee of Ukraine confirm the specific procedure for creating enterprises and companies in the charter fund. This procedure applies when more than 75 percent of the property is state-owned, and applies to splitting-up or spinning-off.

(c) Splitting-Up Procedure Process

The splitting-up procedure should involve the following:

- Making a relevant splitting-up decision by the highest corporate body of the company

- Deciding on the issue of shares of the newly formed companies
- Establishing conditions for the exchange of shares/share interests in the target company to the shares/share interests in the newly created companies
- Confirming the split-up balance
- Buying out shares from shareholders who voted against the split-up (if applicable)
- Exchanging shares of the target company for the written obligations securing the granting of shares in the newly created companies.

(d) Spinning-Off Procedure

Under the spinning-off procedure, the target company passes a certain portion of its rights and obligations to the newly created company(ies) in accordance with the spinning-off balance confirmed by the target company.

The spinning-off procedure should involve the following:

- Making a relevant spinning-off decision by the highest corporate body of the target company
- Deciding the issue of shares for the newly created company(ies)
- Providing conditions for the exchange of shares
- Confirming the spin-off balance
- Valuing and buying out shares from the shareholders who voted against the spinning-off (if applicable)
- Exchanging shares of the target company for the written obligations to grant a relevant number of shares of the newly created company(ies)
- Making decisions by the founders of the newly created companies regarding the establishment of the companies and confirmation of their respective constituent documents
- Making decisions by the highest corporate body of the target company regarding the amendments to be made to the charter of the target company
- Exchanging written obligations for the relevant number of shares in the newly created companies.

(e) Tax Consequences to Distributing Company

Pursuant to the splitting-up scheme, the new companies resulting from dividing the target company succeed to all tax rights and obligations of the target company in accordance with the relevant provisions set forth by the split-up balance sheet. In other words, each of the newly created companies obtains a relevant portion of the tax rights and obligations of the target company, which are equivalent to those possessed by the target company.

In case of spinning-off, the target company, as a legal entity, continues to exist and passes off to each of the newly created companies a certain portion of its tax rights and obligations in accordance with specific provisions of the spinning-off balance. The remaining portion of tax rights and obligations, as contemplated by the spinning-off balance, rest with the target company.

18.8 TAX CONSEQUENCES TO RECIPIENT SHAREHOLDERS

Under Ukrainian law, shareholders in joint stock companies are liable for tax and other obligations of their companies only within the limits of their shareholding. Therefore, either in the event of the splitting-up or the spinning-off scheme, the liability of the shareholders for the tax obligations of their companies should be limited to their relevant shareholding in the companies. Similarly, in companies with limited liabilities, shareholders bear liability for obligations of their companies, including tax obligations, only within the limits of their respective share interests in the company.

(a) Tax Liability

The tax liability of the recipient shareholders in a quasi-LLC should be limited to their contributions to the charter fund of such companies. Where such amounts are not sufficient, the shareholder shall be additionally liable for their own property in proportion to their respective contributions. The limits for shareholders' liability are envisaged by the constituent documents of such a company.

The recipient partners in a general partnership are jointly and severally liable for the tax debts of their company with all their property. Recipient shareholders in a limited partnership company, along with the existence of one or more shareholders, as envisaged by the constituent documents, who act on behalf of the company, bear joint and several liability for the tax debts of their company. One or more participants' liability is limited to their respective contributions to the property of the company.

As to the tax obligations of the companies resulting from the splitting-up and spinning-off, such companies assume these obligations in accordance with the relevant provisions of the splitting-up/spinning-off balances. The recipient shareholders should bear the tax liabilities in accordance with the rules discussed previously.

(b) VAT Issues

In the event of both the splitting-up and spinning-off, the operations involving the transfer of capital assets from the target company to the charter funds of the newly created company should not be subject to VAT and profits tax because pursuant to Article 3.2.8 of the law of Ukraine entitled "On the Value-Added Tax," all operations involving the transfer of capital assets as a contribution into the charter fund of legal entities to create their entire property complexes in exchange for corporate rights issued by such entities are not objects of VAT taxation.

Similarly, pursuant to Article 4.2.5 of the law of Ukraine entitled "On Taxation of Profits of Enterprises," the amounts of funds or the value of assets that a taxpayer obtains are direct investments in exchange for corporate rights. Contributions into the charter fund of the companies do not constitute gross income of the recipient company and therefore should not be subject to profit tax.

(c) Debt Issues

In the event of spinning-off, the owners of the target company often decide that all of the tax and other debts (or a significant part of such debts) of the target company will remain with that company and not be passed to the spinning-off company to give the newly formed company a privileged condition for a "firm and stable start." One needs to make sure, however, that this approach does not result in the bankruptcy of the target company, in which case the court may declare the spinning-off transaction invalid.

When the debts are passed from the target company to the newly created company, Ukrainian law prescribes that requirements of Articles 201 and 202 of the Civil Code must be satisfied. In accordance with Article 201 of the Civil Code, the debt of one company may be transferred to another only upon consent of the creditor. Pursuant to Article 202 of the Civil Code, where the underlying agreement was concluded in a written form, the transfer of the relevant debt must also be executed in writing.

18.9 CARRYOVER OF TAX ATTRIBUTES

In the event of reorganization, both open and closed joint stock companies are required to present to the State Commission on Securities and Stock Market (the Securities Commission), *inter alia,* the following items:

- The balance sheet as approved by auditors
- A document evidencing their financial standing, attested to by auditors
- The auditors' report resulting form the auditors' inspection of such companies

All companies that decide to reorganize must notify the Ukrainian tax administration as to that decision.

In the course of the inspection of the company, the auditors verify and analyze the residual amounts in all settlements with debtors and creditors. In their report, the auditors should make their proposals and recommendations to the highest corporate bodies of such companies (i.e., to the General Meeting of the Shareholders) about the following:

- Carryover of all operational losses
- VAT credits of the target company
- Tax liabilities and penalties that exist as of the date of reorganization

The highest body of the target companies must make a decision about the distribution of the profits resulting from the previous years, specifying sources for writing off the occurred losses. In the event of splitting-up or spinning-off, the distribution of losses and tax liabilities are effectuated in proportion to the value of material and financial assets received by each of the companies as a result of the reorganization. Such a distribution is reflected in the relevant reorganization balance sheet prepared by the company(ies).

18.10 CONSOLIDATION

Pursuant to Article 1 of the law of Ukraine entitled "On Enterprises in Ukraine," a physical person founded by private enterprise is a company. This type of company is relatively uncommon in Ukraine. State-owned enterprises apart, practically all companies are joint stock companies or companies with limited liability.

These entities are owned by more than one person. Strictly from a legal point of view, these entities are based on common ownership. This means that the application of the term *private* regarding such companies should not be viewed as legally accurate.

Ukrainian tax law does not distinguish commonly owned companies and single taxpayers, provided that such taxpayers are entrepreneurs. Pursuant to Article 2 of the Ukrainian law entitled "On Taxation of Profits of Enterprises," a taxpayer is any Ukrainian subject engaged in entrepreneurial activities, as well as budget and public organizations, other enterprises, establishments, and organizations, whose activities are aimed at obtaining profit in Ukraine and abroad. With the exception of diplomatic organizations, foreign physical and legal persons who obtain profit within Ukraine are viewed as taxpayers.

In addition, affiliates, branches, and other similar separate subdivisions of companies located in a different administrative territory (district) and which are not legal entities are viewed as taxpayers. However, in this instance, the company taxpayer that has such an affiliate or a branch is entitled to make a decision and pay a consolidated tax and to pay taxes to the local Treasury at the location of its affiliates/branches. In any event, any company in Ukraine, whether it is owned commonly or not, is viewed as a single taxpayer, provided that such a company is a legal entity.

18.11 FINANCING

Ukrainian law distinguishes the following basic types of financing operations in the area of acquisition financing:

- A bank credit or other financial institution credit
- Commercial credit
- Leasing finance
- An interest-free loan granted by one company to another that does not have the status of a bank or financial institution
- Nonrefundable interest-free financial assistance granted to the company, in most cases by its founders
- Revenues resulting from the sale of newly issued securities

Under Ukrainian law, banks and other financial institutions alone are entitled to extend interest-bearing monetary credits. Pursuant to a bank credit agreement, which must be in writing, a credit is extended only for a particular purpose set forth by the agreement (e.g., for the purpose of acquisition). Foreign currency credits may be granted to Ukrainian legal entities and physical persons, who have the status of entrepreneurs. For nonresidents, foreign currency credits may be extended only to nonresident banks.

As regards creditors, income obtained from bank credits is included the aggregate amount of the taxable gross income. As to borrowers, the payment of interest to the bank for the bank credit is included in the gross expenses of the taxpayer and therefore decreases its taxable basis; however, such an inclusion and decreases are permitted only when the credits are taken to effect economic activities of the taxpayer. This means that a company that takes a credit for acquisition of assets should ensure that such acquisitions are made for business activities of the company as set forth in the company's charter.

Acquisitions can be made through the use of commercial credit. Commercial credits envisage the granting of assets by one company to another under a deferred payment arrangement, which payments can also be made by bills of exchange. When commercial credits payment envisage payment in the form of a bill of exchange, the conclusion of another credit agreement is not required.

Taxation of operations concerning commercial credits has some peculiarities as regards operations involving agricultural companies. A sale to an agricultural company may involve assets connected with the technological process of agricultural production of the borrower. In that event, the gross income of the taxpayer increases, not at the tax period when the assets were delivered, but at the tax period when the payment from the borrower is due.

The date of increase of the balance value of such assets is the date when the borrower actually pays for the commercial credit as regards to purchases made by an agricultural company. There, a company purchases assets with the payments that are subject to depreciation, such as fixed assets. The date of increase of the balance value of such assets is the date when the borrower actually pays for the commercial credit.

Leasing finance is viewed as a commercial operation. A lessor, upon a specific order of the lessee, acquires capital assets and passes these assets on to the lessee for a period that does not exceed full depreciation of such assets. There is an obligation to pass to the ownership rights to the leased assets. According to the tax law it is 60 percent.

In the event of an international leasing, under Article 20 of the law of Ukraine entitled "On Leasing," customs duties, VAT and excise tax on such operations are determined pursuant to Ukrainian law. Indeed, as specified in Article 3.1.2 of the VAT law, the importation in Ukraine of leased assets is subject to VAT. This means that the lessee should be obliged to pay 20 percent VAT on the customs value of the imported assets that are being leased.

The excise tax is payable depending on the applicable rate. For instance, in the event of acquisition of imported vehicles, the excise tax rate should range between Euro 0.05 for each cubic centimeter of the vehicle's engine up to Euro 0.8. The financial lease payments that accrue to the lessor are not subject to VAT under Article 3.2.2 of the VAT law.

18.11 Financing

Expenses incurred by the lessor for the acquisition of financial lease assets are not included in its gross expenses. Such assets are not listed on its balance sheet as its capital assets. Under a financial lease, the leased assets are put on the balance sheet of the lessee but not on that of the lessor.

In the event of an operative lease, where the ownership of the leased object remains with the lessor at all times, the leased assets remain on the balance sheet of the lessor. As a practical matter, this means that expenses incurred by the lessor for the acquisition of objects of financial lease do not decrease the lessor's taxable basis, whereas such a decrease does take place in the event of obtaining assets under an operative lease schedule.

Income obtained by the lessor from the lease operation is included in its gross taxable income in accordance with Article 4.1.4 of the Tax Law. Interest payable by the lessee to the lessor under a financial lease scheme is included in the gross expenses of the lessee. The lessee's taxable basis decreases by the sum equivalent to the amount of the paid interest pursuant to Article 5.5 of the Tax Law and therefore decreases the lessee's taxable basis by the sum equivalent to the amount of the paid interest.

Regarding an interest-free loan or nonrefundable interest-free financial assistance, these types of financing are permitted only for financing arrangements involving companies that do not have the status of banks or financial institutions.

Issues relating to taxation of interest-free refundable loans are under review in Ukraine. The Ukrainian tax authorities use interest-free refundable loans (i.e., loans that must be returned to the creditor). An interest-free refundable loan is to be included in the amount of the gross income of the taxpayer as of the date when such a loan was received. This means that, in the opinion of the tax authorities, the amount thus received under interest-free refundable loans should be subject to taxation at the general profit rate of 30 percent as profits of the company-borrower.

Furthermore, the Ukrainian tax authorities interpret the applicable Ukrainian tax law to mean that the return of such a loan is not to be included in gross expenses of the taxpayer. The view of the Ukrainian legal practitioners is that such an interpretation of the Tax Law is at least erroneous, to avoid potential disputes with tax authorities. We ordinarily do not recommend our clients to undertake such operations unless they are prepared to pay the tax or face a dispute with tax authorities.

A company cannot extend an interest-bearing loan to another company; however, a refundable interest-free loan obtained by a company results (in view of tax authorities) in the obligation to pay profit tax on the income that actually has not been gained. The company has to return the loan to the creditor.

Under Ukrainian law, any operation involving a transfer of funds from one company to another on a nonrefundable basis without compensation is viewed as nonrefundable interest-free financial assistance. Pursuant to such an operation, an amount received by the taxpayer is included in its gross taxable income. This rule does not apply where such financial assistance is extended to nonprofit organizations or where financial assistance is granted by a company to its affiliate that does not have the status of a legal entity. Regarding the financing via the issue of securities (including debentures of the company), the position is as follows.

Pursuant to Article 4.2.9 of the Tax Law, any amounts obtained by the company from the sale of the newly issued securities are not included in its gross income and therefore are not taxable. This means that from the tax point of view, financing of the acquisition of assets by means of an issue of securities with the subsequent sale thereof has certain advantages for the company because the company does not have to pay profits tax on such revenues. Furthermore, when the company that issued securities fails to sell them, the unsold securities that are put on the company's balance sheet are not included in its gross taxable income either.

18.12 REPATRIATION OF CAPITAL AND PROFITS

Any Ukrainian-source revenues obtained by nonresidents are subject to taxation in accordance with the rules set forth by Article 13 of the Tax Law. Ukrainian-source revenues are the following revenues that are due to the nonresident:

(a) Source of Income

- Interest, including the one that arises from a debt obligation
- Dividends
- Royalties, services of the engineering type, and freight services
- Leasing (rent) payments
- Revenues arising from the sale of immovable property located in Ukraine, including the property of the nonresident's permanent establishment in Ukraine
- Profits from the sales operations involving securities or other corporate rights (e.g., share interests in an LLC)
- Income obtained under joint activities agreements with Ukrainian companies and long-term contracts performed in the territory of Ukraine
- Income from cultural, educational, religious, sports, and entertainment activities in Ukraine
- Revenues arising from broker's or agency services; and so forth.

A Ukrainian resident company (or a permanent establishment of the nonresident) that is obliged to pay Ukrainian-source revenues due to the nonresidents for its economic activities in Ukraine must withhold and pay to the Ukrainian State Budget 15 percent of such an income. This general rule applies unless an applicable international treaty provides otherwise. In other words, the aforementioned incomes of nonresidents are generally subject to taxation at the rate of 15 percent.

(b) Exceptions

Article 13 of the Tax Law envisages certain exceptions from the general 15 percent tax rule. These exceptions are as follows.

- Revenues obtained from interest-bearing securities or interest-bearing treasury obligations issued by a Ukrainian resident are subject to the withholding tax at the rate of 30 percent of the amount of such revenues that are due to a nonresident.
- Revenues resulting from freight of means of transportation (vessels and other vehicles) are subject to withholding tax at the rate of 6 percent of the freight due.
- Revenues of nonresidents obtained in the form of interest or discount on the state securities sold outside Ukraine via authorized agents, or interest obtained by nonresidents for loans received by Ukraine that are reflected in the State Budget of Ukraine or in the cost estimates of the NBU are not subject to taxation in Ukraine.

A foreign investor is entitled, within a six-month period, to withdraw and repatriate its investment in-kind or in the currency originally invested free of customs duties in the event of termination of investment activities. Ukrainian law or an applicable international treaty might expressly provide otherwise. The same rule applies to foreign investors' revenues arising from the investment.

Upon payment of taxes and other applicable state duties, foreign investors are granted an unimpeded and immediate opportunity for repatriation of their profits, incomes, and other lawful amounts in foreign currency resulting from their foreign investment. The specific procedure for repatriation of foreign investors' profits and other incomes is determined by the NBU.

18.13 CONCLUSION

Mergers and acquisitions do take place in Ukraine. Ukrainian law in this area is much more developed than even a few years ago. Nevertheless, the restructuring and reorganization of non–state-owned companies in Ukraine continue to remain comparatively infrequent commercial occurrences. A specific single legislative act governing these mergers and acquisitions procedures is lacking.

Ukraine is in its transitional period and is developing in accordance with the market economy principles. The present economic tendency is clearly indicative that mergers and acquisitions will no doubt gain momentum in Ukraine. This conclusion pertains to both foreign and domestic mergers and acquisitions.

Among the various forms of foreign investment, Ukrainian law entitled "On Foreign Investment Regime" expressly envisages the acquisitions by foreign investors of Ukrainian companies or parts thereof, acquisitions of movable or immovable property, including buildings, apartments, premises, equipment, vehicles, and so on. Under Ukrainian law, foreign investors are entitled to make such acquisitions both directly and by acquiring shares, or any other securities contemplated by Ukrainian law.

The experience acquired by Ukraine in the area of foreign investment and privatization of state-owned companies should also be viewed as contributive to the development of merger and acquisition legislation in Ukraine. It seems to be beyond doubt that this experience will serve as firm groundwork for the furthering of the merger and acquisition processes in Ukraine.

CHAPTER 19

Taxation of Mergers and Acquisitions in the United Kingdom

Noel N. Davison
Jim Hillian
Ernst & Young, London

19.1 Introduction
19.2 Domestic (UK to UK) Acquisitions
19.3 UK Outbound Transactions
19.4 UK Inbound Transactions
19.5 Other Tax Issues

19.1 INTRODUCTION

The UK has a well-deserved reputation as a major focus of M & A activity. This reputation applies to the following:

- Transactions by UK parented multinational companies that have invested heavily both in the United States and in the European Union
- U.S. multinationals that have made acquisitions in the UK and have used the UK as a springboard for further investment into Europe

This chapter considers the major tax issues arising in respect of M & A activity in the UK, both domestic transactions and cross-border deals.

19.2 DOMESTIC (UK TO UK) ACQUISITIONS

The arm's-length acquisition of the shares of a UK company by another UK company give rise to a taxable gain in the hands of the shareholders of the acquired company, subject to the deferral provisions described as follows. This acquisition gives the acquiring company a market value tax basis in the shares it has acquired. In the event of any future disposal of the shares, the acquiring company will be able to deduct this tax basis plus an adjustment known as *indexation allowance*. Indexation represents the general rate of inflation in the UK economy during the period of ownership of the asset. Indexation allowance can reduce the amount of the chargeable gain, but cannot turn a taxable gain into a loss or increase a loss.

When a UK company acquires the shares of another UK company, the assets of the acquired company retain their inherited basis for UK tax purposes. There are no opportunities in the UK to generate a step-up in the basis of assets of an acquired company without triggering taxable disposals and possibly the recovery of depreciation allowances.

The acquiring company will generally be able to obtain a deduction for financing costs associated with the acquisition. Unlike many other jurisdictions, the UK does not have a rule restricting the availability of financing deductions for debt to acquire shares, whether in a UK or a non-UK resident company. This lack of limitations on financing exists even though dividends received by a UK resident company from another UK resident company are exempt from UK corporation tax and dividends from overseas acquisitions. These dividends, although subject to tax, perhaps can be wholly or partly sheltered by credits for foreign taxes paid. As a consequence, such costs may be offset against income arising from trading and other taxable activities of the acquiring group.

Whether a company can claim UK tax deductions on interest on borrowed funds is governed by legislation enacted in 1996 on "loan relationships." This legislation provides deductions on an accrual basis, subject to certain exceptions. For example, the debt may have been advanced by a related party. Interest may not be paid by the end of the year following the year in which is accrued. The interest is deductible only on a paid basis when corresponding credits are not brought into charge to UK corporation tax in the hands of the creditor.

Any excess of financing costs over income in the acquiring company may be surrendered as group relief to other companies in the UK group (see definition of "UK group" as follows). Alternately, the excess may be carried back and set off against nontrading income of the previous year or be carried forward indefinitely against nontrading income for future periods.

No interest relief will be available if the acquisition debt has been taken out for an unallowable purpose. This is a widely drawn anti-avoidance provision that is considered in more detail as follows.

Any trading losses of the acquired company are available for continued carry forward within that company provided that two conditions apply:

1. The company continues to carry on the same trade.
2. There is no major change in the nature or conduct of that trade.

In either of the aforementioned circumstances, there would be a disallowance of the carryforward of such losses.

The UK imposes stamp duty or stamp duty reserve tax on the transfer of shares at a rate of 0.5 percent of the consideration given; however, there is no additional real estate transfer tax in the UK for land held in companies and no capital duty on the contribution of capital to a UK company.

A non-UK resident shareholder is not subject to tax on the disposal of shares in a UK company. The transaction is not taxable provided that the nonresident is not disposing of assets used in a UK branch. On the other hand, UK resident share-

19.2 Domestic (UK to UK) Acquisitions

holders are in principle subject to UK tax on the disposal of shares. Although a detailed consideration of the ways in which such shareholders might mitigate their tax liability is outside the scope of this chapter, it is important to note the main deferral mechanisms that are available. These benefits are essentially the same for individual shareholders and corporate shareholders.

A shareholder in a UK company receives an offer of shares or loan stock in an acquiring company. Then, after receiving that offer, subject to certain conditions, it is possible for the shareholder to roll over its capital gain into the new shares or securities issued in exchange. This tax relief will apply in several circumstances, including those in which the offer is made as part of a general offer to all shareholders in the target company.

Capital gains deferral treatment will apply where there is a reconstruction or amalgamation of securities. This situation may apply where there is a combination of two groups and this combination involves a requirement to make a fresh issue of securities to the existing shareholders. Whether this relief will apply depends on the reconstruction or amalgamation being carried out and whether the reconstruction or amalgamation is carried out in a manner consistent with the relevant provisions in UK company law.

These capital gains deferral reliefs apply provided that the transaction in question is carried out for bona fide commercial reasons and is not carried out to avoid liability to UK tax. This motive test will apply only where any shareholder holds more than 5 percent of the shares in the acquired company. A clearance procedure is available under which the Inland Revenue will confirm that they are satisfied that the transactions are being carried out for bona fide commercial reasons. This clearance indicates only that Inland Revenue is satisfied as to motive. This clearance procedure does not confirm that the transaction itself comes within the scope of the rules of capital gains deferral.

The scope of these reliefs has been extended to include circumstances where an earn-out right is issued as part of the consideration for the deal. This will happen when the value of the securities issued to the vendor cannot be determined at the time of issue because that value depends on the future success of the target company. It is possible for the earn-out right to be treated as a security for the purpose of the aforementioned reliefs, provided the other conditions for deferral are met and Inland Revenue provides a clearance for the business purpose of the transaction.

In the event of an asset sale, the buyer will acquire a tax basis in the assets for any future depreciation allowances where such allowances are available. Currently, tax depreciation is not generally available in the UK for investments in intangible assets, including goodwill. The UK Revenue is currently consulting with taxpayers on the possibility of introducing relief for investment in intangibles to bring the UK in line with other jurisdictions.

On the seller's side of the transaction, the sale of depreciable assets is likely to create an adjustment to tax depreciation allowances received for these assets. The adjustment is based on the difference between the tax written-down value of the assets and the consideration received for them. This adjustment would either take the form of a clawback of allowances, a "balancing charge," or an acceleration of allowances, a "balancing allowance." The sale of intangible assets such as goodwill typically creates a taxable gain.

Different rates of stamp duty apply in the event of an asset sale. A asset sale will typically be significantly more expensive from a stamp duty standpoint than a share transaction. In practice, stamp duty is a liability of the purchaser. The liability for stamp duty may have the commercial effect of depressing the sale consideration obtained by the vendor. So far as the allocation of purchase price is concerned between various assets constituting a deal, the allocation agreed by the parties acting at arm's length will typically be respected unless there is some obvious case of abuse.

In a share sale, the business to be sold is often currently carried on in a company that has other activities. As a consequence, it is necessary to distribute the business to a new company before sale of the shares of that company to the acquiror. The distribution can be carried out tax free under the UK's capital gains grouping provisions. The UK permits a carryover of historic basis in tax-depreciable assets and inventory; however, the intra-group transfer provisions provide for a recovery of the tax on the chargeable assets transferred to the new company at the time of the sale of that new company to a buyer. The company will cease to be a member of the UK capital gains group when it is no longer 75 percent controlled by the common parent.

Finally, UK resident individual vendors may claim the benefit of taper relief rather than indexation allowance for capital gains on the sale of assets. The precise terms of this relief vary according to whether a business asset or nonbusiness asset is being sold. Individuals have the opportunity to reduce the taxable gain to 10 percent if the circumstances are right. Taper relief is not available to companies.

19.3 UK OUTBOUND TRANSACTIONS

A UK company making an acquisition overseas will often structure the acquisition through a newly formed subsidiary in the non-UK jurisdiction. If capital is to be provided from the UK, this capital may be raised in the form of either debt or equity.

Interest on any loan financing raised in the UK will be deductible, subject to the anti-avoidance rule briefly referred to previously for loans for unallowable purposes. This interest financing rule was introduced in 1996 and requires that the loan relationship from which the interest arises should not have an unallowable purpose in the accounting period concerned. An unallowable purpose is defined as a tax avoidance purpose where that is the principal purpose or one of the main purposes for which the borrowing company entered into the loan relationship.

The precise scope of this loan financing rule creates considerable uncertainty. Most UK commentators take the view that where a corporate acquisition is the main purpose of the borrowing, then the obtaining of tax relief for interest on the loan cannot be said to be a main purpose of entering into the loan relationship. The position may be less clear where the loan has been taken out for the purposes

19.3 UK Outbound Transactions

of intra-group financing or in any circumstance where an interest deduction has been engineered in an apparently artificial way.

UK companies making foreign acquisitions have for many years looked for opportunities to obtain finance deductions both in the UK and in the target jurisdiction. An example of this is the use of partnerships established in the target jurisdiction. Where a UK company is a partner in such an entity and it can be established that the entity is fully transparent for UK tax, then financing costs in the partnership are deductible against the UK tax liability of the partner. In the non-UK jurisdiction, the interest is deductible on the basis that the partnership is a taxable entity and can be grouped or consolidated with operating subsidiaries of the target group. In this way, a double deduction for financing costs can be achieved.

This planning has been affected by a provision in the Finance Act 2000, which appears to be targeted at hybrid entities of this kind. The new rule prevents the surrender of such losses as group relief in the UK where they have been available for relief in a non-UK jurisdiction. It should be noted that this anti-hybrid rule applies only where the hybrid entity is carrying on a trade. Also, the anti-hybrid rule impacts only on the surrender of losses within a UK group; therefore, the anti-hybrid rule does not prevent the UK partner company from utilizing the losses.

Given the relatively low rate of UK corporate tax (30 percent), it is typically to the advantage of UK companies to fund overseas acquisitions through debt in the local territory, even where no additional planning is involved. In the United States, for example, the effective rate of tax on U.S. profits may be approximately 40 percent after full account is taken of federal and state taxes. There is therefore a benefit in obtaining deductions in the United States and accepting a taxable receipt in the UK. The UK also has an extensive network of double tax treaties under which withholding tax on interest flows is typically, although not always, reduced to zero.

Additional benefits may be available through the use of hybrid instruments, where these instruments would be treated as creating a dividend receipt in the UK but generating tax-deductible interest in the target jurisdiction. Provided that the return was in the legal form of a dividend, it should be possible for foreign tax credits to be available to wholly or partly shelter the taxable receipt in the UK.

UK companies have commonly used offshore financing techniques involving the establishment of a holding company in a jurisdiction, such as the Netherlands or Luxembourg, to provide capital for foreign investments and acquisitions. The usefulness of such structures has been severely curtailed by changes in the Finance Act 2000. The relevant changes fall into two main categories, as follows:

1. *Changes to the double tax relief rules:* The UK system for taxing foreign dividends allows a credit for foreign taxes paid against the UK-taxable income. In principle, the UK's system of double tax credit is operated on a source-by-source basis, so that each source of income could only be relieved from UK tax by the credits associated with that source. It had been possible for UK companies to mix high- and low-taxed income through an offshore "mixer" company to maximize the benefits of the system.

Combined with the capital gains protection available from use of a non-UK resident holding company, this tax credit approach was an attractive structure commonly used by UK multinationals for overseas acquisitions. The changes now implemented have made it no longer feasible to mix high- and low-taxed income in this way. The result is that UK companies deriving profits from overseas are likely to want to hold those investments direct from the UK in order to maximize the benefits of double tax relief.

The primary focus of the group is on capital growth rather than dividend yield. The dividend requirements of shareholders can be satisfied from UK sources. In that event, the offshore holding companies will continue to be attractive for capital gains protection and reinvestment of proceeds outside the UK.

2. *Controlled foreign company changes:* Many non-UK acquisitions were funded through finance branch structures. Under these structures, the interest flows used to finance the acquisitions could be accumulated in a low-taxed environment, using for example, the Swiss branch of a Dutch company. Carefully structured, this arrangement could avoid any requirement to distribute income to the UK under the controlled foreign company (CFC) rules. This is no longer possible under the most recent CFC changes, as a result of which the only good income for CFC purposes is qualifying dividends. Qualifying dividends are defined as dividends that are not deductible in the jurisdiction from which they are paid.

While UK companies investing overseas will continue to look for specific planning opportunities for particular transactions depending on the jurisdiction of residence of the target group, it will be much harder to achieve the tax benefits that were available before the most recent changes.

As mentioned previously, many UK groups will continue to seek protection from UK tax on capital gains by owning overseas subsidiaries through an offshore holding company. Under current law, capital gains are outside the scope of the UK CFC rules. In situations where acquisitions are made direct from the UK, it will be important to establish a full tax basis in the shares acquired. The UK does not have any exemption from tax on capital gains derived from the sale of shareholdings in overseas subsidiaries (i.e., a "participation exemption"), although it may be possible to shelter some or all of the gain by utilizing any available losses in the UK. Previously, capital gains could only be offset against capital losses arising in the same company; however, the recent Finance Act extended this relief so that capital losses can be surrendered to other members of the UK group.

The UK Revenue is also currently considering introducing a form of reinvestment relief whereby the proceeds from the sale of a company could be rolled over into the investment cost in a new investment or acquisition. This program would potentially be of interest to groups that own overseas acquisitions direct from the UK and who engage in a significant number of disposals and acquisitions, although this system would still put the UK at a disadvantage compared to those

European jurisdictions that offer a full exemption from capital gains on the sale of qualifying investments. Full details of this proposed new relief will be made available later in 2001.

Reference was made in the previous section on UK acquisitions to the possibility of undertaking various types of corporate reconstruction as part of an acquisition or the subsequent restructuring of an acquired group. In the context of an overseas acquisition, these reliefs may also be available and may be particularly useful where, for example, it is desired to integrate the acquired group with existing operations in the same jurisdiction. Difficulties can arise because the UK tax reliefs are geared to the types of corporate reconstruction that can be accomplished under specific provisions of UK company law. In the context of an overseas jurisdiction, it is not always clear that the UK tax reliefs apply to a corporate transaction carried out under foreign law. To take one obvious example, there is no provision in UK company law for a true merger of two companies.

The same effect can be achieved by a transfer of assets and subsequent liquidation of the transferor company, but in legal form, a merger under, for example, the law of one of the states of the United States is a quite different transaction. Foreign law is often sufficiently flexible to allow drafting of the necessary agreements to ensure that the correct UK tax answer is achieved, but it is essential to understand the precise details of the proposed transaction.

In considering outbound transactions, it is important to bear in mind the wide scope of the UK's stamp duty and stamp duty reserve tax provisions. Potentially, stamp duty can apply to any document executed in the UK, relating to UK property, or relating to any matter or thing done or to be done in the UK. Careful planning is therefore required, which can involve, for example, executing documents offshore to ensure that wherever possible stamp duty is avoided.

19.4 UK INBOUND TRANSACTIONS

Corporate acquisitions of UK companies by overseas groups are usually made by establishing of a UK acquisition company. The funding provided to this company will generate financing costs that may be deducted against taxable profits of the target under the UK's group relief rules. The ability to obtain deductions for interest costs depends on compliance with the UK's thin capitalization rules and requires that it should be possible to show that the loan does not have an unallowable purpose for the anti-avoidance rule referred to earlier.

The UK has legislation that characterizes excessive interest paid to a related party as a distribution and therefore not deductible for tax purposes. The scope of this legislation has been significantly extended by new transfer pricing rules that will apply to transactions between related parties where there is at least a 40 percent common holding in place. Furthermore, the rules apply where there is a provision between the related parties. This does not just apply to the loan itself but to, for example, parental guarantees provided to support debt from an unrelated lender. In establishing whether a provision is different from that which would be made between unconnected enterprises, the legislation requires that the standards set out in the OECD transfer pricing guidelines for multinational enterprises should be used.

Although the authority for the Inland Revenue to challenge thin capitalization situations is clear, there continues to be uncertainty about what an arm's-length amount of debt is in any particular situation. The UK does not have official safe haven rules in relation to thin capitalization issues, although the Inland Revenue has indicated that it is unlikely that a challenge will be made unless the debt-equity ratio of the combined UK group exceeds 1:1 and interest cover is less than 3:1; however, the Revenue reserves the right to review these guidelines in any situation where the commercial circumstances of the industry concerned would indicate that a different ratio would be appropriate. In property investment, for example, much higher debt-equity ratios would be appropriate and would be acceptable in principle. The Revenue has also indicated that there are other situations where a 1:1 debt-equity ratio might be regarded as excessive.

There is no formal procedure in the UK for obtaining an advance ruling, although the Revenue has indicated its willingness to enter into discussions on what would be an acceptable level of borrowing in any particular transaction. Typically, these discussions result in written confirmation by the Revenue that it would not seek to challenge the thin capitalization position of the borrower for a period provided that certain ratios are met.

The importance of considering thin capitalization issues at an early stage of an acquisition is emphasized by the introduction in the UK of a self-assessment system for companies. The legislation introducing this system now puts the responsibility on the company in preparing its corporation tax return to ensure that any financing or other intra-group transactions are consistent with the arm's-length principle. It is also important to ensure that documentation is retained to demonstrate that financing is on an arm's-length basis because failure to do so may result in the imposition of interest and penalties.

A further issue of concern to foreign companies making acquisitions in the UK is the imposition of withholding taxes on payments made from the UK to a non-resident. As a matter of domestic law, the UK does not impose withholding tax on dividends, and since the abolition of advance corporate tax, the payment of dividends from a UK subsidiary is therefore tax efficient from a UK standpoint. The UK continues to impose withholding tax on remittances of interest and royalties, but these are generally either eliminated or substantially reduced under the double tax agreements negotiated by the UK. Most of these treaties now include an anti-abuse provision that prevents the use of intermediate companies to obtain protection from withholding tax where it would not otherwise be available.

The UK levies stamp duty or stamp duty reserve tax on the consideration given for the transfer of shares or securities. Several exemptions from stamp duty may assist in the context of an acquisition and subsequent reorganization. These exemptions include the following:

- Transfers within groups of companies, which are for this purpose defined as those under a 75 percent common holding company. Anti-avoidance rules are designed to prevent the creation of artificial groups.

- The inter-position of a new holding company in consideration for shares
- Certain schemes of corporate reconstruction

Finally, the UK has relatively stringent corporate law prohibitions on the provision of financial assistance by a company for the acquisition of its own shares. This activity is prohibited both in respect of the acquisition itself and assistance given to pay down liabilities incurred before the acquisition. This situation commonly arises when the lender to a UK acquisition vehicle takes security over the shares of the target company and its subsidiaries.

Company law provides for certain procedures that, if followed, will avoid the prohibition under the financial assistance rules. This requires the directors of the company to make a declaration that the company providing the financial assistance is solvent. This declaration must be certified by the company's auditors. This procedure is only available to private companies. In the context of the takeover of a public company in the UK, it is necessary to convert the target to a private company before the necessary procedures can be carried out.

19.5 OTHER TAX ISSUES

The Finance Act 2000 has introduced some radical changes to the UK corporate tax system. The changes to the double tax relief rules and the CFC code generally restrict the planning options available to UK companies; however, in one important respect, the Finance Act has introduced helpful changes. This relates to the definition of a group for UK tax purposes. It is now possible to trace a UK tax grouping through nonresident holding companies, provided that the 75 percent ownership condition is met and that the companies to be grouped are either UK residents or have a taxable presence in the UK. This option will make it much easier to address the position when, for example, a UK company makes an acquisition of a U.S. group that has a UK subsidiary of its own. Whereas formerly it would be necessary to undertake difficult and potentially expensive restructuring to get the target UK subsidiary out of the United States and into the UK tax group, this will no longer be necessary.

This change has been effected as a result of a decision of the European Court that the previous tax grouping regime in the UK contravened EU law. Other provisions in UK law are also potentially vulnerable to such a challenge, and this is one area of the UK tax regime where we can expect to see further changes in the future.

CHAPTER 20

Taxation of Mergers and Acquisitions in the United States

Marc A. Claybon
Stephen A. Cohen
Robert B. Feinberg
Ernst & Young, LLP.

20.1 Introduction
20.2 Mergers and Acquisitions in the United States
20.3 U.S. Taxation of Corporations and Individuals
    (a) Tax Structures
    (b) Alternative Minimum Tax
    (c) Double Taxation
    (d) State and Local Taxation
20.4 Choice of Legal Entity
    (a) Check-the-Box Options
    (b) Multiple Entities
20.5 Forms of U.S. Acquisitions (U.S. to U.S.)
    (a) Tax Deferral
    (b) Debt-Equity Structure
20.6 Nontaxable Deal Structures
20.7 Nontaxable Asset Acquisition
    (a) Statutory "A" Mergers
    (b) "C" Reorganization
    (c) Acquisitive "D" Reorganization
    (d) 351 Transaction
20.8 Nontaxable Stock Acquisitions
    (a) "B" Reorganization
    (b) The (a)(2)(E) Reorganization
    (c) 351 Transaction
20.9 Taxable Deal Structures
20.10 Taxable Asset Acquisition
    (a) Contractual Asset Acquisition
    (b) Forward Cash Merger
20.11 Taxable Stock Acquisition
    (a) Benefits and Negatives
    (b) Reverse Cash Merger

(c) Section 338 Election
   (d) Practical Consequences of a Section 338 Election
   (e) Timing and Basis of Section 338 Election
   (f) Planning Opportunities
20.12 **Corporate Divisions**
20.13 **International Mergers and Acquisitions Transactions**
20.14 **Outbound Transactions (U.S. to Foreign)**
   (a) Taxable and Tax-Free Outbound Transactions
   (b) Outbound Transfers of Intangible Assets
   (c) Foreign Branches
20.15 **Inbound Transactions (Foreign to U.S.)**
20.16 **Foreign Transactions (Foreign to Foreign)**
20.17 **Consolidated Return Rules**
20.18 **Tax Attributes**

20.1 INTRODUCTION

The 1990s brought with it an extremely large volume of merger and acquisition (M & A) activity in the United States. Often, though, the deals did not involve businesses based solely in the United States. Rather, the trend has been toward global transactions. As a result, both taxpayers and tax collectors need to study and address new and increasingly complex layers of multijurisdictional variables. The tax advisor must strive to fully appreciate the business drivers of the deal, including the related jurisdictional variables, to be in the best position to develop the optimal tax strategy. This conclusion applies whether or not the deal takes place within or outside the United States.

The taxpayer and tax collector should be well versed in the overall business and capital deployment trends that underlie the various deal structures in the market and their impact on deal stakeholders—management, employees, investors, shareholders, creditors, and so forth. Two dominant themes arose across many industries in the 1990s—consolidation and convergence. The message to taxpayers was clear: get big and efficient, or become specialized and grow. M & A activity was a function of several key business environment factors: cheap borrowing rates, the increased valuation of the U.S. stock market, and companies trying to drive maximum shareholder value through globalization and specialization, just to name a few.

M & A activity in the United States slowed considerably early in 2001. While it may be too early to spot significant deal trends, companies are now faced with dramatically different financing challenges. As business strategies begin to take shape around current legal, regulatory, and market conditions, M & A structuring trends will adjust to reflect new priorities. The following outcomes are possible:

- Financial buyers may become more active, with the percentage of cash invested in deals greater than in past acquisitions.
- Companies may be focused more on acquiring selected assets or entering into joint ventures than outright purchases of targets.

20.3 U.S. Taxation of Corporations and Individuals

- Sellers may want less cash and more equity out of deals, hoping for a market reversal.

The value of a target's tax attributes or seller's credit worthiness to stand behind deal representations and warranties may raise new challenges to getting deals done. Perhaps the most important factors will be the need to focus on post-closing activities, such as implementing or monitoring the execution of deal structures, or positioning the tax-efficient integration of the acquired business. Tax advisors now more than ever must rise to meet these challenges.

20.2 MERGERS AND ACQUISITIONS IN THE UNITED STATES

The U.S. tax system has a highly developed series of laws and regulations governing the tax consequences of M & A transactions involving U.S. businesses. At the core is a basic framework for evaluating the federal income tax consequences to corporations and their shareholders from buying and selling businesses. Much of this chapter is devoted to reviewing this framework.

A vast body of other U.S. tax rules—whether they be federal, state, or local—address income taxes as well as nonincome-based taxes. These taxes often become relevant and, in many cases, critical to developing the right deal structure to fit the situation. For example, transactions involving partnerships often raise viable options to both the buyer and seller. A thorough understanding of the U.S. taxation of partnerships is essential to understanding the benefits provided by the use of partnerships in M & A activity. These rules are outside the scope of this chapter, although these provisions certainly should be consulted, as appropriate, with every transaction.

Two additional points should be noted. Transaction financing options and objectives will most likely impact how the deal is structured. The tax advisor must reach out early in the bargaining process to minimize surprises to the decision makers after the terms have been set. Similarly, cross-border acquisitions of U.S. businesses may involve income tax treaty networks and the need to consider, at the time of the structuring, how funds will flow cross-border in a tax-efficient fashion after the closing. Attaining the same level of tax efficiency after closing should not be taken for granted, especially if the value of the acquired business appreciates.

20.3 U.S. TAXATION OF CORPORATIONS AND INDIVIDUALS

The United States generally imposes taxes on entities incorporated under the laws of any state on their entire net income from "whatever source derived" without regard to the country where the income was generated.[1] A highly complex set of foreign income tax credit rules is available to U.S. corporations to prevent, in theory, taxation of the same income twice.

---

[1] IRC § 11.

(a) Tax Structures

The U.S. tax system employs a graduated income tax rate structure[2] based on a company's taxable income. The highest applicable rate to corporations is 35 percent. The character of the income as capital or ordinary is largely irrelevant for corporations in determining the applicable rate of tax; however, the character of the income may be relevant in determining the effective rate of tax on the income, given the importance of asset character in many instances (e.g., in being able to offset capital losses against gains).

The character of the income determines the applicable rate of tax for individuals. Individuals are subject to graduated rates that begin at 15 percent and reach a maximum of 39.6 percent, whereas capital gains are generally taxed at 10 percent to 28 percent.

(b) Alternative Minimum Tax

The alternative minimum tax regime (AMT) is built into the U.S. tax system. The AMT is designed to prevent taxpayers from escaping their fair share of tax liability. The AMT rate is 20 percent for corporations.

The complexities associated with this parallel system of determining U.S. tax become most vexing when year-to-year business results are inconsistent. For example, a common limitation imposed under the AMT rules is on the use of loss carryovers to offset current year income. Under the regular tax rules, a dollar-for-dollar offset is allowed. The AMT rules may limit the offset, requiring the payment of some tax. The AMT paid then becomes a credit carried over to be available to offset regular tax in future years. Unfortunately, matching losses against profits and tax credits against future taxes using these two U.S. systems presents real challenges in practice.

(c) Double Taxation

When it comes to corporations and shareholders, the U.S. tax system can impose a double tax cost on the same corporate earnings—once at the corporate level when earned and again at the shareholder level when distributions are made. Distributions can be in the form of cash or property. Distributions classified as dividends are normally taxed as ordinary income. Distributions not classified as dividends are taxed as either a tax-free return of capital or as gain from a sale or exchange of stock.

Dividends to corporate shareholders may not be fully taxed. Generally, corporate shareholders may deduct 70 percent of dividends received from other domestic corporations, 80 percent for certain corporations that own more than 20 percent of the distributing corporation's stock (by value and vote), or 100 percent if the shareholder and distributing corporations are members of the same "affiliated group." Affiliated group structure is discussed in the consolidated return section of this chapter.[3]

---

2 Id.
3 IRC §243.

(d) State and Local Taxation

In addition to U.S. federal income taxes, many types of state and local taxes may affect a corporation's tax liability:

- State income taxes
- Sales taxes
- Use taxes
- Property taxes
- Payroll taxes
- Excise taxes
- Employment taxes

The state tax rates applicable to income taxes generally range from zero to about 10 percent. State income tax rates are based on taxable income properly apportioned or allocated to the state. The most prevalent apportionment scheme is a three-factor formula involving property, payroll, and sales.

A sampling of other taxes imposed by states includes the following:

- Sales taxes, which can be up to 10 percent and are based on items such as gross proceeds, gross receipts, or gross income within a state
- Use taxes, which can be up to 10 percent and are usually imposed on property bought for storage, use or consumption in the state
- Property taxes, which are based on a percentage of assessed value located within a given locality and can be as much as 100 percent of the assessed value.[4]
- The United States generally does not levy capital duties, stamp taxes, or other transfer taxes (except perhaps on real estate).

20.4 CHOICE OF LEGAL ENTITY

Most U.S. businesses conduct their operations using corporations, partnerships, S-Corporations, or limited liability companies (LLCs). There are numerous other forms or variations in the marketplace. The tax implications may vary depending on the entity classification and will affect items such as corporate liability, taxation at the entity and shareholder level, and elections that the various entities can make.

It may be helpful to think of the entity forms in two broad categories—flow-through forms (e.g., a partnership) and separate entity forms (e.g., a corporation). Flow-through forms often require the income to be passed through and actual tax liabilities to be determined and payable at the investor level. Separate entity forms determine and pay income taxes directly at the entity level. As noted previously,

---

[4] New York, for example, had a range in 1998 of $4.61 to $248.71 per $1,000 of assessed value for city property taxes.

this chapter discusses the framework for M & A purposes involving corporations, whether on the buy or sell side of the deal.

(a) Check-the-Box Options

Planning, especially in the M & A context, has taken on new meaning with the availability of the "check-the-box" (CTB) Treasury Regulations.[5] Now, certain entities may elect the tax classification they desire. This categorization would not only impact how the entity would be taxed going forward, but would also create consequences at the time of the election.

For example, an election under the CTB regulations could trigger the conversion of an association taxable as a corporation into a partnership. This categorization would result in the liquidation of the association, followed by a distribution of all of its assets and liabilities to its shareholders. Immediately thereafter, the shareholders would be treated as having contributed all of the distributed assets and liabilities to a newly formed partnership. If a partnership elects to be treated as an association taxable as a corporation, the partnership would be deemed to contribute all of its assets and liabilities to the association in exchange for stock of the association. Immediately thereafter, the partnership would be liquidated by distributing the stock to the partners.

(b) Multiple Entities

The ordering of the conversions is important if certain CTB elections are made for multiple entities in the same chain of ownership on the same day. The regulations stipulate that, unless otherwise provided in the election forms, the upper-level subsidiary is deemed to liquidate into the parent before the liquidation of the lower-level subsidiary into the parent.

In the case of an association taxable as a corporation electing branch status (also called a *disregarded entity*), the association would be deemed to distribute all of its assets and liabilities to its single owner in liquidation of the association. Or, if a disregarded entity elects treatment as an association taxable as a corporation, the entity would be deemed to contribute all of its assets to a corporation in exchange for stock. Because the implications of these deemed transfers are far reaching, especially if used in the international context, thorough review is essential to minimizing unexpected consequences.[6]

20.5 FORMS OF U.S. ACQUISITIONS (U.S. TO U.S.)

The basic framework to be used in structuring a U.S. acquisition involves a preliminary assessment of factors such as whether assets or stock are to be acquired, and whether the transaction is to be taxable or nontaxable to the sellers. From

---

[5] As discussed in TD 8844 and IRC §7701.
[6] IRC §367.

20.5 Forms of U.S. Acquisitions (U.S. to U.S.)

these factors flow a myriad of tax consequences to buyers and sellers, corporations and shareholders.

Throughout the entire following discussion, it is assumed that 100 percent of the target business, whether stock or assets, is to be acquired by a corporate buyer unless otherwise stated. Assume that the purchase price will be paid in cash if the deal is taxable.

Any gain or loss realized by the seller must be recognized for tax purposes in a taxable acquisition, whether buying assets or stock. The acquiring corporation realizes no gain or loss when it makes the purchase and will take a cost basis in the acquired assets or stock.

(a) Tax Deferral

In a nontaxable acquisition, the seller's disposition does not trigger current gain or loss recognition. Nontaxability in this context merely means tax deferral—the seller will pay tax at some future point with rare exception. From a time value of money concept, though, deferral certainly can be important. Nontaxable deals typically require a significant portion of the purchase price to be paid in buyer equity (i.e., stock) rather than cash or debt. The use of stock may minimize the cash drain to the acquiring corporation, although the parties must consider the dilutive effect (in terms of value and voting control) of the acquiring corporation as well as the impact on earnings per share.

The acquiror will receive a basis in the acquired assets or stock equal to the seller's basis, subject to adjustment for exchanges that are only nontaxable in part. Economically, the cost to the buyer of not getting the tax step-up (in terms of lost future deductions) could warrant a downward adjustment to the purchase price.

(b) Debt-Equity Structure

At the outset of any deal, the parties should pay particular attention to the consideration used by the acquiror in making the purchase. M & A activity in the United States provides fertile ground for the creative use of debt and/or equity to finance transactions. Variations in instruments that blur the distinction between debt and equity inherently raise the risk that the transaction may not qualify for its intended treatment, especially one structured to be nontaxable.

Nontaxable transactions routinely require heavy equity components tied to both vote and value. In most cases, the equity interest must be current to count; warrants and options to acquire stock may not be sufficient. Similarly, equity that is (or may be) meaningfully limited in its ability to share in the earnings and assets of the business may be subject to additional scrutiny.

Certain types of preferred stock could trigger phantom income to the owner under analogies to provisions governing debt securities. This preferred stock could prevent a transaction from being wholly nontaxable. The appropriate choice or mixture of consideration relies on the facts and circumstances of the M & A transaction.

20.6 NONTAXABLE DEAL STRUCTURES

Structuring the tax-free acquisition of businesses in the United States requires an understanding of two distinct acquisition themes:

- Nontaxable asset acquisitions
- Nontaxable stock acquisitions

It is common to think of nontaxable deal structures as involving tax-free reorganizations. As such, qualification involves satisfying certain judicial doctrines, such as the following:

- Continuity of proprietary interest
- Continuity of business enterprise
- Business purpose

In addition, many of the deal structures must satisfy a control requirement under which the buyer in control of the business is involved in the M & A transaction after the transaction is completed. Typically, control is defined as the ownership of stock possessing at least 80 percent of the total combined voting power, plus at least 80 percent of the total number of shares of all other classes of stock.[7]

In general, the continuity of interest doctrine requires the target corporation's shareholders to receive a sufficient equity interest in the acquiring corporation as opposed to a creditor interest. The transaction must actually constitute "a readjustment of continuing interest in the target corporation's property under modified corporate form" as opposed to a sale of property.

A tax-free reorganization also requires that there be a "continuity of the business enterprise under modified corporate form." The acquiring corporation is required either to continue the target corporation's historic business or to use a significant portion of the target's historic business assets.

Finally, to qualify as a tax-free reorganization, there must be a business purpose for the deal. For transactions involving unrelated parties at arm's length, there is little need for caution. Greater attention is warranted when the restructuring of businesses occurs after the deal is completed.

20.7 NONTAXABLE ASSET ACQUISITION

A nontaxable asset acquisition may take the form of one of two types of statutory mergers[8] or the actual contractual acquisition of substantially all the assets of the target corporation.[9] A nontaxable asset acquisition can also be accomplished in

---

[7] IRC §368(c).
[8] IRC §368(a)(1)(A) or §368(a)(2)(D).
[9] IRC §368(a)(1)(C).

20.7 Nontaxable Asset Acquisition

the form of a transfer to a corporation controlled by the transferors after the transaction in what is commonly referred to as a "351 transaction."

(a) Statutory "A" Mergers

The statutory merger can only be achieved by complying with the applicable laws of the United States or a state or territory of the United States or the District of Columbia. The statutory merger can take the form of a merger of one corporation into another corporation, or the consolidation of two or more corporations into one corporation.[10] A second type of statutory merger (an "asset acquisition") generally occurs when the following conditions exist:

- An acquiring corporation acquires substantially all of the assets of a target corporation in a statutory merger.
- The acquisition takes place in exchange for stock of a corporation in control of the acquiring corporation (its parent).
- No stock of the acquiring corporation is used in the transaction.
- The transaction would have qualified under the normal statutory merger provisions had the merger been into the corporation in control of the acquiring corporation.[11]

(b) "C" Reorganization

A third nontaxable asset acquisition scenario occurs when an acquiring corporation acquires substantially all of the assets of a target corporation in exchange solely for the voting stock of the acquiring corporation. Alternately, the transfer takes place in exchange solely for the voting stock of a corporation that is in control of the acquiring corporation.[12] In this scenario, the acquired corporation generally must be liquidated. This type of reorganization is often used in the international arena because foreign corporations cannot execute mergers pursuant to applicable state law. Unlike the first two scenarios, in this scenario, the acquiring corporation may specify whether it will legally assume any of the target corporation's known liabilities.

(c) Acquisitive "D" Reorganization

A fourth type of nontaxable asset deal structure is often used to combine commonly controlled corporations. This structure generally occurs when the following conditions exist:

- A corporation transfers substantially all of its assets to another corporation.
- The transferor corporation distributes the stock of the transferee corporation (as well as other properties) pursuant to a plan of reorganization in liquidation.

---

[10] IRC §368(a)(1)(A).
[11] IRC §368(a)(2)(D).
[12] IRC §368(a)(1)(C).

- The shareholders of the transferor own at least 50 percent of the voting power or stock value of the transferee.[13]

Thus, this acquisitive "D" reorganization normally occurs when a parent ("P") causes its wholly owned subsidiary ("S1") to transfer all its assets to another wholly owned subsidiary ("S2") in exchange for S2 stock, and S1 in turn distributes the S2 stock to P in liquidation. In this scenario, if the liabilities assumed by the transferee exceed the adjusted basis of the assets transferred, and the corporations are not filing a consolidated return, then the transferor would generally recognize gain to the extent of that excess.

The U.S. tax consequences of a nontaxable "D" asset acquisition are generally as follows:

- The target corporations shareholders generally will not recognize gain or loss on the receipt of stock of the acquiring corporation (or stock of the acquiring corporation's parent in the case of a triangular reorganization) in exchange for its shares of target stock.
- The target shareholders' basis in the acquiring corporation's stock received pursuant to the reorganization will be equal to the basis of the target stock surrendered in the exchange.
- The target corporation will not recognize gain or loss on the transfer of its assets to the acquiring corporation in exchange for acquiring stock.
- The acquiring corporation will not recognize gain or loss on the receipt of the target corporation's assets in exchange for the stock of the acquiring corporation.
- The acquiring corporation takes a carryover basis in the assets acquired from the target corporation.
- The target corporation's tax attributes are carried over to the acquiring corporation.

The use of these attributes may be subject to certain limitations (e.g., a limitation on the use of the target corporation's net operating loss carryforwards after a greater than 50 percent point change of ownership).

(d) 351 Transaction

A transfer of property is generally nontaxable when a transferor transfers property in exchange for stock of a corporation and, immediately after the exchange, all transferors of property own at least 80 percent of each class of stock of the transferee corporation.[14] If a transferor receives property other than stock (e.g., cash or corporate debt securities, sometimes called "boot"), the transferor's realized gain (but not loss) should be recognized to the extent of the cash and the fair market value (FMV) of any other boot received.[15] The character of the gain is

---

13 IRC §368(a)(1)(D).
14 IRC §§ 351 and 368(c).
15 IRC §351(b).

determined by reference to the character of the transferred asset to which the gain is attributable, considering the depreciation recapture and other rules. Gain triggered by the receipt of boot increases the shareholder's basis in the stock received and the corporation's basis in the transferred property. In general, if a liability of the transferor is assumed or if property subject to a liability is acquired in the transaction, the assumption is not treated as boot received by the transferor.[16]

20.8 NONTAXABLE STOCK ACQUISITIONS

A nontaxable stock acquisition generally takes the form of one of two types of structures.

(a) "B" Reorganization

The first structure is a "stock-for-stock" exchange. A stock-for-stock exchange requires that the transfer meet two requirements:

1. An acquiring corporation acquires stock of a target corporation in exchange solely for the voting stock of the acquiring corporation or the voting stock of a corporation that is in control of the acquiring corporation.
2. Immediately thereafter, the acquiring corporation owns more than 80 percent of the stock of the target corporation, whether or not the acquiring corporation held the 80 percent control immediately before the acquisition.[17]

(b) The (a)(2)(E) Reorganization

The second type of structure (a "reverse triangular merger") generally occurs when the following conditions exist:

- The controlled subsidiary of an acquiring corporation merges with and into a target corporation, with the target corporation surviving, under applicable state law.
- After the merger, the target corporation holds substantially all of its assets and the assets of the controlled subsidiary (other than stock of the acquiring corporation distributed in the transaction).
- In the transaction, the former shareholders of the target corporation, in exchange solely for voting stock of the acquiring corporation, surrendered more than 80 percent of the stock of the target corporation.[18]

---

[16] IRC §357(a).
[17] IRC §368(a)(1)(B).
[18] IRC §368(a)(2)(E).

(c) 351 Transaction

A nontaxable stock acquisition can also be accomplished using a 351 transaction as described previously. With a transfer of target stock, though, the tax consequences to the parties are as follows:

- Because the acquisition is of the target corporation's stock, no gain or loss will be recognized by the target corporation.
- The target corporation's shareholders will not recognize gain or loss on the disposition of their target corporation stock in exchange for the acquiring corporation stock.
- The acquiring corporation will either take a carryover basis in the target corporation stock (first and third scenarios) or the acquiring corporation will generally take a basis in the target corporation stock equal to the net inside basis of the target corporation's assets (second scenario).

Where a structure qualifies under more than one scenario, in some instances, the acquiring corporation may elect whether to take a carryover basis or a net inside asset basis in the target corporation's stock.

20.9 TAXABLE DEAL STRUCTURES

Structuring the taxable acquisition of businesses in the United States can, similarly, be divided into two distinct acquisition themes:

1. Taxable asset acquisitions
2. Taxable stock acquisitions

Unless otherwise stated, the following discussion assumes that the purchase price is paid in cash.

20.10 TAXABLE ASSET ACQUISITION

A taxable asset acquisition can involve acquisition of the following:

- Specific assets
- Business divisions
- Branch operations
- Entire operations of a target corporation

(a) Contractual Asset Acquisition

A common form of a taxable asset acquisition (a "contractual asset acquisition") involves a purchase of assets that, pursuant to state law, is treated as a sale. This type of transaction offers flexibility regarding the selection of particular assets and liabilities. A contractual asset acquisition, however, has several disadvantages. For instance, each asset must be transferred individually, which may involve substantial expense.

20.11 Taxable Stock Acquisition

In addition, some assets may be nontransferable or may be transferable only with the consent of a third person. An acquisition of specific assets or branch operations will generally result in the recognition of gain or loss, as well as triggering potential recapture tax. Because the target is often the seller, its existence as a separate legal entity is not disturbed.

(b) Forward Cash Merger

The second approach used to effect a taxable asset acquisition is a "forward cash merger." In this form of taxable asset acquisition, the target corporation is generally merged into the acquiring corporation or into a subsidiary of the acquiring corporation. The Internal Revenue Service (IRS) has ruled that such mergers will be treated as the acquisition of the target's assets for cash followed by a liquidation of the target corporation. Thus, a forward cash merger generally results in two levels of tax:

1. The target corporation will recognize gain or loss on the deemed sale of its assets to the acquiring corporation.
2. The target shareholders will recognize gain or loss on the receipt of the proceeds in cancellation of their stock.

In contrast to the contractual asset acquisition, the transfer of assets in a forward cash merger is effectuated by operation of state or federal law, which eliminates the need for individual transfers of assets.

20.11 TAXABLE STOCK ACQUISITION

A taxable acquisition of stock can simply be made by the direct purchase of shares, triggering recognition of gain or loss to the selling shareholders. The basis of the target corporation's assets and its tax attributes will not be affected by such a stock acquisition. From a purely business perspective, target shareholders are not liable for the debts or contingent liabilities of the target corporation, although the acquiring corporation may negotiate an indemnification from the target shareholders for debts or contingent liabilities. This type of stock sale is easily administered in that there is no need to change titles of underlying corporate assets; however, no rights of dissent and appraisal are available for shareholders who want to hold shares.

(a) Benefits and Negatives

Other potential benefits of a stock acquisition include the following:

- The preservation of the target corporation's legal identity
- Avoiding the need to seek consent associated with certain intangible assets such as favorably negotiated leases, employment contracts, and nontransferable copyrights, patents, franchises, trade names, or licenses

- Reduced disruption to existing organizational structures affecting management and employees
- Preservation of public recognition of the corporate name and other types of goodwill

Potential negative aspects include the following:

- All liabilities (disclosed, undisclosed, and contingent) are retained by the target corporation and, economically, are inherited by the buyer.
- If the assets of the target corporation are highly appreciated, the buyer inherits the tax cost of this "built-in gain" unless the built-in gain has been accounted for in the purchase price.

(b) Reverse Cash Merger

Stock purchases can be accomplished either by extending a tender offer to the target shareholders, who individually may either accept or reject the offer, or through a "reverse cash merger." In the reverse cash merger, a new transitory subsidiary of the acquiring corporation merges into the surviving target corporation. The existence of the transitory subsidiary is disregarded, and the acquiring parent corporation is viewed as purchasing the target corporation's stock. Such transaction can be used to acquire 100 percent of the target corporation's stock or to squeeze out a minority interest.

The buyer obtains a cost basis in the purchased stock, not in the target's assets. As a result, the ease of using a stock purchase form brings with it a distinct disadvantage—the target's assets are not stepped up to fair value with the corresponding increase in tax depreciation and amortization deductions.

(c) Section 338 Election

For certain qualified stock purchases, an election is available to treat the stock purchase as, in effect, a deemed purchase of assets that results in a basis step-up for tax purposes. This election is commonly called a "Section 338 election."[19] Only a corporation that makes a qualified stock purchase is eligible to make the Section 338 election. A qualified stock purchase is a transaction or series of transactions in which at least 80 percent of the stock in a target corporation is acquired by purchase within a 12-month acquisition period.

If a Section 338 election is made, the following recast of the transaction is deemed to have occurred:

- The target corporation (the "Old Target") is deemed to have sold all its assets to itself (a sale by Old Target to "New Target") at the close of the acquisition date.

---

[19] IRC §338.

20.11 Taxable Stock Acquisition

- New Target is deemed to have a purchase price and cost basis in the assets equal to the purchasing corporation's grossed-up basis in its target stock plus the amount of Old Target's liabilities (including any tax liability resulting from the deemed sale).

(d) Practical Consequences of a Section 338 Election

Old Target would close its taxable year at the end of the acquisition date. Old Target then must file a final short-period tax return on which it reports the gain or loss realized from the deemed sale. Old Target's tax attributes would be eliminated, and New Target would be "born" on the very next day with a stepped-up (or stepped-down) basis in its assets and no tax attributes. The election must be filed by the fifteenth day of the ninth month from the month in which the acquisition occurred.

From both a legal and accounting standpoint, the Section 338 election is meaningless. This transaction is for tax purposes only and impacts the target and the buyer alone. The seller is still viewed as selling stock. Because the buyer shoulders the economic cost of the section 338 election, the buyer would ordinarily not be made aware barring unusual circumstances. The current tax cost to obtain future tax benefits attributable to the step-up in the basis would be prohibitive. Still, the election can be a useful planning alternative under the right conditions, especially if the target's tax carryovers enhance the present value of the tax benefits.

Of greater usage in today's tax planning is another type of election permissible under Section 338. If the target corporation is a member of an affiliated group of corporations, typically filing a consolidated tax return or is classified as an "S" corporation, the target can make a Section 338(h)(10) election.[20] Both the purchaser and the seller consolidated group (or the "S" corporation shareholders) must agree for the Section 338 election to be made.

(e) Timing and Basis of Section 338(h)(10) Election

Although many of the rules governing the timing and availability of this election are the same as with a Section 338 election, the impact to the parties is materially different. The seller now becomes a party to the election and the economic cost. Generally, only in cases where the outside basis of the target stock exceeds the inside basis of the target assets will a seller resist joining in the election unless the buyer increases the purchase price to make up the difference.

The Section 338(h)(10) election allows a basis step-up in the assets of an acquired target corporation and permits the affiliated group—out of which the target subsidiary is sold—and the purchaser to jointly elect to treat the sale of the target's stock as an asset sale. Other consequences include the following:

- The gain on the constructive asset sale is included in the selling group's consolidated return.

---

[20] IRC §338(h)(10). In this scenario, the seller must be U.S. based, although the buyer can be foreign.

- No gain or loss is recognized on the sale of the target subsidiary's stock.
- After the constructive asset sale, Old Target is deemed to be liquidated into its parent, a member of the consolidated group in a nontaxable liquidation, and Old Target's tax attributes carry over to its parent.

(f) Planning Opportunities

Finally, evaluating the treatment of a taxable stock purchase should not stop at closing. If the purchase is but the first of a series of steps to liquidate the target corporation or merge it upstream into the purchasing corporation, the liquidation may be tax-free. If so, the acquiring corporation will take a carryover basis in the target corporation's assets, and its tax attributes will carry over to the acquiring corporation. The impact of making or not making a Section 338 election for the target needs to be considered. For example, if the election is not made, there may be a disallowance of the use of the target corporation's net operating loss carryovers if the liquidation occurs within two years of the stock purchase.[21]

20.12 CORPORATE DIVISIONS

Although a detailed discussion of corporate divisions is outside the scope of this chapter, the United States provides an extensive body of law governing the tax-free division of a single corporation (or corporate group) into two or more corporations (or corporate groups).[22] The benefits of qualifying can be significant to both corporations and their shareholders. The division is tax free at both levels. The U.S. Treasury has undertaken steps to reduce the tax efficiency of combining tax-free divisions with M & A strategies involving unrelated parties. Nevertheless, significant opportunities remain and should be explored under the right circumstances.

A corporate division may be effected pursuant to any one of three basic transactions. In discussing each of these transactions, it is assumed that the distributing corporation ("Distributing") owns all of the stock of the controlled corporation(s) ("Controlled").

- The most common type of division is a "spin-off." In a spin-off, stock of Controlled is distributed to shareholders of Distributing without any surrender of stock by them.
- A second approach is the "split-off." In a split-off, stock of Controlled is distributed to some shareholders of Distributing in exchange, generally, for all of their stock in Distributing.
- Finally, in a "split-up" transaction, stock of two or more Controlled corporations is distributed to the shareholders of Distributing in complete liquidation of Distributing.

---

[21] IRC §269(b).
[22] IRC §355.

Corporate divisions must meet the following requirements to be eligible for tax-free treatment:

1. The requisite "control" must exist. The control requirement for corporate divisions is met if Distributing owns at least 80 percent of the voting power of all the outstanding Controlled stock and at least 80 percent of each class of Controlled nonvoting stock.

2. Distributing must distribute either all of its Controlled stock or an amount of Controlled stock that represents control (i.e., greater than 80 percent of the voting and nonvoting stock).

3. The business involved in the corporate division must have been owned and been in active operation for at least five years.

Recent tax legislation now imposes tax recognition upon Distributing if the corporate division is part of a plan pursuant to which a third party acquires a greater than 50 percent or more interest in Distributing or Controlled within a two-year period from the date of the corporate division. Although these rules raise new obstacles to achieving tax-free treatment, M & A in connection with corporate divisions continue to attract considerable interest in the business and financial communities because of their potential to yield significant value to deal stakeholders.

20.13 INTERNATIONAL MERGERS AND ACQUISITIONS TRANSACTIONS

Much of the law governing M & A involving foreign-owned U.S. corporations or U.S.-owned foreign corporations stems from a policy to prevent the avoidance of U.S. tax that could otherwise arise when the corporate tax provisions apply to transactions that involve foreign corporations.[23] To effect this general policy of anti-avoidance, the U.S. tax regulations essentially prevent a foreign corporation from being able to benefit from tax-free treatment otherwise available under the normal rules applicable to U.S. corporations unless certain conditions (often with tax consequences) are met.

The regulations target three types of corporate transactions:

1. Outbound transfers of appreciated assets
2. Inbound asset repatriations that bring into U.S. corporate solution certain carryover earnings that have not been subject to U.S. corporate taxation
3. Foreign-to-foreign transfers that may impair the ability to tax a foreign corporation's earnings.[24]

---

[23] T.D. 8862.
[24] See Reg. §§ 367(b)-3 – (b)-5.

Unique rules exist for transactions involving real property entities, "passive foreign investment companies,"[25] and "controlled foreign corporations."

20.14 OUTBOUND TRANSACTIONS (U.S. TO FOREIGN)

In an outbound transaction, a U.S. person transfers property to a foreign entity. The transfer event can be either taxable or nontaxable. The consideration could be stock, assets, or some combination of both. With some exception, transfers to foreign entities that come within certain categories are taxable under the U.S. tax system. For example, when a U.S. person transfers appreciated stock in a U.S. corporation to a foreign corporation that the U.S. persons thereafter controls, the transaction is taxable.

(a) Taxable and Tax-Free Outbound Transactions

The U.S. tax rules do provide for tax-free transfers of a U.S. corporation's stock to a foreign corporation under limited circumstances. Generally, this exception allows for a widely held U.S. corporation to be acquired by a larger foreign corporation in a share-for-share transaction. Recent examples of the utilization of this exception are the DaimlerChrysler and Vodafone/Airtouch transactions. Furthermore, the provisions applicable to outbound transfers trigger only gain and do not operate to trigger built-in losses.[26]

Transactions that normally would be nontaxable face special scrutiny, such as those dealing with corporate formations, reorganizations, and liquidations.[27] The system is designed to essentially prevent the built-in appreciation on the property involved in the outbound transfer from escaping U.S. taxation. The character and source of the gain is determined by reference to the results of a hypothetical taxable sale in that the gain recognized is the same character and source that would have arisen had that property been disposed of in a taxable exchange with the foreign corporate transferee.

Corporate status will not be disregarded in all situations. For example, gain may not be triggered if property is transferred outside of the United States for use in the active conduct of the foreign corporate transferee's trade or business.

(b) Outbound Transfers of Intangible Assets

Outbound transfers of intangible assets are generally recast as taxable sales of intangibles in exchange for payments contingent upon the use, productivity, or disposition of such property.[28] Generally, payments must be contingent upon the productivity, use, or disposition of the intangible property; the amounts must rea-

---

[25] IRC §1297(f).
[26] IRC §367(a).
[27] IRC §367(a). Some provisions specifically mentioned are §§332, 351, 354, 356, and 361.
[28] IRC § 367(d) and Reg. §1.367(d).

20.15 Inbound Transactions (Foreign to U.S.)

sonably reflect the amounts that would have been paid annually over the useful life of the property; and finally, the amounts deemed received must be commensurate with the income attributable to the intangible.[29] Unlike an actual royalty payment under the U.S. tax system, this deemed and imputed royalty stream will typically not give rise to a corresponding deduction for foreign tax purposes. These rules should be reviewed before undertaking a transaction involving the outbound transfer of intangibles.

(c) Foreign Branches

In the context of M & A deals, many U.S. companies often open a foreign branch (to benefit from a flow-through of losses) with the goal of incorporating the branch once the foreign operations become profitable. The U.S. outbound transfer rules includes the incorporation of a foreign branch. The incorporation would be considered an "outbound transfer of assets" subject to special rules mentioned previously, among others.

20.15 INBOUND TRANSACTIONS (FOREIGN TO U.S.)

Complex U.S. tax rules address inbound transactions.[30] Outbound U.S. tax rules seek to prevent the expatriation of assets with built-in gains. The inbound rules seek to avoid the repatriation of earnings on a tax-free basis.

The general rule with regard to inbound transfers is that the transferor foreign corporation does not recognize gain in the United States. The transferor foreign corporation may be engaged in a U.S. trade or business. In that event, the reorganization does not affect the transferor's branch profits tax liability as long as the transferee domestic corporation executes an agreement with the IRS. This agreement would provide that the earnings and profits carry over from the foreign corporation to the domestic corporation.

Subject to certain exceptions, a shareholder may exchange the stock of a foreign corporation for the stock of an acquiring domestic corporation in a reorganization without recognizing gain. Unique rules, though, such as those governing treatment of a foreign investment company or a passive foreign investment company, raise many obstacles to tax-free treatment. Gain may be recognized in many instances.[31]

An inbound reorganization of a foreign corporation into a U.S. corporation raises fundamental questions of whether the U.S. corporation should receive a tax basis (even a carryover basis) in the assets of the foreign corporation if the foreign corporation's earnings have not been subject to U.S. tax. Under the current

---

[29] IRC § 367(d)(2)(A).
[30] IRC § 367(b) and related Treasury Regulations. Transactions covered are certain inbound reorganizations, certain § 351 contributions to U.S. corporations, certain § 332 liquidations, and certain § 355 distributions and transfers between foreign entities.
[31] IRC § 1297(f).

tax regulations, inbound liquidations of a foreign corporation generally require an inclusion of all or a portion of the foreign corporation's historic earnings as a dividend. The amount of the inclusion varies depending on whether the foreign corporation qualifies as a controlled foreign corporation and whether the shareholder receiving assets in the liquidation qualifies as a 10 percent shareholder. If the shareholder includes in income the appropriate earnings amount, the transaction, if otherwise tax-free under the general U.S. principles, will be tax-free.

20.16 FOREIGN TRANSACTIONS (FOREIGN TO FOREIGN)

The general rule relating to foreign-to-foreign transfers of stock and assets is that the transferor foreign corporation does not recognize gain, unless the regulations provide to the contrary.[32] In general, an exchanging shareholder must include in income as a deemed dividend the IRC Section 1248 amount[33] attributable to the stock that it exchanges in a foreign-to-foreign nonrecognition transaction when any of the following circumstances occur:

- Either the U.S. shareholder loses its Section 1248 shareholder status or the foreign acquired corporation ceases to be a controlled foreign corporation as a result of the exchange,[34] or the U.S. shareholder receives domestic stock in the exchange.
- When the exchanging shareholder receives preferred or other stock.[35]
- If certain recapitalizations occur.[36]

The section 1248 amount relates to the foreign corporation's earnings that were generated during the period the shareholder held the foreign corporation's shares. Transfers by significant shareholders (generally 5 percent or more) may require the filing of a gain recognition agreement (GRA). Under a GRA, the gain on the transaction is deferred as long as the acquiring entity retains the transferred property for five years or does not enter into a transaction that "triggers" the gain. The regulations include a list of factors to evaluate in determining whether a triggering transaction has occurred.

In the case of a second-tier (or lower) reorganization, the Section 1248 amount is moved up the chain by a preorganization deemed dividend (which is excluded from Subpart F income). As a result, the Section 1248 amount is not triggered into income but is preserved and deferred as an adjustment to the earnings and profits pool of the foreign exchanging shareholder.

---

[32] IRC § 367(b) and Reg. §1.367(b)-4.
[33] As defined in Reg. §1.367(b)-2(b) and (c). An IRC § 1248 shareholder is a U.S. person that satisfies the ownership requirements of § 1248(a)(2) or § 1248(c)(2) with respect to a foreign corporation. In the case of a foreign exchanging shareholder, the foreign shareholder's § 1248 amount is generally determined as if the foreign shareholder were a U.S. person.
[34] As defined in Reg. § 1.367(b)-2(a).
[35] As described in Reg. Section 1.367(b)-4(b)(2).
[36] As described in Reg. Section 1.367(b)-4(b)(3).

20.17 CONSOLIDATED RETURN RULES

In the United States, members of an affiliated group of corporations are allowed to elect to file a consolidated federal income tax return. The following requirements must be met to constitute an affiliated group of corporations.:

- A corporation must be an "includible corporation."
- All includible corporations must pass a "stock ownership test."[37]

An "includible corporation" (subject to some exceptions) is generally any corporation *other than:*

- A corporation exempt from tax
- A foreign corporation
- A regulated investment company
- A life insurance company
- A domestic international sales corporation (DISC)
- A foreign sales corporation (FSC)
- A company electing a Section 936 credit[38]

A company meets the "stock ownership test" if there is an "includible parent corporation" and there is an includible corporation other than a parent corporation (i.e., a subsidiary). The parent requirement is met when a single corporation directly "controls" the stock of at least one of the other includible corporations.[39] The subsidiary requirement is met when one or more of the other members of the affiliated group "controls" a subsidiary. "Control" means the direct possession of at least 80 percent of the voting stock and at least 80 percent of the value of stock in a corporation.[40]

The major benefit of filing a consolidated return is that the losses incurred by one member of the group may be used to offset the income of other group members. This availability of losses has the effect of the group receiving a current tax benefit for the loss without having to carry over any unused losses to other years. Other benefits include the following:

- The deferral of taxation on intercompany profits from the sale of services and property between members of the affiliated group
- Intercompany dividends between group members
- Deductions and credits ordinarily subject to percentage limitations on a separate company basis are now limited on a consolidated basis

---

37 IRC §1504.
38 IRC §1504(b).
39 IRC §1504(a)(1).
40 IRC §1504(a)(2).

There are, however, some disadvantages of electing to file a consolidated tax return:

- Once the election is made, it is irrevocable unless terminated by disbanding the group or by IRS permission.
- This election may have the effect of requiring certain subsidiaries to change their tax years to conform to the common parent's year.
- The election may limit carryover of tax attributes.
- The election potentially may cause other attributes to expire.
- In addition, losses on the sale of a subsidiary's stock are generally not deductible in computing a parent's taxable income.
- Maybe most important, each member of the group is jointly and severally liable for the group's entire federal tax liability, not just its pro-rata share of that liability.

20.18 TAX ATTRIBUTES

This chapter briefly touches upon the impact of various structures on the ability to use the target's tax attributes after it has been acquired. The term *tax attributes* tends to refer to tax loss and credit carryovers of the target, but tax attributes can mean much more. Tax attributes can include the following:

- The target's tax year
- Its tax accounting elections
- Depreciation methodologies
- Tax basis
- Earnings and profits history
- A favorable tax ruling

At times, the value of these attributes is not really reflected on the balance sheet. Additional probing is necessary to make sure all material tax variables have been priced into the deal.

Given that operating losses in the United States may be carried forward 20 years (as well as carried back two years), acquisition agreements should be specific regarding the party entitled to the benefits. Furthermore, numerous U.S. rules may limit the use of carryovers or carrybacks after an acquisition, especially for a target becoming a member of a group filing U.S. consolidated returns.

One attribute deserving of special note because of its frequent applicability in M & A transactions involves the imposition of an annual limitation on the use of a target's loss carryovers after a more than 50 percent point change in the target's ownership within a three-year testing period. The limit is equal to the value of target's stock immediately before the ownership change times the long-term tax exempt bond rate for the month in which the change occurred.

Index

A

(a)(2)(E) reorganization, U.S., 20-11
Abnormal Management Act, France, 6-21–6-22
Abuse of law theory, France, 6-21
Accrual tax rule, Australia, 2-16–2-17
Acquisition of control rules, Canada, 4-8
Acquisition tax, Korea, 12-2
Acquisitive "D" reorganization, U.S., 20-9–20-10
Active entity requirement, Argentina, 1-12
Ad valorem duty, Australia, 2-22
Advance pricing agreements, Netherlands, 14-12–14-13
Advertising tax:
    Russia, 16-5
    Ukraine, 18-5
Alternative minimum tax (AMT), U.S., 20-4
Amalgamation transactions, *see* Mergers
Anti-avoidance provisions:
    Australia, 2-25–2-26
    France, 6-21
    Germany, 7-40, 7-45
    Ireland, 8-10
    Italy, 9-8–9-9
    Mexico, 13-24, 13-25
    Norway, 15-10
    Spain, 17-16
    United Kingdom, 19-3, 19-4
Anti-monopoly regulations:
    Australia, 2-25–2-26
    Azerbaijan, 3-7–3-8
    Japan, 10-16
    Kazakhstan, 11-11–11-12
    Russia, 16-7–16-8, 16-10, 16-17
    Ukraine, 18-10–18-12
Argentina, 1-1–1-18
    asset acquisition, 1-5–1-8
    reorganization, 1-10–1-16
    sales/transfers within business group, 1-16–1-17
    share acquisition, 1-8–1-10
    tax law, 1-3–1-5
Arm's length transactions:
    Australia, 2-9, 2-19
    Mexico, 13-22
    Netherlands, 14-4, 14-17
    United Kingdom, 19-8
Asset acquisitions:
    Argentina, 1-5–1-8
    Australia, 2-7–2-9, 2-16, 2-22–2-23
    Azerbaijan, 3-11–3-15
    Canada, 4-12–4-14
    Finland, 5-5–5-6
    France, 6-29–6-33
    Germany, 7-18–7-27
    Ireland, 8-10–8-12
    Japan, 10-6, 10-8–10-11, 10-16
    Kazakhstan, 11-14–11-19
    Korea, 12-1–12-2, 12-3
    Mexico, 13-21–13-26
    Netherlands, 14-14–14-17
    Norway, 15-4–15-5
    Russia, 16-8–16-9, 16-12–16-16
    Ukraine, 18-12–18-15
    United States, 20-8–20-13
Assets tax, Mexico, 13-11, 13-17, 13-18–13-19, 13-26
Asset step-up, Germany, 7-18–7-19
Australia, 2-1–2-26
    asset acquisition, 2-7–2-9, 2-16, 2-22–2-23
    Australia to foreign investment, 2-15–2-17
    business tax reform, 2-14, 2-15, 2-16, 2-17–2-19
    foreign to Australia investment, 2-14–2-15
    goods and services tax, 2-20–2-22
    merger and acquisition options, 2-6–2-7
    scrip acquisition, 2-2, 2-9–2-14
    share acquisition, 2-16–2-17, 2-21–2-22, 2-23
    stamp duty, 2-22–2-24
    tax law, 2-24–2-26

I-1

Australia *(cont'd)*
Average cost per share, Mexico, 13-20–13-21, 13-29–13-31
Azerbaijan, 3-1–3-24
    asset acquisition, 3-11–3-15
    financing structures, 3-19–3-21
    reorganization, 3-15–3-19
    repatriation of capital/profits, 3-21–3-24
    share acquisition, 3-9–3-11
    tax law, 3-2–3-3

B

Barter exchange, Kazakhstan, 11-17
Bonds, France, 6-32
"Boot," U.S., 20-10–20-11
"B" reorganization, U.S., 20-11
Business succession principle, Finland, 5-9, 5-10

C

Canada, 4-1–4-23
    amalgamation transactions, 4-19–4-20
    asset acquisition, 4-12–4-14
    business structure alternatives, 4-8–4-10
    disposition of taxable property by nonresidents, 4-10–4-12
    exchange of shares, 4-17–4-21
    FIE rules, proposed, 4-21–4-22
    financing structures, 4-22
    foreign purchasers, 4-20
    repatriation of profit, 4-16–4-17
    share acquisition, 4-14–4-16
    tax law, 4-3–4-8
    thin capitalization rules, 4-22–4-23
Capital cost allowances (CCA), Canada, 4-4, 4-7–4-8
Capital duty, Ireland, 8-5
Capital expenditures, Australia, 2-5–2-6
Capital gains tax:
    Argentina, 1-4
    Australia, 2-10–2-14
    Canada, 4-10
    Finland, 5-2–5-4
    Germany, 7-11–7-12, 7-24, 7-25–7-27
    Ireland, 8-4–8-5, 8-11
    Korea, 12-3
    Russia, 16-4
    Spain, 17-5–17-6
    United Kingdom, 19-3
    United States, 20-4
Capital investment relief, Azerbaijan, 3-13
Capital redemptions, Mexico, 13-17, 13-24–13-25
Carryover of tax attributes:
    Germany, 7-21–7-22
    Japan, 10-8
    Kazakhstan, 11-21
    Mexico, 13-10
    Russia, 16-18
    Spain, 17-11–17-12
    Ukraine, 18-24
    United States, 20-22
Check-the-box regulations, U.S., 14-21, 20-6
Chernobyl Disaster Fund, 18-5
Choice of entity:
    Azerbaijan, 3-6–3-7
    Germany, 7-43
    Japan, 10-3
    Kazakhstan, 11-7–11-9
    Korea, 12-4
    Netherlands, 14-20–14-21
    United States, 20-5–20-6
Church tax, Germany, 7-7
Chusik Hoesa (CH), Korea, 12-4
Clearance certificate, Canada, 4-12
Closed joint stock company:
    Kazakhstan, 11-8–11-9
    Russia, 16-6
    Ukraine, 18-7–18-8
Competition policy, Australia, 2-25–2-26
Consolidated return rules, U.S., 20-21–20-22
Consolidation, *see also* Mergers
    Kazakhstan, 11-21–11-22
    Mexico, 13-12
Consortium, Kazakhstan, 11-21–11-22
Consumption tax, Japan, 10-5, 10-10, 10-11
Continuity of business doctrine:
    Argentina, 1-12
    United States, 20-8
Contractual asset acquisition, U.S., 20-12–20-13
Contribution of assets:
    Finland, 5-9–5-10
    France, 6-12–6-16

Index

Conversion, Argentina, 1-11
Convertible bonds, France, 6-32
Corporate income tax:
    Argentina, 1-3–1-4, 1-4, 1-6, 1-7–1-8
    Australia, 2-3–2-4
    Azerbaijan, 3-11
    Canada, 4-2–4-3
    Finland, 5-2–5-4
    Germany, 7-8
    Kazakhstan, 11-15–11-16, 11-18
    Korea, 12-2
    Mexico, 13-17–13-18
    Norway, 15-2–15-3, 15-4–15-6
    Spain, 17-5–17-7
    United States, 20-4
Corporate profits tax:
    Azerbaijan, 3-3
    Russia, 16-4, 16-11, 16-13, 16-14–16-15
    Ukraine, 18-4
Corporate tax:
    Ireland, 8-3–8-4
    Japan, 10-3–10-4
    Ukraine, 18-4–18-6
"C" reorganization, U.S., 20-9
Cross-border transactions, Norway, 15-10
Currency control:
    Australia, 2-26
    Azerbaijan, 3-7
    Japan, 10-16
    Kazakhstan, 11-6–11-7, 11-22–11-23
    Russia, 16-7, 16-10, 16-21, 16-22
    Ukraine, 18-6–18-7
Customs duties:
    Azerbaijan, 3-4
    Russia, 16-4
    Ukraine, 18-4

    Germany, 7-9, 7-11, 7-16–7-17, 7-23, 7-43
    Ireland, 8-4, 8-5–8-6, 8-14
    Japan, 10-4
    Korea, 12-2
    Netherlands, 14-4, 14-13, 14-19
    Norway, 15-7
    Russia, 16-9, 16-23
    United Kingdom, 19-2
    United States, 20-4
Division, of company:
    Finland, 5-8–5-9
    France, 6-16–6-17
    Italy, 9-2–9-3
    Japan, 10-12–10-13
    Kazakhstan, 11-20–11-21
    Norway, 15-9–15-10
    Russia, 16-16–16-17
    Ukraine, 18-21–18-24
    United States, 20-16
Double taxation:
    Australia, 2-6, 2-13, 2-14
    Canada, 4-3, 4-13
    France, 6-3, 6-10, 6-14, 6-27, 6-30
    Germany, 7-9, 7-11
    Ireland, 8-14
    Netherlands, 14-4, 14-8, 14-13, 14-19
    Norway, 15-5
    Spain, 17-13–17-15
    United Kingdom, 19-5–19-6
    United States, 20-4
Dropdown, Ireland, 8-9–8-10
Due diligence:
    Germany, 7-5–7-6
    Japan, 10-10
    Russia, 16-12

D

Deemed dividends, Canada, 4-14–4-15
Deferral instruments, Germany, 7-37–7-38
Demergers, *see* Division, of company
Depreciation deduction, Australia, 2-8–2-9
Dividends:
    Argentina, 1-9
    Australia, 2-12–2-16
    Azerbaijan, 3-9, 3-24
    Canada, 4-14–4-15
    Finland, 5-2–5-4
    France, 6-24–6-25

E

88(1)(d) bump, Canada, 4-16
Employee entitlements, Australia, 2-9
Employee profit-sharing, Mexico, 13-14
Estimated tax payments, Mexico, 13-11–13-12, 13-17–13-19
European Union Directive on Mergers:
    France and, 6-11–6-12
    Germany and, 7-40–7-41
    Norway and, 15-7
Exchange of shares:
    Canada, 4-17–4-21
    Finland, 5-10–5-11
    Ireland, 8-7

Exchange of shares (*cont'd*)
    Italy, 9-7–9-8
    Japan, 10-11
    Spain, 17-4, 17-8, 17-13
    United States, 20-11
Excise taxes:
    Azerbaijan, 3-4
    Kazakhstan, 11-5
    Russia, 16-5
    Ukraine, 18-5
Exempt entities, Australia, 2-9
Exit tax:
    Germany, 7-24, 7-43
    Ireland, 8-16
    Japan, 10-14–10-15
    Netherlands, 14-16

F

Fair market value:
    Azerbaijan, 3-5–3-6
    France, 6-6
    Japan, 10-9–10-10
Fictional interposition, Italy, 9-8
FIE rules, Canada, 4-21–4-22
Finance leasing law, Kazakhstan, 11-15
Financing structures, *see also* Thin capitalization rules
    Australia, 2-9–2-11, 2-15–2-16, 2-19
    Azerbaijan, 3-19–3-21
    France, 6-18–6-23, 6-27–6-28, 6-31–6-33
    Germany, 7-16–7-17, 7-28–7-37, 7-43–7-44, 7-47–7-48
    Ireland, 8-12–8-14
    Kazakhstan, 11-14–11-15, 11-22
    Netherlands, 14-5–14-7, 14-18–14-20
    Russia, 16-19–16-21
    Ukraine, 18-25–18-28
    United Kingdom, 19-2, 19-4–19-5, 19-7–19-8
    United States, 20-7–20-8
Finland, 5-1–5-11
    asset acquisition, 5-5–5-6
    contribution of assets, 5-9–5-10
    divisions, 5-8–5-9
    exchange of shares, 5-10–5-11
    imputation system, 5-2–5-4
    mergers, 5-6–5-8
    share acquisition, 5-4–5-5
    tax law, 5-2

Fiscal unity, Netherlands, 14-6–14-7, 14-11–14-12, 14-17
Fixed assets:
    Argentina, 1-7
    Australia, 2-5–2-6, 2-8–2-9
    Azerbaijan, 3-12–3-13
    Canada, 4-4, 4-7–4-8
    Finland, 5-6
    Ireland, 8-4
    Mexico, 13-21
    Norway, 15-2–15-3
    Russia, 16-15
Foreign ownership/investment policy:
    Australia, 2-24–2-26
    Azerbaijan, 3-8
    Canada, 4-2
    Ireland, 8-15–8-16
    Japan, 10-3
    Kazakhstan, 11-13
    Netherlands, 14-7, 14-8, 14-9
    Russia, 16-8
    Ukraine, 18-12–18-14, 18-29
Foreign tax credits, Mexico, 13-11, 13-17
Forward cash merger, U.S., 20-13
France, 6-1–6-33
    asset acquisition, 6-29–6-33
    divisions, 6-16–6-17
    hybrid financing instruments, 6-31–6-33
    mergers, 6-4–6-16
    share acquisition, 6-18–6-28
    tax law, 6-3–6-4
Franking account, Australia, 2-3–2-4
Fraud, *see* Anti-avoidance provisions

G

Gain recognition agreement (GRA), U.S., 20-20
General partnership, *see* Partnerships
Germany, 7-1–7-48
    2001 tax reform highlights, 7-10–7-13
    asset step-up, 7-18–7-19
    carryover of tax attributes, 7-21–7-22
    consolidation requirements, revised, 7-13
    deferral instruments, 7-37–7-38
    financing structures, 7-16–7-17
    joint ventures and mergers of equals, 7-41–7-45
    M & A market in, 7-3–7-5

M & A tax consulting in, 7-5–7-7
partnership acquisition, 7-31–7-33
pooling of profits and losses,
    7-19–7-20
public offering, 7-45–7-48
real estate transfer tax, 7-20–7-21
reorganization, 7-38–7-41
sale of shares, 7-25–7-27
share acquisition, 7.27, 7-33–7-37
tax law, 7-7–7-13
thin capitalization rules, 7-13–7-15
Gift tax, Germany, 7-9, 7-48
Going concern sale:
    Argentina, 1-5–1-6
    Australia, 2-21
    Azerbaijan, 3-13
    France, 6-23–6-24
    Italy, 9-5–9-7
    Mexico, 13-23
    Netherlands, 14-15
Goods and services tax (GST), Australia,
    2-20–2-22
Goodwill:
    Argentina, 1-8, 1-10
    Australia, 2-6, 2-22–2-23
    Canada, 4-10
    Finland, 5-6
    France, 6-23
    Germany, 7-18–7-19
    Japan, 10-7, 10-8–10-9, 10-11
    Kazakhstan, 11-19
    Korea, 12-3
    Mexico, 13-22
    Netherlands, 14-3, 14-14, 14-18
    Norway, 15-5
    Russia, 16-15
    Spain, 17-8–17-11
    Ukraine, 18-15
    United Kingdom, 19-3–19-4
Group relief:
    Finland, 5-4
    Ireland, 8-7–8-8, 8-13
    United Kingdom, 19-2, 19-9
    United States, 20-21

H

Holding company:
    Germany, 7-15
    Korea, 12-4
    Netherlands, 14-19–14-20
    Russia, 16-9–16-10
    United Kingdom, 19-5, 19-6
Holding requirement, Argentina, 1-12
Hybrid financing instruments:
    France, 6-31–6-33
    Germany, 7-23
    United Kingdom, 19-5

I

Imputation system:
    Australia, 2-3–2-4
    Finland, 5-2–5-4
    Germany, 7-10
Income attribution, Australia, 2-16–2-17
Income tax, *see* Corporate income tax;
    Individual income tax
Increased Value of Immovable Goods
    (NVIM), Italy, 9-4–9-5
Indexation allowance, United Kingdom,
    19-1
Individual income tax:
    Australia, 2-3–2-4
    Azerbaijan, 3-4
    France, 6-7–6-8
    Germany, 7-7
    Kazakhstan, 11-4
    Russia, 16-5, 16-11
    Spain, 17-5–17-7
    Ukraine, 18-5, 18-23–18-24
Inheritance tax, Germany, 7-9, 7-48
Initial public offering, Japan, 10-15
In-kind contribution, Spain, 17-13, 17-4
Input tax credits, Australia, 2-20–2-22
Intangible assets, *see also* Goodwill
    Argentina, 1-7
    Azerbaijan, 3-13
    Canada, 4-10
    France, 6-23
    Germany, 7-19
    Mexico, 13-27
    Netherlands, 14-3
    United Kingdom, 19-3–19-4
    United States, 20-19–20-20
Intellectual property, *see* Intangible
    assets
Interest:
    Azerbaijan, 3-20, 3-23–3-24
    Canada, 4-4, 4-22
    France, 6-18–6-19

Interest (cont'd)
    Germany, 7-9, 7-16, 7-22–7-23, 7-32, 7-36
    Ireland, 8-6
    Japan, 10-5, 10-7, 10-15
    Netherlands, 14-4, 14-5–14-7, 14-15, 14-16, 14-18–14-19, 14-20
    Russia, 16-20–16-21, 16-23
    Ukraine, 18-26
    United Kingdom, 19-2, 19-5, 19-7
Invalid duty, Azerbaijan, 3-4
Inventory:
    Australia, 2-8
    Mexico, 13-11, 13-22
    Norway, 15-2
    Russia, 16-14
Ireland, 8-1–8-16
    asset acquisition, 8-10–8-12
    financial structures, 8-12–8-14
    mergers, 8-15
    other legal structures, 8-15–8-16
    outbound investment, 8-14–8-15
    share acquisition, 8-8–8-10, 8-12–8-14
    tax law, 8-2–8-8
    transaction structures, 8-8–8-10
Italy, 9-1–9-9
    anti-avoidance provisions, 9-8–9-9
    capital contributions, 9-6–9-7
    direct taxation, 9-2–9-4
    exchange of shares, 9-7–9-8
    going concern sale, 9-5–9-6
    indirect taxation, 9-4–9-5

J

Japan, 10-1–10-16
    asset acquisition, 10-6, 10-8–10-11, 10-16
    exchange of shares, 10-11
    exit strategies, 10-14–10-15
    legal preparation, 10-15–10-16
    reorganization, 10-12–10-14
    share acquisition, 10-6–10-8
    tax laws, 10-2–10-6
Joining, Ukraine, 18-19–18-21
Joint stock company:
    Azerbaijan, 3-6–3-7, 3-11
    Russia, 16-6
    Ukraine, 18-7–18-8, 18-15–18-18, 18-19

Joint ventures:
    Australia, 2-5–2-6
    Germany, 7-41–7-45
    Ireland, 8-15

K

Kazakhstan, 11-1–11-25
    anti-monopoly provisions, 11-11–11-12
    asset acquisition, 11-14–11-19
    consolidation, 11-21–11-22
    corporate law, 11-7–11-9
    divisions, 11-20–11-21
    financing structures, 11-22
    mergers, 11-20
    repatriation of capital/profits, 11-22–11-23
    securities law, 11-9–11-11
    share acquisition, 11-10–11-11, 11-18, 11-19
    tax law, 11-3–11-5
Korea, 12-1–12-4
    asset acquisition, 12-1–12-2, 12-3
    financial structures, 12-4
    share acquisition, 12-1, 12-2–12-3

L

Land-rich provisions, Australia, 2-23
Land tax, see Real estate tax
Large Corporations Tax (LCT), Canada, 4-6
Leasing:
    Azerbaijan, 3-22–3-24
    Mexico, 13-26
    Russia, 16-23
    Ukraine, 18-26–18-27
Legal entity, see Choice of entity
Legal reserve, Argentina, 1-3, 1-10
Limited liability company (LLC):
    Azerbaijan, 3-7
    Kazakhstan, 11-8–11-9
    Korea, 12-4
    Russia, 16-6–16-7
    Ukraine, 18-7–18-9
Limited partnerships, see Partnerships
Loans, see Financing structures

Index

Local taxes:
    Azerbaijan, 3-5
    Canada, 4-3, 4-4–4-5
    Germany, 7-7, 7-8–7-9
    Russia, 16-5–16-6
    United States, 20-5
Location of business, Germany,
    7-42–7-45
Loss carryforwards:
    Australia, 2-11–2-12
    Canada, 4-7
    Germany, 7-45
    Ireland, 8-7, 8-11
    Italy, 9-3
    Japan, 10-4–10-5
    Kazakhstan, 11-15–11-16
    Korea, 12-3
    Mexico, 13-11, 13-13, 13-23–13-24
    Netherlands, 14-4
    Norway, 15-8, 15-9
    Russia, 16-19
    Spain, 17-11–17-12
    United States, 20-4, 20-22
Loss integrity measures, Australia, 2-12

M

Management fees:
    Azerbaijan, 3-22
    Russia, 16-22
Mergers, *see also* Consolidation;
    Contribution of assets
    Argentina, 1-11
    Canada, 4-19–4-20
    Finland, 5-6–5-8
    France, 6-4–6-9
    Germany, 7-41–7-45
    Ireland, 8-15
    Italy, 9-2–9-4
    Japan, 10-14
    Kazakhstan, 11-20
    Mexico, 13-2–13-5, 13-8–13-14
    Netherlands, 14-10–14-11
    Norway, 15-7–15-9
    Russia, 16-16–16-17
    Spain, 17-2, 17-7
    Ukraine, 18-9–18-10, 18-18–18-21,
        18-19–18-21
Mexico, 13-1–13-31
    asset acquisition, 13-21–13-26
    mergers, 13-2–13-5, 13-8–13-14

    selection of purchaser, 13-25–13-27
    share acquisition, 13-20–13-23,
        13-25–13-26, 13-29–13-31
    spin-offs, 13-5–13-8, 13-14–13-20
Minerals resource tax, Azerbaijan, 3-4

N

Nakhichevan, Republic of, 3-5
Net after-tax profits account (CUFIN),
    Mexico, 13-11, 13-16
Netherlands, 14-1–14-22
    asset acquisition, 14-14–14-17
    partnerships, 14-21
    planning opportunities, 14-20–14-21
    share acquisition, 14-14, 14-17–14-20
    tax law, 14-2–14-14
Noncompete agreements:
    Argentina, 1-8
    Germany, 7-19
Norway, 15-1–15-10
    anti-avoidance rules, 15-10
    asset acquisition, 15-4–15-5
    cross-border transactions, 15-10
    divisions, 15-7–15-10
    share acquisition, 15-5–15-7
    tax law, 15-1–15-3
Notarization, Ukraine, 18-13,
    18-14–18-15
Nova Scotia unlimited liability company
    (NS ULC), 4-9–4-10, 4-17

O

Offshore holding company, Ireland, 8-14
Open joint stock company:
    Russia, 16-6
    Ukraine, 18-7–18-8
Organschaft, 7-20, 7-13, 7-34–7-35

P

Partial merger, *see* Contribution of assets
Participation exemption, Netherlands,
    14-8, 14-9, 14-13, 14-18
Participation requirement, Argentina,
    1-12

Partnerships:
    Australia, 2-4–2-5, 2-18
    Germany, 7-31–7-33
    Ireland, 8-15
    Kazakhstan, 11-7–11-8, 11-21–11-22
    Netherlands, 14-21
    Ukraine, 18-7, 18-23
    United States, 20-6
Plant and equipment, *see* Fixed assets
Pooled development fund, Australia, 2-4
Pooling of profits and losses, Germany, 7-19–7-20
Prior activity requirements, Argentina, 1-12–1-13
Production cooperative, Kazakhstan, 11-8
Production sharing agreements (PSAs), Azerbaijan, 3-2, 3-3
Profit-sharing, Mexico, 13-14
Property tax, *see* Real estate tax
Publication/registration requirements, Argentina, 1-13–1-14
Public offering:
    France, 6-30–6-31
    Germany, 7-45–7-48
    Japan, 10-15

Q

Quasi-ownership right, Australia, 2-9

R

Rapid merger alternative, France, 6.26-23
Real estate tax:
    Argentina, 1-9
    Australia, 2-23
    Azerbaijan, 3-4, 3-12, 3-14
    Canada, 4-10–4-12
    France, 6-4, 6-5, 6-23
    Germany, 7-9, 7-10, 7-20–7-21
    Korea, 12-2
    Mexico, 13-9, 13-15
    Netherlands, 14-4, 14-13–14-14
    Russia, 16-5, 16-16
    Spain, 17-5, 17-13
    Ukraine, 18-5
Redemption of shares:
    Azerbaijan, 3-24
    Russia, 16-23

Registration duty, *see* Stamp tax
Reinvested net after-tax profits account (CUFINRE), Mexico, 13-10, 13-16
Reinvestment reserve, Netherlands, 14-15–14-16
Related persons, Azerbaijan, 3-5, 3-20–3-21
Reorganization:
    Argentina, 1-10–1-16
    Australia, 2-24
    Azerbaijan, 3-15–3-19
    Germany, 7-38–7-41, 7-43
    Ireland, 8-7
    Japan, 10-12–10-14
    Russia, 16-8–16-9, 16-16–16-19
    Ukraine, 18-9
    United States, 20-8
Repatriation of capital/profits:
    Azerbaijan, 3-21–3-24
    Canada, 4-16–4-17
    Japan, 10-8, 10-15
    Kazakhstan, 11-22–11-23
    Russia, 16-22–16-24
    Ukraine, 18-28–18-29
Reverse cash merger, U.S., 20-14
Reverse triangular merger, U.S., 20-11
RISK adjustments, Norway, 15-5, 15-6
Road use tax:
    Azerbaijan, 3-4
    Russia, 16-5, 16-14
Rollover regime, *see* Spain
Rollover relief:
    Australia, 2-5, 2-7, 2-10, 2-13
    Canada, 4-13–4-14, 4-17–4-19
    Ireland, 8-11
Royalties, *see also* Intangible assets
    Australia, 2-14
    Azerbaijan, 3-22
    Germany, 7-9, 7-19
    Russia, 16-22
Russia, 16-1–16-24
    anti-monopoly regulation, 16-7–16-8
    asset acquisition, 16-8–16-9, 16-12–16-16
    commercial/corporate law, 16-6–16-7
    currency control, 16-7, 16-10, 16-21, 16-22
    financing structures, 16-19–16-21
    foreign ownership restrictions, 16-8
    reorganization, 16-8–16-9, 16-16–16-19

Index

repatriation of capital/profits, 16-22–16-24
share acquisition, 16-8–16-12
tax law/legal system, 16-3–16-6

S

"S," corporation, 20-15
Safe harbor debt ratio, Australia, 2-19
Safe harbors, Germany, 7-14–7-15, 7-44
Sale of enterprise, Kazakhstan, 11-17–11-18
Sale of shares:
    Germany, 7-25–7-27
    Russia, 16-24
Sale of substantial participation, Italy, 9-5–9-6
Sales tax, Russia, 16-5
Same business test, Australia, 2-11–2-12
Scrip acquisition, Australia, 2-2, 2-9–2-14. *See also* Share acquisition
Section 338 election, U.S., 20-14–20-16
Securities law, Kazakhstan, 11-9–11-11
Share acquisition, *see also* Scrip acquisition
    Argentina, 1-8–1-10
    Australia, 2-16–2-17, 2-21–2-22, 2-23
    Azerbaijan, 3-9–3-11
    Canada, 4-14–4-16
    Finland, 5-4-5-5
    France, 6-18–6-28
    Germany, 7-27, 7-33–7-37
    Ireland, 8-8–8-10, 8-12–8-14
    Japan, 10-6–10-8
    Kazakhstan, 11-10–11-11, 11-18, 11-19
    Korea, 12-1, 12-2–12-3
    Mexico, 13-20–13-23, 13-25–13-26, 13-29–13-31
    Netherlands, 14-14, 14-17–14-20
    Norway, 15-5–15-7
    Russia, 16-8–16-12
    Ukraine, 18-15–18-18
    United States, 20-11–20-16
Share-for-share transactions, *see* Exchange of shares
Shareholders, *see* Individual income tax
"Significant" investments, Germany, 7-25–7-26

Social program liabilities:
    Argentina, 1-9–1-10
    Azerbaijan, 3-4
    Russia, 16-5
    Ukraine, 18-6
Societas Europeae (SE), France, 6-10
Solidarity surcharge, Germany, 7-8
Spain, 17-1–17-16
    allocation of income, 17-16
    corporate/personal income tax, 17-5–17-7
    double taxation avoidance, 17-13–17-15
    entity definitions, 17-1–17-4
    goodwill, 17-8–17-11
    in-kind contributions, 17-4, 17-13
    shareholders/partners, 17-7–17-8
Spin-offs:
    Argentina, 1-15–1-16
    France, 6-16–6-17
    Germany, 7-39–7-40
    Japan, 10-14
    Kazakhstan, 11-20–11-21
    Russia, 16-17–16-18
    Spain, 17-3–17-4, 17-7
    Ukraine, 18-22–18-24
    United States, 20-16
Split-offs:
    Mexico, 13-5–13-8, 13-14–13-20
    Netherlands, 14-11
Split-ups:
    Kazakhstan, 11-20–11-21
    Netherlands, 14-11
    Russia, 16-17–16-18
    Ukraine, 18-21–18-24
Stamp tax/duty:
    Argentina, 1-5, 1-8, 1-15
    Australia, 2-22–2-24
    France, 6-3, 6-5, 6-14
    Ireland, 8-5, 8-7, 8-8–8-9, 8-11
    Italy, 9-4, 9-6
    Japan, 10-5
    Korea, 12-2
    Norway, 15-3
    United Kingdom, 19-2, 19-4, 19-7, 19-8–19-9
Statutory "A" mergers, U.S., 20-9
Subsoil use contract, Kazakhstan, 11-4, 11-5, 11-22
Superannuation fund, Australia, 2-4

T

Taper relief, United Kingdom, 19-4
Tax law:
    Argentina, 1-3–1-5
    Australia, 2-24–2-26
    Azerbaijan, 3-2–3-8
    Canada, 4-3–4-8
    Finland, 5-1–5-2
    France, 6-3–6-4
    Germany, 7-7–7-13
    Japan, 10-2–10-6
    Kazakhstan, 11-3–11-5
    Netherlands, 14-4–14-14
    Russia, 16-3–16-6
    Ukraine, 18-2–18-12, 18-25
    United States, 20-3–20-5
Tax on minimum presumed income (TMPI), Argentina, 1-4, 1-14–1-15
Tax planning, Germany, 7-5–7-7
Tax treaties:
    Canada, 4-2, 4-8–4-9, 4-12, 4-15
    Germany, 7-24, 7-44
    Ireland, 8-13–8-14
    Japan, 10-7, 10-14–10-15
    Mexico, 13-24, 13-26
    Russia, 16-9, 16-20–16-21
    United Kingdom, 19-5, 19-8
Thin capitalization rules:
    Australia, 2-15, 2-18–2-19
    Azerbaijan, 3-21
    Canada, 4-22–4-23
    France, 6-19–6-20
    Germany, 7-13–7-15, 7-33, 7-34, 7-44
    Japan, 10-5, 10-10
    United Kingdom, 19-7–19-8
351 transaction, U.S., 20-10–20-11, 20-12
Trade debts, Australia, 2-8
Trademarks, France, 6-23
Trade tax:
    France, 6-5
    Germany, 7-8–7-9
Transfer of rights/obligations, Argentina, 1-14, 1-17
Transfer pricing regulations:
    Australia, 2-15
    Azerbaijan, 3-5
    Kazakhstan, 11-16–11-17
    Mexico, 13-22
    Netherlands, 14-4
    Russia, 16-6, 16-21
Transformation, Ukraine, 18-20
Trusts, Australia, 2-4

U

Ukraine, 18-1–18-29
    asset acquisition, 18-12–18-15
    carryover of tax attributes, 18-24
    divisions, 18-21–18-24
    financing structures, 18-25–18-28
    mergers, 18-18–18-21
    repatriation of capital/profits, 18-28–18-29
    share acquisition, 18-15–18-18
    tax law, 18-2–18-12, 18-25
Unfranked dividend, Australia, 2-13
Unified social tax, Russia, 16-5
Uniform entity regime, Australia, 2-19
United Kingdom, 19-1–19-9
    foreign to UK acquisitions, 19-7–19-9
    UK to foreign acquisitions, 19-4–19-7
    UK to UK acquisitions, 19-1–19-4
United States, 20-1–20-22
    choice of entity, 20-5–20-6
    consolidated return rules, 20-21–20-22
    divisions, 20-16
    foreign to foreign transactions, 20-20
    foreign to U.S. transactions, 20-19–20-20
    tax attributes, 20-22
    tax law, 20-3–20-5
    U. S. to foreign transactions, 20-18–20-19
    U.S. to U.S. acquisitions, 20-6–20-17
    asset, 20-8–20-13
    stock, 20-13–20-16
Unitrusts, Australia, 2-4
Unlimited liability company (ULC), Canada, 4-9–4-10, 4-17
Urban land appreciation tax, Spain, 17-5, 17-13

V

Value-added tax (VAT), *see also* Goods and services tax (GST)
    Argentina, 1-4, 1-6–1-7, 1-8, 1-9, 1-15
    Azerbaijan, 3-4, 3-3, 3-11–3-14, 3-22

Index

Finland, 5-6
France, 6-4, 6-5, 6-8, 6-9, 6-22–6-23, 6-24, 6-26
Germany, 7-9–7-10
Ireland, 8-6, 8-11
Italy, 9-4, 9-6
Kazakhstan, 11-5, 11-16, 11-17, 11-18
Korea, 12-2
Mexico, 13-11, 13-12, 13-17, 13-19, 13-26–13-27
Netherlands, 14-17, 14-19
Norway, 15-3, 15-4, 15-5
Russia, 16-4, 16-13–16-14, 16-15, 16-22
Spain, 17-5, 17-13
Ukraine, 18-4, 18-14, 18-15, 18-17, 18-18, 18-23

W

Withholding:
    Australia, 2-14–2-15
    Azerbaijan, 3-3, 3-9–3-10, 3-20
    Canada, 4-6–4-7
    Germany, 7-9, 7-22–7-23, 7-44
    Ireland, 8-5–8-6
    Japan, 10-4
    Kazakhstan, 11-4
    Netherlands, 14-13
    Norway, 15-7
    Russia, 16-11
    United Kingdom, 19-8

Y

Yuhan Hoesa (YH), Korea, 12-4